Transition report 2002

Agriculture and rural transition

Contents

Chapter 1. Transition, welfare and sustainable development

Part I: Transition and economic performance

Chapter 2. Progress in transition and the business environment

Chapter 3. Macroeconomic performance and prospects

Part II: Agriculture and rural transition

Chapter 4. Agriculture

Chapter 5. Rural transition

Country assessments

Foreword

This *Transition Report*, with its special topic of agriculture and rural transition, is the ninth in an annual series. Taken together, the nine Reports have charted since 1994 the progress of transition from a command to a market economy in each of the 27 countries of central and eastern Europe and the Commonwealth of Independent States in which the European Bank for Reconstruction and Development (EBRD) operates. They also identify and analyse the challenges of the coming years.

The EBRD seeks to foster the transition to an open market-oriented economy and to promote private and entrepreneurial initiative in all 27 of its countries of operations. It does this through investment with a private sector focus. The Bank works with its partners on projects that are financially sound and advance the transition, and that would be unlikely to emerge or to realise their full potential without its participation. For the EBRD to perform this task effectively, it needs to analyse and understand the complex process of transition and to share the Bank's analyses with its partners, other investors and policy-makers in the region. The EBRD's *Transition Reports* therefore take an investment perspective on the transition. They focus on both the business environment and the contribution that investment shaped by market forces can make to the transition and to overall economic performance.

The structure of the *Transition Report* mirrors its purpose: to understand the dynamic process of market reforms in transition economies and the key requirements for a successful transition. Part I of the Report focuses on the impact of initial conditions, reform choices and the political process on the evolution of reforms and economic performance. It also examines the pitfalls in transition that have impeded reforms in some countries. Central to this analysis is an assessment of the role of economic liberalisation and democratic political processes in helping to sustain progress in market-oriented reform and in laying the foundations for sustainable development in the region. The Report also recognises that the quality of the business environment in areas such as regulation, taxation, the rule of law and corruption can have a strong influence on the effectiveness of other structural and institutional reforms.

To assess the quality of the business environment, the EBRD and the World Bank implemented jointly in 2002 the second round of the Business Environment and Enterprise Performance Survey (BEEPS), covering close to 6,000 enterprises in 26 countries of the region. The survey provides useful insights into the quality of the business environment in the region and the ways in which firms seek to influence the environment and markets in which they operate. Preliminary findings from the second round of the BEEPS are reported in this *Transition Report*. The findings of the first round of the BEEPS, which was implemented in 1999, are reported in the *Transition Report* 1999.

Each *Transition Report* has a special theme. These themes have developed a detailed analysis of the transition and the forces shaping its progress. They have also examined the policies that foster the development of the institutions and practices that are required to support well-functioning markets and private enterprise. It is important therefore to consider the Reports as a series in which each edition contributes in its own right to our understanding of the transition process and forms part of an inter-related and cross-referenced sequence of analyses.

The special themes of the previous *Transition Reports* have been:

▌ 1994 – Institutional reform and economic openness;
▌ 1995 – Fixed investment and enterprise development;
▌ 1996 – Commercial infrastructure and contractual savings institutions;
▌ 1997 – Enterprise performance and growth;
▌ 1998 – Financial sector in transition;
▌ 1999 – Ten years of transition (a special issue);
▌ 2000 – Employment, skills and transition; and
▌ 2001 – Energy in transition

This year's *Transition Report* draws from and builds on this previous work.

Part II of this year's *Transition Report* contains an analysis of the agricultural sector and the rural economy in transition countries. Recognising the relatively slow progress in reforming the agricultural sector and in developing rural areas in most transition economies, the Report highlights the policy challenges that must be addressed. It emphasises in particular the importance of land reform and the creation of markets for agricultural land. The problem of low productivity in agriculture – caused by incomplete reforms – also remains a major factor limiting the export of agricultural products from the region.

The agricultural sector and the rural economy are held back by relatively poor physical and market infrastructure and lack of access to finance. A key requirement for rural development is the attraction of investment and skills, and a significant improvement in the rural business environment. One way to achieve this is through policies that strengthen linkages between rural firms and their customers and suppliers.

The assessments and views expressed in this *Transition Report* are not necessarily those of the EBRD. The responsibility for them is taken by myself on behalf of the Office of the Chief Economist. While we have attempted to be as up to date as possible, the "cut-off" date for most of the information in the Report is early October 2002.

Willem Buiter
Chief Economist and Special Counsellor to the President
18 October 2002

Executive summary

Chapter 1: Transition, welfare and sustainable development

The recent World Summit on Sustainable Development hosted by the United Nations in Johannesburg refocused attention on achieving development "which will last" and on ensuring that future generations have the potential to enjoy at least the present-day level of welfare. Since the debates at the summit were largely dominated by concerns of industrialised and developing countries, there remains a need to examine sustainable development from a transition perspective.

Communism and central planning were unsustainable systems, making transition to market economies necessary for the region to achieve sustainable development. However, transition has been associated with at least temporary setbacks in some key aspects of sustainable development, notably in terms of poverty and living standards. The concept of sustainability must therefore be refined to reflect the constraints imposed by conditions at the start of transition and to address adequately the issue of fairness towards present and future generations.

It is important to recognise that sustainability implies neither an unchanging economic and political system nor a stable growth path. In addition, while transition has put pressure on living standards, it has not necessarily involved a departure from the broad principle of sustainable development or a decline in well-being if this is defined in terms of expanding human potential. This perspective places political issues, such as freedoms and rights, at the centre of the sustainability debate. These include the right to support policies that promote environmental sustainability and fairness. In many countries, transition has brought marked increases in political freedoms and civil rights. Political and democratic transition, however, is only one aspect of sustainability. Democratic and market

systems also require sound economic and corporate governance to help ensure sustainable development.

Part I: Transition and economic performance

Chapter 2: Progress in transition and the business environment

The past year has seen sustained reform momentum across many countries and areas of transition, as measured by the EBRD's transition indicators. A number of countries that had been lagging in reform, such as Bosnia and Herzegovina, the Federal Republic of Yugoslavia and Russia, have made significant progress over the past year as a result of favourable political and economic developments. At the same time, several advanced transition countries that are candidates for accession to the European Union continued to make steady progress in strengthening the performance of their market-supporting institutions. The greatest advances over the past year have been in the financial sector in both leading and less advanced countries.

To complement the insights provided by the transition indicators, the EBRD and the World Bank launched the second stage of the Business Environment and Enterprise Performance Survey this year. The survey asked enterprises to evaluate economic governance and state institutions and to assess the extent to which the business environment creates obstacles to the growth of their business.

The 2002 survey shows that the business environment has improved significantly across most countries of the region since 1999 and that this is not solely due to the upswing in the business cycle. Moreover, some of the less advanced transition economies in south-eastern Europe (SEE) and the Commonwealth of Independent States (CIS) have seen strong improvements in economic

governance, helping them to close the gap with the more advanced reformers. This mirrors the findings of the EBRD transition indicators. The unevenness of the business environment for different types of firms – such as small, newly established private firms and large, state-owned enterprises – has also diminished. These developments suggest that less advanced transition economies may now be able to move beyond the stage of partial reforms characterised by insecure property rights, corruption and limited investment, which have held back their progress over the first decade of transition.

Chapter 3: Macroeconomic performance and prospects

The past year has been turbulent for the global economy, and the increased uncertainty among the world's major economic blocks has affected all emerging markets, including the transition economies. Nonetheless, macroeconomic performance in most transition countries continues to be robust, and the region as a whole is expected to record its fourth year of successive growth in 2002, at 3.5 per cent. Net foreign direct investment to the region is likely to achieve a record level in 2002, with many countries continuing to reap the rewards of an improved business environment and a sustained commitment to structural reforms.

In central eastern Europe and the Baltic states (CEB), growth is expected to slow to 2.3 per cent in 2002, as these countries are most affected by the EU slow-down. High fiscal deficits are posing a significant challenge for a number of these countries. Prospects for the SEE region continue to improve, reflecting significant improvements in regional stability and cooperation, and growth in 2002 is projected to reach 3.6 per cent. In the CIS, where GDP growth is forecast at 4.4 per cent for 2002, countries that benefit from significant natural resources wealth continue to grow rapidly while in the region's largest economy, Russia, growth is expected to ease to just below 4 per cent in 2002.

Over the medium term, the economies of the region face several significant macro-economic challenges. The countries that are on track to join the EU in 2004 have to balance the fiscal demands of accession with the need to bring the general government budget to balance or surplus over the medium term, as required by the EU's Stability and Growth Pact. To reach EU living standards, the accession countries will need to achieve a higher productivity growth than the rate recorded by current EU members and to ensure careful management of exchange rate policy in advance of eventual eurozone membership. High-quality investment, including foreign direct investment, is fundamental to achieving these productivity gains.

In SEE, large fiscal and external imbalances continue to cause concern. The declines in both donor assistance and private remittances also highlight the need to improve regional cooperation and stability and to attract greater inflows of foreign investment. For CIS countries, the recent period of growth facilitated by a competitive currency and high oil prices may be ending and greater economic diversification is needed to maintain growth. Building state capacity and managing high levels of external debt are key challenges in several of the poorer CIS countries.

Part II: Agriculture and rural transition

Chapter 4: Agriculture

The region has experienced significant and persistent declines in agricultural output since the start of transition, from 15 to 30 per cent in central Europe to more than 50 per cent in some of the Baltic and CIS countries. A number of factors have contributed to these differing trends. Countries with better conditions at the start of transition have subsequently achieved the most reforms and experienced the highest growth in agricultural output. Other reforms have also generally had a positive effect, particularly on productivity. Liberalisation and

privatisation of the economy have, on the whole, had positive consequences for the agricultural sector. Equally important are changes in land ownership and control – particularly the extent to which farms are owned by individuals or households. The higher the share of farmland in individual hands, the higher the level of growth in output and productivity. Moreover, the method for implementing the privatisation of land has had a clear impact on productivity. Countries that followed land distribution policies have performed the worst.

Progress in agricultural reform is strongly linked to the methods of political decision-making. The most committed reformers have been stable democracies with high levels of political competition and an active civil society while the least effective reformers have lacked democracy and exerted weak influence on the power of government. Nevertheless, countries at intermediate stages of reform – such as Kazakhstan and Russia – have begun to break down the resistance of vested interests.

In the course of reform, transition countries have experienced a major shift in their agricultural trade. They have seen a substantial rise in agricultural trade deficits, mostly due to low agricultural productivity, which remains a major factor limiting trade with the rest of the world. They were also affected by differences between their trade policies and those of OECD countries. However, in some transition countries support for producers of some of the main agricultural products is already approaching EU levels.

Chapter 5: Rural transition

Over a third of the population of the region live in rural areas. Yet rural issues have not featured prominently during the first decade of transition. Consequently, rural areas lag behind urban areas in many respects. Poverty and unemployment are at significantly higher levels in rural than in urban areas. The rural investment climate is also less business-friendly, particularly in terms of access to finance and quality of infrastructure. The disadvantage experienced by rural areas is relatively modest on average but it can be large for specific countries and

particular aspects of the business environment. It is often similar to the disadvantage experienced by small firms. The shortcomings in the investment climate have resulted in rural enterprises recording less growth, investing less and restructuring more slowly than urban firms.

In view of the importance of the farm sector, reforming agriculture, increasing farm productivity and promoting land reform remain the dominant rural transition issues. But rural areas also need to promote non-farm activities to diversify their economic activities. A key way of achieving these goals is to exploit and strengthen market linkages. Market economies have a complex web of economic relationships, and in many rural areas these linkages have not been fully developed. As a consequence, economic activity has been held back, and rural economies have not experienced the benefits of new investment. Improved links between rural firms and their clients and suppliers can help to bring about enterprise reform, develop skills and provide working capital. Linkages between firms are equally important to develop skills and to encourage the expansion of non-farm activities.

Another crucial link is between rural firms and financial institutions. Rural enterprises have particular credit needs and limited collateral, especially in the farming sector. Transition countries are still in the process of reforming their rural banking sector and developing the legal and institutional framework that would allow banks to increase lending to the rural market.

Acknowledgements

The *Transition Report* was prepared primarily by the EBRD's Office of the Chief Economist with important contributions by the Office of the General Counsel – Annex 2.2 – and by the Environment Department – Annex 5.1. The editorial team, under the general direction of Willem Buiter, consisted of Steven Fries, Simon Commander, Samuel Fankhauser, Martin Raiser and Peter Sanfey.

The authors of the chapters and annexes are:

Contents	Authors
1. Transition, welfare and sustainable development	Willem Buiter, Samuel Fankhauser and Steven Fries

Part I: Transition and economic performance

Contents	Authors
2. Progress in transition and the business environment	Steven Fries, Joel Hellman and Martin Raiser
Annex 2.1: Progress in infrastructure reform	David Kennedy and Martin Raiser
Annex 2.2: Legal transition indicators	David Bernstein, Anita Ramasastry and Olivia Oddi
Annex 2.3: Qualitative assessment of the business environment in 1999 and 2002	Saso Polanec
3. Macroeconomic performance and prospects	Willem Buiter and Peter Sanfey
Annex 3.1: Macroeconomic performance tables	Katrin Tinn

Part II: Agriculture and rural transition

Contents	Authors
4. Agriculture	Alan Bevan, Elisabetta Falcetti, Vanessa Mitchell-Thomson, Alan Rousso, Franklin Steves and Marian Rizov
5. Rural transition	Liesbeth Dries, Rika Ishii, Libor Krkoska, Vanessa Mitchell-Thomson, Mark Schankerman and Anita Taci
Annex 5.1: Agriculture, rural development and the environment	Mark Hughes and Mark King

Anita Taci prepared Box 2.1 and provided substantial input to Chapter 4. Kjetil Tvedt prepared the backdated infrastructure indicators for 1994 to 1998. Saso Polanec provided valuable research support for Chapter 2, Gernot Müller for Chapter 3, and Katrin Tinn for Chapters 2 and 5.

The transition assessments and the macroeconomic indicators were prepared by the economists of the EBRD's Office of the Chief Economist. Country responsibilities are as follows: Albania – Anita Taci; Armenia – Samuel Fankhauser; Azerbaijan – Alan Bevan; Belarus – Alan Bevan; Bosnia and Herzegovina – Peter Sanfey; Bulgaria – Elisabetta Falcetti; Croatia – Rika Ishii; Czech Republic – Libor Krkoska; Estonia – Vanessa Mitchell-Thomson; FR Yugoslavia – Peter Sanfey; FYR Macedonia – Peter Sanfey;

Georgia – David Kennedy; Hungary – Francesca Pissarides; Kazakhstan – Martin Raiser; Kyrgyz Republic – Clemens Grafe; Latvia – Vanessa Mitchell-Thomson; Lithuania – Rika Ishii; Moldova – Maria Vagliasindi; Poland – Libor Krkoska; Romania – Elisabetta Falcetti; Russia – Ivan Szegvari; Slovak Republic – Libor Krkoska; Slovenia – Rika Ishii; Tajikistan – Toshiaki Sakatsume and Martin Raiser; Turkmenistan – Martin Raiser; Ukraine – Julian Exeter; and Uzbekistan – Clemens Grafe.

Libor Krkoska coordinated the data gathering for the structural and institutional indicators tables, which were prepared by Katrin Tinn. Katrin Tinn also coordinated and prepared the macroeconomic indicators tables and Lucie Ryan prepared the text tables and charts for publication.

Sandy Donaldson, Anthony Martin and Angela Hill of the EBRD's Publishing Unit expertly prepared the text for publication and managed the publication process. Richard Bate, Steven Still, Jon Page and Adrian Jonker of the Design Unit designed the Report and saw it through the production process.

The Report benefited significantly from the input of and comments from colleagues in the EBRD. Many helpful comments and suggestions were received from members of the EBRD's Board of Directors and Executive Committee. The Country Teams and Resident Offices made important contributions to the preparation of the Country Assessments. The teams from Power and Energy, Municipal and Environmental Infrastructure, Telecommunications and

Transport provided valuable contributions to infrastructure transition indicators and to the structural and institutional indicators for infrastructure. The Agribusiness Team and the Group for Small Business provided extensive feedback and material on Chapters 4 and 5.

Staff from the International Monetary Fund and the World Bank generously provided valuable comments and information on the entire Report. Philippe Aghion commented extensively on the Report. Chapters 4 and 5 also benefited from feedback by Sophia Davidova, Carol Leonard, Karen Macours and Jo Swinnen as well as staff from the UK Department for International Development and from the Food and Agricultural Organization (FAO). LMC International and staff from the Dnipropetrovsk Oil Extraction Plant provided information for Box 5.1.

Background studies for this *Transition Report*, including implementation of the Business Environment and Enterprise Performance Survey (BEEPS), were funded by the Japan-Europe Co-operation Fund. The World Bank also contributed to the funding of the BEEPS. The governments of the United States and Taipei China provided generous support for the Legal Indicator Survey and its analysis. This funding is gratefully acknowledged.

Agriculture and rural transition

Chapter 1

Transition, welfare and sustainable development

Transition, welfare and sustainable development

1

The World Summit on Sustainable Development hosted by the United Nations in Johannesburg in September 2002 marks the tenth anniversary of the UN Conference on Environment and Development held in Rio de Janeiro. Participants at the Rio summit, which included almost all countries in the world, committed to the Rio Declaration on Environment and Development and adopted *Agenda 21*, a detailed road map for achieving sustainable development – that is, development "which will last". The Johannesburg summit reaffirmed the commitments made ten years earlier and sought to accelerate the pace of reform in several key aspects of the sustainable development agenda.

The debate in Johannesburg was dominated mostly by the concerns of industrialised and developing countries. The post-communist countries of central and eastern Europe and the Commonwealth of Independent States all attended the summit but the issues arising from transition towards democracy and an open market economy did not feature prominently in public discussions. This chapter therefore examines transition from a sustainable development perspective and *vice versa*.

The chapter argues that communism and central planning were unsustainable systems, making transition essential for the region to achieve sustainable development. However, transition has been associated with at least temporary setbacks in some key areas of sustainable development, notably poverty levels and living standards. The concept of sustainability must therefore be refined to address adequately the issue of fairness towards both present and future generations and to reflect the constraints imposed by conditions at the start of the transition process and ongoing changes in the global environment. It is important to recognise that a sustainable process is not necessarily a stable growth path.

Indeed, it could not be stable if the initial conditions were inconsistent with sustainable development, as was the case with the transition countries.

While some aspects of sustainable development in the transition countries have worsened, it is not clear whether transition has actually involved a departure from the principles of sustainable development and to an overall lowering of living standards since setbacks in some areas may have been offset by gains in others. We argue, along the lines of Sen (1999), that progress in development or transition must be evaluated in terms of fulfilling human potential. This places political issues, such as freedoms and rights, at the centre of the sustainability debate, especially the right to support institutions and policies that promote environmental sustainability and fairness in the distribution of resources within and across generations. In many countries, transition has brought marked improvements in political freedoms and individual rights.

Political and economic transition, however, is only one aspect of sustainability. Even in fully democratic and market-based systems, additional measures are needed to ensure sustainable development. Markets need to be underpinned by adequate laws, regulations and institutions, and enterprises need to have incentives to follow the rules of good corporate governance and to apply sound business and environmental practices. There is a need, therefore, to assess progress in transition alongside achievement in sustainable development. This chapter evaluates sustainable development in transition economies in terms of overall levels of development, distributional issues and impacts on future generations.

1.1 Welfare and sustainable development

The prominence of sustainable development owes much to the 1987 Report of the World Commission on Environment and Development (WCED), *Our Common Future* – the so-called Brundtland Report.[1] This report sought to forge a broad policy agenda around the single concept of "sustainable development". The agenda included human development (population growth, education and health), food security, biological diversity, energy and climate change, industrialisation and environmental impact, urbanisation and management of global concerns. All of these issues have a significant impact on the "welfare" or "well-being" of current and future generations. The WCED used the concept of sustainable development to combine these issues into a more coherent agenda for change.

Conditions for sustainable development

The WCED defined sustainable development as "meeting the needs of the present without compromising the ability of future generations to meet their own needs". Expanding on this definition, the Commission emphasised two key concepts: (i) need – in particular, the essential needs of the world's poor; and (ii) limitations – how the level of technology and social organisation limits the environment's ability to meet present and future needs. The definition also gives prominence to how the benefits of development are distributed. In particular, it emphasises the importance of meeting the essential needs of the poor among current and future generations (a key dimension of "intra-generational fairness") and of not compromising the interests of future (or existing) generations in meeting the needs of existing (or future) generations ("intergenerational equity").

While there are many interpretations of sustainable development, most now centre on the concept of maintaining at least the current level of welfare or well-being of the population.[2] This formulation extends the definition in the WCED report, which focused on needs, and goes

---

[1] See WCED (1987). The Report is named after the Norwegian Prime Minister Gro Harlem Brundtland, who was the chairperson of the Commission.

[2] Among the first to interpret sustainable development as a problem of non-decreasing welfare (or utility) was Pezzey (1989).

beyond conventional measures of material development, such as per capita gross national income. It acknowledges that needs are met through goods and services included in the national income accounts, mainly those traded and valued in markets, but it also goes further by allowing for the non-market provision of goods and services (such as public provision, subsistence production and household production). It also includes the cost of damage to the environment and the cost of depleting non-renewable or slowly renewable natural resources (such as forests, fish stocks and biodiversity). In principle, catch-all terms such as welfare or well-being include anything that may be valued by current or future generations and this can include factors such as inter-personal relationships and individual freedoms.

The broadness of the terms helps to enrich the analysis of sustainable development but it also complicates the practical evaluation of whether certain policies are consistent with sustainable development. One approach is to consider the different aspects of sustainable development under the broad headings of economic, environmental and social sustainability.[3] Each element is seen as important but no attempt is made to produce an overall measure of sustainability. Sustainable progress in each of these elements is sufficient, but not necessary, for overall sustainability. Other approaches attempt to take account of the various elements to arrive at an overall index of development, such as the United Nations Development Programme (UNDP) Human Development Index.[4] However, the ways of calculating these overall indexes are inevitably arbitrary.

A more practical, although perhaps narrower, approach to defining sustainable development is to maintain that future generations need to be bequeathed the same amount of assets or wealth as enjoyed by the current generation.[5]

Assets in this context are broadly defined as the natural environment (natural resources and ecosystems), human capital (health, skills and education), social capital (organisations, institutions and culture, including trust among citizens and between citizens and the state) and physical assets (infrastructure, factories and equipment). These assets will provide future goods and services – including those from the earth's environment.

There are, however, difficulties about how to assess such disparate and often intangible assets. A key issue is the extent to which one type of asset (for example, education and accumulated knowledge) can be offset against or replaced by another (such as a better preserved or safer environment).[6] For example, a development strategy that severely damages the environment while investing heavily in education may not be sustainable because an increasingly deteriorating environment will ultimately undermine the benefits gained from improvements in education. The assumption that the different types of assets listed above can be substituted for each other is likely to lead to costly mistakes. For example, the assumption that technological progress and the accumulation of physical assets will always be able to overcome the constraints of depletable or slowly renewable resources is just that – an assumption.

Importance of rights and freedom

Most definitions of sustainable development allow for the fact that welfare or well-being is derived not only from the satisfaction of material needs (conventionally defined as living standards) but also from other aspects of existence, such as the freedom to improve the quality of life. This aspect of sustainable development is particularly relevant for transition countries, where individual freedom was severely limited under communism and a culture of freedom and rights is only now emerging.

There is ample evidence that individuals value basic freedoms, such as the freedom to participate in markets and other forms of trade (economic freedom), including the labour market. The value of economic freedom is perhaps most powerfully demonstrated by the experiences of African-American slaves in nineteenth-century America. Their living standards in terms of average consumption may well have equalled or even exceeded those of free agricultural labourers. Yet many slaves sought to escape servitude, aware that a successful escape could well mean a lower standard of living (conventionally measured) while a failed attempt would mean severe penalties, including maiming or loss of life.[7]

Other freedoms are also important, especially political freedom and civil liberties. These give people the right to determine who governs them and on what basis, to judge those in authority and to express their political views. These political freedoms provide the foundations for self-expression and for exercising political choice. This cannot be left solely to those in authority. Collective choice must be developed and implemented by ensuring that there is widespread participation in decision-making. Political freedoms and civil liberties can provide authorities with vital information about people's views and impose constraints on the power of the state, provided that the political system is open and holds the state accountable for its actions.

Political freedom and civil liberties are important because they are needed to develop social values and to implement collective choice.[8] When combined with transparent government, they provide the people with some protection against arbitrary or excessive use of power by the state. However, the extent to which political freedom (such as the principles of democracy, pluralism, civil liberties and transparency) and economic freedom (the right to participate in markets and

---

[3] See, for example, Munasinghe (1993).

[4] See United Nations Development Programme (2002).

[5] The formal demonstration that a constant stock of capital, or assets, is necessary to ensure non-decreasing consumption over time goes back to Hartwick (1977) and Solow (1986).

[6] The extent to which these various types of assets are perfect substitutes (weak sustainability) or imperfect substitutes (strong sustainability) is largely an empirical issue. For a discussion of weak versus strong sustainability, see Pearce and Atkinson (1993) and Beckerman (1994).

[7] See Fogel and Engerman (1974).

[8] A related issue is the intrinsic value of political freedom and civil liberties to individuals, regardless of what they imply for the quality of social choice and collective action. This issue is beyond the scope of this chapter but further analysis is available in Rawls (1971), Nozick (1974) and Sen (1999), Chapter 3.

engage in voluntary trade) improve the welfare of individuals is complex. In particular, this depends on whether certain conditions are present that allow individuals to benefit from this freedom.[9] For example, to participate in the political process, knowledge and basic skills are needed. The freedom to choose is only as valuable as the extent of choice available.

Political and economic freedoms can be instrumental in promoting better living standards and greater fairness for present and future generations. This can be achieved through the processes of competition, investment, innovation and sound economic governance in order to provide the public services that are necessary to support a market economy. However, open, democratic and market-oriented systems differ significantly in how much they promote better living standards, reflecting in part differing social values and cultural norms. In addition, political freedoms can help to distribute the benefits of development more fairly, at least by avoiding some of the extreme inequalities that have occurred under autocratic regimes. The extreme disregard of the environment in the former Soviet Union is one example. It is much harder to pursue a large-scale and sustained act of environmental "vandalism" when there is an active democratic society, including a free press.

Transition and sustainable development

For the countries of central and eastern Europe and the CIS economic and political transition is an essential requirement on their road towards sustainable development. The point of departure for transition was communism and central planning – a system that was unsustainable economically, environmentally, politically and socially. Central planning used natural resources wastefully and allocated them inefficiently. Heavy reliance on natural resources and disregard for the environment resulted in the extensive depletion of natural assets and widespread pollution of soil, water and air resources. Misguided investment decisions meant that, despite high education levels, the

region's natural assets were not replaced with an adequate combination of physical assets, such as infrastructure, human capital, such as job skills, and social capital, including institution-building. Central planning was unable to sustain an improvement in living standards and popular political support and was incapable of satisfying the key sustainability requirement of maintaining the country's assets.

While communism did not provide a blueprint for sustainable development, it is possible to question whether the post-communist transition towards an open market economy, democracy and pluralism does so. This process has led to an at least temporary decline in overall living standards in all countries of the region and, in some countries, significant increases in income inequality and poverty. The issue therefore arises as to whether transition represents a movement in the direction of or away from sustainable development and whether the concept of sustainability needs to be refined in view of the experiences of transition.

Sustainable development, as defined by the WCED, would require well-being – or living standards – to remain at the same level or improve over time. However, the case of transition countries shows that this requirement may be too strict if an economic and political system is in a state of flux due to internal contradictions or outside factors. A system is unlikely to be stable if the fundamentals of that system (resources, technologies, organisations and institutions) cannot sustain current living standards. Moreover, even if the system is stable in this sense, it may be subject to variations in climate, natural disasters, disease and other calamities that are not "man-made". Sustainable development, therefore, does not require an unchanging system or stable growth.

While in principle a steady increase in well-being is obviously better, the evidence of transition shows that this may not always be feasible, or indeed desirable. Transition may also be consistent with sustainable development to the extent

that other relevant issues – such as political freedoms – improve and help to offset any decline in living standards.

1.2 Measuring sustainable development

Well-being extends beyond material living standards, which can be measured at least in part through per-capita income (or consumption). The concept also includes basic capabilities (such as health and education) and freedoms (such as political freedoms and civil rights). If the definition of well-being also takes account of the issue of fairness from one generation to the next, there are inherently difficult problems of measurement and social valuation. There is no simple way of evaluating the well-being of individuals or groups of individuals (countries). The best we can do is to examine the main aspects of sustainable development, using simple measures. The relevant social values placed on these developments are expressed by the people of the region through open political processes.

The focus of the following analysis is on the social and economic aspects of sustainability and on the political dimension that is central to sustainable development in the transition process. Environmental indicators for transition economies were discussed in the *Transition Report* 2000,[10] while Annex 5.1 of this Report examines the impact of agriculture on the environment in the region.

Measures of overall country conditions

Political freedom and civil liberties in transition economies can be assessed over time using the measures of autocracy and democracy from the Polity IV database, developed at the University of Maryland's Center for International Development and Conflict Management. For this purpose, autocracy is defined in terms of whether specific political characteristics are present. For example, autocracies sharply restrict or suppress competitive participation in politics. Their chief executives are chosen from within the political elite and, once in office, they exercise power with few institutional constraints. The degree of autocracy is measured on a ten-point

---

[9] See Sen (1999), Chapter 4.

[10] Annex 2.4. See also OECD (1996) and Ichikawa et al. (2002).

Chart 1.1

Autocracy and democracy, 1985–2000

Polity index

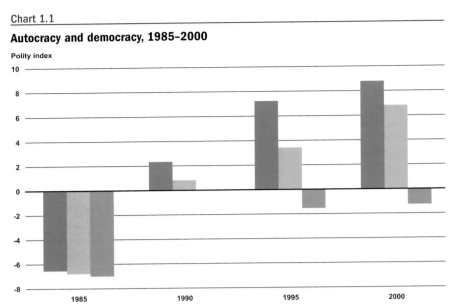

■ CEB ■ SEE ■ CIS

Source: Center for International Development and Conflict Management at the University of Maryland.
Note: Regional indices are calculated as unweighted averages using the Polity II index. The values of the Polity II index range from –10 to 10, with the highest value denoting the most democratic political regime and the lowest the most autocratic regime.

Chart 1.2

Political and civil freedom, 1985–2000

Freedom House index (adjusted)

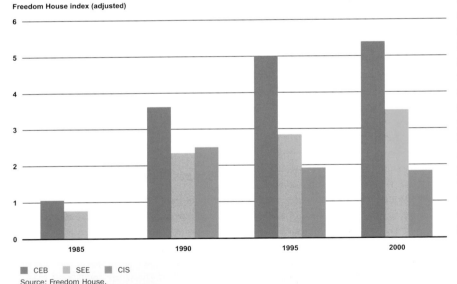

■ CEB ■ SEE ■ CIS

Source: Freedom House.
Note: Regional indices are calculated as unweighted averages of country values. The Freedom House index ranges from 1 to 7, with 1 indicating the most free and 7 the least free. However, for the purpose of this chart, the range has been inverted and modified to 0 to 6, with 6 indicating the most free and 0 the least free.

scale, with a value of ten representing the most extensive (and intensive) form of autocracy. Similarly, democracy is defined as three essential elements. The first is the presence of institutions and procedures that allow individual citizens and minorities to express their preferences for alternative policies and leaders. The second element is the competitive selec-

tion of the chief executive and the existence of institutional constraints on the exercise of power by the executive. The third is the guarantee of civil liberties to all citizens in their daily lives and in political participation. Unfortunately, this dimension of democracy, which is perhaps the most fundamental of the three because without it the other two cannot

be effective, is not singled out in the database. As with autocracy, the degree of democracy is measured on a ten-point scale. The balance between autocracy and democracy in a political system is indicated by an overall score, which shows the difference between the democracy and autocracy measures.

Since this index does not take into account political freedom and civil liberties, two measures of civil liberties and political rights compiled by Freedom House are also reported. Civil liberties is defined as the freedom to develop views, institutions and personal autonomy apart from the state, and political rights is defined as the freedoms that enable individuals to participate freely in political processes. These liberties and rights are reported on a scale of zero (not free society) to six (free).

Charts 1.1 and 1.2 show the levels of autocracy/democracy and civil liberties and political rights from 1985 to 2000 for three groups of transition economies: central eastern Europe and the Baltic states (CEB), south-eastern Europe (SEE) and the Commonwealth of Independent States (CIS). The charts show the high degree of autocracy and lack of political freedom under the old communist regime and the significant movement towards democracy and greater freedom since the political revolutions in central and eastern Europe of 1989 and the advent of *glasnost* in the former Soviet Union. This progress has been greatest in CEB countries and least evident in the CIS. In fact, the CIS as a whole has backtracked on these measures since 1990, reflecting in particular developments in Belarus, Turkmenistan and Uzbekistan, which have failed to maintain the level of political reform achieved in the former Soviet Union. There are, of course, other CIS countries that have continued to advance the process of political reform, although this process has had its setbacks.

Changes in life expectancy and education are highlighted using components of the United Nations Development Programme's Human Development Index (HDI). The HDI measures the overall achievements in a country in three basic areas – longevity, knowledge and living standards. Life

Chart 1.3

Longevity, 1985–2000

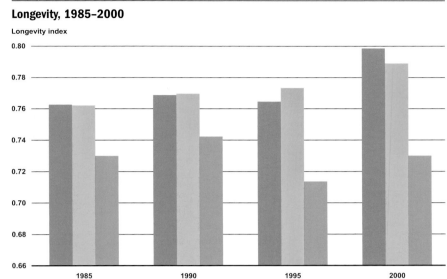

Longevity index

■ CEB   ■ SEE   ■ CIS

Source: World Development Indicators Database 2002.

Note: Regional indices are calculated from country indices. Country indices of longevity are calculated following the Human Development Index methodology: (life expectancy–25) divided by (85-25). Data for FYR Macedonia were not available for 1985.

Chart 1.4

Enrolment in formal education, 1990–2000

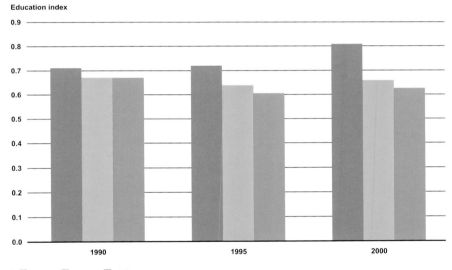

Education index

■ CEB   ■ SEE   ■ CIS

Sources: Trans-Monee Database 2002 and UNICEF.

Note: Regional indices are calculated as unweighted averages of country indices. The country indices are calculated by weighting the basic, secondary and tertiary enrolments with the number of years in each education level. The higher the index, the greater the level of formal education. Data for FR Yugoslavia and Georgia were not available.

expectancy and education correspond to the first two measures. Longevity is measured by life expectancy at birth and knowledge by educational attainment (adult literacy with a weight of two-thirds combined with primary, secondary and tertiary education enrolment with a weight of one-third). Performance in both these

areas is measured by an index with a scale of 0 to 1, with 1 representing the maximum value (for example, life expectancy at birth of 85 years). A score of zero is the minimum value that could conceivably be achieved by a country (for example, life expectancy at birth of 25 years).

Charts 1.3 and 1.4 show life expectancy and education from 1985 to 2000 for three groups of transition economies, CEB, SEE and the CIS. These indicators show significant improvements in longevity on average in CEB and SEE but a significant decline in the CIS. This decline in life expectancy was associated primarily with adult males in Kazakhstan, Russia and Ukraine although there has been some improvement in recent years. The stresses associated with transition, high levels of alcohol consumption and the rapid spread of HIV/AIDS in some CIS countries have contributed to the decline in adult male life expectancy. At the same time, overall school enrolment rates improved on average in CEB countries but have declined at least temporarily in SEE and the CIS, particularly in the Caucasus and Central Asia. However, there has been some improvement in school enrolment rates in SEE and the CIS in recent years.

Changes in living standards are shown by using gross national income (GNI) per capita at both real exchange rates (World Bank Atlas method) and at purchasing power parity (PPP) exchange rates (International Comparison Programme conversion rate). In principle, living standards are more accurately measured using PPP exchange rates because they take into account variation in the relative price of non-tradable goods and services across countries. However, the quality of data used in estimating PPP exchange also varies widely across countries, and a feature of available PPP calculations for transition economies is a particularly wide discrepancy between nominal exchange rates and PPP exchange rates for some countries of the former Soviet Union. For example, the estimates of GNI at PPP in 2000 for Russia (8,010 international dollars) place it ahead of Croatia (7,960 international dollars). However, according to the World Bank Atlas method, Russian GNI per capita was US$ 1,660 in 2000 and Croatian GNI per capita was US$ 4,620. The extent of the implied correction for the relative price of non-tradable goods and services in Russia may be excessive.

Chart 1.5

GDP per capita, 1990–2000

US dollars (1995 exchange rate)

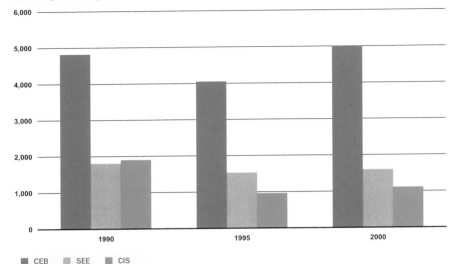

■ CEB   ■ SEE   ■ CIS

Source: World Development Indicators Database 2002.
Note: Regional values are calculated as unweighted averages of country values. Data for Bosnia and Herzegovina and FR Yugoslavia were not available.

Chart 1.6

GNI per capita (PPP adjusted), 1990–2000

International US dollars

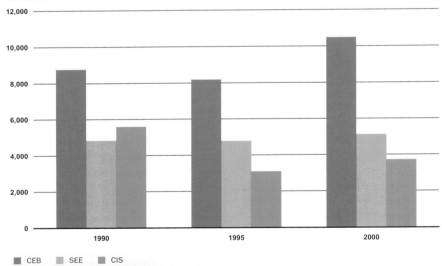

■ CEB   ■ SEE   ■ CIS

Source: World Development Indicators Database 2002.
Note: Regional values are calculated as unweighted averages of country values. Data for Bosnia and Herzegovina and FR Yugoslavia were not available.

Charts 1.5 and 1.6 show living standards in transition economies from 1990 to 2000, using the two measures of income per capita, GDP per capita at constant 1995 US dollars and GNI per capita at PPP exchange rates. As with the measures of life expectancy and education, CEB countries on average have achieved an increase in living standards during the

transition process, not withstanding an initial decline in the first five years of reform. However, countries of SEE and the CIS have not experienced such improvements. In fact, CIS countries on average have seen significant declines in living standards, at least as measured by recorded output per capita. No allowance has been made for informal activity.

This analysis of changes in the quality of life in transition economies points to a complex pattern. Substantial political freedoms have been gained in many – but not all – transition economies, adding significantly to the quality of life. But at the same time, there have been significant setbacks in terms of lower levels of education and life expectancy in certain countries, in particular lower life expectancy for adult males in the CIS and, to a lesser extent, lower levels of education in Central Asia and the Caucasus. There has also been a significant decline in living standards in CIS countries although the extent of the decline depends on how it is measured. However, these patterns do not show that if there is less political freedom, there will be greater life expectancy or education and higher living standards. In fact, they show that it is costly to move from one economic and political system to another, but the costs are less in the countries that have more fully embraced new political (and economic) freedoms.

The impact that freedoms and other benefits/costs of the transition process have had on the quality of life has to be judged by the people of the region, taking account of political freedom and civil liberties. It is, of course, possible to compare measures of well-being achieved under communism and central planning with those same indicators during the transition process. Such a comparison can help to explain why people feel better or worse off and this can affect the choice of transition strategy. However, it does not affect the decision to abandon communism and central planning as a political and economic system, which collapsed because it was unsustainable. The continuation of that regime was not a feasible option.

In judging current policies and transition strategies, the people of the region may consider not only their experience since the start of transition but also look ahead to possible improvements in life expectancy, education and living standards. In this regard, it is important to recognise the important role of political and economic freedom in helping to bring about these improvements. While the relationship between freedom and development is affected by many factors, including

Chart 1.7

Institutional development

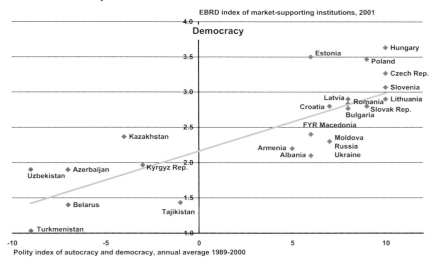

EBRD index of market-supporting institutions, 2001

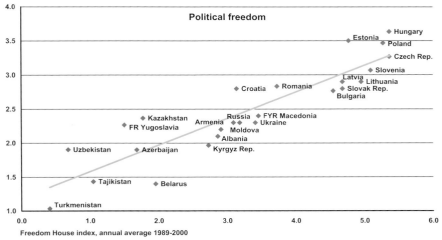

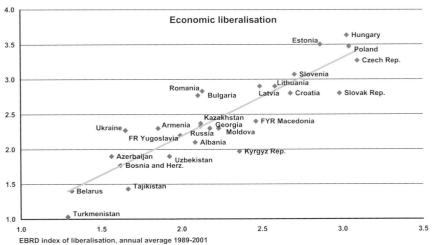

Sources: EBRD staff calculations; Center for International Development and Conflict Management at the University of Maryland; and Freedom House.

Note: Both the EBRD transition indicators and the index of liberalisation range from 1 to 4, with 1 indicating little or no change from rigid central planning and 4 indicating the level of reform is consistent with a well-functioning market economy. The index of market-supporting institutions combines four equally weighted dimensions: large-scale privatisation, enterprise restructuring, infrastructure and financial market reforms. For details of the Polity index, refer to Chart 1.1. Data relating to democracy and freedom were not available for Bosnia and Herzegovina, FR Yugoslavia and Georgia.

existing social and cultural norms, and by the international environment, previous *Transition Reports* have identified how economic and political freedoms in transition help to strengthen the process of structural and institutional change.

Chart 1.7 shows how the introduction of democratic reforms, greater political freedom and economic openness are strongly linked with sustained progress in structural and institutional reform, as measured by EBRD transition indicators. These fundamental reforms have tended to create forward momentum in many transition economies, helping to sustain progress in other aspects of reform, particularly institutional development. One reason for this is the way that these measures are mutually supportive in strengthening economic performance.[11]

Fairness among current population groups

Our analysis of the improvements in the quality of life in transition has so far focused on country-wide conditions without considering distributional issues within countries. In some countries there have been significant gains in political freedom and civil liberties while improvements in life expectancy, education and living standards have been uneven. It is therefore important to examine how these aspects of transition have affected particular population groups. One way of assessing these aspects is to examine the performance of transition economies with respect to the Millennium Development Goals (MDGs), adopted by the United Nations General Council in 2000. These goals, which are quantifiable and measurable, focus on life expectancy, education and living standards of the poor and vulnerable groups, such as children, women and those suffering from avoidable illnesses. This approach extends the general concern of WCED for meeting the essential needs of the world's poor into specific performance targets.

The United Nations has set a number of goals for development and poverty reduction by 2015. Using 1990 as the starting point, these include:

---

[11] See *Transition Report* 2001, Chapter 2.

Table 1.1

Transition economies and the Millennium Development Goals

	1989-90	1999-2000
Poverty rates (percentage of the population living below the international poverty line of 4.30 international dollars per day at PPP exchange rates) [1]		
CEB	na	13.8
SEE	na	41.3
CIS	na	56.8
Distribution of income (Gini coefficient) [2]		
CEB	0.27	0.30
SEE	0.23	0.34
CIS	0.27	0.70
Enrolment in primary education (gross rate as a percentage of the relevant population)		
CEB	94.6	97.7
SEE	97.4	91.7
CIS	92.5	90.4
Female / male enrolments (percentage of female to male enrolment rates in primary and secondary schools) [3]		
CEB	95.7	96.5
SEE	94.8	94.5
CIS	na	na
Maternal mortality rate (per thousand live births)		
CEB	14.2	14.0
SEE	29.2	15.8
CIS	37.6	36.3
Under-five mortality rate (per thousand live births)		
CEB	15.2	9.4
SEE	28.8	16.4
CIS	34.4	24.5
HIV/AIDS (newly registered cases)		
CEB	64	1,653
SEE	55	411
CIS	461	63,503

Sources: United Nations Children's Fund Innocenti Research Centre, *Social Monitor 2002* and World Bank, *World Development Indicators* 2002.

Note: Regional values are calculated as the unweighted averages of country values.

[1] Data on poverty rates for 1999-2000 are for the most recent year available. Comparable poverty rates are not available for 1989-90.

[2] The Gini coefficient is the measure of inequality in income distribution. It ranges from 0 to 1, with 0 indicating low inequality and 1 indicating high inequality.

[3] Female / male enrolment ratio is not available for most CIS countries.

▮ halving the proportion of people whose income is less than US$ 1 per day;

▮ halving the proportion of people who suffer from hunger;

▮ halving the proportion of people without safe access to drinking water;

▮ achieving universal completion of primary education;

▮ achieving gender equality in access to education;

▮ reducing by three-quarters the maternal mortality ratio;

▮ reducing by two-thirds the under-five mortality rate;

▮ halting and beginning to reverse the spread of HIV/AIDS, malaria and other major diseases.

We have based these assessments as far as possible on the data identified in the goals themselves. To make comparisons more reliable and comprehensive, a different international poverty line has been used from that specified in the MDGs, which uses the international poverty line for low-income developing countries. The poverty rate used is the share of the population below an international poverty line of 4.30 international dollars per day at PPP exchange rates for the most recent year available (1995 to 1999). This is the international poverty line used by the UNDP and World Bank for middle-income developing countries. Equivalent poverty rates are not available for 1990 but some pre-transition poverty rates based on national poverty lines at the time are reported in Atkinson and Mickelwright (1992) for four countries. They are former Czechoslovakia (7 per cent in 1988), Hungary (13 per cent in 1987), Poland (15 per cent in 1988) and the former Soviet Union (14 per cent in 1989). However, in the latter, there was wide variation in poverty rates among the republics – lower in the Baltic states, Belarus, Russia and Ukraine (1 to 6 per cent) and highest in Azerbaijan and four of the five Central Asian republics (30 to 50 per cent), with Armenia, Georgia, Kazakhstan and Moldova in between (10 to 16 per cent).

Table 1.1 shows the performance of three groups of transition economies (CEB, SEE and CIS) for six of the eight MDGs. Data on malnutrition and access to safe drinking water are not available for most transition economies. Overall, transition economies have experienced a significant increase in poverty since the start of transition, particularly in SEE and the CIS. However, the accuracy of these comparisons is limited by the lack of data. The poverty rates in 2000 (or the most recent year available) are much higher in SEE and the CIS than in CEB countries. This is in line with the lower average per capita incomes and more unequal distribution of income in SEE and the CIS. The view that poverty rates have increased during the transition is also consistent with the declines in average per capita incomes in SEE and the CIS since the start of transition and the rise in income inequality in these regions.

There is also evidence that the costs associated with transition are affecting some groups (such as women and children) considered to be vulnerable to particular hardship in developing countries. The decline in primary school enrolment rates in SEE and the CIS is a particular concern. Another is the rapid increase in the number of reported new cases of HIV/AIDS in Russia and some other CIS countries. In other issues considered by the MDGs, the transition economies have shown some improvement although data on gender balance in primary and secondary education in CIS countries are not available.

The costs of transition have therefore been unevenly distributed, with significant increases in poverty in most transition economies. There is of course considerable variation between countries. UNICEF (2002) and the World Bank (2002) provide a more detailed analysis of transition economies and their record in terms of the MDGs. The UNICEF report also takes a close look at other aspects of social trends that go beyond the MDGs.

Availability of assets for future generations

While benefits and costs of transition have been unevenly distributed among the region's population, these costs and benefits can also be transferred to future generations. This could occur if current generations accumulate or consume assets that contribute to the well-being of future generations. In the former communist countries, for example, there was extensive investment in developing skills, substantial but misdirected investment in infrastructure and social capital (organisations and institution-building) and overuse of natural assets.

Transition represents a new approach to investment, particularly in social capital. The EBRD transition indicators measure progress in some aspects of this social capital, such as institution-building. In addition, the joint EBRD-World Bank Business Environment and Enterprise

Performance Survey provides further insight into social capital, drawing on the views of close to 6,000 businesses in the region on the quality of economic governance (see Chapter 2). While the value of these aspects of social capital is difficult to weigh up, both types of assessment point to significant gains in institution-building and economic governance in the region and, as a result, greater investment, innovation and growth by firms.

At the same time, the extent of investment (or disinvestment) in other types of assets has also changed in transition economies. One measure of the value of these investments is adjusted net savings developed by the World Bank.[12] These savings are derived from standard national income account measures of gross savings by making four types of adjustment. First, estimates of the depreciation of physical capital, such as infrastructure, are deducted to obtain net national savings. Second, expenditure on education is added to net national savings because these expenditures are counted as consumption in national income accounts rather than investment in human capital. Third, estimates of the value of natural resource depletion in the energy, minerals and forestry sectors are deducted to account for the decline in asset value associated with their extraction or harvest. These estimates are based on the calculation of income earned from natural resources (that is, the difference between the world market value of the resources and the cost of their extraction or harvest). Fourth, a deduction is made for the value of environmental damage from carbon dioxide emissions. This is calculated as the marginal social cost of a unit of pollution multiplied by the amount of emissions.

This is of course only a partial (and tentative) accounting of the annual net change in physical, human and natural assets. Several important factors are omitted from the calculations, owing primarily to difficulties in measurement. There are also gaps in the accounting of natural assets. For example, the depletion and

degradation of soils and net depletion of fishing stocks are not included in the estimates nor are the costs of air and water pollution from industry, agriculture and households. Annex 5.1 examines the environmental impact of agriculture in the region, including the intensive use of water in some countries.

While recognising the partial nature of the adjusted net savings calculations, Charts 1.8 to 1.11 show the composition of these savings rates for three groups of transition economies from 1995 to 2000. Data for earlier years are not available. Net savings as a percentage of GNI in 2000 ranged from a high of about 10 per cent on average in CEB countries to about 4 per cent in SEE and the CIS. At the same time, education expenditure as a share of GNI ranged from just over 5 per cent in CEB to about 3.5 per cent in SEE.[13] This accumulation of assets in CEB and SEE is offset partially by resource depletion and the estimated cost of carbon dioxide damage, leaving adjusted net savings rates in the range of 14 per cent of GNI in CEB and 4 per cent in SEE. In the CIS, however, the offset is greater, owing to extensive resource depletion and extremely inefficient use of energy. Both are persistent legacies from the period of communism and central planning. The adjusted net savings rate for the CIS is on average minus 10 per cent of GNI.

Some CIS countries have yet to achieve a degree of sustainability therefore that may result in sustained increases in the quality of life over time. In some of these countries the accumulation of social capital through institution-building and improvements in economic governance may help to redress the imbalance. However, the quality of these social assets will depend fundamentally on the nature of the region's political systems and respect for basic rights and freedoms. This remains a significant concern in some CIS countries.

[12] The adjusted net savings measure assumes that the current relative prices of different types of assets reflect their appropriate social valuation. See Hamilton and Clemens (1999) and Kunte et al. (1998). Adjusted savings estimates for the hydrocarbon-rich countries of the region were also reported in the *Transition Report* 2001, Chapter 4.

[13] It is important to recognise that some of the variation across countries reflects the variation in the relative salary of teachers, which is not related directly to the extent of accumulation of human capital.

Chart 1.8

Net national savings, 1995–2000

Share of GNI (in per cent)

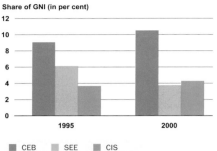

■ CEB ■ SEE ■ CIS

Source: World Development Indicators Database 2002.
Note: Regional values are calculated as unweighted averages of country values. Data for Bosnia and Herzegovina, FR Yugoslavia, Turkmenistan and Ukraine were not available.

Chart 1.10

Depletion of natural resources, 1995–2000

Share of GNI (in per cent)

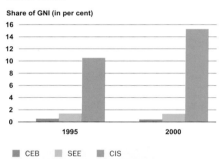

■ CEB ■ SEE ■ CIS

Source: World Development Indicators Database 2002.
Note: Regional values are calculated as unweighted averages of country values. Data for FR Yugoslavia were not available.

Chart 1.9

Education expenditure, 1995–2000

Share of GNI (in per cent)

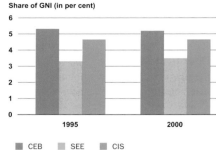

■ CEB ■ SEE ■ CIS

Source: World Development Indicators Database 2002.
Note: Regional values are calculated as unweighted averages of country values.

Chart 1.11

Environmental damage from carbon dioxide emissions, 1995–2000

Share of GNI (in per cent)

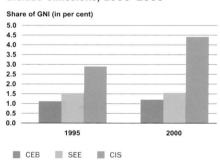

■ CEB ■ SEE ■ CIS

Source: World Development Indicators Database 2002.
Note: Regional values are calculated as unweighted averages of country values. Data for FR Yugoslavia were not available.

1.3 Conclusion

There is a strong overlap between the objectives of sustainable development and transition to open market economies, democracy and pluralism in the countries of central and eastern Europe and the CIS. However, the experience of transition poses fundamental challenges in assessing sustainability, recognising that sustainability implies neither an unchanging economic and political system nor a stable growth path. In responding to these challenges, our assessment is based on a comprehensive understanding of the factors that contribute to the welfare or well-being of individuals.

This perspective highlights the importance of civil rights and political freedom. We also emphasise the complex nature of making judgements about fairness within current and future generations and the appropriate distribution of the benefits

of development. Transition has been associated with increases in poverty and a lowering of life expectancy and educational standards, particularly in CIS countries. A priority should be to reverse this. Transition has also been associated with the continuing depletion of assets in some CIS countries, particularly those with abundant natural resources.

In the right political, legal and regulatory framework, market forces can provide a powerful incentive for resource efficiency, skill enhancement and long-term investment – important ways of ensuring the welfare of future generations. Market distortions (such as misplaced subsidies and the failure to reflect environmental costs and benefits in commercial and economic decision-making) often pose the main challenges to achieving long-term sustainable development. Many of these distortions in transition economies

are persistent legacies of the previous communist regime – an approach to development that proved unsustainable. The energy sector, where low tariffs and poor collection rates are a key reason for high energy intensity in the region, is an example of a sector where market reform can go hand-in-hand with some requirements of sustainability.

However, these concerns can conflict with affordability and fairness to the poorer sections of the community (see *Transition Report* 2001). Agriculture is another area where market distortions and lack of reform not only sustain inefficient agricultural practices but also impose a high cost on the natural environment. Chapters 4 and 5 discuss these issues in more detail. A challenge for transition economies is, therefore, to provide social protection to poor urban households and rural communities in ways that are less detrimental to long-term sustainability.

Sustainable development requires individuals and social groups to have the opportunity and freedom to realise their potential under sound social, economic and environmental conditions, and within a system of markets and market-supporting institutions and regulations. This system must support private investment, encourage entrepreneurship and permit the markets to respond freely to price signals and economic incentives. The expectation, based on experience, is that this will lead to sustainable employment and widely shared prosperity. Again, there is a strong overlap with the objectives of transition, and Chapters 2 and 3 of this Report provide evidence on progress in this regard.

Policies and safeguards are nevertheless needed to ensure that resources are used efficiently. The benefits of resources must be shared fairly and society needs to maintain a sufficient stock of natural and man-made assets and skills for future generations. Social "safety nets" have to be in place to protect those unable to take advantage of market opportunities. Prices must not only reflect the actual costs of production but also the social worth of scarce resources and place adequate weight on the well-being of future generations.

Enterprises should comply with international standards and best practice as reflected in laws and regulations concerning waste management, control of pollution emissions, transparency and integrity, and compliance with labour standards and health and safety regulations. This is an important task in promoting sustainable development. Organisations such as the EBRD can contribute to this through the conditions associated with its investments and by setting a firm example of best practice.

References

G. Atkinson, R. Dubourg, K. Hamilton, M. Munasinghe, D. Pearce and C. Young (1999), *Measuring Sustainable Development: Macroeconomics and the Environment,* Edward Elgar, Cheltenham.

W. Beckerman (1994), "'Sustainable development': Is it a useful concept?", *Environmental Values,* Vol.3, pp.191-209.

R. Fogel and S. Engerman (1974), *Time on the Cross: The Economics of American Negro Slavery,* Little Brown, Boston.

K. Hamilton and M. Clemens (1999), "Genuine saving in developing countries", *World Bank Economic Review,* Vol.13, No.2, pp.33-56.

J.M. Hartwick (1977), "Intergenerational equity and the investing of rents from exhaustible resources", *American Economic Review,* Vol.67, No.5, pp.972-74.

N. Ichikawa, R. Tsutsumi and K. Watanabe (2002), "Environmental indicators of transition", *European Environment,* Vol.12, pp.64-76.

A. Kunte, K. Hamilton, J. Dixon and M. Clemens (1998), "Estimating natural wealth: Methodology and results", Environment Department Papers No.57, Environmental Economics Series, World Bank, Washington D.C.

M. Munasinghe (1993), *Environmental Economics and Sustainable Development,* World Bank, Washington D.C.

R. Nozick (1974), *Anarchy, State and Utopia,* Basic Books, New York.

OECD (1994), *Environmental Indicators: OECD Core Set,* Organisation for Economic Cooperation and Development, Paris.

OECD (1996), *Environmental Indicators: A Review of Selected Central and Eastern European Countries,* Organisation for Economic Cooperation and Development, Paris.

D.W. Pearce and G. Atkinson (1993), "Capital theory and the measurement of sustainable development: An indicator of 'weak' sustainability", *Ecological Economics,* Vol.8, pp.103-08.

J. Pezzey (1989), "Economic analysis of sustainable growth and sustainable development", Environment Department Working Paper No.15, World Bank, Washington D.C.

J. Rawls (1971), *A Theory of Justice,* Harvard University Press, Cambridge MA.

A. Sen (1999), *Development as Freedom,* Alfred Knopf, New York.

R. Solow (1986), "On the intergenerational allocation of natural resources", *Scandinavian Journal of Economics,* Vol.88, No.1.

United Nations Development Programme (UNDP) (2002), *Human Development Report,* Oxford University Press, Oxford.

United Nations Children's Fund (UNICEF) (2002), *Social Monitor 2002: The Monee Project CEE/CIS/Baltics,* UNICEF Innocenti Research Centre, Florence.

World Commission on Environment and Development (WCED) (1987), *Our Common Future,* Oxford University Press, Oxford.

Transition and economic performance

Part I

Chapter 2

Progress in transition and the business environment

Chapter 3

Macroeconomic performance and prospects

Progress in transition and the business environment

2

In 2002 many countries of central and eastern Europe and the Commonwealth of Independent States have continued to make significant progress in structural and institutional reforms. The positive momentum over the past three years has been maintained, allowing some of the less advanced transition economies to close the gap with the front-runners, which are now focusing on institutional reforms that inevitably take longer to achieve.

In central eastern Europe and the Baltic states (CEB), the EU accession process remains the main driving force for reform as eight countries in this sub-region – with the exception of Croatia – aim for EU accession by 2004. The Copenhagen summit at the end of 2002 is to announce the list of countries officially invited to join, signalling a landmark in these efforts. For these countries, negotiations on most accession issues related to adopting the *acquis communautaire* have been completed. In south-eastern Europe (SEE), political and regional stability has changed fundamentally the prospects of the countries in the region. As economic prospects have improved, the interest of investors has increased and this has helped to demonstrate the benefits of economic reform. As in 2001, the Federal Republic of Yugoslavia has made the most reform gains in SEE, albeit from a low starting point. In the Commonwealth of Independent States (CIS), Russia continues to lead reform efforts and its example is closely watched by reformers elsewhere in the sub-region. However, in parts of the CIS, the reform momentum has slowed down, particularly in Central Asia, where the commitment to economic and political openness is weaker.

The EBRD's Office of the Chief Economist has assessed progress in structural and institutional reform across the region since 1994 based on its assessment of progress in key aspects of the transition process. However, these assessments do not fully address important aspects of economic governance, such as taxation, business regulation, corruption and the rule of law, and do not take account of the two-way relationship between enterprises and the state. To cover these crucial areas, the EBRD and the World Bank launched the Business Environment and Enterprise Performance Survey (BEEPS) in 1999. The BEEPS asks enterprises to evaluate economic governance and state institutions and to assess the extent to which the business environment creates obstacles to the operation and growth of their businesses. In 2002 the EBRD and the World Bank undertook a second stage of the BEEPS, surveying close to 6,000 firms across 26 countries of the region. The results indicate the progress that has been made in economic governance over the past three years, complementing the EBRD's assessment of progress in transition.

The 2002 BEEPS shows that the business environment has improved significantly across most countries in the region since 1999 and that this is not due solely to the recovery in the business cycle since 1999. Moreover, some of the less advanced transition economies in SEE and the CIS have seen some of the strongest improvements in economic governance, closing the gap with the advanced reformers. This mirrors the findings of the EBRD transition indicators. The unevenness of the business environment for different types of firms – such as small, newly established private firms and large state-owned enterprises – has also diminished. These developments suggest that less advanced transition economies might be able to move beyond the partial or incomplete reforms, including insecure property rights, corruption and limited investment, that have held back their progress over the first decade of transition.

An analysis of reform patterns since 1989 suggests that three factors are critical for sustaining progress in reform.

First, comprehensive economic liberalisation is necessary to create market competition and to generate the demand for market-supporting institutions. This demand arises from the fact that to prosper in competitive markets and to benefit from international trade, businesses must be supported by sound institutions and fair state practices. Second, market liberalisation is more effective when combined with political competition. The strongest and most sustained reform gains have been achieved in countries that elect their governments through a free public vote (see Chapter 1). Third, the process of transition is influenced by international integration (see *Transition Report* 2001, Chapter 2). This has been clearly demonstrated by the countries of CEB and SEE that are not EU accession candidates. In the countries of SEE and the CIS that are not candidate countries for EU accession, it will be important to promote other processes, such as accession to the World Trade Organization and possibly the voluntary adoption of at least some aspects of EU law. While free markets and private enterprise now seem to be relatively well-established across the region – with the exceptions of Belarus, Turkmenistan and to a lesser extent Uzbekistan – progress in democracy and the establishment of political competition remain much more uneven, as does the process of international integration.

This chapter begins with a review of reform progress as indicated by the EBRD's transition assessments (see Sections 2.1 and 2.2). Section 2.3 introduces the findings of the BEEPS and explains how they complement the transition indicators. Section 2.4 examines the variation in the business environment as perceived by firms across 26 countries of the region. Section 2.5 looks at the number of business obstacles faced by enterprises to verify the qualitative assessments provided in the survey. Section 2.6 examines these business obstacles as experienced by different types of firm. The concluding section summarises why the business environment may have improved significantly between 1999 and 2002 and suggests areas where additional analysis is needed.

2.1 Transition indicators and progress in 2002

The EBRD's *Transition Reports* have provided assessments of progress in transition for CEB, SEE and the CIS since 1994. Assessments are made for four main elements of a market economy – markets and trade, enterprises, infrastructure and financial institutions. The transition indicators measure how much progress has been made in each of these areas towards achieving a well-functioning market economy. Progress is measured against the standards of industrialised market economies, recognising that there is neither a perfectly functioning market economy nor a unique end-point for transition. The measurement scale for the indicators ranges from 1 to 4+, where 1 represents little or no change from a rigidly planned economy and a 4+ represents the standard of an industrialised market economy.

Table 2.1 presents the scores for reform progress in nine areas. The reform of markets and trade is measured by the liberalisation of prices (including the extent that utility prices reflect economic costs[1]), the liberalisation of trade and access to foreign exchange, and the effectiveness of competition policy in combating the abuses of market dominance and anti-competitive practices. The reform of enterprises includes two indicators for privatisation, measuring progress in transferring state-owned small and large-scale enterprises into private ownership. For large-scale privatisation, the scores also reflect the standards of corporate behaviour among privatised large corporations. The governance and enterprise restructuring score indicates progress in cutting production subsidies and introducing effective bankruptcy procedures and sound corporate governance practices.

Regarding infrastructure, Table 2.1 summarises the extent of tariff reform, the commercialisation of infrastructure enterprises and the extent of regulatory and institutional development. The summary indicator reflects progress in five areas of infrastructure: telecommunications, electric power, railways, roads, and water and waste water. A detailed assessment is contained in Annex 2.1, which also reports individual scores for these five areas. Regarding financial institutions, the indicators measure reform and development of the banking sector (including the extent to which interest rates have been liberalised) as well as the creation of securities markets and non-bank financial institutions. They also show the extent to which banking and financial regulations have been raised to international standards, whether they have been enforced effectively and if procedures exist for resolving the failure of financial institutions.

Detailed definitions of the scores can be found in the notes to Table 2.1 and Annex 2.1. The country pages at the back of the Report contain further country-by-country assessments that support the scores presented here. They also contain key dates in the transition process for each country since 1991. For the first time this year, the series of infrastructure transition indicators has been backdated to 1989.

Looking across the nine indicators presented in Table 2.1, there is significant variation in reform progress across the sub-regions. The countries of CEB have clearly progressed furthest in all aspects of reform while countries in the CIS continue to lag behind. Those in SEE continue to lie in the middle, with Bulgaria closing on the group of advanced reformers while Romania and the southern Balkan countries are still at earlier stages of reform. These geographical differences have now persisted for several years, reflecting the much more rapid progress in reforms in CEB during the mid-1990s. However, over the past three years several of the less advanced transition economies have started to catch up with the front-runners. This mirrors the gradual progress in economic performance in SEE and the CIS.

Chart 2.1 documents the average change in the transition indicator scores between 2001 and 2002. Fifteen out of 27 countries recorded average increases in their reform scores last year, with 12 countries remaining at the same level. Out of these 15 improving countries, nine are located either in SEE or in the CIS, confirming that less advanced reformers have continued to catch up this year.

The largest gains were made in the Federal Republic of Yugoslavia. The democratic government elected in Serbia in December 2000 has taken significant strides in creating the foundations for a market economy and in overcoming the distortions arising from conflicts. Price liberalisation is almost complete (excluding utility price reform), the trade regime is generally open and current account convertibility has been established. Over the past 12 months, early gains in liberalisation have been accompanied by progress in the sale of large enterprises, the consolidation and privatisation of the banking sector, the re-establishment of a capital market (currently trading mainly government securities) and the beginnings of reform in infrastructure. Reform momentum has also been maintained in Montenegro, allowing FR Yugoslavia to close the gap in reform progress that separated the country from its neighbours in SEE. Box 2.1 describes recent progress in reform in Kosovo. The reform momentum has also extended to other countries in SEE, with Bosnia and Herzegovina and Bulgaria recording significant progress.

In the CIS the most significant progress was recorded in Russia. Since the adoption of the Government's economic reform programme in May 2000, Russia has pressed ahead with structural reforms in a number of areas. In 2001 significant progress was made in strengthening financial discipline through an overhaul of the tax system and in improving corporate governance standards through the adoption of new company and bankruptcy legislation and a corporate governance code. In 2002 some preliminary steps have been taken to reform public infrastructure, in particular electric power and railways, although implementing

---

[1] As reported in the notes to Table 2.1, a transition indicator score of 4 in price liberalisation would reflect full economic pricing of utility services. A 3+ is allocated to those few countries that have achieved significant progress in tariff reform in the energy sector, the sector in which initial under-pricing was probably most extreme.

Box 2.1

Recent developments in Kosovo

The province of Kosovo continues to be run according to the UN Security Council Resolution that placed Kosovo under the authority of the United Nations Interim Administration Mission in Kosovo (UNMIK). A new Constitutional Framework was adopted in May 2001, under which a number of responsibilities were delegated to the Provisional Institutions of Self-Government (Assembly, President, and Government) that were formed after the elections on 17 November 2001 in Kosovo. These responsibilities relate to economic and financial policy, trade, industry and investments, transport and telecommunications. However, the ultimate authority for the implementation of the UN Security Council Resolution remains with UNMIK.

Economic activity has picked up markedly over the past two years but GDP per capita, roughly estimated at around US$ 900 in 2001, is significantly lower than in the rest of the Federal Republic of Yugoslavia. In view of the province's low revenue, a major macroeconomic challenge faced by UNMIK is the control and financing of current public expenditure. Revenue collection improved in 2001, due mainly to a sharp increase in import duties and excise taxes, and UNMIK introduced new taxes in April 2002, including profit and wage taxes. However, local revenue growth is unlikely to compensate for the expected decline in donor grants. The IMF has projected that foreign grants, including humanitarian assistance, donor grants and private remittances, will decrease from an estimated 67 per cent of GDP in 2001 to 15–20 per cent of GDP by 2004.

UNMIK is slowly establishing a legal framework in Kosovo that would allow normal investment activity, including new regulations on banking, taxation, business registration, pledges and foreign investment. However, one of the biggest challenges is to tackle the issue of property rights for the 300–350 state and socially owned enterprises. To address this issue, in June 2002 UNMIK signed two regulations that pave the way for privatisation of socially owned enterprises in Kosovo. These regulations establish the Kosovo Trust Agency (KTA) and set up a Special Chamber of the Supreme Court of Kosovo to deal with KTA matters. The KTA is an independent body that will administer public and socially owned enterprises in trade, industry or agriculture as well as public utilities (power, water, post and telecommunications, and transport).

The KTA will also act as a trustee for the owners of the property and will have the right to undertake all necessary corporate activities, including management, reorganisations, spin-offs, concessions, liquidations and, for the socially owned enterprises, privatisation. Despite the fact that only 20 to 40 companies are expected to attract outside investors, the privatisation process should help to overcome the uncertainty over ownership. If successful, it will also unlock the potential assets that many of these enterprises hold, restore a level playing field between enterprises, eliminate a source of quasi-fiscal liabilities and send a signal to domestic and foreign investors about progress in reform.

Chart 2.1

Change in average transition indicator scores, 2001–02

Increase in scores

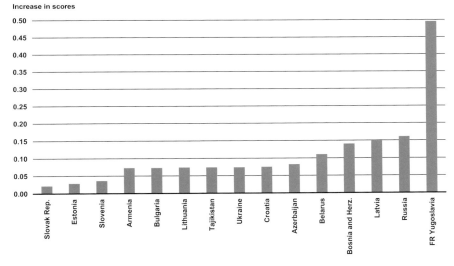

Source: EBRD.
Note: The chart reports the change in the simple unweighted average across all nine dimensions of transition reported in Table 2.1. No change was recorded for Albania, Czech Republic, FYR Macedonia, Georgia, Hungary, Kazakhstan, Kyrgyz Republic, Moldova, Poland, Romania, Turkmenistan and Uzbekistan.

reforms remains a priority. Elsewhere in the CIS there was a lack of reform progress in Central Asia in 2002. While military intervention in Afghanistan may have increased uncertainty within the region, the slow-down in reforms reflects domestic political factors and a weak commitment to economic and political openness in some countries.

Among CEB countries likely to accede to the EU, progress was made in the Baltic states, the Slovak Republic and Slovenia. These countries were lagging behind the Czech Republic, Hungary and Poland in some areas and progress reflects further efforts to meet the requirements of the *acquis communautaire*. Croatia has also

continued to achieve significant reform gains, despite not being an EU accession candidate.

In addition to the core areas of transition measured by the *Transition Reports*, Annex 2.1 summarises progress in five infrastructure sectors: telecommunications, electric power, railways, roads, and water and waste water. Annex 2.2 presents the results of the EBRD's legal transition survey of 165 practising lawyers in 27 countries in the region. The EBRD's Office of the General Counsel implemented and analysed this survey, which measures the extensiveness and effectiveness of commercial and financial laws, with a particular focus on laws and regulations that are fundamental to investment and financing decisions. They include company law, bankruptcy and secured transactions laws as well as banking and securities laws and regulations. The survey examines both the content of the law and the effectiveness of judicial enforcement, providing a valuable supplement to the EBRD's economic transition indicators.

Table 2.1

Progress in transition in central and eastern Europe and the CIS

Countries	Population mid-2001 (million)	Private sector share of GDP mid-2001 (EBRD estimate in %)	Enterprises			Markets and trade			Financial institutions		Infrastructure
			Large-scale privatisation	Small-scale privatisation	Governance & enterprise restructuring	Price liberalisation	Trade & foreign exchange system	Competition policy	Banking reform & interest rate liberalisation	Securities markets & non-bank financial institutions	Infra-structure reform
Albania	3.4	75	2+	4	2	3	4+	2-	2+	2-	2
Armenia	3.0	70	3+	4-	2+	3	4	2	2+	2	2+
Azerbaijan	8.1	60	2	4-	2	3	4-	2	2+	2-	2-
Belarus	10.0	20	1	2	1	2	2+	2	2-	2	1+
Bosnia & Herzegovina	4.3	45	2+	3	2-	3	3	1	2+	2-	2+
Bulgaria	8.1	70	4-	4-	2+	3	4+	2+	3+	2+	3-
Croatia	4.6	60	3	4+	3-	3	4+	2+	4-	3-	3-
Czech Republic	10.3	80	4	4+	3+	3	4+	3	4-	3	3
Estonia	1.4	80	4	4+	3+	3	4+	3-	4-	3+	3+
FR Yugoslavia	8.6	40	2	3	2	3	3+	1	2+	2-	2
FYR Macedonia	2.0	60	3	4	2+	3	4	2	3	2-	2
Georgia	5.4	65	3+	4	2	3+	4+	2	2+	2-	2+
Hungary	10.0	80	4	4+	3+	3+	4+	3	4	4-	4-
Kazakhstan	14.9	65	3	4	2	3	3+	2	3-	2+	2
Kyrgyz Republic	4.7	60	3	4	2	3	4	2	2+	2	1+
Latvia	2.4	70	3+	4+	3-	3	4+	2+	4-	3	3
Lithuania	3.7	75	4-	4+	3	3	4+	3	3	3	3-
Moldova	4.3	50	3	3+	2	3+	4+	2	2+	2	2+
Poland	38.7	75	3+	4+	3+	3+	4+	3	3+	4-	4-
Romania	22.3	65	3+	4-	2	3+	4	2+	3-	2	3
Russia	145.4	70	3+	4	2+	3	3	2+	2	2+	2+
Slovak Republic	5.4	80	4	4+	3	3	4+	3	3+	2+	2+
Slovenia	2.0	65	3	4+	3	3+	4+	3-	3+	3-	3+
Tajikistan	6.2	50	2+	4-	2-	3	3+	2-	2-	1	1+
Turkmenistan	5.4	25	1	2	1	2	1	1	1	1	1
Ukraine	49.3	65	3	4-	2	3	3	2+	2+	2	2
Uzbekistan	25.0	45	3-	3	2-	2	2-	2	2-	2	2-

Note: The private sector share of GDP is calculated using available statistics from both official (government) and unofficial sources. The share includes income generated from the formal activities of registered private companies, as well as informal activities where reliable information is available. The term "private company" refers to all enterprises in which private individuals or entities own the majority of shares.

The accuracy of EBRD estimates is constrained by data limitations, particularly in the area of informal activity. EBRD estimates may, in some cases, differ markedly from official data. This is usually due to differences in the definition of "private sector" or "non-state sector". For example, in the CIS, "non-state sector" includes collective farms, as well as companies in which only a minority stake has been privatised.

Classification system for transition indicators[1]

Large-scale privatisation

1 Little private ownership.

2 Comprehensive scheme almost ready for implementation; some sales completed.

3 More than 25 per cent of large-scale enterprise assets in private hands or in the process of being privatised (with the process having reached a stage at which the state has effectively ceded its ownership rights), but possibly with major unresolved issues regarding corporate governance.

4 More than 50 per cent of state-owned enterprise and farm assets in private ownership and significant progress on corporate governance of these enterprises.

4+ Standards and performance typical of advanced industrial economies: more than 75 per cent of enterprise assets in private ownership with effective corporate governance.

Small-scale privatisation

1 Little progress.

2 Substantial share privatised.

3 Comprehensive programme almost ready for implementation.

4 Complete privatisation of small companies with tradable ownership rights.

4+ Standards and performance typical of advanced industrial economies: no state ownership of small enterprises; effective tradability of land.

Governance and enterprise restructuring

1 Soft budget constraints (lax credit and subsidy policies weakening financial discipline at the enterprise level); few other reforms to promote corporate governance.

2 Moderately tight credit and subsidy policy but weak enforcement of bankruptcy legislation and little action taken to strengthen competition and corporate governance.

3 Significant and sustained actions to harden budget constraints and to promote corporate governance effectively (e.g. privatisation combined with tight credit and subsidy policies and/or enforcement of bankruptcy legislation).

4 Substantial improvement in corporate governance, for example, an account of an active corporate control market; significant new investment at the enterprise level.

4+ Standards and performance typical of advanced industrial economies: effective corporate control exercised through domestic financial institutions and markets, fostering market-driven restructuring.

Price liberalisation

1 Most prices formally controlled by the government.

2 Price controls for several important product categories; state procurement at non-market prices remains substantial.

3 Substantial progress on price liberalisation; state procurement at non-market prices largely phased out.

4 Comprehensive price liberalisation; utility pricing reflects economic costs.

4+ Standards and performance typical of advanced industrial economies: comprehensive price liberalisation; efficiency-enhancing regulation of utility pricing.

Trade and foreign exchange system

1 Widespread import and/or export controls or very limited legitimate access to foreign exchange.

2 Some liberalisation of import and/or export controls; almost full current account convertibility in principle but with a foreign exchange regime that is not fully transparent (possibly with multiple exchange rates).

3 Removal of almost all quantitative and administrative import and export restrictions; almost full current account convertibility.

4 Removal of all quantitative and administrative import and export restrictions (apart from agriculture) and all significant export tariffs; insignificant direct involvement in exports and imports by ministries and state-owned trading companies; no major non-uniformity of customs duties for non-agricultural goods and services; full and current account convertibility.

4+ Standards and performance norms of advanced industrial economies: removal of most tariff barriers; membership in WTO.

Competition policy

1 No competition legislation and institutions.

2 Competition policy legislation and institutions set up; some reduction of entry restrictions or enforcement action on dominant firms.

3 Some enforcement actions to reduce abuse of market power and to promote a competitive environment, including break-ups of dominant conglomerates; substantial reduction of entry restrictions.

4 Significant enforcement actions to reduce abuse of market power and to promote a competitive environment.

4+ Standards and performance typical of advanced industrial economies: effective enforcement of competition policy; unrestricted entry to most markets.

Banking reform and interest rate liberalisation

1 Little progress beyond establishment of a two-tier system.

2 Significant liberalisation of interest rates and credit allocation; limited use of directed credit or interest rate ceilings.

3 Substantial progress in establishment of bank solvency and of a framework for prudential supervision and regulation; full interest rate liberalisation with little preferential access to cheap refinancing; significant lending to private enterprises and significant presence of private banks.

4 Significant movement of banking laws and regulations towards BIS standards; well-functioning banking competition and effective prudential supervision; significant term lending to private enterprises; substantial financial deepening.

4+ Standards and performance norms of advanced industrial economies: full convergence of banking laws and regulations with BIS standards; provision of full set of competitive banking services.

Securities markets and non-bank financial institutions

1 Little progress.

2 Formation of securities exchanges, market-makers and brokers; some trading in government paper and/or securities; rudimentary legal and regulatory framework for the issuance and trading of securities.

3 Substantial issuance of securities by private enterprises; establishment of independent share registries, secure clearance and settlement procedures, and some protection of minority shareholders; emergence of non-bank financial institutions (e.g. investment funds, private insurance and pension funds, leasing companies) and associated regulatory framework.

4 Securities laws and regulations approaching IOSCO standards; substantial market liquidity and capitalisation; well-functioning non-bank financial institutions and effective regulation.

4+ Standards and performance norms of advanced industrial economies: full convergence of securities laws and regulations with IOSCO standards; fully developed non-bank intermediation.

Infrastructure

The ratings are calculated using the average reform process ratings in telecommunications, electric power, water and waste water, roads and railways. (See Annex 2.1 for the individual scores and the definitions of thresholds.) "+" and "−" ratings are treated by adding 0.3 and subtracting 0.3 from the full value. The average is obtained by rounding down, e.g. a score of 2.6 is treated as 2+, but score of 2.8 is treated as 3−.

---

[1] The classification system is a stylised reflection of the judgement of the EBRD's Office of the Chief Economist. More detailed descriptions of country-specific transition progress has been provided at the back of this Report. The classification system builds on the 1994 *Transition Report*. To refine further the classification system, pluses and minuses have been added to the 1–4 scale to indicate countries on the borderline between two categories. The classification 4* which was used in previous years has been replaced with 4+, though the meaning of the score remains the same.

Chart 2.2

Reform progress since 1989

Average transition score

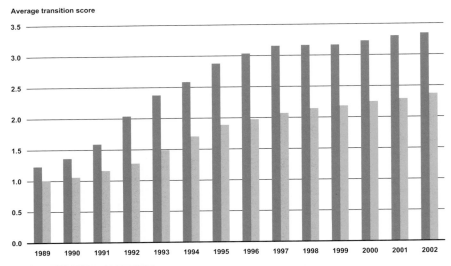

■ Initial phase   ■ Second phase

Source: EBRD.

Note: The chart reports the average score across all 27 countries of operations in the two broad dimensions of reform between 1989-2002. Initial phase reforms include price liberalisation, foreign exchange and trade liberalisation and small-scale privatisation. Second phase reforms include large-scale privatisation, governance and enterprise restructuring, competition policy, infrastructure reforms, banking and interest rate liberalisation and non-bank financial institutions. Reforms are measured using the EBRD transition indicators. Scores range from 1 to 4. For a full explanation of the classification system, refer to Table 2.1.

2.2 Patterns in reform

The transition indicators in Table 2.1 not only reveal significant variation across countries but also between various aspects of reform. This variation reflects a largely consistent pattern in the order of reforms in the transition, which has been analysed in depth in previous *Transition Reports*. This analysis has established a distinction between "initial phase" reforms, which take priority during the early years of transition, and subsequent "second phase" reforms. Initial phase reforms include price and trade liberalisation as well as small-scale privatisation, and are relatively straightforward (in the sense of reducing state intervention) and simple to implement. These reforms have been largely completed in most countries in the region, with the exception of Belarus and Turkmenistan. Uzbekistan also lags behind in market liberalisation but has advanced with small-scale privatisation.

The second phase of transition, which has begun at different times across the region, focuses on institution-building. These reforms comprise competition policy, enterprise restructuring, the development of market-based financial institutions and the reform of infrastructure. They are considerably more complex,

require significant implementation capabilities from the state, and in many instances face stiff resistance from vested interest groups clinging to the benefits of the status quo. Large-scale privatisation generally straddles these two phases of reform. In some countries mass privatisation of large enterprises was carried out very early in the transition but in the majority of countries, large-scale privatisation has been slow, involving political struggles with insiders in state-owned companies. Large-scale privatisation has therefore remained on the policy agenda in the second phase of transition and can be grouped together with enterprise reform, financial markets and infrastructure.

Chart 2.2 shows the overall transition indicator scores from 1989 to 2002 averaged across all countries of the region, covering liberalisation and small-scale privatisation on the one hand and large-scale privatisation and institutional development on the other. These averages provide a summary of region-wide progress in reform. The chart shows a period of rapid progress from 1989 to 1995, a marked slow-down from 1996 to 1999 in initial phase reforms, including some backtracking in liberalisation following the Russia crisis in August 1998,

followed by an upturn beginning in 2000. During 2000 and 2001 this upturn was driven largely by accelerated liberalisation and privatisation by laggards in reform, such as Bosnia and Herzegovina, FR Yugoslavia and Tajikistan, where the start of economic transition was delayed by military conflict or civil war. In 2002, however, progress in institutional reforms has been more pronounced than initial phase reforms.

Chart 2.3 shows the change between 2001 and 2002 in the transition scores for the aspects of transition recorded in Table 2.1, averaged across all transition economies. The largest increase on average was recorded in banking reform, with eight countries being upgraded this year. This was mostly due to significant financial progress following early efforts to consolidate the banking sector and to sell off the largest domestic banks to foreign financial institutions. The EBRD has actively supported this process as an equity investor in the banking sector in many countries, including investments in 2002 in Bulgaria, FR Yugoslavia and Tajikistan, which received upgrades in their scores.

Seven countries were upgraded for progress in the reform of capital markets. Particularly notable were developments in the Baltic states, where the Riga and Tallinn stock exchanges merged with the Helsinki bourse, and regulations were brought into line with EU requirements. The new regional exchange will provide Baltic companies with access to a broader pool of investment funds and increase the range of financing available to them. It will also provide a more attractive exit option for private equity investors seeking to create value from lower-risk premia and greater growth prospects following EU accession. Russia's capital markets have recorded very significant gains in recent months and the country has benefited from more credible regulatory institutions and improved corporate governance, leading to an upgrade in this area.

A notable feature of transition progress in 2002 has been the improvement in governance and enterprise restructuring. Four countries were upgraded for progress in this area, including Armenia,

Chart 2.3

Change in average reform scores by dimension, 2001-02

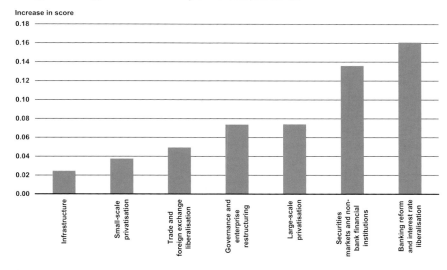

Source: EBRD.
Note: The chart reports the average change in the transition scores across all 27 countries of operations for each of the nine dimensions in Table 2.1. No change was recorded in price liberalisation and competition policy.

Chart 2.4

Reform patterns in transition, 2002

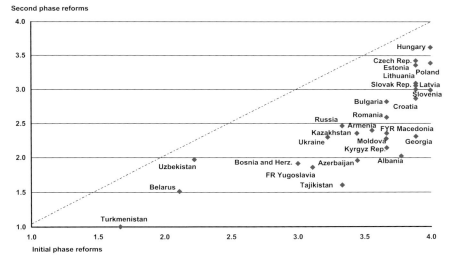

Source: EBRD.
Note: The chart reports the average score across all 27 countries of operations in the two broad dimensions of reform for 2002. Initial phase reforms include price liberalisation, foreign exchange and trade liberalisation and small-scale privatisation. Second phase reforms include large-scale privatisation, governance and enterprise restructuring, competition policy, infrastructure reforms, banking and interest rate liberalisation and non-bank financial institutions. Reforms are measured using the EBRD transition indicators. Scores range from 1 to 4. For a full explanation of the classification system, refer to Table 2.1.

FR Yugoslavia, Lithuania and Slovenia. In Armenia this reflects government efforts to reduce "red tape" and to improve the business environment for private enterprises. In FR Yugoslavia major improvements have been made in tightening financial discipline while Lithuania enforced new bankruptcy legislation and undertook several initiatives to reduce corruption and the tax burden.

Both Lithuania and Slovenia are aiming to become more attractive for foreign direct investment (FDI), which has lagged behind levels achieved in other EU accession countries.

The least progress in reform in 2002 was recorded in price liberalisation and competition policy. With the exception of Belarus, Turkmenistan and Uzbekistan,

prices are already largely liberalised across the region. Further progress in this area would require decisive moves towards cost-reflective tariffs in infrastructure. As Chart 2.3 reveals, and Annex 2.1 further explains, these reforms have not progressed much over the past year, with the exception of the electric power sector. In the area of competition policy, the lack of progress reflects the considerable resources and time required to develop effective capacity in this area. Competition authorities throughout the region often remain under-funded and under-staffed. For the EU accession countries a key consideration in this area is the need to comply with EU regulations on state aid.

How far has the progress in institutional reforms over the past year reduced the imbalance between liberalisation and privatisation on the one hand and institution-building on the other, which was so evident in the first decade of transition? Chart 2.4 summarises reform patterns across the region by presenting the average reform scores in initial phase and second phase reforms by country in 2002. The chart also shows points on a 45-degree line, which represents a hypothetical reform path in the sense that steps towards a well-functioning market economy would occur simultaneously. Points to the right of this line show the inevitable imbalance in reforms in favour of liberalisation and small-scale privatisation. Chart 2.4 shows that in the most advanced and least advanced transition economies, the distances to the 45-degree line are relatively small. In countries at an intermediate stage of transition, reform imbalances are large. These are evident in Albania, the Caucasus, FR Yugoslavia, FYR Macedonia, the Kyrgyz Republic, Moldova and Tajikistan.

While there are sound reasons why institutional reforms tend to advance more slowly than initial phase reforms, particularly when reform outcomes are highly uncertain or when state capacity is weak,[2] the lack of well-functioning institutions can create significant business obstacles and reduce investment and economic growth. Often in these circumstances, some of the most significant obstacles

[2] See Dewatripont and Roland (1995), Roland (2000), Chapter 2, and *Transition Report* 2001, Chapter 2.

are the lack of secure property rights, arbitrary business regulations and taxation, and corruption. Moreover, although there is a strong connection between both areas of reform (see Chapter 1 of this Report), progress in liberalisation and privatisation alone may not be enough to generate momentum for institutional reforms. Other crucial factors include political liberalisation and competition, international integration (for example, through EU accession) as well as cultural and social changes that make it easier for market-oriented institutions to become accepted.[3] For instance, FR Yugoslavia and Russia made the largest reform gains in 2002 and both countries have undergone significant political changes since 2000. The challenge over the coming years will be to maintain the momentum towards more complex areas of economic transition and institution-building.

2.3 Transition, economic governance and the business environment

The transition indicators focus on markets, enterprises, infrastructure and financial institutions, reflecting in part the particular mandate and role of the EBRD. However, the transition indicators do not provide a comprehensive assessment of all aspects of transition relevant to investment and growth. One area not covered fully by the transition indicators is economic governance. This covers macroeconomic stability, laws and their enforcement, effective business regulation and fair taxation. Reforms in these areas can be complementary to progress in transition, as measured by the transition indicators. At the same time, failure to reform these aspects of economic governance can impose significant obstacles to the operation and growth of firms despite other market-oriented reforms.

In view of the importance of economic governance and institutions for a successful transition, the EBRD and the World Bank have conducted periodic business surveys to assess how businesses in the region perceive the quality of public goods and services provided by the state. The

first survey was undertaken by the World Bank in late 1996 and early 1997 as part of the World Business Environment Survey (WBES) and findings from this survey were published in the World Bank's 1997 *World Development Report*. Building on this initial work, the EBRD and World Bank have conducted jointly two subsequent Business Environment and Enterprise Performance Surveys (BEEPS) in 1999 and 2002. Findings from the 1999 survey were published in the EBRD's *Transition Report* 1999. This year's Report updates and develops that analysis, using the findings of this year's BEEPS.

The 1999 and 2002 BEEPS asked firms to assess how the functioning of the state, physical infrastructure and financial institutions affect their business operations. Seven broad areas related directly or indirectly to the functioning of the state and public administration are assessed. They comprise macroeconomic management, taxation, business regulation, corruption, crime, the judiciary, finance and infrastructure. Firms were asked to assess how problematic these factors are for the operation and growth of their business on a scale of one to four. A score of one represents a minor obstacle and four indicates a major obstacle. In addition to these qualitative assessments, the BEEPS also asked respondents to indicate the quality of other aspects of economic governance using quantitative indicators.

The qualitative assessments of business obstacles provide a useful summary of the quality of the business environment. However, like any qualitative rating, they have potential drawbacks. For instance, different cultural traditions may influence the assessments of enterprise managers when judging how well the state and other institutions perform. Moreover, assessments could be influenced by the prevailing sense of economic optimism and could therefore be closely related to a country's current macroeconomic performance. In comparing the qualitative assessments of the business environment over

time and across countries, it is important to take into account the potential impact of such factors.

The BEEPS also contains a number of questions asking firms about quantitative measures of obstacles faced in their operations (see Section 2.5 for a detailed analysis of some of these measures). These measures of the business climate provide a useful cross-check to the qualitative ratings. For example, firms that spend more time dealing with public officials and regulatory matters may perceive business regulation as a more significant obstacle. Moreover, the qualitative assessment of the business environment across countries can also be compared with actual macroeconomic performance. Firms operating in countries with high growth and low inflation should perceive macroeconomic instability as less of an obstacle. By and large, such consistency checks did not identify particular exceptions to this.

A comparison of the 1999 and 2002 BEEPS, however, suggests that the business cycle has a strong effect on perceptions of the business environment. Therefore, in order to compare the underlying quality of the business environment across countries and over time, it is necessary to isolate from the qualitative assessments the influence of the business cycle. To do this, statistical adjustments were undertaken.[4] The adjusted results were used to construct corrected business environment scores, reflecting the business climate that would prevail if all countries shared the same macroeconomic performance.

Chart 2.5 shows the impact of correcting for business cycle effects (leaving out the dimension of macroeconomic management). The horizontal axis of these charts show the business environment scores (ranging from one – no obstacle – to four – major obstacle) for each country averaged across seven areas (taxation, business regulation, corruption, crime, the judiciary, finance and infrastructure) and allowing macroeconomic performance

---

[3] See *Transition Report* 2001, Chapter 2, and Raiser, di Tomasso and Weeks (2002).

[4] This involved running a regression of the qualitative assessments of the business environment at the firm level on the characteristics of firms (size, ownership and location within a country), reported quantitative measures of the businesses environment that relate to the qualitative assessments, the average growth rate over the past year and country dummy variables to allow for any other country-specific effects. The results from this analysis were then used to construct the qualitative business environment assessments, controlling for the business cycle by setting the macroeconomic growth rate to be the average value for all countries and to use the predicted values from the regressions using this average growth rate.

Chart 2.5

Qualitative assessments of the business environment

Assessments with controls for macroeconomic performance

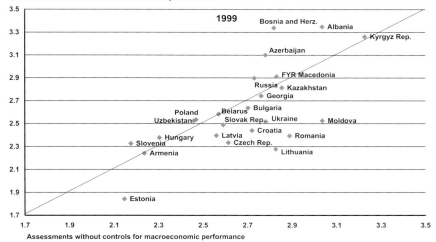

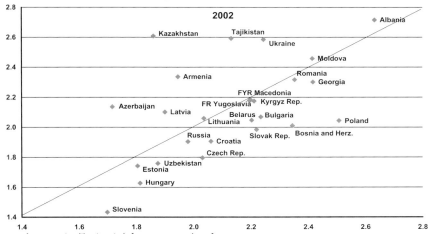

Sources: Business Environment and Enterprise Performance Survey, 1999 and 2002.

Note: The combined measure of qualitative assessments of the business environment is calculated as an unweighted average across seven dimensions: finance, infrastructure, taxes, regulation, judiciary, crime and corruption. The values range from 1 to 4, with 1 indicating no obstacles to business growth and operation and 4 indicating major obstacles. The qualitative assessments of business environment with controls for variation in macroeconomic performance are estimated qualitative assessments at the average growth rate in the sample of surveyed countries. Data for FR Yugoslavia, Tajikistan and Turkmenistan were not available for 1999. Data for Turkmenistan were not available for 2002.

to differ across countries. On the vertical axis this score has been adjusted for the influence of the business cycle. The primary effects of this adjustment in 2002 are to increase (worsen) the average business environment scores for some rapidly growing CIS countries (Azerbaijan and Kazakhstan) and to reduce (improve) the scores for one CEB country (Poland) that has experienced slow growth. Similar effects can be seen in the adjustments to the 1999 data.

2.4 Qualitative assessments of the business environment

Chart 2.6 shows the qualitative assessments of the business environment along the seven broad areas of economic governance for three country groups (CEB, SEE and the CIS) for 1999 and 2002. These measures take account of the systematic influence of the business cycle. Even after adjusting for business cycle effects, the most striking finding from the two surveys is the overall improvement in the business environment from 1999 to 2002 by about 0.55 (on an unweighted average) on the one-to-four scale. The improvements have been greater in SEE and the

CIS than in CEB, which is consistent with a gradual catching-up process for these two regions, with particularly strong gains being seen in SEE. The results for the CIS exclude Turkmenistan, where implementation of the 2002 BEEPS was terminated prior to completion. Overall, the CIS and SEE achieved about the same average business environment scores in 2002 as the CEB recorded in 1999. However, such a comparison based on the EBRD transition indicators suggests that this overestimates the current level of reform in SEE and the CIS. Within the CIS and SEE there was also considerable variation among countries (see Annex 2.3 for charts depicting individual country scores).

In CEB, the Czech Republic, Hungary and Slovenia witnessed the most significant improvements in how the business environment is perceived. Estonia, which had achieved the most favourable perceptions in 1999, saw relatively little improvement in 2002. Nevertheless, these four countries are the clear front-runners among CEB countries, with Croatia, Latvia, Lithuania, Poland and the Slovak Republic achieving lower ratings. In SEE, Albania, Bosnia and Herzegovina, Bulgaria and FYR Macedonia witnessed significant gains in ratings of the business environment while in Romania perceptions remained largely unchanged.

Among SEE countries in 2002 Bosnia and Herzegovina and Bulgaria achieved the most favourable levels of perception and Albania the least, with FR Yugoslavia, FYR Macedonia and Romania occupying the middle ground. In the CIS, Azerbaijan, the Kyrgyz Republic, Russia and Uzbekistan saw business environment ratings improve the most and Armenia, Kazakhstan, Moldova and Ukraine made the least improvement. The CIS countries with the most favourable ratings in 2002 were Azerbaijan, Belarus, Russia and Uzbekistan while the laggards were Kazakhstan, Tajikistan and Ukraine. Armenia, Georgia, the Kyrgyz Republic and Moldova occupied the middle ground among the CIS countries.

A consistent finding in both the 1999 and 2002 BEEPS is the unexpectedly favourable perceptions of the business environment in Belarus and Uzbekistan,

Chart 2.6

Qualitative assessments of the business environment, 1999 and 2002

CEB	SEE	CIS

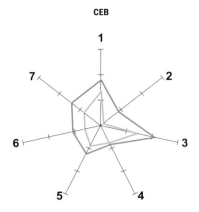
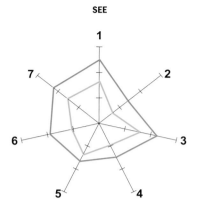
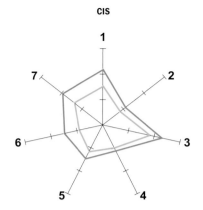

— 1999   — 2002

1 – Access to financing
2 – Quality of infrastructure
3 – Taxes
4 – Regulations
5 – Quality of judiciary
6 – Crime
7 – Corruption

Sources: Business Environment and Enterprise Performance Survey, 1999 and 2002.

Note: Regional values were calculated using unweighted averages of country values. For an explanation of the qualitative assessment of the business environment, refer to Chart 2.5. The extremity of each axis represents a score of 4, indicating a less favourable investment climate.

A fuller circle indicates a more challenging investment climate. Data for FR Yugoslavia, Tajikistan and Turkmenistan were not available.

particularly given the limited extent of market-oriented reforms in these countries, including liberalisation of markets and trade. One interpretation of this finding is that existing businesses are being sheltered from competitive pressures and that they, therefore, have relatively positive perceptions of the business environment. The survey, of course, does not include those enterprises and entrepreneurs that would like to enter these markets but are prevented from doing so by the restrictive policies of these countries.

When adjusting for the effects of the business cycle, most gains between 1999 and 2002 in how the business environment is perceived are concentrated in five of the seven areas. Finance, infrastructure, taxation, corruption and crime each saw improvements between 1999 and 2002 of about 0.5 to 0.8 on the scale of one to four. These gains were fairly uniformly distributed across the three broad country groups except for finance and crime, where SEE and CIS countries scored relatively strong gains. Perceptions of business regulation and the judiciary saw less improvement, in the range of 0.2 to 0.3 overall.

Only SEE countries saw significant improvement in business perceptions of regulation, albeit from a low level. Perceptions of the judiciary improved only moderately in all three sub-regions. The SEE and CIS countries therefore made headway in catching up with the more advanced CEB countries, primarily in the areas of finance and crime. In SEE these gains also extended to business regulation.

Notwithstanding these improvements, the aspects of the business environment that continue to pose the most serious obstacles to the operation and growth of firms are finance, taxation and corruption. Infrastructure is the least problematic area of the business environment. These findings are true of both the 1999 and 2002 BEEPS.

2.5 Quantitative measures of the business environment

In addition to the qualitative assessments provided in the survey, it is important to assess developments in the business environment using quantitative measures of economic governance. These measures provide a means of cross-checking the findings from the qualitative assessments. A drawback to the use of

quantitative measures, however, is that they focus on relatively narrow aspects of the business environment. Some caution is therefore required in drawing general conclusions from these specific measures.

This section focuses on taxation, regulation, corruption, crime and the judiciary aspects of the business environment. For finance and infrastructure, the EBRD's transition indicators already provide significant data. From the 1999 survey, quantitative measures are available for only taxation, regulation and corruption.

Tax

One way of assessing if tax administration and tax rates create an obstacle to the operation and growth of firms is to examine to what extent firms seek to avoid taxes. The BEEPS asked businesses to indicate to what extent firms like theirs under-reported sales for tax purposes, recognising the difficulty that many firms face in complying with taxes. A high proportion of reported sales would indicate a low level of tax avoidance and more effective tax compliance. Chart 2.7 shows the average reporting rates by country in 2002 and in 1999. Countries with average rates above 80 per cent in

Chart 2.7

Reported sales to tax authorities as a percentage of total sales, 1999 and 2002

Percentage of sales reported

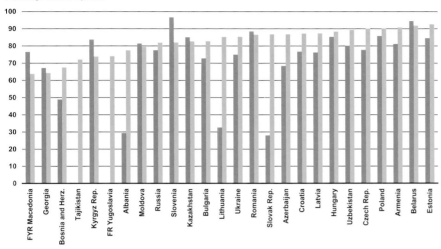

■ 1999   ■ 2002

Sources: Business Environment and Enterprise Performance Survey, 1999 and 2002.

Note: Firms were asked to estimate the percentage of reported sales to tax authorities by a typical firm in their sector. The average ratio for each country is calculated as an unweighted average of individual firms' responses. Data for Turkmenistan were not available.

Chart 2.8

Average senior management time spent dealing with public officials, 1999 and 2002

Percentage of total working time

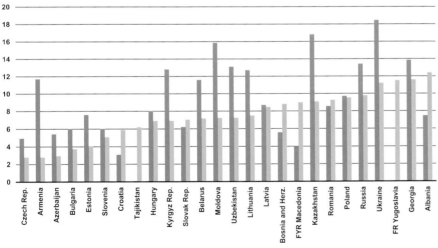

■ 1999   ■ 2002

Sources: Business Environment and Enterprise Performance Survey, 1999 and 2002.

Note: Firms were asked to report the percentage of time senior management spent on dealing with public officials over the application and interpretation of laws and regulations and access to public services. The average ratio for each country is calculated as an unweighted average from individual firms' responses. Data for Turkmenistan were not available.

2002 include all CEB countries as well as Bulgaria and Romania in SEE. Average rates above 80 per cent were also achieved by seven CIS countries (Armenia, Azerbaijan, Belarus, Kazakhstan, Russia, Ukraine and Uzbekistan). The largest increases in tax compliance between 1999 and 2002 were primarily in SEE and the CIS. Lithuania and the Slovak Republic also show large increases in tax compliance but this may be partly due to implausibly low rates (30 to 40 per cent) reported in the 1999 BEEPS for these two countries.

Business regulation

The level of business regulation that firms undergo is shown by the amount of time senior managers spend in dealing with public officials regarding the application of laws and regulations. The greater the amount of time spent by managers – the so-called "time tax" – the greater is the cost of complying with laws and regulations. While some cost is inevitable, very high costs can weaken the performance of firms. In 2002 senior managers in 11 countries spent on average more than 8 per cent of their time dealing with public officials. These included Latvia and Poland among CEB countries and five SEE countries (Albania, Bosnia and Herzegovina, FR Yugoslavia, FYR Macedonia and Romania – see Chart 2.8). Four CIS countries also had relatively high time tax rates (Georgia, Kazakhstan, Russia and Ukraine). The largest reductions in time tax rates between 1999 and 2002 were achieved in the CIS while a number of SEE countries (Albania, Bosnia and Herzegovina, FYR Macedonia and Romania) saw an increase in the cost of complying with laws and regulations over this period.

Corruption

Corruption can constitute a significant cost on firms, and one measure of this cost is the proportion of sales that are paid in the form of unofficial payments to public officials – the so-called "bribe tax". According to the 2002 BEEPS, the heaviest bribe taxes in the region are in SEE and the CIS (see Table 2.2). Firms pay on average more than 2 per cent of their total sales in unofficial payments in Albania, Azerbaijan, Georgia, Kazakhstan, the Kyrgyz Republic, Moldova, Romania, Tajikistan and Ukraine. No CEB country had a bribe tax of more than 2 per cent of sales in 2002.

Overall, there were significant reductions in the burden imposed by corruption across the region between 1999 and 2002. In 2002 the unweighted average bribe tax rate was 1.6 per cent of sales compared with 1.9 per cent in 1999.[5] Moreover, the largest reductions in the bribe tax rates were in the CIS, albeit from high levels. However, there is wide

---

[5] In the 1999 BEEPS, survey respondents were asked to report bribes paid as a percentage of total sales in terms of ranges. The average reported in the text is based on the minimum points of the reported ranges. If the mid-points of the ranges are used, the average bribe tax in 1999 is 6.9 per cent. The *Transition Report* 1999, Chapter 6, reported the average bribe tax based on the range mid-points. In the 2002 BEEPS, specific values were reported.

Table 2.2

Frequency and extent of the "bribe tax"

Countries	Percentage of firms making bribes frequently		Average bribe tax as a percentage of annual firm revenues	
	1999	2002	1999	2002
Albania	46.7	36.4	1.7	3.3
Armenia	40.3	14.3	4.2	0.9
Azerbaijan	59.5	27.5	3.7	2.7
Belarus	14.8	24.0	1.6	1.5
Bosnia and Herzegovina	20.5	22.4	2.1	0.9
Bulgaria	23.0	32.8	1.3	1.9
Croatia	17.7	12.9	0.6	0.6
Czech Republic	26.0	13.3	1.7	0.9
Estonia	12.9	12.1	0.9	0.3
FR Yugoslavia	na	15.9	na	1.5
FYR Macedonia	33.0	22.7	1.4	0.8
Georgia	36.8	37.8	3.5	2.7
Hungary	32.3	22.6	0.9	1.0
Kazakhstan	26.1	29.7	1.9	2.1
Kyrgyz Republic	28.2	43.7	2.4	3.7
Latvia	22.0	17.9	0.9	0.9
Lithuania	23.2	20.6	1.6	0.7
Moldova	34.4	34.3	3.2	2.1
Poland	33.2	18.6	0.7	1.2
Romania	50.9	36.7	1.7	2.6
Russia	30.6	38.7	1.7	1.4
Slovak Republic	33.6	36.0	1.3	1.4
Slovenia	7.7	7.1	1.4	0.8
Tajikistan	na	35.1	na	2.6
Ukraine	39.1	34.9	3.1	2.2
Uzbekistan	46.2	20.2	2.5	1.5

Source: Business Environment and Enterprise Performance Survey, 2002.

Note: Data for Turkmenistan were not available. The country averages reported for 1999 are based on the minimums of the reporting ranges in that survey. In the 2002 survey, specific values were reported.

Chart 2.9

Average time needed to resolve overdue payments, 2002

Number of weeks

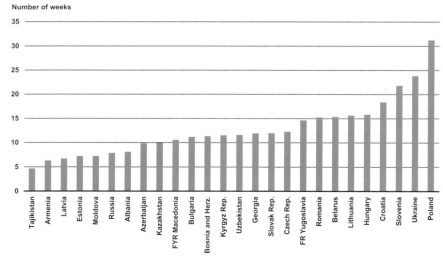

Source: Business Environment and Enterprise Performance Survey, 2002.

Note: Firms were asked to report the average time needed to resolve overdue payments. The average time for each country is calculated as an unweighted average from individual firms' responses. Data for Turkmenistan were not available.

variation among countries in this sub-region. The levels of corruption as measured by the percentage of firms that pay bribes also shows some improvement between 1999 and 2002, particularly in Albania, Armenia, Azerbaijan, the Czech Republic, FYR Macedonia, Hungary, Poland, Romania and Uzbekistan. There was in fact a significant increase in the incidence of corruption in Belarus, Bulgaria, the Kyrgyz Republic and Russia. This suggests that the burden of corruption has been partly reduced by economic growth and rising sales while some of the fundamental factors that contribute to corruption remain.

The judiciary and crime

Two measures of the impact of the judiciary and crime are the average time needed to resolve overdue payments (delays in contract enforcement) and losses to businesses as a result of crime, expressed as a percentage of sales. The average time to resolve overdue payments in 2002 exceeded three months in Belarus, Croatia, FR Yugoslavia, Hungary, Lithuania, Poland, Romania, Slovenia and Ukraine (see Chart 2.9). It is surprising that relatively long delays were experienced in a number of CEB countries, which are often regarded as having some of the best law enforcement institutions in the region. However, in Poland the long delays may be partly due to the adverse impact of slow growth. The average losses from crime (theft, vandalism or arson) in 2002 exceeded 2.5 per cent as a percentage of sales in Armenia, Azerbaijan, FR Yugoslavia, FYR Macedonia, Georgia, the Kyrgyz Republic, Moldova, Ukraine and Uzbekistan (see Chart 2.10). Perhaps unsurprisingly, the countries of SEE and the CIS appear to have relatively weaker institutions in this respect.

Overall pattern

The objective measures therefore show a similar pattern to the subjective measures. In particular, they point to consistent improvement in the business environment across the region. At the same time, many countries of SEE and the CIS appear to be closing – but not entirely eliminating – the gap between them and CEB in terms of the quality of economic

Table 2.3

Variation in the business environment between two types of firm, 1999–2002

| | | 1999 | | | 2002 | | | |
		Small new private	Large state-owned	Difference	Small new private	Large state-owned	Difference	Variation between 1999 and 2002
Bribe tax [1]	CEB	6.7	1.2	5.5	1.2	0.1	1.1	4.4
	SEE	7.3	2.7	4.6	2.2	1.3	0.9	3.8
	CIS	9.6	6.3	3.3	2.5	0.8	1.6	1.6
Time tax [2]	CEB	6.9	6.9	0.1	5.9	9.5	-3.7	3.7
	SEE	5.4	5.4	0.0	8.7	10.5	-1.9	1.9
	CIS	12.3	16.4	-4.0	6.8	6.6	0.2	4.3
Reported sales	CEB	68.8	67.8	1.1	85.5	93.8	-8.3	9.4
for tax purposes [3]	SEE	60.4	65.9	-5.5	71.3	85.4	-14.2	8.7
	CIS	73.7	86.4	-12.7	71.6	84.3	-12.6	0.0

Sources: Business Environment and Enterprise Performance Survey, 1999 and 2002.

Note: Due to data unavailability in 1999 and/or 2002 the following countries have been excluded from the respected sub-regional averages: FR Yugoslavia, Tajikistan and Turkmenistan.

[1] Percentage of total sales.
[2] Percentage of total working time.
[3] Percentage of total sales.

Chart 2.10

Losses due to crime as a share of sales, 2002

Percentage of total sales

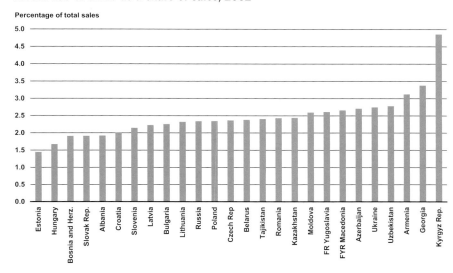

Source: Business Environment and Enterprise Performance Survey, 2002.

Note: Firms were asked to report the losses in total sales as a result of theft, robbery, vandalism or arson against their establishments. The average loss for each country is calculated as an unweighted average from individual firms' responses. Data for Turkmenistan were not available.

governance. In addition, it is important to recognise that the quality of the business environment varies not only among countries but between different types of firms (see *Transition Report* 1999, Chapter 6). The following section examines this variation in more detail.

2.6 Variation in the business environment for different types of firms

One of the important findings of the 1999 round of the BEEPS was that the quality of economic governance experienced by enterprises varied according to firm ownership and size. By and large, certain aspects of the business

environment were far more difficult for new private firms and small firms than for state-owned and larger firms. It is important to assess whether these patterns have persisted and whether the overall improvement in the business environment has benefited all firms to a similar degree. This is particularly significant because it is not only the overall quality of the business environment that influences the performance of firms but also the evenness of the so-called "playing field". In other words, all firms need to be treated in a similar way. In particular, a level playing field is necessary for the process of competition, innovation and investment to work effectively and to

sustain high rates of growth. It is important to recognise, however, that an uneven playing field can arise not just from the uneven provision of goods and services by the state but also by uneven access to market opportunities that are not measured by the business environment.

Table 2.3 examines the variation in business obstacles between two types of firms: small, new private firms (with no state-owned predecessor) and large state-owned firms. These two types are used to reflect how the business environment varies according to the size of firms and their ownership. The table reports results for the bribe tax, time tax and extent of tax avoidance. For these three measures, data are available for both 1999 and 2002, which allows an assessment to be made of how the business environment has developed over the past three years.

The table reveals that in 1999 the business environment varies depending on the type of firm and that small, new private firms tended to face more significant obstacles than large, state-owned enterprises. Small private firms tended to pay a higher percentage of their sales in bribes and to incur about the same time tax as large, state-owned enterprises, except in the CIS where the time tax was significantly higher. In addition, the same or a smaller proportion of sales were reported for tax purposes by small new private firms than by large, state-owned enterprises, indicating greater tax avoidance and possibly a greater share of activity in the shadow economy. At least in these three aspects, therefore, small new private firms faced greater business obstacles than large, state-owned firms, with the possible exception of the CIS.

The table indicates that between 1999 and 2002, some improvements have taken place in these aspects of the business environment and that the playing field has become less uneven for small, new private firms. For example, the difference between the levels of bribe tax paid by small new private firms and by large state-owned firms has diminished significantly, and bribe tax has decreased overall. At the same time, the time tax incurred by new private firms in CEB and the CIS has diminished. For large, state-owned enterprises in CEB the time tax has increased as well. Again, these changes have tilted the balance back towards small, new private enterprises. The share of total sales reported for tax purposes increased significantly between 1999 and 2002 in CEB and SEE, especially for large state-owned enterprises, but it has remained largely unchanged in the CIS for both types of firms. This suggests that differences between the two types of firms regarding the degree of tax avoidance may have increased in recent years.

This analysis of variations in the business environment for different types of firms shows that the variation is diminishing. This mirrors the trend between countries although even in 2002, significant differences remain between small, new private firms on the one hand and large, state-owned firms on the other.

2.7 Conclusion

Over the past three years the transition economies have achieved solid economic growth and progress in economic reform. At the end of the first decade of transition, reform efforts shifted increasingly towards institution-building, and this year has seen strong progress in this area. Moreover, there is clear evidence that the less advanced transition economies are starting to catch up with the

front-runners. These positive trends are mirrored by evidence emerging from the second round of the BEEPS. The business environment has improved significantly across the region, and improvements have been particularly notable in SEE and the CIS. To some extent, these improvements simply reflect the better macroeconomic environment, which may encourage firms to be more optimistic. However, there have been some actual improvements too, as the burden of taxation and corruption has declined. Moreover, a more level playing field for different types of firms is beginning to emerge.

This concluding section looks at the factors that may account for these improvements, recognising that a more detailed analysis of the BEEPS data is needed to substantiate the views offered here. To begin, it is necessary to consider why the business environment differed so much between countries during the first decade of transition. In brief, two theories have been put forward:

▌ The first theory suggested that vested interests had "captured" the state. Using the payments made available to them as a result of partial liberalisation, insider privatisation and the wealth acquired from poorly protected property rights, these vested interests used their economic power to prevent improvements in governance that would have threatened their privileged position.[6]

▌ The second theory asserted that state capture in the less advanced transition economies, particularly in the CIS, was caused by a lack of political competition and a weak state. Unelected public officials who were too weak to assert their authority were easily bought off by powerful vested interests in pursuit of short-term gains.[7]

The experiences of recent years suggest that the degree of state capture was not as stable as earlier analyses indicated. Two developments may have helped to spur change and to support recent improvements in economic governance and institutions.

First, economic competition and increased international integration may have created new constituencies in favour of a sound business environment and eroded the strength of vested interests. Since markets were only recently created in transition economies, it may take some time for certain countries to benefit from competition, particularly Russia and the rest of the CIS, where international trade has had less impact than in CEE. In general, the large exchange rate devaluations and the resumption of economic growth after 1998 provided a more stable economic environment for new businesses to enter the market and for existing private firms to grow. A growing economy may have boosted the returns from investment and innovation relative to that of contesting property rights and corruption. This shift may have changed the relationship between influential firms and the state. Moreover, when growth prospects are good, the security of property rights and access to public goods and services may become a greater concern, even for powerful oligarchs.

The second parallel development was change in the political process and the attitude of the political leadership. In Russia such a change took place with the beginning of the Putin presidency and his insistence on protecting property rights and curbing the influence of the oligarchs. In SEE the fall of the Milosevic regime may have had a similar effect. A change in political thinking is less obvious in other countries of the CIS, where ruling elites have increased in general their tendency to seize domestic assets. But even in the CIS, the process of privatisation has passed its peak and the consolidation of ownership has taken place to some extent, even if in some cases only the privileged few have benefited. Governments across the region may have had strong incentives to replace the "grabbing hand" of the state with the "taxing hand" – recognising that it is in their best interest to provide the right conditions for firms to invest, innovate and grow.[8]

---

[6] See Hellman (1998) and *Transition Report* 1999, Chapter 6.

[7] See World Bank (2000).

[8] On roving versus stationary bandits, see Ohlson (2000), Chapter 1.

There is reason to believe that the trends observed over the past three years are sustainable. The levelling of the playing field that seems to have taken place across the region suggests that the forces of economic and political competition may provide an impetus for progress in reform and better governance. Moreover, as business obstacles faced by new private and small firms have been reduced, competition has been boosted. Yet, there is no room for complacency. There is still a gap between the advanced and less-advanced reformers, and the current positive trend has yet to stand the test of a downturn. It is far from clear whether the current reform momentum would be maintained in the face of recession or significantly lower growth as the gains from reform would become less immediately apparent. When the going is good, enterprise managers demand secure property rights and reinvest their profits. But the same managers could return to asset-stripping and corrupt practices if economic prospects decline. Moreover, they could succeed if domestic institutions have not been strengthened sufficiently to resist these pressures.

Developments in the EU accession countries suggest that the task of institution-building will remain at the core of the policy agenda for all transition economies for some time to come. Even with the strong influence provided by the *acquis communautaire*, institutional weaknesses remain in regulation, competition policy, the judicial system and often in local government administration. The improvement of the past three years calls for continued progress and awareness that the task of transition has not been completed. Much remains to be done.

References

M. Diewatripont and G. Roland (1995), "Design of reform packages under uncertainty", *American Economic Review*, Vol.85, No.5, pp.1207–23.

J. Hellman (1998), "Winners take all: The politics of partial reform in post-communist transition", *World Politics*, Vol.50, No.2, pp.203–34.

H. Kitschelt (2001), "Post-communist economic reform: Causal mechanisms and concomitant properties", mimeo, Duke University.

M. Ohlson (2000), *Power and Prosperity: Outgrowing Communist and Capitalist Dictatorships*, Basic Books, New York.

M. Raiser, L.M. di Tommaso and M. Weeks (2002), "Measurement and determinants of institutional change in transition economies", mimeo, EBRD.

G. Roland (2000), *Transition and Economics: Politics, Markets and Firms*, MIT Press, Cambridge, MA.

World Bank (2000), *Anti-corruption: A Contribution to the Policy Debate*, World Bank, Washington D.C.

Annex 2.1: Progress in infrastructure reform

Infrastructure networks and services in the transition economies, which were originally designed for central planning and authoritarian political regimes, are poorly suited to the needs and standards of market economies. Use of electric power and water, for example, is excessive due to a structure of production and prices that paid scant regard to the costs of production. Rail networks are extensive and heavily staffed while road networks remain inadequate. Telecommunications services are still vastly under-supplied.

The transition economies face considerable challenges in replacing old technology and building new infrastructure networks. This requires tariff reform, increased commercialisation and competition in the provision of infrastructure services, and regulatory and institutional development. The EBRD transition scores in infrastructure reflect these major challenges. This year these scores have been backdated to 1989 for all 27 of the EBRD's countries of operations (see the country assessments at the back of the Report).[1]

Viewed against the need for reform in infrastructure, progress in 2002 was modest (see Table A.2.1). Ten rating upgrades were made for four countries, and one downgrade was recorded. Improvements were concentrated in the power and transport sectors, prompted by the EU accession process in central eastern Europe and the Baltic states (CEB) and the urgent need for efficiency improvements in south-eastern Europe (SEE) and the Commonwealth of Independent States (CIS) following years of under-investment. The attraction of private investment through tariff and institutional reforms is seen by many countries as the best way to save scarce public resources while guaranteeing higher levels of efficiency. Yet, attracting private investment has been difficult over the past year due to general concern among investors over emerging market risks.

Power sector

The greatest progress over the past year was achieved in the power sector. Five countries received a rating upgrade but one country, Estonia, was downgraded in 2002. In Azerbaijan the Government adopted a financial recovery plan for the energy sector, and brought in a private Turkish investor under a long-term concession for the power distribution network in Baku. The challenge for Azerbaijan is to build on this progress with regulatory strengthening, further industry restructuring and extension of private sector participation to remaining state-owned generation and distribution companies. The tendering process for these remaining assets had begun by late summer 2002.

Bosnia and Herzegovina has progressed by adopting legislation for setting up a state regulator to oversee the operation of an integrated transmission network and has developed electricity privatisation plans. In the Kyrgyz Republic the electricity industry has been unbundled, with a view to privatisation. In Russia legislation for regulatory development and opening up of the electricity market has been drafted but implementation will be a key issue.

The Slovak Republic has been given a higher rating following the sale to strategic investors of 49 per cent stakes in three electricity distribution companies within the context of independent and incentive-based regulation. Armenia recently privatised its distribution networks, selling a majority stake to a foreign investor but an improved performance is still to be demonstrated and as a result its rating has remained unchanged. Estonia has taken a step backwards regarding privatisation following the breakdown in negotiations for the sale of the Narva power plant to a strategic investor.

Municipal sector

In the municipal sector there has been some progress in reform during the past year but not enough to warrant a higher rating for any countries. In Romania, legislation has been passed to set up an independent water sector regulator, to commercialise water companies (by requiring relations between municipalities and municipal companies to be on a contract basis) and to introduce private sector participation. In Russia the implementation of legislation to increase tariffs to cost-recovery levels for all types of customer by 2004 is on track.

Private sector participation in the municipal sector is anticipated in Russia in 2003, particularly in St Petersburg, where private sector involvement is likely in the construction of new waste-water treatment facilities. In Georgia a tender process for a water and waste-water concession is under way and there are plans to introduce management contracts for some Ukrainian utilities by mid-2003. In Kazakhstan, negotiations over a private sector concession in the waste-water sector have not progressed. Private sector participation has been introduced under concession contracts in Bulgaria, the Czech Republic and Estonia, with all parties fulfilling their contractual obligations.

Telecommunications

The lack of upgrades in ratings for the telecommunications sector is largely due to the extremely difficult global business environment. Privatisation has been delayed due to the lack of interest from strategic investors. The majority of telecommunications operators who could be potential investors face increasing levels of indebtedness, most notably in western Europe, in part due to the purchase of expensive third generation (3G) cellular UMTS (universal mobile telecommunications system) licences.

---

[1] In some limited cases, the backdating exercise revealed some inaccurate ratings in certain countries, as additional information has become available. The dataset of infrastructure ratings is available from the EBRD's Office of the Chief Economist on request.

Table A.2.1

Infrastructure transition indicators, 2002

Country	Telecommunications	Electric power	Railways	Roads	Water and waste water
Albania	3+	2+	2	2	1
Armenia	2+	3+	2	2+	2
Azerbaijan	1	2+	2+	2+	2
Belarus	2	1	1	2	1
Bosnia and Herzegovina	3+	3	3	2	1
Bulgaria	3	3+	3	2+	3
Croatia	3+	3	2+	2+	3+
Czech Republic	4	3	2+	2+	4
Estonia	4	3	4+	2+	4
FR Yugoslavia	2	2	2+	2+	2
FYR Macedonia	2	2+	2	2+	2
Georgia	2+	3+	3	2	2
Hungary	4	4	3+	3+	4
Kazakhstan	2+	3	3-	2	1
Kyrgyz Republic	2+	2+	1	1	1
Latvia	3	3	3+	2+	3+
Lithuania	3+	3	2+	2+	3+
Moldova	2+	3+	2	2	2
Poland	4	3	4	3+	4
Romania	3	3	4	3	3
Russia	3	2+	2+	2+	2+
Slovak Republic	2+	4	2+	2+	2+
Slovenia	3	3	3+	3	4
Tajikistan	2+	1	1	1	1
Turkmenistan	1	1	1	1	1
Ukraine	2+	3+	2	2	1
Uzbekistan	2	2	3	1	1

Source: EBRD.

Classification system for transition indicators[1]

Telecommunications

1 Little progress has been achieved in commercialisation and regulation. There is a minimal degree of private sector involvement. Strong political interference takes place in management decisions. There is a lack of cost-effective tariff-setting principles, with extensive cross-subsidisation. Few other institutional reforms to encourage liberalisation are envisaged, even for mobile phones and value-added services.

2 Modest progress has been achieved in commercialisation. Corporatisation of the dominant operator has taken place and there is some separation of operation from public sector governance, but tariffs are still politically set.

3 Substantial progress has been achieved in commercialisation and regulation. There is full separation of telecommunications from postal services, with a reduction in the extent of cross-subsidisation. Some liberalisation has taken place in the mobile segment and in value-added services.

4 Complete commercialisation (including privatisation of the dominant operator) and comprehensive regulatory and institutional reforms have been achieved. There is extensive liberalisation of entry.

4+ Implementation of an effective regulation (including the operation of an independent regulator) has been achieved, with a coherent regulatory and institutional framework to deal with tariffs, interconnection rules, licensing, concession fees and spectrum allocation. There is a consumer ombudsman function.

Electric power

1 The power sector operates as a government department. There is political interference in running the industry, with few commercial freedoms or pressures. Average prices are below costs, with external and implicit subsidy and cross-subsidy. Very little institutional reform has been achieved. There is a monolithic structure, with no separation of different parts of the business.

2 The power company is distanced from government. For example, it operates as a joint-stock company, but there is still political interference. There has been some attempt to harden budget constraints, but management incentives for efficient performance are weak. Some degree of subsidy and cross-subsidy exists. Little institutional reform has been achieved. There is a monolithic structure, with no separation of different parts of the business. Minimal, if any, private sector involvement has occurred.

3 A law has been passed providing for full-scale restructuring of the industry, including vertical unbundling through account separation and setting-up of a regulator. Some tariff reform and improvements in revenue collection have been achieved, and there is some private sector involvement.

4 A law for industry restructuring has been passed and implemented, with separation of the industry into generation, transmission and distribution. A regulator has been set up. Rules for cost-reflective tariff-setting have been formulated and implemented. Arrangements for network access (negotiated access, single buyer model) have been developed. There is substantial private sector involvement in distribution and/or generation.

4+ Business has been separated vertically into generation, transmission and distribution. An independent regulator has been set up, with full power to set cost-reflective effective tariffs. There is large-scale private sector involvement. Institutional development has taken place, covering arrangements for network access and full competition in generation.

Railways

1 Monolithic organisational structures still exist. State railways are still effectively operated as government departments. Few commercial freedoms exist to determine prices or investments. There is no private sector involvement. Cross-subsidisation of passenger service obligations with freight service revenues is undertaken.

2 New laws distance rail operations from the state, but there are weak commercial objectives. There is no budgetary funding of public service obligations in place. Organisational structures are still overly based

Classification system for transition indicators[1] (continued)

on geographic or functional areas. Ancillary businesses have been separated but there is little divestment. There has been minimal encouragement of private sector involvement. Initial business planning has been undertaken, but the targets are general and tentative.

3 New laws have been passed that restructure the railways and introduce commercial orientation. Freight and passenger services have been separated and marketing groups have been grafted onto traditional structures. Some divestment of ancillary businesses has taken place. Some budgetary compensation is available for passenger services. Business plans have been designed with clear investment and rehabilitation targets, but funding is unsecured. There is some private sector involvement in rehabilitation and/or maintenance.

4 New laws have been passed to fully commercialise the railways. Separate internal profit centres have been created for passenger and freight (actual or imminent). Extensive market freedoms exist to set tariffs and investments. Medium-term business plans are under implementation. Ancillary industries have been divested. Policy has been developed to promote private rail transport operations.

4+ Railway law has been passed allowing for separation of infrastructure from operations, and/or freight from passenger operations, and/or private train operations. There is private sector participation in ancillary services and track maintenance. A rail regulator has been established. Access pricing has been implemented. Plans have been drawn up for a full divestment and transfer of asset ownership, including infrastructure and rolling stock.

Roads

1 There is a minimal degree of decentralisation and no commercialisation has taken place. All regulatory, road management and resource allocation functions are centralised at ministerial level. New investments and road maintenance financing are dependent on central budget allocations. Road user charges are based on criteria other than relative costs imposed on the network and road use. Road construction and maintenance are undertaken by public construction units. There is no private sector participation. No public consultation or accountability take place in the preparation of road projects.

2 There is a moderate degree of decentralisation and initial steps have been taken in commercialisation. A road/highway agency has been created. Initial steps have been undertaken in resource allocation and public procurement methods. Road user charges are based on vehicle and fuel taxes but are only indirectly related to road use. A road fund has been established but it is dependent on central budget allocations. Road construction and maintenance is undertaken primarily by corporatised public entities, with some private sector participation. There is minimal public consultation/participation and accountability in the preparation of road projects.

3 There is a fairly large degree of decentralisation and commercialisation. Regulation, resource allocation, and administrative functions have been clearly separated from maintenance and operations of the public road network. Road user charges are based on vehicle and fuel taxes and fairly directly related to road use. A law has been passed allowing for the provision and operation of public roads by private companies under negotiated commercial contracts. There is private sector participation either in road maintenance works allocated via competitive tendering or through a concession to finance, operate and maintain at least a section of the highway network. There is limited public consultation and/or participation and accountability in the preparation of road projects.

4 There is a large degree of decentralisation of road administration, decision-making, resource allocation and management according to government responsibility and functional road classifications. A transparent methodology is used to allocate road expenditures. A track record has been established in implementing competitive procurement rules for road design, construction, maintenance and operations. There is large-scale private sector participation in construction, operations and maintenance directly and through public-private partnership arrangements. There is substantial public consultation and/or participation and accountability in the preparation of road projects.

4+ A fully decentralised road administration has been established, with decision-making, resource allocation and management across road networks and different levels of government. Commercialised road maintenance operations are undertaken through open competitive tendering by private construction companies. Legislation has been passed allowing for road user charges to fully reflect costs of road use and

associated factors, such as congestion, accidents and pollution. There is widespread private sector participation in all aspects of road provision directly and through public-private partnership arrangements. Full public consultation is undertaken in the approval process for new road projects.

Water and waste water

1 There is a minimal degree of decentralisation and no commercialisation has taken place. Water and waste-water services are operated as a vertically integrated natural monopoly by a government ministry through national or regional subsidiaries or by municipal departments. There is no, or little, financial autonomy and/or management capacity at municipal level. Heavily subsidised tariffs still exist, along with a high degree of cross-subsidisation. There is a low level of cash collection. Central or regional government controls tariffs and investment levels. No explicit rules exist in public documents regarding tariffs or quality of service. There is no, or significant, private sector participation.

2 There is a moderate degree of decentralisation and initial steps have been taken in commercialisation. Water and waste-water services are provided by municipally owned companies, which operate as joint-stock companies. There is some degree of financial autonomy at the municipal level but heavy reliance on central government for grants and income transfers. Partial cost recovery is achieved through tariffs and initial steps have been taken to reduce cross-subsidies. General public guidelines exist regarding tariff-setting and service quality but these are both still under ministerial control. There is some private sector participation through service or management contacts or competition to provide ancillary services.

3 A fairly large degree of decentralisation and commercialisation has taken place. Water and waste-water utilities operate with managerial and accounting independence from municipalities, using international accounting standards and management information systems. A municipal finance law has been approved. Cost recovery is fully operated through tariffs and there is a minimum level of cross-subsidies. A semi-autonomous regulatory agency has been established to advise on tariffs and service quality but without the power to set either. More detailed rules have been drawn up in contract documents, specifying tariff review formulae and performance standards. There is private sector participation through the full concession of a major service in at least one city.

4 A large degree of decentralisation and commercialisation has taken place. Water and waste-water utilities are managerially independent, with cash flows – net of municipal budget transfers – that ensure financial viability. A municipal finance law has been implemented, providing municipalities with the opportunity to raise finance. Full cost recovery exists and there are no cross-subsidies. A semi-autonomous regulatory agency has the power to advise and enforce tariffs and service quality. There is substantial private sector participation through build-operator-transfer concessions, management contacts or asset sales to service parts of the network or entire networks. A concession of major services has taken place in a city other than the country's capital.

4+ Water and waste-water utilities are fully decentralised and commercialised. Large municipalities enjoy financial autonomy and demonstrate the capability to raise finance. Full cost recovery has been achieved and there are no cross-subsidies. A fully autonomous regulator exists with complete authority to review and enforce tariff levels and performance quality standards. There is widespread private sector participation via service management/lease contracts, with high-powered incentives and/or full concessions and/or divestiture of water and waste-water services in major urban areas.

[1] The classification system is a stylised reflection of the judgement of the EBRD's Office of the Chief Economist. More detailed descriptions of country-specific transition progress has been provided at the back of this Report. The classification system builds on the 1994 *Transition Report*. To refine further the classification system, pluses and minuses have been added to the 1–4 scale to indicate countries on the borderline between two categories. The classification 4* which was used in previous years has been replaced with 4+, though the meaning of the score remains the same.

Despite the difficult conditions, some countries are at an advanced stage of privatisation – for example, Bulgaria, where a tender for the dominant telecommunications company was concluded in September 2002, with two investors (a consortium of Turktelecom and Koc Holding and a UK-based financial investor) submitting bids. Other countries have made strong commitments to privatisation in the short term. Republika Srpska (part of Bosnia and Herzegovina), for example, plans to privatise the main fixed line operator by 2004. Moreover, many EU accession countries, including Poland and the Slovak Republic, have amended their legislation to meet EU requirements for the telecommunications industry.

Transport

Progress has been mixed in the reform of the railways in several countries. Reforms have focused on legislative changes and commercialisation, including the introduction of business plans and privatisation in six countries, three of which received a rating upgrade in 2002. In two other countries, corporate restructuring of the railways did not progress as planned although neither case was considered sufficiently serious to warrant a rating downgrade.

The railways of Bosnia and Herzegovina and FR Yugoslavia have made notable progress with the enactment of new railway laws, the preparation of business plans and the funding of loss-making passenger services with subsidies based on the "public sector obligation" concept. Estonian railways, on the other hand, has completed the privatisation of both its freight and passenger operations. Consequently, Estonia has become the first country to achieve a railways rating of 4+. Polish railways has completed its unbundling and is expected to continue the sale of assets and the introduction of private sector operations in 2003. However, these changes were not sufficient to warrant a rating upgrade. The railways of Lithuania, Ukraine and Uzbekistan have made progress in legislation and commercialisation but not enough for a rating upgrade.

The railways in the Czech Republic and Kazakhstan, on the other hand, have experienced a slow-down in reform. In Kazakhstan the review of the existing corporate restructuring plans took a long time to be agreed and approved, and there has been very slow progress with the unbundling of passenger and freight operations. Little reform activity, increasing operating losses and a controversial restructuring law have stalled the slow-moving reform of the railways in the Czech Republic, which will be subject to increasing pressures to reform as a result of the EU accession process.

Progress in the reform of the road sector has been modest, focusing on the areas of institutional reform and road sector financing. This slow progress reflects the scale of the challenges, which involve public administration reform and changes in taxation and budget financing. FR Yugoslavia has separated the administrative function of the Roads Directorate from the policy and legislative role of the Government. The next steps include transforming the Directorate into a public enterprise and introducing planning and management systems to identify expenditure priorities. Russia also made some progress in 2002, as the federal and regional road sector funds, which used to be financed through an enterprise turnover tax, are now funded via general taxation. The next step involves proposals to fund a system of road user charges via dedicated duties and taxes.

Annex 2.2:
Legal transition indicators

The EBRD conducted a Legal Indicator Survey (LIS) for the eighth consecutive year in 2002 to measure progress in legal reform in central and eastern Europe and the Commonwealth of Independent States, as viewed by local lawyers. The EBRD's Office of the General Counsel has developed measures to assess the extent to which key commercial and financial laws have reached internationally acceptable standards (extensiveness) and the degree to which these laws are implemented and enforced (effectiveness). The survey can also be used to analyse the perceived role of legal reform in promoting investment and growth in the region.

The results of this year's LIS reflect how lawyers and other experts familiar with the region perceive the state of commercial and financial legal reform in 2002.[1] These perceptions do not always correspond directly with the written legislation or regulations that exist in the various jurisdictions. Table A.2.2.1 provides an assessment of commercial laws, including pledge, bankruptcy and company law. Table A.2.2.2 provides an assessment of banking and capital markets laws.

The LIS results presented in the tables assess perceptions of legal reform in terms of both the extensiveness of legal reform and its effectiveness.[2] For commercial law, extensiveness measures the impact of the jurisdiction's pledge, bankruptcy and company law on commercial transactions.[3] For financial markets, extensiveness assesses whether banking and capital market legal rules approach minimum international standards, such as the Basel Committee on Banking

Supervision's Core Principles or the Objectives and Principles of Securities Regulation developed by the International Organisation of Securities Commissions (IOSCO). Effectiveness of legal reform measures the degree to which commercial and financial legal rules are clear, accessible and adequately implemented, both administratively and judicially.

Extensiveness indicators must be read in conjunction with effectiveness indicators to reach a more complete understanding of how legal reform appears to be progressing in any jurisdiction. Countries that exhibit a high extensiveness indicator in conjunction with a low effectiveness indicator reveal that, while the relevant legislation may be viewed as broadly in line with international standards, poor implementation may be preventing the proper utilisation of the legislation. For example, Azerbaijan and FYR Macedonia have had persistent and significant gaps between extensiveness and effectiveness for their commercial laws while Armenia and Georgia have significant gaps in their financial market indicators this year. These gaps indicate that relatively extensive laws are not perceived as being properly applied or enforced. When such gaps are extremely large, the value of extensive substantive legal reforms may be negated through poor implementation.[4]

The legal indicators reflect the subjective assessments of survey respondents as well as the views of EBRD lawyers with experience in working on commercial and financial transactions in the region. For a few countries the LIS respondents provided a wide range of assessments. In

these cases or where there were significant gaps between the extensiveness and effectiveness indicators, the EBRD's in-house knowledge of that country's legal system was utilised to take an overall assessment of the differing views. The LIS should not be considered a stand-alone tool for measuring legal reform. It is intended to supplement other forms of data. Accordingly, while the purpose of the LIS and the resulting analysis is to provide an impression of how local lawyers perceive the quality of laws and how well these laws work in practice, some caution must be exercised in interpreting the results.[5]

Results of the LIS 2002

In 2001, LIS respondents noted for the first time that the effectiveness of legal reforms had improved for the majority of survey countries in both commercial law and in financial markets. As a result, the implementation gap between extensiveness and effectiveness indicators that the survey has consistently revealed began to close in both legal sectors. In 2002 this trend continued but to a lesser degree. The average implementation gap for commercial law decreased somewhat while the average gap remained relatively stable for financial markets.

For commercial law, a few large decreases in Armenia, the Czech Republic, Poland and the Slovak Republic accounted for a large part of the average change. The narrowing of the implementation gap in commercial law was due as much to a reduction in the extensiveness indicators as it was to increasing effectiveness. In 2002, 13 countries experienced a

---

[1] The survey was made available to respondents in both English and Russian.

[2] The scores for commercial law and financial markets are aggregate indicators that do not segregate the individual subject areas surveyed (e.g. commercial law results are not further broken down into pledge, company, bankruptcy etc). More in-depth analysis of the LIS sector indicators and data is presented in the EBRD's legal journal Law in transition, published by the EBRD's Office of the General Counsel.

[3] The LIS secured transactions questions focus on the ability of parties to contract for non-possessory pledges in movable property, to protect their pledges through registration in a centralised collateral registry and to enforce their pledges effectively. The LIS company law questions focus on the ability of parties to form a joint-stock company and for shareholders to effectively enforce their rights with respect to management and majority owners, and the accountability of directors and company management. The LIS bankruptcy questions focus on the ability of creditors to pursue insolvency proceedings and to utilise reorganisation and liquidation procedures in the event of an enterprise's insolvency.

[4] The EBRD factors in significant gaps between extensiveness and effectiveness when developing the legal indicators for each country.

[5] The EBRD endeavours each year to achieve as broad a response as possible for each country. In certain circumstances, the political situation in a country or a lack of available practitioners with the requisite qualifications has created a lower response rate. Those countries with less than four responses to the 2002 LIS were Albania, Armenia, Belarus, Bosnia and Herzegovina, FYR Macedonia, the Kyrgyz Republic, Latvia, Tajikistan and Uzbekistan. Results for these countries should be interpreted with caution. No responses were received for Turkmenistan.

reduction in their commercial law extensiveness indicators while the same number maintained or increased commercial law effectiveness indicators. This paradox can be explained in many countries by practitioners' increasing familiarity with commercial laws, revealing shortcomings in the legislation. At the same time, improvements have continued to be made in implementation and enforcement.

In general, perceptions of banking and finance were less positive this year. This may reflect increasing use of banking laws as well as increasing frustration with bank failures, insolvencies and other problems in various jurisdictions. Albania, Azerbaijan, Belarus, Croatia, Lithuania, Moldova and Slovenia recorded lower scores this year for the extensiveness and effectiveness of financial markets. For each of these jurisdictions, there was a decline in banking indicators, sometimes accompanied by a smaller decline in perceptions of capital markets. In contrast to this downward trend, Latvia's ratings for financial markets improved significantly. It has amended its banking legislation and made minor changes to securities clearance and settlement rules. Latvia amended its laws on credit institutions in an effort to harmonise with the banking laws of the European Union.

In addition to these general trends, some countries were perceived as having changed significantly in certain sectors. Croatia experienced declines this year in both its commercial and financial markets. With respect to commercial law, the decline in extensiveness and effectiveness may relate to perceived delays in both court and administrative processes. For example, in its recent strategy paper for Croatia, the European Commission found that the courts and judiciary are in need of substantial reform.

Other countries in central eastern Europe and the Baltic states (CEB) continue to be perceived as having relatively strong laws compared with other sub-regions. The Czech Republic's extensiveness scores in commercial law (which had been declining) increased this year, perhaps reflecting a recent change to its Civil Code and pledge law (see below). In contrast, Poland's extensiveness scores continue

to decline. Although standards for corporate governance increased as a result of changes in Poland's Commercial Code in 2001, some commentators have noted that minority shareholders remain critical of shareholder safeguards. Poland's bankruptcy law continues to be perceived as inadequate, and there is some disagreement whether secured creditors receive the highest priority in a liquidation proceeding. The law was also the subject of a legal challenge in the Polish Supreme Court, which was asked for an interpretative ruling on the constitutionality of the existing law's punitive provisions (these were ultimately upheld).

Bosnia and Herzegovina was perceived as having made significant improvement in its commercial and financial markets, albeit from a low starting point. Although Bosnia and Herzegovina only received a 1 for the effectiveness of its financial markets, there was a substantial increase in perceptions relating to implementation of its laws. It also received an upgraded rating for commercial law extensiveness. In line with World Bank recommendations, Bosnia and Herzegovina adopted a new law on registered pledges and pledge registry.

Developments in commercial law

Civil and commercial codes

Several jurisdictions undertook major reforms of civil codes or procedural codes in 2002. Estonia adopted a new general part of its Civil Code that has an impact on the formation of contracts. Moldova also adopted a new Civil Code in April 2002, which replaces the 1964 Soviet-era Code. Judges and other legal experts have criticised the legislation, however. The version adopted by the Moldovan Parliament differs considerably from earlier versions that were commented on by interested parties. In response, the International Monetary Fund (IMF) has stated that future financing is conditional on the new Code being revised. Moldova's commercial law indicators improved slightly.

In Ukraine the Parliament approved new Civil and Commercial Codes in December 2001 but these were vetoed by the President. Ukraine's indicator for the

extensiveness of commercial law declined but its effectiveness rating increased slightly, leading to a smaller implementation gap for 2002. In contrast, earlier this year Lithuania adopted a new Code of Civil Procedure that is not due to enter into force until January 2003, leaving Lithuania's commercial law indicators virtually unchanged.

Pledge law

While there have been several reforms to pledge law during the year, these have been accompanied by implementation problems, such as delays in the creation of a registry system or failure to repeal previous legislation.

The Czech Republic amended the Civil Code, Notarial Code and Civil Procedure Code regarding pledge law. The amendments make it possible to pledge certain objects and property rights, including movables, immovables and receivables. The Czech amendments also make it possible to pledge all the assets of an enterprise. Lawyers may have taken account of the potential benefits of these changes when assessing Czech pledge law. However, the effectiveness of these new pledges depends on whether the newly created Electronic Register of Pledges is well-implemented by the Czech Chamber of Notaries.

In Azerbaijan confusion among practitioners is the probable cause of a lower rating for pledge law. Azerbaijan's new Civil Code, which includes pledge provisions, came into force on 1 September 2001 but it did not revoke the earlier Law on Mortgages, leaving it unclear which law governs pledges. In addition, the Azeri Government has issued a Presidential decree covering the registration of pledges over some assets (for example, securities and immovables) but it has yet to establish a registration system for most movable property.

In Moldova, as of 30 July 2001, a newly enacted Pledge Law governs security over movable assets. The Moldovan legislation is intended to improve on previous provisions governing pledges in movable property, but plans to create a new registry system for pledges have stalled, leaving a legal vacuum. Pledges under the new

Table A.2.2.1

Legal transition indicators: commercial law

Country	2002			2001		
	Overall	Extensiveness	Effectiveness	Overall	Extensiveness	Effectiveness
Albania	3	3	3	2+	2+	2
Armenia	3+	3+	3+	2+	3-	2
Azerbaijan	2	2+	2	3-	3	2
Belarus	3	3+	2	3	3	3
Bosnia and Herzegovina	3	3	3	2-	1+	2
Bulgaria	4-	4-	4	4-	4	4-
Croatia	3+	3+	3+	4-	4-	4-
Czech Republic	4-	4-	4-	3	3	3
Estonia	4-	4-	4	4-	3+	4
FR Yugoslavia	3	3	3	3+	3+	3
FYR Macedonia	3+	3+	4-	4-	3+	4-
Georgia	3-	3-	3-	3	3	3
Hungary	4-	4-	4-	4-	4-	4-
Kazakhstan	4-	4-	4-	4	4	4
Kyrgyz Republic	3+	3+	3+	na	na	na
Latvia	3+	4-	3+	4-	4-	4
Lithuania	4-	4-	4-	4-	4-	4-
Moldova	4-	4-	4-	4-	3+	4-
Poland	3+	3+	4-	3+	4-	3
Romania	4-	4-	4	4	4	4
Russia	3+	3	4-	3+	3	4-
Slovak Republic	3+	3	3+	3+	3+	3+
Slovenia	3+	3+	4-	4-	4-	4
Tajikistan	1+	2-	1	2	2	2
Turkmenistan	na	na	na	2+	2	3
Ukraine	3	3	3	3	3+	3
Uzbekistan	3-	2+	2+	3	3	3

Source: EBRD.

law are valid only if registered but the registry does not exist. Moldova's pledge extensiveness indicator has increased while its effectiveness indicator has decreased. Similarly, the Slovak Republic adopted a new set of Civil Code provisions in summer 2002, including wide-ranging changes in its pledge law. However, these changes came too late to be captured in the 2002 LIS.

Bankruptcy

Very little bankruptcy reform took place over the past year but it is notable that several jurisdictions have begun to review and draft new bankruptcy legislation. The governments of Armenia, Croatia, FYR Macedonia and Poland are all preparing new bankruptcy legislation. In Armenia and Croatia these reforms are the result of public recognition of the shortcomings of existing bankruptcy legislation.

The Moldovan Parliament passed a new law on bankruptcy in November 2001, which was a condition of the IMF for future lending. The Ukrainian Parliament also amended its Law on Bankruptcy, in March 2002. The amendments define the qualifications, rights and duties for bankruptcy administrators and include procedures for a moratorium on satisfying creditor claims, conducting a creditors' meeting and undertaking reorganisation. The Slovak Republic has amended its bankruptcy laws to abolish the tax authorities' priority lien on movable and immovable assets. The existence of this priority has contributed to banks' reluctance to provide credit. The new provision is expected to become effective in January 2003.

Company law

As with bankruptcy, there was little activity in company law and corporate governance during 2002. Amendments to Russia's Federal Law on Joint Stock Companies, which provides for increased minority shareholder rights, became effective in late summer 2001. The new law states that a company's charter may not set general assembly (that is, annual meeting of shareholders) voting requirements at greater than a simple majority vote unless specified by the amended Joint Stock Companies Law. Under the amendments, shareholders are now given six months to file a complaint with a court in order to challenge a general assembly decision. As of 1 January 2002, the Joint Stock Companies Law no longer limits the number of issues that a shareholder with at least 2 per cent of the company's stock may propose for consideration by the general assembly. The amended law also allows shareholders to nominate candidates for all of the company's management bodies, including the audit commission.

On the management side, the amendments prevent the use of proxy voting by management and limit management's representation on the board of directors to one-quarter. However, these major changes do not appear to have improved practitioners' views of the extensiveness or effectiveness of Russia's company law

Classification system for transition indicators: commercial law

Extensiveness

1 Legal rules concerning pledge, bankruptcy and company law are perceived as very limited in scope. Laws appear to impose substantial constraints on the creation, registration and enforcement of security over movable assets and can impose significant notarisation fees on pledges. Company laws do not ensure adequate corporate governance or protect shareholders' rights. Bankruptcy laws are perceived as unable to provide with certainty or clarity the definition of an insolvent debtor, the scope of reorganisation proceedings or the priority of distribution to creditors following liquidation. Laws in these substantive areas may not have been amended to approximate those of more developed countries or these laws have been amended but are perceived to contain ambiguities or inconsistencies.

2 Legal rules concerning pledge, bankruptcy and company law are limited in scope and are subject to conflicting interpretations. Legislation may have been amended but new laws do not appear to approximate those of more developed countries. Specifically, the registration and enforcement of security over movable assets may not have been adequately addressed, leading to uncertainty. Pledge laws may impose significant notarisation fees on pledges. Company laws may not ensure adequate corporate governance or protect shareholders' rights. Laws appear to contain inconsistencies or ambiguities concerning, among other things, the scope of reorganisation proceedings and/or the priority of secured creditors in bankruptcy.

3 New or amended legislation may have been recently enacted (i.e., within the past five years) in at least two of the three commercial legal sectors that were the focus of the survey. However, the legislation could benefit from further refinement and clarification. Legal rules appear to permit a non-possessory pledge over most types of movable assets. However, the mechanisms for registration of security interests may still be rudimentary and appear not to provide parties with adequate protection. There may be scope for enforcement of pledges without court assistance. Company laws appear to contain limited provisions for corporate governance and the protection of shareholders' rights. Bankruptcy legislation appears to contain provisions for both reorganisation and liquidation but may place claims of other creditors above those of secured creditors in liquidation.

4 Comprehensive legislation exists in at least two of the three commercial legal sectors that were the focus of the survey. Pledge law appears to allow parties to take non-possessory pledges in a wide variety of movable property and contains mechanisms for enforcement of pledges without court assistance. The legal infrastructure, however, may not be fully developed to include a centralised or comprehensive mechanism for registering pledges. Company laws may contain provisions for corporate governance and the protection of shareholders' rights. Director and officer duties appear to be clearly defined. Bankruptcy law appears to include detailed provisions for reorganisation and liquidation. Liquidators appear to possess a wide variety of powers to deal with the property and affairs of a bankrupt.

4+ Comprehensive legislation exists in all three commercial legal sectors that were the subject of the survey. Legal rules are perceived as closely approaching those of more developed countries. These legal systems appear to have a uniform (that is, centralised registration) system for the taking and enforcement of a security interest in movable assets and also provide for adequate corporate governance and protect shareholders' rights. In particular, the rights of minority shareholders appear to be protected in the event of the acquisition by third parties of less than all of the shares of a widely held company. Bankruptcy law seems to provide in a comprehensive manner for both reorganisation and liquidation. Liquidators appear to possess a wide variety of powers and duties to deal with the property and affairs of a bankrupt, including wide powers of investigation of pre-bankruptcy transactions carried out by the debtor. There may be specialised courts that handle bankruptcy proceedings. Liquidators are required to possess certain minimum qualifications.

Effectiveness

1 Commercial legal rules are perceived as usually unclear and sometimes contradictory. The administration and judicial support for the law is perceived as rudimentary. The cost of transactions, such as creating a pledge over a movable asset, is perceived as prohibitive so as to render the law ineffective. There appear to be no meaningful procedures in place in order to make commercial laws operational and enforceable. There also appear to be significant disincentives for creditors to seek the commencement of bankruptcy proceedings in respect of insolvent debtors.

2 Commercial legal rules are perceived as generally unclear and sometimes contradictory. There appear to be few, if any, meaningful procedures in place to make commercial laws operational and enforceable.

3 While commercial legal rules are perceived as reasonably clear, administration or judicial support of the law appears to be often inadequate or inconsistent, creating a degree of uncertainty (for example, substantial discretion in the administration of laws and few up-to-date registries for pledges).

4 Commercial laws are perceived as reasonably clear and administrative and judicial support of the law is reasonably adequate. Specialised courts, administrative bodies or independent agencies may exist for the liquidation of insolvent companies, the registration of publicly traded shares or the registration of pledges.

4+ Commercial laws are perceived as clear and readily ascertainable. Commercial law appears to be well-supported administratively and judicially, particularly regarding the efficient functioning of courts, liquidation proceedings, the registration of shares and the orderly and timely registration of security interests.

Overall score

The overall score is the average of the scores given for the two indicators, rounded up where the average did not fall exactly into the existing categories. A "+" after a number is used to indicate countries that have just made it to the highest tier of one category and are within a few points of reaching the next category in the scale. A "–" indicates countries that are at the bottom of a category where a significant improvement is required for that jurisdiction to fall more comfortably within the middle range for that category.

---

and corporate governance practices. This may be due to survey respondents being unfamiliar with such far-reaching changes.

Developments in financial law

Across the region a number of countries were perceived as having worse financial laws in 2002 than in 2001. Azerbaijan, Belarus, FR Yugoslavia/Serbia, Georgia, Kazakhstan and Uzbekistan experienced a decline in their financial market ratings this year. As noted above, much of this change is due to declining ratings for banking – a trend that has continued from the 2001 LIS. As lawyers become more familiar with banking laws and regulations, they appear to perceive these laws as less extensive than they originally thought when the laws were initially adopted. Recently the IMF has published detailed assessments of various countries' compliance with the Basel and IOSCO principles, providing information that allows lawyers to compare their financial market regulations with international benchmarks and regulations of other countries.

Banking

In 2002 Albania considered a legislative amendment to create a deposit insurance scheme in its banking sector. The ensuing debate concerning the legislation caused depositors to panic and withdraw funds from the banking sector. In March the Supervisory Council of the Bank of Albania issued a press release aimed at calming public concerns surrounding the proposed insurance scheme.

Table A.2.2.2

Legal transition indicators: financial regulations

Country	2002			2001		
	Overall	Extensiveness	Effectiveness	Overall	Extensiveness	Effectiveness
Albania	1+	2	1	2-	2	2-
Armenia	3-	3+	2	3	3+	3
Azerbaijan	1	1	1	2	2+	2
Belarus	2	2	2	3-	3	2+
Bosnia and Herzegovina	1	1	1	1+	1+	1
Bulgaria	3	3	3	3	3	3
Croatia	2	3	2-	3	3	3
Czech Republic	3	3+	3	3+	3+	3
Estonia	4-	4	3+	4-	4	3+
FR Yugoslavia	2-	2	2-	3-	3+	2
FYR Macedonia	3-	3-	3-	3	3+	2
Georgia	2+	3+	2	3-	3	2+
Hungary	3+	3+	4-	4-	4-	4-
Kazakhstan	3-	3	3-	3+	4	3
Kyrgyz Republic	2-	2	1	na	na	na
Latvia	4-	4	4-	3	3	3
Lithuania	3+	4-	3	3+	3+	4-
Moldova	3	4-	3-	3+	4	3
Poland	3+	4-	3+	3+	4	3
Romania	3+	4-	3	3+	4	3
Russia	3-	3-	3-	3-	3-	2+
Slovak Republic	3-	3	2+	3	3	3
Slovenia	3	3+	3	4-	4	4-
Tajikistan	3	3+	2-	2	2	2-
Turkmenistan	na	na	na	1	1	1
Ukraine	2+	3	2	2+	2+	2+
Uzbekistan	2-	2	2-	2+	3-	2

Source: EBRD.

In Azerbaijan at least three foreign banks are leaving the country, including HSBC, which announced its departure in March 2002. Commentators have noted that these departures are due to discriminatory treatment of foreign investors in Azerbaijan. For example, HSBC has been drawn into court disputes by the tax authorities even though the bank proved that it had not violated Azerbaijan's laws. The Azerbaijan Government announced in early 2002 that it would reform its laws to bring its banking supervision scheme in line with international standards but no new legislation has been adopted so far.

In October 2001 the IMF noted that Georgia had significant weaknesses in its banking sector. The National Bank of Georgia must seek court permission to suspend banking licences, greatly limiting its enforcement ability. The IMF also noted that Georgia needs to refine its "fit and proper" criteria for ownership of banks. The IMF also stated that Georgia must adopt anti-money laundering measures. The Georgian Parliament is

currently considering revisions to its law on commercial banking to rectify these deficiencies.

In Serbia (FR Yugoslavia) there have been important reforms in the banking sector, from the introduction of a new banking law to the closure of many insolvent banks, including (in January 2002) the four largest banks in Serbia. Despite these achievements, the banking system is still experiencing problems, with a low level of deposits and limited provision of credit. Donor organisations have identified the development of international accounting standards as a crucial next step for the Serbian financial sector.

In Ukraine new banking regulations came into effect in November 2001 and January 2002, relating to the establishment and registration of banks – including banks with foreign capital, affiliates, representative offices, branches and bank holding groups. Ukrainian respondents probably recognised these new regulations (resulting in an increase in Ukraine's banking

extensiveness rating) but they also continued to perceive a decline in the effectiveness of Ukraine's banking laws.

Armenia is taking action to strengthen confidence in its financial and banking sector. The Armenian Parliament is currently considering amendments to the law on credit organisations, which was adopted recently. These are intended to reduce perceived risk in the Armenian banking sector. In addition, Armenia has published the list of 26 banks that have been liquidated and had their registration revoked over the past few years.

Capital markets

A greater improvement was achieved in the regulation of capital markets than in the banking sector in 2002. This activity was recognised by respondents in a number of countries. However, in many countries this improvement in capital market perceptions was not enough to offset the general decline in banking ratings.

favourable growth trajectory. The country's stability was boosted in mid-2002 by the peaceful re-shuffle of the government and election of a new president with cross-party support, and by the signing of a new IMF programme. For Bosnia and Herzegovina and FYR Macedonia, however, the short-term prospects are less clear. In both countries, growth has fallen sharply over the past couple of years, and investor confidence is low. The outcome of elections in both countries in autumn 2002 will help to determine the way ahead, and whether internal inter-ethnic tensions can be resolved, or whether they will continue to divert attention from much-needed economic reforms.

CIS: Russia slows down, diverse growth elsewhere

Recent economic performance in the CIS has been even more diverse than in the other two main sub-regions. The region as a whole grew by 5.9 per cent in 2001 but growth is likely to drop to above 4 per cent in 2002 and 2003. Some countries in the region are enjoying high growth: Armenia, Azerbaijan, Kazakhstan, Tajikistan, Turkmenistan and Ukraine all achieved growth rates close to or at double-digit levels in 2001, and most are predicted to come close to repeating that performance in 2002. Others, such as Belarus and Uzbekistan, two of the slowest reformers in the region, are performing sluggishly. The region's largest economy, Russia, now in its fourth year of sustained growth since the 1998 crisis, is expected by most forecasters to have growth of between 3.5 and 4 per cent in 2002, compared with 4.9 per cent in 2001 and 8.3 per cent in 2000. The recovery in Russia since the August 1998 crisis is seen as one of the main reasons for high growth in other CIS countries so a sustained slowdown in Russia would be a major source of concern for the region as a whole.

In Russia growth has stabilised and some of the foundations for sustained long-term growth are being put in place. Capital inflows have increased significantly, which shows the growing confidence in the country's economy and currency. However, the structure of growth in Russia is still rather uneven across sectors and across regions. In terms of sectors, the recovery

has been led by the export-oriented fuel and metal sectors, agro-processing and the service sector. The natural resources-based sectors have benefited from higher margins, due to a more competitive cost base and higher oil prices, while agro-processing has attracted substantial inflows of FDI. Recent fiscal performance in the Russian economy has also been good. The increase in revenues over the past two years has been partially due to the sharply increased oil prices and may be difficult to maintain if oil prices start to fall. However, the authorities have taken advantage of high oil prices and strong growth by pushing through an extensive reform of the tax system and running surpluses to build up reserves and repay debt to cushion the effects of large debt servicing requirements in coming years.

One of the countries where recovery has been most rapid in the last two years is Ukraine although growth has slowed in the past year. The slowdown was not unexpected as the external market has been weaker but domestic demand has remained robust, boosted by strong consumer spending (on the back of substantial real wage growth) and higher levels of investment. One of the main uncertainties for Ukraine, as for many other oil and gas importing countries in the CIS, concerns the effect of the level of oil prices on the external account.

As a net importer of oil (and gas), the direct effect on the trade balance (through the import bill for oil and gas whose demand is largely independent of price) would be negative if oil prices were to stay well above US$ 20 per barrel. High oil and gas prices would benefit Russia, as a major oil and gas exporter. This would boost Russian demand for Ukrainian exports. The net effect on the trade balance is uncertain.

Elsewhere in the CIS, economic growth is likely to continue in all cases, but at varying speeds. The highest growth rates are currently observed in countries rich in natural resources. Kazakhstan and Turkmenistan are benefiting from high oil prices and gas exports respectively, with growth in 2002 expected to be above 7 and 13 per cent respectively. Azerbaijan

is performing similarly, with increasing investments for the exploration and export of its huge hydro-carbon reserves.

Other countries in the region, which do not benefit to the same extent from natural resources, are growing more slowly. Projected growth in the Kyrgyz Republic has been revised downwards due to lower gold production and a sharp fall in electricity production, reflecting a renewed drive towards energy efficiency. The growth potential of the Kyrgyz Republic and Tajikistan remains limited due to low investor interest and restrictions on regional trade and transit, in particular for food products, although Tajikistan has benefited from recent growth in the production and export of aluminium and cotton. Armenia has enjoyed a boom in the important diamond processing business and a continuing recovery of industry. Growth prospects in the region of 7–8 per cent for 2002 and 2003 reflect this. However, growth has been rather slower in Georgia, which remains highly dependent on agriculture, and in Moldova. The Belarussian authorities continue to try to micro-manage the economy, to the detriment of private sector activity.

3.2 Medium-term policy challenges

EU accession: managing the fiscal-monetary balance

EU accession is approaching for a number of countries in CEB and SEE. Ten transition countries are in the formal accession process, and, with the exception of Bulgaria and Romania, all are hoping to join in 2004. In addition to the structural reform challenges associated with meeting the requirements of the *acquis communautaire*, accession is associated with formidable macroeconomic and budgetary challenges.

Rapid growth over a sustained period is necessary for the accession countries to catch up with the EU average for productivity and living standards. The extent to which living standards in accession countries lag behind the EU is illustrated in Chart 3.5, which presents GDP per capita in PPP terms as a percentage of the EU average. In 2001 the average PPP per capita income in accession countries was €9,700, representing 40 per cent of the EU average. All countries except the two that lag behind in the process – Bulgaria and Romania – are above 30 per cent but only three countries – the Czech Republic, Hungary and Slovenia – are above 50 per cent. As a comparison, the PPP-adjusted income levels at the time of accession for Greece (1981), Portugal (1986) and Spain (1986) were between 60 and 70 per cent of the EU average.[4]

For EU accession to be a success, therefore, the accession countries will have to continue on a growth path with a much higher growth rate than that found in the west European countries. At the same time they will be subject to the demands of the *acquis*, the Stability and Growth Pact and, for those countries striving for early adoption of the euro, the Maastricht criteria. EMU membership is part of the *acquis*. There will be no more EMU "opt-outs" of the kind obtained by the UK and Denmark. When they become EU members, the accession countries will obtain derogations from EMU membership (like Sweden today) until they satisfy all the Maastricht criteria.

The obligation to strive to meet these criteria is clear from the Treaties. While the Maastricht criteria will have greater weight in the run-up to EU accession for those candidates aiming for early admission to EMU, no candidate for EU membership can afford to ignore the implications of the obligation to meet the Maastricht criteria for participation in the eurozone following EU accession. The requirements of the Stability and Growth Pact and the Maastricht Treaty were designed for the relatively homogeneous group of countries in the existing European Union. A key policy challenge for the more heterogeneous current group of accession candidates is the implementation, country-by-country, of a medium-term fiscal and monetary framework and policies that respect the Stability and Growth Pact (and the Maastricht criteria for those countries aiming for early eurozone membership) and support growth during the protracted real convergence process.

Chart 3.5

GDP relative to the European Union

As a percentage of euro area average

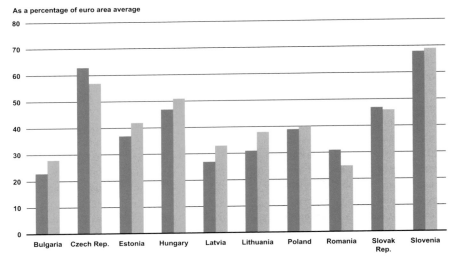

■ 1997 ■ 2001
Source: European Commission.
Note: Data refer to Purchasing Power Parity standard.

As noted earlier, fiscal deficits are already worryingly high in several accession countries, and *acquis*-related public expenditure is certain to grow further in the years to come (see Box 3.1). Even without the demands of the Stability and Growth Pact, significant budgetary retrenchment on a cyclically corrected basis would be desirable, or even unavoidable. The looming requirement of a general government budget that is close to balance or in surplus in the medium term further points to the need for early fiscal consolidation in many of the accession candidates.[5]

As regards the Maastricht criteria and the prospects for early eurozone membership, with the exception of the Baltic states and Slovenia, the accession countries currently do not satisfy the Maastricht deficit criterion, which states that the general government deficit to GDP ratio should be below 3 per cent.[6] The necessary fiscal retrenchment will be difficult politically and inevitably painful for those affected by spending cuts or tax increases. With respect to its effect on real convergence, there can be indirect (often longer-term) benefits if spending

priorities are re-targeted towards productive expenditure (education, for example) and away from wasteful spending. However, the degree of fiscal tightening that would be indicated by a strict interpretation of the Stability and Growth Pact budgetary criterion may be excessive from the point of view of successful real convergence. The ability of the accession countries to attract foreign capital, FDI in particular, will be key to successful convergence.

Successful convergence is also likely to be associated with sustained appreciation of the accession countries' real exchange rates *vis-à-vis* the existing EU members. With a stable nominal exchange rate, real exchange rate appreciation means a higher rate of inflation for the accession countries than for the existing EU. Higher real growth and higher inflation mean higher nominal income growth for the accession countries relative to the existing EU. Other things being equal, a higher growth rate of nominal GDP implies that a country can, up to a point, support a higher government deficit without necessarily imperilling government

---

[4] See ECB (2002).

[5] While there are no reliable estimates of cyclically adjusted general government budget deficits for the accession countries, the juxtaposition of robust growth with large deficits suggests that most of the accession countries do not satisfy the Stability and Growth Pact condition. Much of the high unemployment in many accession countries is likely to be non-cyclical in nature.

[6] Bulgaria's current gross general government debt to GDP ratio is above the 60 per cent Maastricht debt ceiling, although it is projected to fall below this threshold by end-2002. Bulgaria, however, is not expected to be part of the first wave of accession.

Box 3.1

Environmental compliance costs

It is now clear to the candidates for EU membership that, while membership is likely to bring long-term benefits, joining the EU brings with it considerable up-front costs. Some chapters of the *acquis* are relatively straightforward to adopt, but others entail substantial investment. The overall amount of investment required is difficult to quantify. One early study estimated a total amount of €225 billion for environment, transport, the steel sector and nuclear safety issues. Environmental compliance costs alone were estimated in this study at around €120 billion.[1]

All estimates have since been revised with newly calculated unit costs, and the new estimates take account of the substantial investment that has already taken place in recent years. This makes it difficult to judge by how much compliance costs create an increased burden for the budgets in the medium term. Several countries have made good progress in improving environmental standards, and current spending of the accession countries on environmental protection is, at 2 per cent of GDP, on average twice as high as the EU average.[2] Nevertheless, the costs for environmental compliance remain high, amounting to about 1.5 per cent of GDP on average for each of the next 15 years. Some of the costs are borne by the private sector and an annual pre-accession aid of €3.1 billion is provided by the EU, which is, however, only partly earmarked for environmental issues. Overall, the fiscal burden for the accession

countries remains high and may even increase in the years to come. After accession, grants from the EU will increase further but will not be allowed to exceed 4 per cent of GDP of the accession countries.

[1]   See Walldén (1998).

[2]   See DANCEE (2001).

Environmental compliance costs

Country	Total cost 1997 (estimate in € millions)	Total cost 1999-2000 (estimate in € millions[1])	Percentage of GDP 2001[2]
Bulgaria	15,000	8,610	3.8
Czech Republic	13,400	6,600 - 9,400[3]	0.7 - 1.0[3]
Estonia	1,500	4,406	4.8
Hungary	13,700	4,118 - 10,000[3]	0.5 - 1.1[3]
Latvia	1,710	1,480 - 2,360[3]	1.2 - 1.9[3]
Lithuania	2,380	1,600	0.8
Poland	35,200	22,100 - 42,800[3]	0.7 - 1.4[3]
Romania	22,000	22,000	3.4
Slovak Republic	5,400	4,809	1.4
Slovenia	1,840	2,430	0.8
Total	**112,130**	**78,153 - 108,415[3]**	**1.2 - 1.6[3]**

Sources: European Commission (2001) and the EBRD.
[1]   Estimates are from different studies.
[2]   Calculated after spreading total costs over 15 years.
[3]   Total cost or percentage of GDP falls within stated range.

solvency or crowding out private sector investment.[7] Furthermore, most *acquis*-related expenditure constitutes a form of investment that can be expected to generate real returns in the future. Borrowing to finance productive investment in general and *acquis*-related expenditure in particular can be consistent with fiscal prudence.

While an increase in the per capita income levels of new members may ease the difficult task of operating within tighter budgets, it would also imply a challenge for monetary policy. The reason is that productivity differentials between the accession countries and the EU are likely to be greater in the traded (internationally exposed) sectors than in the non-traded (sheltered) sectors, and therefore the relative price of non-traded goods will be rising faster in the accession countries. With traded goods prices at an equal level through international competition, the real exchange rate of the accession countries will appreciate.[8] This is an equilibrium phenomenon, and is consistent with (indeed necessary for) efficient growth and convergence. Its magnitude

has been estimated to be between 2 and 3 per cent per annum for the duration of the convergence process.[9] It should not, of course, be used to rationalise every appreciation of the real exchange rate in the accession countries. There are many other short-term and cyclical influences on the real exchange rate, some benign or unavoidable, others undesirable and avoidable.

The monetary authorities in candidate accession countries have to address these issues. When a country pursues stability of its nominal exchange rate, real exchange rate appreciation can only occur through a rate of inflation in excess of that of its trading partners. Successful convergence, under conditions of nominal exchange rate stability, therefore means that the accession candidate will have a higher rate of productivity growth and a higher rate of inflation than the existing EU average. This may cause the country to fall foul of the Maastricht inflation criterion, which states that the annual inflation rate cannot exceed the average of the three best performing countries by more than 1.5 per cent. To prevent this, mone-

tary authorities would have to engineer a temporary contractionary policy to bring the inflation rate below the threshold for at least one year prior to eurozone membership – at the expense of real convergence. The only alternative is to accept an appreciating nominal exchange rate.

Chart 3.6 shows that disinflation efforts among the eight front-runners have been quite successful so far. However, inflation in Hungary and Slovenia (as well as in Bulgaria and Romania) is still significantly above the level in the euro area. In the short-run, a number of factors are likely to impede further reductions in inflation in some of these countries – for example, nominal wage growth based on backward-looking indexation and stubborn inflation expectations.

In the context of accession, the choice of an appropriate exchange rate policy is also an important decision facing the monetary authorities of candidate countries. Currently, the tendency among candidate countries is towards the two polar regimes, i.e. either free float or hard pegs. Bulgaria, Estonia and Lithuania

[7]   To a first approximation the extra leeway is given by the product of the nominal income growth differential (*vis-à-vis* the country with lower growth) and the outstanding government (net) debt to GDP ratio. For example, if two countries have identical net public debt to annual GDP ratios of 60 per cent, and if nominal income growth is 4 per cent higher in one country than in the other, then the 'safe' level of the government deficit as a share of GDP is approximately 2.4 per cent of GDP higher in the high-growth country.

[8]   This is known as the "Balassa-Samuelson" effect.

[9]   See Begg et al. (2002) and Halpern and Wyplosz (2001).

Chart 3.6

Inflation in eight EU accession countries

Year on year in per cent

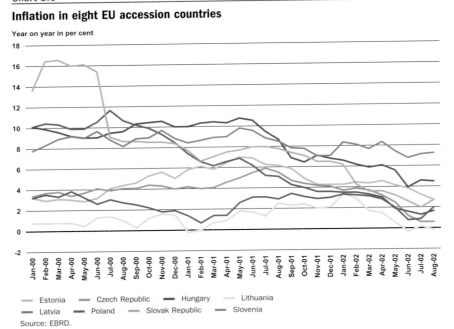

Estonia — Czech Republic — Hungary — Lithuania
Latvia — Poland — Slovak Republic — Slovenia

Source: EBRD.

operate a currency board while Latvia maintains a peg to a currency basket. The Czech Republic, Poland, Romania, the Slovak Republic and Slovenia all operate a managed float, and Hungary adopted an inflation targeting framework and widened its exchange rate band to ± 15 per cent, with a central parity set against the euro.

For eurozone participation, the Maastricht Treaty requires that the exchange rates of new members remain, for a period of two years prior to the examination, within the margins provided for by the exchange rate mechanism (ERM) of the European Monetary System. Floating within a band of 15 per cent around a fixed central parity vis-à-vis the euro, with intervention at or within the margins of the band, is permissible (ERM II). A conventional fixed exchange rate regime or a currency board with the euro are also permissible.

For those countries that currently adopt a managed float, two alternatives are available. One option is to maintain the float and to postpone ERM II until more real convergence has been achieved with the euro area regarding real exchange rate behaviour and capital inflows. This could mean that the adoption of the euro might be delayed substantially. If, alternatively, ERM II is joined at an early stage, the

appropriate economic policy should include enhanced fiscal discipline and a credible nominal anchor for monetary policy in order to reduce vulnerability to speculative attacks and sudden large-scale capital outflows.[10] More is required, however. Further strengthening of the domestic financial sector is key to successful EU accession and eventual adoption of the euro for all accession countries but it takes on special significance for those who pursue euro adoption through the wide-band ERM II route. For those countries that already operate a successful currency board, it may be sensible to maintain the board and use the strong exit option of euro adoption once all the Maastricht criteria have been met.[11] Key to the success of this option is rigorous budgetary control.

Fostering trade, investment and regional cooperation within south-eastern Europe

For most of the past decade, the region of south-eastern Europe has lagged behind its transition neighbours in the rest of Europe in terms of economic growth, foreign investment and poverty reduction. Recent developments give grounds for optimism that this pattern can be reversed. As noted earlier, in 2001 the growth rate in SEE exceeded that of CEB for the first time during the transition

and this result is likely to be repeated in 2002. More significantly, there is a strong reform momentum in the region, most notably in FR Yugoslavia after ten years of war, sanctions and isolation, but also in Bulgaria and Romania. This suggests that the groundwork for sustainable growth is, at last, being put in place. Finally, the collapse of the Milosevic regime in FR Yugoslavia in October 2000 was a major boost not only to that country but more generally to prospects for enhanced regional cooperation. All transition countries in the region, plus Croatia from the CEB group and (since June 2001) Moldova from the CIS, are now active participants in the Stability Pact for South-eastern Europe. For countries not yet formally in the EU accession process, the EU has devised the Stabilisation and Association Process (SAP), which stresses the importance of regional cooperation as a preliminary step to greater integration with the EU.

One reason for the region's slower progress is that external trade and investment levels are low relative to those in CEB. Foreign trade, both intra-regional and to Western markets, has been restricted by a range of problems, from sanctions and wars to corrupt customs officials and the failure of goods (such as livestock) to meet EU standards. Potential foreign investors have been deterred by the poor investment climate and (perceived or actual) threat of regional instability. Instead, several countries in the region rely heavily on other sources of income, both from official sources and private remittances from emigrants.

Chart 3.7 highlights these points by showing exports, FDI and transfers (official and private) for 1999–2001 for five non-accession countries of the Stability Pact: Albania, Bosnia and Herzegovina, Croatia, FR Yugoslavia and FYR Macedonia. In all cases, the ratio of exports to GDP is below 35 per cent. Only Croatia, by far the richest of these five countries, has attracted substantial amounts of FDI. The country where private remittances are most important is Albania, where they exceed exports by about 50 per cent on average. Private remittances are also a key source of

---

[10] See Begg et al. (2002).

[11] See Buiter and Grafe (2002) for a discussion of the importance of a strong exit from a currency board.

Chart 3.7

Net transfers from abroad, exports and foreign direct investment in selected non-accession countries

Percentage of GDP

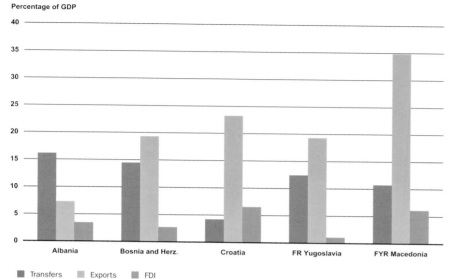

■ Transfers ■ Exports ■ FDI
Sources: IMF staff reports and the EBRD.
Note: Values shown are averages for 1999-2001.

Chart 3.8

Main export destinations for selected countries

Percentage of total exports

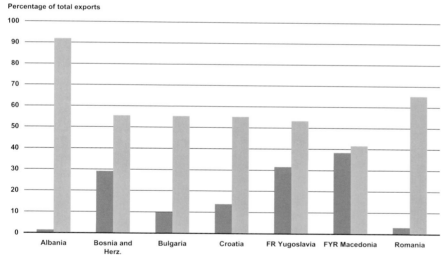

■ SEE countries ■ EU countries
Sources: IMF Direction of Trade Statistics 2002 and IMF staff reports for Bosnia and Herzegovina and FR Yugoslavia.

foreign currency revenue in FR Yugoslavia and FYR Macedonia although they are subject to considerable volatility. There was a notable drop in remittances in FYR Macedonia during 2001 as a result of the turmoil during much of the year and the temporary closure of the border with Kosovo. However, this was counterbalanced by a large jump in FDI due to

the sale of a majority stake in the national telecommunications company. Private remittances are less important in Bosnia and Herzegovina but official aid flows are still substantial, although on a declining trend.

The macroeconomic challenge illustrated by this chart is clear. Official grants

cannot be relied on indefinitely as a source of finance for a large trade deficit, and private remittances mostly go towards the consumption of imports.[12] For long-term sustainability, enhancing trade opportunities and attracting FDI are the key objectives. To date, however, levels of trade and investment have been disappointing, and in SEE generally, fiscal and current account deficits have generally been high. Concrete measures to enhance trade and investment flows are therefore urgently needed and have been the focus of much of the debate within the Stability Pact.

Turning to external trade, Chart 3.8 shows that the main trading partner of the SEE countries is already the EU. For some countries intra-regional trade is important but in other cases it is noticeable how little trade actually occurs between some countries of the region.[13] Both Bosnia and Herzegovina and FYR Macedonia, for example, conduct about a third of their trade with SEE countries. For Albania in contrast, trade with Italy alone accounted for more than 70 per cent of total exports in 2000 while for Romania a mere 2.7 per cent of exports go to other SEE countries. Trade between the two accession countries in the region, Bulgaria and Romania, has historically been limited and is currently at negligible levels, even though the two countries share a land border.

In an effort to promote intra-regional trade, the Stability Pact has sponsored a free trade initiative. A memorandum of understanding, facilitating and liberalising trade among the countries of SEE, was signed on 27 June 2001 in Brussels within the framework of the Stability Pact. Its aim was to promote regional trade through a network of 21 bilateral agreements on free trade among Albania, Bosnia and Herzegovina, Bulgaria, Croatia, FR Yugoslavia, FYR Macedonia and Romania by the end of 2004. Moldova, which was not formally a part of the Stability Pact at the time, has since joined this process. As of end-September 2002, ten bilateral Free Trade Agreements (FTAs) had been signed, including several revisions to FTAs that were signed prior to June 2001. The remaining 11 Agreements

---

[12] In Albania a recent survey shows about 17 per cent of remittances go to productive activities, mostly micro-enterprises and small-scale farming activities. See Kule et al. (2002).

[13] Christie (2000) shows, using a "gravity" model of trade, that intra-regional trade in SEE is low relative to other countries.

Chart 3.9

Net foreign direct investment in CIS

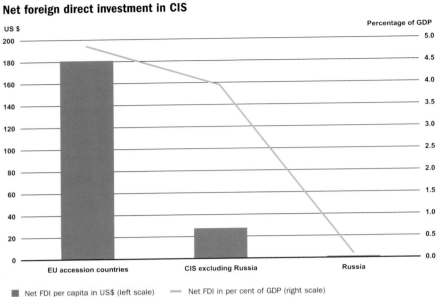

Net FDI per capita in US$ (left scale) ■ — Net FDI in per cent of GDP (right scale)
Source: EBRD.
Note: Average values for 1999-2001.

through a reduction in the high fiscal deficits, as relying on the current sources of finance is not a viable option in the medium term.

Sustainability of growth and debt in the CIS

The period of recovery after the Russia crisis of 1998 was, to some extent, a period of easy growth. The combination of a large real depreciation (first of the Russian rouble and then of other currencies in the region), a high oil price and significant initial slack in the system all permitted production to rise without any corresponding increase in productive capacity. The benefits of these favourable factors are ending. With the real exchange rate approaching its pre-collapse level, CIS countries have to expand their capacity to produce and sell goods.

A high rate of sustainable growth requires high rates of investment, at significantly higher levels than those seen throughout the transition period. That in turn requires both new capital and high volumes of FDI, with the related expertise and know-how. Chart 3.9 shows that net FDI into Russia remains extremely low.[15] Similarly, FDI inflows into the other CIS countries are well below the levels in the ten accession countries. Increased efforts to improve the investment climate will be necessary to change this picture over the medium term.

Moreover, gross capital formation has to be raised in order to engineer sustainable growth. This is true for Russia in particular, where – despite available means of financing – investment has been low because of capital outflows. If the average investment ratio after the crisis, i.e. over the years 1999-2001, is considered, investment in Russia falls short of the levels in Ukraine and Azerbaijan. However, only Azerbaijan among CIS countries has reached investment ratios close to those in East Asian economies (Hong Kong, Korea, Singapore and Taiwan), which experienced high growth for several decades (see Chart 3.10).

(among the seven original signatories) are expected to be finalised in 2002. All the FTAs are in conformity with World Trade Organization regulations and in line with EU partnerships.

The FTAs should enable the SEE countries to create a liberalised market of about 55 million customers and to attract more investments in the region. Alongside the preferential export conditions from the European Union, the free trade regional regime is an instrument to create open economies and enhance international competition. However, FTAs are not a panacea, and other obstacles to trade still remain. In particular, problems can still arise even among countries that have had an FTA for years. For example, in March 2002 the Serbian government banned the import of oil and oil-related products from FYR Macedonia, claiming that such imports had violated the existing FTA. In retaliation, FYR Macedonia banned the import of a range of products from Serbia, including oil products, construction materials, cakes and sweets. The dispute has since been resolved but it is an important reminder of the potential obstacles to implementing these agreements.

To attract more FDI, a second initiative sponsored by the Stability Pact – the South East Europe Compact for Reform, Investment, Integrity and Growth (the "Investment Compact") – was set up to encourage countries in the region to improve their investment climates. It is currently led jointly by the OECD and the Austrian government, and all countries in the region signed up to a declaration on common principles and best practices for attracting investment to SEE. Partly as a consequence of these efforts, investment in the SEE region is expected to increase in the medium term. Another important factor is the low wage level relative to the CEB countries. Annual wages in the larger countries of the region – Bulgaria, FR Yugoslavia and Romania – were still below US$ 2,000 in 2000, compared with over US$ 4,000 in the Czech Republic and over US$ 5,000 in Poland.[14]

However, FDI is likely to remain well below the levels in CEB for the foreseeable future, as is the extent of foreign trade. Domestic investment will also continue to be constrained by the low level of savings and weak financial sectors although these are also improving. This leaves macroeconomic policy with the challenge of reducing external imbalances

---

[14] See Chart 1.6 of the EBRD *Transition Report Update* 2002.

[15] While in the case of Russia, gross FDI differs significantly from net FDI, it is still far below the levels in the accession countries.

Chart 3.10

Savings and investment in selected countries

Percentage of GDP

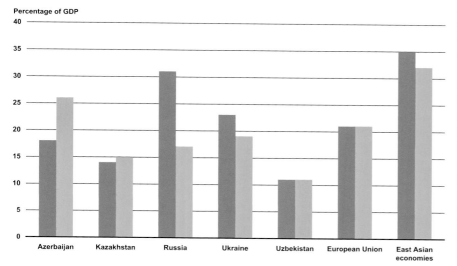

■ Savings ■ Investment
Source: IMF World Economic Outlook.

Note: All data are averages for 1999-2001, except East Asian economies which refer to 1988-95. Investment is equal to gross fixed capital formation (current prices) divided by gross domestic product (current prices). Savings is equal to gross national savings (current prices) divided by gross domestic product (current prices).

Chart 3.11

Debt versus income in 2000 in CIS countries

Present value of total debt service to export (in per cent)

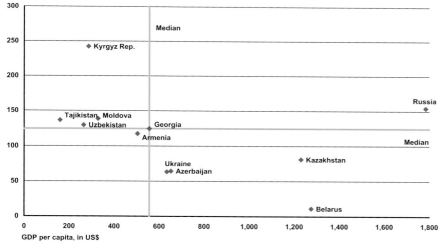

GDP per capita, in US$

Sources: Global Development Finance 2002 and EBRD.
Note: Data not available for Turkmenistan.

Chart 3.10 demonstrates that for Russia in particular, lack of savings is not the problem. On the contrary, Russia has been running very large current account surpluses for several years. From 1994 until 2001 the cumulative surplus is around US$ 136 billion. Therefore, domestic investment can be boosted only by an improvement in the investment climate, which would help to reduce net capital outflows, and consequently the current account surplus. The intermediation role of banks also needs to be enhanced. Political influence over bank lending has expanded with the growing dominance of Sberbank following the August 1998 crisis while commercially motivated loans to private non-financial enterprises remain more the exception than the rule.[16]

Similarly, in Ukraine capital formation was below desirable levels and fell short of savings from 1999 to 2001 but it was high by CIS standards. In Kazakhstan both savings and investment have been at low levels relative to the successful growth economies in East Asia. The need for more diversified growth outside the oil sector remains a particular issue in Kazakhstan. In both Ukraine and Kazakhstan, however, the gap between investment and savings could be financed externally over the medium term in view of the large resource endowment of each country and the associated long-term prospects. This highlights the need to stimulate investment.

The situation is more difficult for some of the poorer countries in the CIS, where external sources of investment are depleted. Here the low savings rate is a constraint on investment. Particularly low rates, as a percentage of GDP, are observed in Armenia (8 per cent), the Kyrgyz Republic (-2 per cent) and Tajikistan (2 per cent).[17] This is not very surprising because these countries are among the poorest in the region and the low incomes prevent the recovery of savings rates. To gauge the extent to which particular countries are constrained in accumulating capital through savings or external means, Chart 3.11 displays both debt and current income for the CIS countries. The Kyrgyz Republic, Moldova, Tajikistan and, to a lesser extent, Armenia and Georgia are both poor and severely indebted by CIS standards. Unlike Uzbekistan (which is also relatively highly indebted), they do not have the advantage of significant marketable natural resources.[18]

Recent progress in rescheduling debt for these five countries is discussed in Box 3.2. Despite some progress, a debt sustainability analysis by the IMF and

---

[16] See Buiter and Szegvari (2002) for a more detailed discussion of capital flight from Russia.

[17] Data are from the World Economic Outlook, April 2002.

[18] The vast fresh water reserves of Armenia, Georgia, the Kyrgyz Republic and Tajikistan have not yet become a direct source of export revenues for these countries.

Box 3.2

External debt of Armenia, Georgia, the Kyrgyz Republic, Moldova and Tajikistan

The high external indebtedness of five countries – Armenia, Georgia, the Kyrgyz Republic, Moldova and Tajikistan – has attracted the attention of the international community in recent years. The chart shows that as of end-2000 the largest part of the debt in all five countries is owed to multilateral creditors. The biggest bilateral creditor is Russia (a Paris Club member), except in Georgia where most of the bilateral debt is owed to Turkmenistan (not a Paris Club member). While some of the bilateral debt is negotiated separately, the Paris Club of creditors is usually considered as the forum to seek rescheduling and/or restructuring of bilateral debt.

So far, the five countries have taken different approaches to seeking debt relief. In summary:

■ Armenia agreed with Russia on a debt-for-equity swap in 2001: an outstanding debt of US$ 98 million was waived in exchange for full ownership of the Hrasdan I–IV power generation complex and four companies in the industry/defence field. Armenia is not expected to seek debt relief from Paris Club creditors in the near future.

■ Georgia reached an official agreement with the Paris Club in March 2001. The agreement consolidated roughly US$ 58 million (total debt owed to Paris Club was US$ 482 million by January 2000). It reduced debt service to Paris Club creditors during 2001 and 2002 from US$ 88 million to US$ 33 million. Further negotiations with the Paris Club are possible in 2003. There was no debt reduction in present value terms – the Georgia agreement simply rolled the debt forward. Progress was made in 2002 in reducing arrears to Turkmenistan through offset operations involving aircraft services and sugar and railcar deliveries.

■ The Kyrgyz Republic reached an official agreement with the Paris Club in March 2002. The agreement consolidated roughly US$ 99 million (total debt owed to the Paris Club was US$ 450 million by November 2001). It reduces debt service to Paris Club creditors during 2002, 2003 and 2004 from US$ 101 million to US$ 5.6 million. Creditors agreed to consider a concessional treatment of the stock of the external debt upon successful implementation of the current IMF programme and the Paris Club agreement.

■ Moldova's approach to the Paris Club was delayed because of a suspension of the IMF programme during the last year. In July 2002 an evaluation by the IMF of the situation in Moldova was positive. In particular the development of the Poverty Reduction Strategy Paper was judged as satisfactory and regarded as a sound basis for continued access to concessional assistance by the Fund. A US$ 75 million Eurobond was successfully restructured in August 2002.

■ Tajikistan's debt burden was reduced by more than US$ 100 million in early 2002. Uzbekistan agreed to write off large parts of the debt owed. Negotiations with Belarus, Kazakhstan and Russia are in progress. According to preliminary information, Russia appears to have agreed to reduce its debt stock by US$ 50 million and to discuss a restructuring of the remaining debt. Nevertheless, the present value of public debt relative to government revenues is expected to remain high.

Structure of external debt end-2000

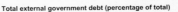

Total external government debt (percentage of total)

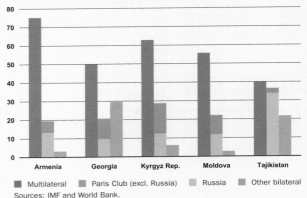

■ Multilateral   ■ Paris Club (excl. Russia)   ■ Russia   ■ Other bilateral

Sources: IMF and World Bank.

World Bank based on data for 2000 found that even if maximum debt relief is provided by Paris Club creditors to the Kyrgyz Republic, Moldova and Tajikistan, this may not be enough for these countries to achieve medium and longer-term public and external debt sustainability.[19] The scenario underlying the analysis appears conservative against the background of recent growth.

Such high growth is doubly welcome for the poorer countries of the CIS, not only for alleviating poverty but also for reducing the pressure of high external debt. If these countries can transfer abroad an amount equal to the product of their external debt and the excess of the interest rate on their debt over the growth rate of GDP, they will maintain the existing debt to GDP ratio. Any greater external transfer will generate a declining debt-GDP ratio. However, as argued earlier, high debt together with a low level of income may prevent the accumulation of capital that is necessary to maintain sustainable growth. An early resolution of the uncertainty surrounding the rescheduling and restructuring of the debt of these countries is therefore needed to clarify their medium-term prospects.

3.3 Conclusion

The main message of this chapter is that the transition economies continue to show resilience in the face of the global slowdown and increased economic and political uncertainty. All countries in the region are likely to record positive growth in 2002, macroeconomic stability is deeply rooted in most countries and capital inflows, including FDI, are rising, despite the global contraction in FDI flows during 2002. Ultimately, however, each country's long-term growth will depend to a large extent on the extensiveness of, and commitment to, deep structural and institutional reforms. Early reforms, such as price and trade liberalisation and small-scale privatisation, while necessary for sustainable growth, are not sufficient to put a country on the path to prosperity.[20] As the previous chapter showed, most countries continue to make

---

[19] The sustainability criteria used in these studies are those used by the IMF and the World Bank to determine eligibility for treatment under the Heavily Indebted Poor Country (HIPC) initiative (see IMF and World Bank (2002)). For HIPC treatment, the ratio of the present value of external debt to annual exports has to exceed 150 per cent while for very open economies, the criterion is that the ratio of the present value of debt to annual government revenues exceeds 250 per cent. Further eligibility requirements include poverty (International Development Association status) and willingness and ability to implement appropriate monetary, fiscal and social policies to pursue structural reform.

[20] See Falcetti, Raiser and Sanfey (2002).

progress in structural and institutional reform, and the benefits are evident in better macroeconomic performance.

Short-term prospects differ widely across the region. Several countries in CEB are facing serious fiscal challenges in the run-up to EU accession, and Poland's economic performance remains weak, largely due to domestic factors. Other problems facing this region include the prolonged slowdown in the EU, which is negatively affecting exports. Nevertheless, most economies in CEB look relatively healthy and growth is likely to pick up in 2003. For SEE, the improved performance of Bulgaria and Romania in recent years is being sustained but growth in FR Yugoslavia is rather sluggish after years of neglect and decline. In the CIS many countries continue to grow at quite a rapid pace but from a low level. The major oil and gas exporters – Russia and the other Caspian nations – continue to be vulnerable to a sharp decline in oil and gas prices. While such a turnaround in oil and gas prices does not seem likely in the near future, oil and gas prices are traditionally highly volatile. Careful management of the current windfall is key to the medium-term sustained prosperity of the oil and gas exporting nations.

The chapter outlined some of the main medium-term macroeconomic challenges facing the region. Throughout the region, the ability to attract growing amounts of foreign capital, FDI in particular, is key to sustained growth in the medium and long term. For EU accession countries, it is difficult to achieve the right fiscal-monetary balance but most countries are reasonably well prepared for the challenge. However, coordination of fiscal and monetary policy is an area where weaknesses have been evident in some of the larger countries of CEB. For SEE countries not yet in the accession process, an opportunity beckons to build on the new spirit of regional cooperation and to promote trade and investment.

High fiscal and current account deficits in this region do not pose a major threat in the short term but the current sources of financing are unlikely to last in the long term. In the CIS the benefits of the recent Russian boom both for Russia and for the rest of the region are starting to fade. In all CIS countries there is scope to improve investment levels but the situation is particularly critical for poorer countries, which are trying to grapple with a large debt burden, artificial restrictions on regional export markets and volatile (and currently low) primary export prices.

References

D. Begg, B. Eichengreen, L. Halpern, J. von Hagen and C. Wyplosz (2002), "Sustainable regimes of capital movements in accession countries", CEPR Final Report, revised version.

W.H. Buiter and C. Grafe (2002), "Anchor, float or abandon ship: Exchange rate regimes for the accession countries", EBRD mimeo.

W.H. Buiter and I. Szegvari (2002), "Capital flight and capital outflows from Russia: Symptom, cause and cure", EBRD Working Paper No.73.

E. Christie (2000), "Potential trade in southeast Europe: a gravity model approach", Vienna Institute for International Economic Studies Working Paper.

DANCEE (2001), "The environmental challenge of EU enlargement in central and eastern Europe", Thematic Report, Danish Ministry of the Environment.

European Bank for Reconstruction and Development (2002), *Transition Report Update 2002*, London.

European Central Bank (2002), *Monthly Bulletin,* July.

European Commission (2001), "The challenge of environmental financing in the candidate countries", Communication 304 final, Brussels.

E. Falcetti, M. Raiser and P. Sanfey (2002), "Defying the odds: Initial conditions, reforms, and growth in the first decade of transition", *Journal of Comparative Economics*, Vol.30, pp.229–50.

L. Halpern and C. Wyplosz (2001), "Economic transformation and real exchange rates in the 2000s: the Balassa-Samuelson Connection", UN/ECE.

International Monetary Fund and World Bank (2002), "Poverty reduction, growth and debt sustainability in low-income CIS countries", Working Paper, February, Washington D.C.

D. Kule, A. Mançellari, H. Papapanagos, S. Qirici and P. Sanfey (2002), "The causes and consequences of Albanian emigration during transition: evidence from micro-data", *International Migration Review,* Vol.36, No.1, pp.229–39.

A.S. Walldén (1998), "EU enlargement: how much it will cost and who will pay", Hellenic Foundation for European and Foreign Policy (ELIAMEP), Occasional Papers OP98.14.

World Bank (2002), "Global Development Finance", Washington D.C.

Annex 3.1:
Macroeconomic performance tables

Table A.3.1

Growth in real GDP in central and eastern Europe and the CIS

	1990	1991	1992	1993	1994	1995	1996	1997	1998	1999	2000	2001	2002	Estimated level of real GDP in 2001
					(in per cent)									*(1989=100)*
Croatia	-7.1	-21.1	-11.7	-8.0	5.9	6.8	6.0	6.5	2.5	-0.9	2.9	3.8	3.5	85
Czech Republic	-1.2	-11.6	-0.5	0.1	2.2	5.9	4.3	-0.8	-1.0	0.5	3.3	3.3	2.5	106
Estonia	-6.5	-13.6	-14.2	-8.8	-2.0	4.3	3.9	9.8	4.6	-0.6	7.1	5.0	4.0	90
Hungary	-3.5	-11.9	-3.1	-0.6	2.9	1.5	1.3	4.6	4.9	4.2	5.2	3.8	4.0	112
Latvia	2.9	-10.4	-34.9	-14.9	2.2	-0.9	3.7	8.4	4.8	2.8	6.8	7.7	4.0	75
Lithuania	-5.0	-5.7	-21.3	-16.2	-9.8	3.3	4.7	7.3	5.1	-3.9	3.8	5.9	5.2	72
Poland	-11.6	-7.0	2.6	3.8	5.2	7.0	6.0	6.8	4.8	4.1	4.0	1.0	1.0	129
Slovak Republic	-2.5	-14.6	-6.5	-3.7	4.9	6.7	6.2	6.2	4.1	1.9	2.2	3.3	3.5	110
Slovenia	-4.7	-8.9	-5.5	2.8	5.3	4.1	3.5	4.6	3.8	5.2	4.6	3.0	2.7	121
Central eastern Europe and the Baltic states	*-6.6*	*-10.3*	*-2.2*	*0.3*	*3.9*	*5.4*	*4.7*	*5.0*	*3.6*	*2.8*	*4.0*	*2.5*	*2.3*	*113*
Albania	-10.0	-28.0	-7.2	9.6	8.3	13.3	9.1	-7.0	8.0	7.3	7.8	6.5	6.0	116
Bosnia and Herzegovina	-23.2	-12.1	-30.0	-40.0	-40.0	20.8	86.0	37.0	9.9	10.6	4.5	2.3	3.0	na
Bulgaria	-9.1	-11.7	-7.3	-1.5	1.8	2.9	-9.4	-5.6	4.0	2.3	5.4	4.0	4.0	80
FR Yugoslavia	-7.9	-11.6	-27.9	-30.8	2.5	6.1	7.8	10.1	1.9	-18.0	5.0	5.5	3.0	50
FYR Macedonia	-9.9	-7.0	-8.0	-9.1	-1.8	-1.2	1.2	1.4	3.4	4.3	4.6	-4.1	2.0	77
Romania	-5.6	-12.9	-8.8	1.5	3.9	7.1	3.9	-6.1	-5.4	-3.2	1.8	5.3	3.5	84
South-eastern Europe	*-7.3*	*-14.8*	*-9.6*	*-2.4*	*3.0*	*6.4*	*3.5*	*-0.5*	*-0.7*	*-3.4*	*3.6*	*4.5*	*3.6*	*79*
Armenia	-7.4	-11.7	-41.8	-8.8	5.4	6.9	5.9	3.3	7.3	3.3	6.0	9.6	8.0	74
Azerbaijan	-11.7	-0.7	-22.6	-23.1	-19.7	-11.8	1.3	5.8	10.0	7.4	11.1	9.9	8.8	62
Belarus	-3.0	-1.2	-9.6	-7.6	-12.6	-10.4	2.8	11.4	8.4	3.4	5.8	4.1	3.0	91
Georgia	-12.4	-20.6	-44.8	-25.4	-11.4	2.4	10.5	10.8	2.9	3.0	2.0	4.5	3.5	37
Kazakhstan	-0.4	-11.0	-5.3	-9.3	-12.6	-8.2	0.5	1.7	-1.9	2.7	9.8	13.2	7.6	84
Kyrgyz Republic	3.0	-5.0	-19.0	-16.0	-20.1	-5.4	7.1	9.9	2.1	3.7	5.1	5.3	2.0	71
Moldova	-2.4	-17.5	-29.1	-1.2	-31.2	-1.4	-5.9	1.6	-6.5	-3.4	2.1	6.1	3.5	37
Russia	0.0	-5.5	-18.6	-13.0	-13.5	-4.1	-3.4	0.9	-4.9	5.4	8.3	4.9	4.1	64
Tajikistan	-1.6	-7.1	-29.0	-11.0	-18.9	-12.5	-4.4	1.7	5.3	3.7	8.3	10.3	7.0	56
Turkmenistan	2.0	-4.7	-5.3	-10.0	-17.3	-7.2	-6.7	-11.3	5.0	16.0	17.6	12.0	13.5	96
Ukraine	-4.0	-10.6	-9.7	-14.2	-22.9	-12.2	-10.0	-3.0	-1.9	-0.2	5.9	9.1	4.5	46
Uzbekistan	1.6	-0.5	-11.1	-2.3	-4.2	-0.9	1.6	2.5	4.4	4.1	4.0	4.5	2.5	105
Commonwealth of Independent States	*-0.4*	*-6.0*	*-17.4*	*-12.7*	*-14.1*	*-4.9*	*-3.4*	*1.0*	*-3.7*	*4.5*	*7.9*	*5.9*	*4.4*	*64*
Central and eastern Europe and the CIS[1]	**-3.3**	**-8.1**	**-11.0**	**-6.9**	**-6.1**	**-0.2**	**0.1**	**2.3**	**-1.0**	**3.0**	**5.5**	**4.2**	**3.4**	**76**

Note: Data for 1990-2000 represent the most recent official estimates of outturns as reflected in publications from the national authorities, the IMF, the World Bank and the OECD. Data for 2001 are preliminary actuals, mostly official government estimates. Data for 2002 represent EBRD projections.

[1] Estimates for real GDP represent weighted averages. The weights used for the growth rates were EBRD estimates of nominal dollar-GDP lagged by one year; those used for the index in the last column were EBRD estimates of GDP converted at PPP US$ exchange rates in 1989.

Table A.3.2

GDP growth by components

(real change in per cent)

	1998	1999	2000	2001		1998	1999	2000	2001
Bulgaria					**Poland**				
Real GDP growth	4.0	2.3	5.4	4.0	Real GDP growth	4.8	4.1	4.0	1.0
Private consumption	2.6	9.3	4.9	4.5	Private consumption	4.8	5.2	2.6	2.1
Public consumption	23.4	4.1	13.3	4.7	Public consumption	1.4	1.0	1.1	2.0
Gross fixed investment	35.2	20.8	15.4	19.9	Gross fixed investment	14.2	6.8	2.7	-9.8
Exports of goods and services	-4.7	-5.0	16.6	8.5	Exports of goods and services	11.0	1.0	17.5	8.0
Imports of goods and services	12.1	9.3	18.6	13.0	Imports of goods and services	14.0	6.0	12.0	7.0
Croatia					**Romania**				
Real GDP growth	2.5	-0.9	2.9	3.8	Real GDP growth	-5.4	-3.2	1.8	5.3
Private consumption	-0.6	-2.9	4.2	4.6	Private consumption	-4.6	-4.9	-1.2	6.4
Public consumption	2.3	2.8	-1.5	-4.3	Public consumption	14.1	-2.5	4.2	-1.9
Gross fixed investment	2.5	-3.9	-3.8	9.7	Gross fixed investment	-18.1	-5.1	5.5	6.6
Exports of goods and services	3.9	0.7	12.0	8.7	Exports of goods and services	na	9.7	23.9	10.6
Imports of goods and services	-4.9	-3.5	3.7	9.3	Imports of goods and services	na	-5.1	29.1	17.5
Czech Republic					**Russia**				
Real GDP growth	-1.0	0.5	3.3	3.3	Real GDP growth	-4.9	5.4	8.3	4.9
Private consumption	-1.6	1.7	2.5	3.9	Private consumption	-2.4	-4.2	8.5	8.4
Public consumption	-4.4	2.3	-1.0	0.3	Public consumption	0.6	3.0	1.6	-1.1
Gross fixed investment	0.7	-1.0	5.3	7.2	Gross fixed investment	-9.8	4.7	15.5	11.5
Exports of goods and services	10.0	6.1	17.0	12.3	Exports of goods and services	2.7	-4.5	6.0	na
Imports of goods and services	6.6	5.4	17.0	13.6	Imports of goods and services	-14.1	-21.7	16.0	na
Estonia					**Slovak Republic**				
Real GDP growth	4.6	-0.6	7.1	5.0	Real GDP growth	4.1	1.9	2.2	3.3
Private consumption	4.3	-2.9	6.5	4.9	Private consumption	5.3	0.1	-3.4	4.0
Public consumption	4.5	3.8	0.1	2.1	Public consumption	4.0	-6.9	-0.9	5.2
Gross fixed investment	11.3	-14.8	13.3	9.1	Gross fixed investment	11.1	-18.8	-0.7	11.6
Exports of goods and services	12.0	0.5	28.6	-0.2	Exports of goods and services	12.2	3.6	15.9	6.5
Imports of goods and services	12.9	-5.4	27.9	2.1	Imports of goods and services	19.9	-6.1	10.2	11.7
Hungary					**Slovenia**				
Real GDP growth	4.9	4.2	5.2	3.8	Real GDP growth	3.8	5.2	4.6	3.0
Private consumption	4.9	4.6	4.1	5.1	Private consumption	3.3	6.0	0.8	1.7
Public consumption	-0.3	1.8	1.2	0.4	Public consumption	5.8	4.6	3.1	3.2
Gross fixed investment	13.3	5.9	7.7	3.1	Gross fixed investment	11.3	19.1	0.2	-1.9
Exports of goods and services	16.7	13.1	21.8	9.1	Exports of goods and services	6.7	1.7	12.7	6.2
Imports of goods and services	10.1	12.3	21.1	6.3	Imports of goods and services	10.4	8.2	6.1	2.1
Latvia									
Real GDP growth	4.8	2.8	6.8	7.7					
Private consumption	1.1	3.7	7.4	7.1					
Public consumption	6.1	0.0	-1.9	-2.1					
Gross fixed investment	44.0	-4.0	20.0	17.0					
Exports of goods and services	4.9	-6.4	12.0	6.9					
Imports of goods and services	19.0	-5.2	4.9	12.6					

Source: EBRD.

Note: Data for 1998-2000 represent the most recent official estimates of outturns as reflected in publications from the national authorities, the IMF, the World Bank and the OECD. Data for 2001 are preliminary actuals, mostly official government estimates.

Table A.3.3

Inflation in central and eastern Europe and the CIS

(change in annual average retail/consumer price level, in per cent)

	1990	1991	1992	1993	1994	1995	1996	1997	1998	1999	2000	2001	2002
Central eastern Europe and the Baltic states													
Croatia	609.5	123.0	665.5	1,517.5	97.6	2.0	3.5	3.6	5.7	4.2	6.2	4.9	2.3
Czech Republic	9.7	52.0	11.1	20.8	9.9	9.1	8.8	8.5	10.7	2.1	3.9	4.7	2.3
Estonia	23.1	210.5	1,076.0	89.8	47.7	29.0	23.1	11.2	8.1	3.3	4.0	5.8	3.8
Hungary	28.9	35.0	23.0	22.5	18.8	28.2	23.6	18.3	14.3	10.0	9.8	9.2	4.9
Latvia	10.5	172.2	951.2	109.2	35.9	25.0	17.6	8.4	4.7	2.4	2.6	2.5	2.3
Lithuania	8.4	224.7	1,020.5	410.4	72.1	39.6	24.6	8.9	5.1	0.8	1.0	1.3	0.9
Poland	585.8	70.3	43.0	35.3	32.2	27.8	19.9	14.9	11.8	7.3	10.1	5.5	2.1
Slovak Republic	10.8	61.2	10.0	23.2	13.4	9.9	5.8	6.1	6.7	10.6	12.0	7.3	3.1
Slovenia	549.7	117.7	207.3	32.9	21.0	13.5	9.9	8.4	7.9	6.1	8.9	8.4	7.4
Median [1]	*23.1*	*117.7*	*207.3*	*35.3*	*32.2*	*25.0*	*17.6*	*8.5*	*7.9*	*4.2*	*6.2*	*5.5*	*2.3*
Mean [1]	*204.0*	*118.5*	*445.3*	*251.3*	*38.7*	*20.5*	*15.2*	*9.8*	*8.3*	*5.2*	*6.5*	*5.5*	*3.2*
South-eastern Europe													
Albania	0.0	35.5	226.0	85.0	22.6	7.8	12.7	33.2	20.6	0.4	0.1	3.1	5.3
Bulgaria	26.3	333.5	82.0	73.0	96.3	62.0	123.0	1,082.0	22.2	0.7	9.9	7.4	6.1
FR Yugoslavia	593.0	121.0	9,237.0	116.5x10^{12}	3.3	78.6	94.3	21.3	29.5	37.1	60.4	91.3	21.5
FYR Macedonia	608.4	114.9	1,664.4	338.4	126.5	16.4	2.5	0.8	2.3	-1.3	6.5	5.3	3.6
Romania	5.1	170.2	210.4	256.1	136.7	32.3	38.8	154.8	59.1	45.8	45.7	34.5	22.7
Median [1]	*26.3*	*121.0*	*226.0*	*170.6*	*96.3*	*32.3*	*38.8*	*33.2*	*22.2*	*0.7*	*9.9*	*7.4*	*6.1*
Mean [1]	*246.6*	*155.0*	*2,284.0*	*188.1*	*77.1*	*39.4*	*54.3*	*258.4*	*26.8*	*16.5*	*24.5*	*28.3*	*11.8*
Commonwealth of Independent States													
Armenia	10.3	274.0	1,346.0	1,822.0	4,962.0	175.8	18.7	14.0	8.7	0.7	-0.8	3.2	1.4
Azerbaijan	7.8	107.0	912.0	1,129.0	1,664.0	412.0	19.7	3.5	-0.8	-8.5	1.8	1.5	2.8
Belarus	4.7	94.1	970.8	1,190.2	2,221.0	709.3	52.7	63.8	73.2	293.8	168.9	61.4	41.4
Georgia	3.3	79.0	887.4	3,125.4	15,606.5	162.7	39.4	7.1	3.6	19.2	4.1	4.7	5.5
Kazakhstan	na	78.8	1,381.0	1,662.3	1,892.0	176.3	39.1	17.4	7.3	8.3	13.2	8.4	6.0
Kyrgyz Republic	na	85.0	855.0	772.4	228.7	40.7	31.3	25.5	12.0	35.8	18.7	7.0	2.5
Moldova	4.2	98.0	1,276.4	788.5	329.7	30.2	23.5	11.8	7.7	39.0	31.3	9.8	9.0
Russia	5.6	92.7	1,526.0	875.0	311.4	197.7	47.8	14.7	27.6	86.1	20.8	21.6	16.3
Tajikistan	4.0	112.0	1,157.0	2,195.0	350.0	609.0	418.0	88.0	43.2	27.6	32.9	38.6	12.8
Turkmenistan	4.6	103.0	493.0	3,102.0	1,748.0	1,005.3	992.4	83.7	16.8	24.2	8.3	11.6	9.6
Ukraine	4.2	91.0	1,210.0	4,734.0	891.0	377.0	80.0	15.9	10.5	22.7	28.2	12.0	1.6
Uzbekistan	3.1	82.2	645.0	534.0	1,568.0	304.6	54.0	58.9	17.8	29.1	24.2	26.2	22.8
Median [1]	*na*	*93.4*	*1,064*	*1,426*	*1,616*	*251*	*44*	*17*	*11*	*26*	*20*	*11*	*7*
Mean [1]	*na*	*108.1*	*1,055*	*1,827*	*2,648*	*350*	*151*	*34*	*19*	*48*	*29*	*17*	*11*
Central and eastern Europe and the CIS													
Median [1]	*24.7*	*100.5*	*899.7*	*534.0*	*131.6*	*40.2*	*24.1*	*14.8*	*10.6*	*9.2*	*9.9*	*7.3*	*5.1*
Mean [1]	*219.2*	*120.7*	*1,080.3*	*997.8*	*1,250.2*	*176.2*	*85.6*	*68.6*	*16.8*	*27.2*	*20.5*	*15.3*	*8.5*

Note: Data for 1990-2000 represent the most recent official estimates of outturns as reflected in publications from the national authorities, the IMF, the World Bank and the OECD. Data for 2001 are preliminary actuals, mostly official government estimates. Data for 2002 represent EBRD projections.

The figure for Albania for 1997 is based on the limited country data available. Estimates of inflation from parts of Bosnia and Herzegovina (for the Federation and Republika Srpska separately) are provided in the selected selected economic indicators at the back of this Report.

[1] The median is the middle value after all inflation rates have been arranged in order of size. The mean (unweighted average) tends to exceed the median, due to outliers caused by very high inflation rates in certain countries.

Table A.3.4

General government balances in central and eastern Europe and the CIS

	1990	1991	1992	1993	1994	1995	1996	1997	1998	1999	2000	2001 Estimate	2002 Projection	Change 2000-01	Change 2001-02
	(in per cent of GDP)													*(in percentage points)*	
Croatia	na	na	-3.9	-0.8	1.2	-1.4	-1.0	-1.9	-1.0	-6.5	-7.1	-5.8	-4.6	1.3	1.3
Czech Republic	-0.2	-1.9	-3.1	0.5	-1.9	-1.6	-1.9	-2.0	-2.4	-2.0	-4.2	-5.2	-9.3	-1.0	-1.0
Estonia	na	na	na	na	1.3	-1.3	-1.5	2.2	-0.3	-4.6	-0.7	0.4	-1.0	1.1	1.1
Hungary	0.0	-2.9	-6.1	-6.0	-7.5	-6.7	-5.0	-4.8	-4.8	-3.4	-3.3	-4.7	-6.0	-1.5	-1.5
Latvia	na	na	na	na	-4.4	-4.0	-1.8	0.3	-0.8	-3.9	-3.3	-1.9	-2.5	1.4	1.4
Lithuania	na	na	na	-5.3	-4.8	-4.5	-4.5	-1.8	-5.9	-8.5	-2.8	-1.9	-1.4	0.8	0.8
Poland	3.1	-2.1	-4.9	-2.4	-2.2	-3.1	-3.3	-3.1	-3.2	-3.7	-3.2	-6.0	-5.0	-2.8	-2.8
Slovak Republic	na	na	-11.9	-6.0	-1.5	0.4	-1.3	-5.2	-5.0	-3.6	-3.6	-3.9	-4.5	-0.3	-0.3
Slovenia	na	2.6	0.3	0.6	-0.2	-0.3	-0.2	-1.7	-1.4	-0.9	-1.3	-1.2	-2.9	0.1	0.1
Central eastern Europe and the Baltic states [1]	*1.0*	*-1.1*	*-4.9*	*-2.8*	*-2.2*	*-2.5*	*-2.3*	*-2.0*	*-2.8*	*-4.1*	*-3.3*	*-3.4*	*-4.1*	*-0.1*	*-0.1*
Albania	-6.1	-20.7	-23.1	-15.5	-12.6	-10.1	-12.1	-12.6	-10.4	-11.4	-9.1	-8.5	-8.0	0.6	0.6
Bosnia and Herzegovina	na	na	na	na	na	-0.3	-4.4	-0.5	-8.0	-9.1	-10.1	-6.3	-5.5	3.8	3.8
Bulgaria	-8.1	-4.5	-2.9	-8.7	-3.9	-5.7	-10.3	-2.0	0.9	-0.9	-1.0	-0.9	-0.8	0.1	0.1
FR Yugoslavia	na	na	na	na	na	-4.3	-3.8	-7.6	-5.4	na	-0.8	-1.9	-5.6	-1.1	-1.1
FYR Macedonia	na	-4.5	-9.8	-13.4	-2.7	-1.0	-1.4	-0.4	-1.7	0.0	2.5	-6.3	-4.4	-8.8	-8.8
Romania	na	na	-4.6	-0.4	-2.2	-2.5	-3.9	-4.6	-5.0	-3.5	-3.7	-3.5	-3.0	0.2	0.2
South-eastern Europe [1]	*-7.1*	*-9.9*	*-10.1*	*-9.5*	*-5.3*	*-4.0*	*-6.0*	*-4.6*	*-4.9*	*-5.0*	*-3.7*	*-4.6*	*-4.6*	*-0.9*	*-0.9*
Armenia	na	-1.9	-13.9	-54.7	-16.5	-9.0	-8.5	-5.8	-4.9	-7.4	-6.3	-3.8	-3.2	2.5	2.5
Azerbaijan	na	na	2.7	-15.3	-12.1	-4.9	-2.8	-1.6	-3.9	-4.7	-0.6	1.4	-0.1	2.1	2.1
Belarus	na	na	-2.0	-5.5	-3.5	-2.7	-1.8	-1.2	-0.5	-1.8	0.3	-0.4	-0.7	-0.7	-0.7
Georgia	na	-3.0	-25.4	-26.2	-7.4	-5.3	-7.3	-6.7	-5.4	-6.7	-4.1	-2.0	-1.7	2.1	2.1
Kazakhstan	1.4	-7.9	-7.3	-4.1	-7.7	-3.4	-5.3	-7.0	-8.0	-5.2	-1.0	-1.1	-2.0	-0.1	-0.1
Kyrgyz Republic	na	na	na	-14.4	-8.6	-17.3	-9.5	-9.1	-9.4	-11.8	-9.6	-6.0	-4.9	3.6	3.6
Moldova	na	0.0	-26.6	-7.5	-19.2	-13.1	-15.2	-14.1	-5.7	-6.1	-2.6	-0.5	-2.7	2.1	2.1
Russia	na	na	-18.9	-7.3	-10.4	-6.1	-8.9	-8.0	-8.0	-3.3	3.0	2.9	1.5	-0.1	-0.1
Tajikistan	-3.0	-20.2	-30.5	-20.9	-4.6	-3.3	-5.8	-3.3	-3.8	-3.1	-0.6	-0.1	-1.0	0.5	0.5
Turkmenistan	1.7	3.0	-9.4	-4.1	-2.3	-2.6	0.3	0.0	-2.6	0.0	0.4	0.8	-2.0	0.4	0.4
Ukraine	na	na	-25.4	-16.2	-8.7	-6.1	-3.2	-5.4	-2.8	-2.4	-1.3	-1.6	-1.8	-0.3	-0.3
Uzbekistan	-1.1	-3.6	-18.3	-10.4	-6.1	-4.1	-7.3	-2.4	-3.0	-2.7	-1.2	-0.5	-2.5	0.7	0.7
Commonwealth of Independent States [1]	*-0.2*	*-4.8*	*-15.9*	*-15.6*	*-8.9*	*-6.5*	*-6.3*	*-5.4*	*-4.8*	*-4.6*	*-2.0*	*-0.9*	*-1.8*	*1.1*	*1.1*

Note: Data for 1990-2000 represent the most recent official estimates of outturns as reflected in publications from the national authorities, the IMF, the World Bank and the OECD. Data for 2001 are preliminary actuals, mostly official government estimates. Data for 2002 represent EBRD projections.

[1] Unweighted average for the region.

Table A.3.5

General government revenue
(in per cent of GDP)

	1995	1996	1997	1998	1999	2000	2001
Croatia	43.5	44.3	42.5	45.6	43.2	41.7	40.2
Czech Republic	41.9	40.5	39.4	38.4	40.0	38.8	40.3
Estonia	40.3	39.0	39.8	39.3	38.1	37.9	38.2
Hungary	49.5	49.6	47.7	44.2	44.0	42.7	39.8
Latvia	37.6	37.7	41.4	42.6	40.1	37.3	35.7
Lithuania	32.3	29.6	32.6	32.6	32.1	30.4	29.8
Poland	47.4	43.1	42.7	41.4	40.2	39.4	39.2
Slovak Republic	47.0	45.6	41.1	38.3	39.7	41.8	43.5
Slovenia	43.1	42.7	42.1	43.0	43.6	42.8	43.1
Central eastern Europe and the Baltic states [1]	*42.5*	*41.3*	*41.0*	*40.6*	*40.1*	*39.2*	*38.9*
Albania	23.4	18.3	16.9	20.3	21.3	22.4	23.0
Bosnia and Herzegovina	39.0	0.5	39.2	57.3	60.4	56.3	55.0
Bulgaria	35.7	31.7	30.7	35.4	40.7	41.4	36.6
FR Yugoslavia	na	na	na	na	na	39.2	41.5
FYR Macedonia	37.9	35.7	34.8	33.3	35.4	36.7	34.3
Romania	31.4	28.9	27.1	28.1	31.1	31.5	31.2
South-eastern Europe [1]	*33.5*	*23.0*	*29.7*	*34.9*	*37.8*	*37.9*	*36.9*
Armenia	19.9	17.6	19.7	20.7	22.7	19.6	16.5
Azerbaijan	17.6	17.6	19.1	19.6	18.5	21.2	22.1
Belarus	36.1	39.4	43.6	43.4	44.6	44.6	42.6
Georgia	7.1	13.8	14.3	13.7	15.4	15.3	na
Kazakhstan	16.9	13.2	13.5	18.0	17.9	21.9	21.3
Kyrgyz Republic	24.8	23.9	23.9	24.4	24.0	19.6	22.2
Moldova	26.5	23.5	29.1	33.1	30.4	27.6	26.9
Russia	34.1	33.5	37.1	33.4	35.1	38.8	38.7
Tajikistan	17.5	13.2	13.7	12.0	13.5	13.6	15.2
Turkmenistan	20.5	16.6	25.4	22.0	19.4	25.8	25.2
Ukraine	37.8	36.7	38.8	36.0	33.8	35.1	35.0
Uzbekistan	34.6	34.3	30.1	31.1	29.3	31.1	32.0
Commonwealth of Independent States [1]	*24.4*	*23.6*	*25.7*	*25.6*	*25.4*	*26.2*	*27.1*
Memorandum:							
Germany	43.1	43.9	43.7	43.8	44.6	na	45.6
Greece	36.4	36.9	38.9	40.1	41.9	na	42.9
Japan	32.0	31.7	31.6	31.6	31.1	na	32.1
Portugal	38.8	40.1	41.0	41.3	42.8	na	43.8
United States	29.8	30.2	30.5	30.9	31.1	na	32.1

Sources: EBRD for transition economies and *OECD Economic Outlook* for OECD countries.
Note: Data for 1995-2000 represent the most recent official estimates of outturns as reflected in publications from the national authorities, the IMF, the World Bank and the OECD. Data for 2001 are preliminary actuals, mostly official government estimates.

[1] Unweighted average for the region.

Table A.3.6

General government expenditure
(in per cent of GDP)

	1995	1996	1997	1998	1999	2000	2001
Croatia	44.9	45.3	44.4	46.7	49.7	48.8	46.0
Czech Republic	44.1	42.9	42.3	41.6	43.0	44.2	45.2
Estonia	41.5	40.5	37.6	39.6	42.7	38.6	37.8
Hungary	52.6	48.8	49.5	50.4	44.8	46.0	43.0
Latvia	41.5	39.5	41.0	43.3	44.1	42.0	37.6
Lithuania	36.8	34.2	33.7	38.1	40.2	33.2	31.4
Poland	49.2	46.4	45.8	44.6	43.9	42.6	45.2
Slovak Republic	45.2	47.0	45.5	42.9	43.3	45.4	47.7
Slovenia	43.4	42.9	43.8	44.4	44.5	44.1	44.3
Central eastern Europe and the Baltic states [1]	*44.4*	*43.1*	*42.6*	*43.5*	*44.0*	*42.8*	*42.0*
Albania	33.4	30.3	29.4	30.7	32.7	31.4	31.5
Bosnia and Herzegovina	39.3	52.7	39.7	65.3	69.5	66.4	61.3
Bulgaria	41.3	42.0	32.7	34.5	41.6	42.4	37.4
FR Yugoslavia	na	na	na	na	na	40.1	42.8
FYR Macedonia	39.0	37.1	35.1	35.0	35.4	34.2	40.6
Romania	34.7	33.8	34.0	34.9	35.6	35.1	34.6
South-eastern Europe [1]	*37.6*	*39.2*	*34.2*	*40.1*	*43.0*	*41.6*	*41.4*
Armenia	28.9	26.1	25.5	25.6	30.1	25.9	23.9
Azerbaijan	22.5	20.3	20.8	23.7	23.6	20.8	19.9
Belarus	43.0	41.2	44.8	43.9	46.4	44.3	31.3
Georgia	12.3	21.1	21.0	19.1	22.1	19.4	18.2
Kazakhstan	20.8	18.6	20.4	26.1	23.1	22.8	22.4
Kyrgyz Republic	42.1	33.4	33.0	33.8	35.8	29.9	28.0
Moldova	39.6	38.7	43.2	38.7	36.4	30.2	27.4
Russia	40.2	42.4	45.1	41.4	38.4	35.8	35.8
Tajikistan	20.8	19.0	17.0	15.8	16.6	15.2	16.3
Turkmenistan	23.1	16.3	25.3	24.6	19.4	25.3	24.4
Ukraine	37.8	39.9	44.2	38.7	36.1	36.4	36.6
Uzbekistan	38.7	41.6	32.5	33.1	32.0	30.4	32.5
Commonwealth of Independent States [1]	*30.8*	*29.9*	*31.1*	*30.4*	*30.0*	*28.0*	*26.4*
Memorandum:							
Germany	43.1	43.9	43.7	43.8	44.6	na	na
Greece	36.4	36.9	38.9	40.1	41.9	na	na
Japan	32.0	31.7	31.6	31.6	31.1	na	na
Portugal	38.8	40.1	41.0	41.3	42.8	na	na
United States	29.8	30.2	30.5	30.9	31.1	na	na

Sources: EBRD for transition economies and *OECD Economic Outlook* for OECD countries.

Note: Data for 1995-2000 represent the most recent official estimates of outturns as reflected in publications from the national authorities, the IMF, the World Bank and the OECD. Data for 2001 are preliminary actuals, mostly official government estimates. General government expenditure includes net lending.

[1] Unweighted average for the region.

Table A.3.7

Current account balance in central and eastern Europe and the CIS

	1990	1991	1992	1993	1994	1995	1996	1997	1998	1999	2000	2001	2002	Change 2000-01	Change 2001-02
						(in per cent of GDP)								*(in percentage points)*	
Croatia	na	-3.4	3.2	5.7	5.9	-7.7	-5.5	-11.6	-7.1	-7.0	-2.3	-3.3	-3.5	-0.9	-0.2
Czech Republic	na	na	na	1.3	-1.9	-2.6	-7.1	-6.7	-2.2	-2.7	-5.3	-4.6	-3.6	0.7	1.0
Estonia	na	na	3.3	1.3	-7.2	-4.4	-9.2	-12.1	-9.2	-4.7	-5.7	-6.2	-6.7	-0.5	-0.5
Hungary	0.4	0.8	0.9	-9.0	-9.4	-5.6	-3.7	-2.1	-4.9	-4.3	-2.8	-2.1	-2.4	0.7	-0.3
Latvia	na	na	na	19.1	5.5	-0.4	-5.5	-6.1	-10.7	-9.8	-6.9	-9.7	-8.5	-2.8	1.2
Lithuania	na	na	na	-3.2	-2.2	-10.2	-9.2	-10.2	-12.1	-11.2	-6.0	-4.8	-5.8	1.2	-1.0
Poland	1.0	-2.6	1.1	-0.7	0.7	4.5	-1.0	-3.2	-4.4	-7.5	-6.3	-3.9	-3.8	2.3	0.1
Slovak Republic	na	na	na	-4.7	4.6	2.1	-10.6	-9.6	-9.7	-5.5	-3.7	-8.8	-9.1	-5.1	-0.3
Slovenia	3.0	1.0	7.4	1.5	4.0	-0.5	0.2	0.1	-0.8	-3.9	-3.4	-0.4	1.2	3.0	1.6
Central eastern Europe and the Baltic states [1]	*1.4*	*-1.0*	*3.2*	*1.3*	*0.0*	*-2.8*	*-5.7*	*-6.8*	*-6.8*	*-6.3*	*-4.7*	*-4.9*	*-4.7*	*-0.2*	*0.2*
Albania	na	na	na	-30.1	-14.4	-7.2	-9.1	-12.1	-6.1	-7.2	-6.9	-6.3	-6.0	0.6	0.3
Bosnia and Herzegovina	na	na	na	na	-14.1	-10.3	-27.3	-31.0	-17.1	-20.7	-21.4	-23.1	-20.3	-1.8	2.8
Bulgaria	-8.2	-1.0	-4.2	-10.1	-0.3	-0.2	0.2	4.1	-0.5	-5.3	-5.6	-6.5	-5.9	-0.9	0.6
FR Yugoslavia	na	na	na	na	na	na	-11.6	-7.7	-4.8	-7.5	-7.4	-10.7	-12.9	-2.4	-0.4
FYR Macedonia	-9.1	-5.5	-0.8	0.6	-5.3	-5.0	-6.5	-7.7	-10.1	-3.4	-3.1	-9.8	-10.2	-7.6	-2.3
Romania	-9.6	-3.5	-8.0	-4.5	-1.4	-5.0	-7.3	-6.1	-7.0	-3.7	-3.7	-6.1	-5.0	-2.4	1.1
South-eastern Europe [1]	*-9.0*	*-3.4*	*-4.3*	*-11.0*	*-7.1*	*-5.5*	*-10.3*	*-10.1*	*-7.6*	*-8.0*	*-8.0*	*-10.4*	*-10.0*	*-2.4*	*0.4*
Armenia	na	na	na	-14.3	-16.0	-17.0	-18.2	-18.0	-21.3	-16.6	-14.6	-9.5	-8.9	5.2	0.6
Azerbaijan	na	19.3	-12.2	-12.2	-9.4	-13.2	-25.8	-23.1	-30.7	-13.1	-3.2	-0.9	-22.4	2.3	-21.5
Belarus	na	na	na	-11.9	-9.1	-4.4	-3.6	-6.1	-6.7	-1.6	-2.1	0.8	-0.4	2.9	-1.2
Georgia	na	na	-33.5	-40.2	-22.3	-7.5	-9.1	-10.6	-9.4	-8.2	-5.5	-6.8	-6.2	-1.3	0.5
Kazakhstan	-85.9	-50.0	0.0	-7.9	-7.8	-1.3	-3.6	-3.6	-5.6	-1.0	2.2	-7.8	-5.5	-10.1	2.3
Kyrgyz Republic	na	na	na	na	-6.9	-13.9	-21.4	-7.8	-25.0	-19.5	-11.6	-3.4	-2.9	8.1	0.6
Moldova	na	na	-3.0	-11.9	-7.0	-6.8	-9.8	-12.6	-16.7	-2.9	-8.4	-9.1	-9.2	-0.6	-0.1
Russia	na	na	na	na	3.0	2.2	2.8	0.5	0.3	12.7	17.9	11.3	8.0	-6.5	-3.3
Tajikistan	na	na	na	-28.8	-17.8	-16.0	-7.1	-5.4	-9.1	-3.4	-6.4	-6.9	-4.1	-0.5	2.8
Turkmenistan	na	88.6	68.5	14.1	4.0	0.9	0.1	-25.3	-37.4	-24.8	15.2	-2.5	0.8	-17.7	3.3
Ukraine	na	na	na	na	-4.9	-3.1	-2.7	-2.7	-3.1	2.6	4.7	3.7	4.0	-1.0	0.2
Uzbekistan	na	395.6	-12.0	-8.4	2.1	-0.2	-7.8	-5.4	-0.4	-2.0	2.8	-0.5	0.6	-3.3	1.1
Commonwealth of Independent States [1]	*na*	*na*	*1.3*	*-13.5*	*-7.7*	*-6.7*	*-8.8*	*-10.0*	*-13.7*	*-6.5*	*-0.8*	*-2.6*	*-3.9*	*-1.9*	*-1.2*
Central and eastern Europe and the CIS [1]	**na**	**na**	**0.8**	**-7.0**	**-4.9**	**-5.1**	**-8.1**	**-9.0**	**-10.1**	**-6.7**	**-3.7**	**-5.1**	**-5.5**	**-1.4**	**-0.4**

[1] Unweighted average for the region.

Note: Data for 1990-2000 represent the most recent official estimates of outturns as reflected in publications from the national authorities, the IMF, the World Bank and the OECD. Data for 2001 are preliminary actuals, mostly official government estimates. Data for 2002 represent EBRD projections.

Table A.3.8

Indicators of competitiveness
(change as a percentage, unless indicated)

	1997	1998	1999	2000	2001	1997-2001
Bulgaria						
Industrial gross output	-13.7	-5.8	-4.3	12.0	0.7	-12.3
Productivity in industry	-6.9	1.4	-1.8	18.7	5.1	15.7
Real wage in industry (PPI-based)	16.2	14.1	7.5	-5.4	-0.5	34.1
EUR unit labour costs	24.3	26.6	15.0	na	-9.3	na
Real EUR exchange rate index (1995=100)	117.6	136.9	137.4	147.3	154.3	-
Wage share	0.41	0.39	0.48	0.51	0.53	-
Croatia[1]						
Industrial gross output	6.8	3.7	-1.4	1.7	6.0	17.8
Productivity in industry	6.6	7.4	1.7	4.3	9.3	32.6
Real wage in manufacturing (PPI-based)	8.2	11.4	2.8	-1.6	5.0	28.0
EUR unit labour costs	-0.9	0.1	-1.9	-0.6	0.9	-2.4
Real EUR exchange rate index (1995=100)	101.3	103.8	100.5	103.6	108.4	-
Wage share	0.50	0.53	0.51	0.53	0.59	-
Czech Republic						
Manufacturing gross output	6.4	2.5	-2.7	4.8	7.8	19.9
Productivity in manufacturing	11.1	5.6	2.2	5.8	6.6	35.1
Real wage in manufacturing (PPI-based)	8.4	5.6	6.3	0.7	8.2	32.6
EUR unit labour costs	-1.9	4.1	2.0	4.1	8.9	18.0
Real EUR exchange rate index (1995=100)	109.7	119.5	118.3	124.4	132.9	-
Wage share	0.25	0.24	0.24	na	na	-
Estonia						
Manufacturing gross output	14.5	5.4	-2.3	16.7	8.2	49.0
Productivity in manufacturing	18.4	9.2	4.8	10.8	4.5	56.9
Real wage in manufacturing (PPI-based)	11.5	10.7	3.5	9.3	4.3	45.6
EUR unit labour costs	1.1	4.5	-3.8	4.6	3.3	9.8
Real EUR exchange rate index (1995=100)	131.9	141.1	144.2	146.5	151.2	-
Wage share	0.51	0.49	0.48	0.47	na	-
Hungary						
Manufacturing gross output	14.8	16.2	12.5	11.0	6.2	76.9
Productivity in manufacturing	13.0	10.1	0.2	10.7	2.4	41.4
Real earnings in manufacturing (PPI-based)	3.6	7.4	8.5	3.4	4.8	30.8
EUR unit labour costs	-2.1	-9.0	10.2	1.4	13.5	12.9
Real EUR exchange rate index (1995=100)	108.6	107.5	111.6	116.4	125.6	-
Wage share	0.27	0.27	0.27	0.25	0.26	-
Latvia						
Manufacturing gross output	17.1	4.0	-5.9	6.8	9.5	34.0
Productivity in manufacturing	12.7	13.2	-1.6	4.4	na	na
Real wage in manufacturing (PPI-based)	17.8	4.8	7.7	2.0	na	na
EUR unit labour costs	15.1	-7.3	9.9	9.6	na	na
Real EUR exchange rate index (1995=100)	128.8	133.0	142.8	159.7	158.9	-
Wage share	0.39	0.43	0.45	0.44	na	-
Lithuania[2]						
Manufacturing gross output	8.0	9.3	-9.6	8.8	17.0	35.8
Productivity in manufacturing	5.7	8.0	-6.1	14.7	20.3	47.9
Real wage in manufacturing (PPI-based)	18.1	28.6	-10.4	-16.3	3.7	18.1
EUR unit labour costs	30.4	12.5	3.4	15.3	-12.8	52.5
Real EUR exchange rate index (1995=100)	151.5	159.7	168.1	192.5	195.8	-
Wage share	0.33	0.35	0.33	0.32	na	-

Table A.3.8 (continued)

Indicators of competitiveness
(change as a percentage, unless indicated)

	1997	1998	1999	2000	2001	1997-2001
Poland						
Manufacturing gross output	12.8	5.1	5.3	7.3	0.0	34.0
Productivity in manufacturing	12.1	4.7	9.5	8.3	1.9	41.7
Real wage in manufacturing (PPI-based)	12.1	8.4	5.8	8.1	4.8	45.6
EUR unit labour costs	0.1	4.7	-6.4	12.8	18.1	30.6
Real EUR exchange rate index (1995=100)	113.2	119.0	116.9	132.8	149.4	-
Wage share	0.34	0.34	0.33	0.34	na	-
Romania						
Manufacturing gross output	-6.8	-18.1	-6.1	8.9	na	na
Productivity in manufacturing	-1.4	-15.9	14.7	15.5	na	na
Real wage in manufacturing (PPI-based)	-23.7	10.7	1.9	-14.2	na	na
EUR unit labour costs	-6.5	46.7	-22.2	-2.7	na	na
Real EUR exchange rate index (1995=100)	111.5	143.6	125.9	146.6	147.8	-
Wage share	0.28	0.31	0.26	0.23	na	-
Russia[3]						
Manufacturing gross output	1.9	-5.2	8.1	na	na	na
Productivity in manufacturing	12.0	19.1	7.3	na	na	na
Real wage in manufacturing (PPI-based)	1.6	-5.9	-2.7	na	na	na
EUR unit labour costs	7.7	-43.6	-39.7	na	na	na
Real EUR exchange rate index (1995=100)	148.5	110.2	86.4	103.1	121.3	-
Wage share	na	na	na	na	na	-
Slovak Republic						
Manufacturing gross output	1.6	6.5	-3.0	10.0	6.0	22.4
Productivity in manufacturing	4.1	11.5	2.0	7.8	3.9	32.6
Real wage in manufacturing (PPI-based)	7.5	6.1	-3.9	1.9	6.2	18.7
EUR unit labour costs	9.1	-6.0	-5.8	5.7	4.3	6.5
Real EUR exchange rate index (1995=100)	115.8	118.3	115.1	130.4	134.3	-
Wage share	0.30	0.29	0.29	0.33	0.36	-
Slovenia						
Manufacturing gross output	0.2	3.9	0.0	7.0	2.8	14.5
Productivity in manufacturing	4.5	5.4	1.8	7.3	1.8	22.3
Real wage in manufacturing (PPI-based)	6.2	5.0	6.3	3.3	0.7	23.3
EUR unit labour costs	1.9	2.5	3.0	-1.5	2.8	8.8
Real EUR exchange rate index (1995=100)	98.3	102.1	102.9	103.4	103.3	-
Wage share	0.37	0.36	0.35	0.35	0.35	-

Sources: Production, employment and wages figures are taken from various issues of monthly, quarterly and annual publications from national authorities, the IMF, the OECD, the ILO and the Vienna Institute for International Economic Studies.

Note: Data for 1997-2000 represent the percentage change of annual averages based on actual data. Figures for 2001 represent preliminary official estimates.

Productivity is calculated as the ratio of manufacturing / industry production over manufacturing / industry employment.

Data on the exchange rate to the EUR, on CPI and PPI are based on national authorities, the IMF and EBRD estimates. Prior to 1999, D-Mark is used instead of euro.

The real EUR exchange rate is calculated as the domestic CPI divided by the product of the euro area HICP index and the exchange rate. An increase in the index represents a real appreciation.

EUR unit labour costs are calculated as wages in EUR divided by productivity. The wage share is the ratio of wages and value added in manufacturing.

Real wages are calculated as average monthly wages deflated by PPI. Average monthly wages in manufacturing are deflated by PPI in manufacturing, while average monthly earnings in industry are deflated by PPI in industry.

[1] Figures for 1997 refer to industry and thereafter to manufacturing. PPI refers to industry in 1997 and to manufacturing thereafter.

[2] Output and PPI refers to mining, quarrying and manufacturing. Production data for 1999 refer to sales.

[3] From 1997 figures refer to industry.

Table A.3.9

Foreign direct investment
(net inflows recorded in the balance of payments)

	1990	1991	1992	1993	1994	1995	1996	1997	1998	1999	2000	2001 (estimate)	2002 (projection)	Cumulative FDI-inflows 1989-2001 (in US$ mln)	Cumulative FDI-inflows per capita 1989-2001 (US$)	FDI-inflows per capita 2000 (US$)	FDI-inflows per capita 2001 (US$)	FDI-inflows 2000 (in per cent of GDP)	FDI-inflows 2001 (in per cent of GDP)
Croatia	na	na	13	102	110	109	486	347	835	1,445	1,086	1,325	970	5,858	1,315	248	297	5.9	6.8
Czech Republic	na	na	983	563	749	2,526	1,276	1,275	3,591	6,234	4,943	4,820	8,000	26,960	2,615	479	468	9.6	8.5
Estonia	na	na	80	156	212	199	111	130	574	222	324	343	300	2,351	1,727	237	252	6.3	6.2
Hungary	311	1,459	1,471	2,328	1,097	4,410	2,279	1,741	1,555	1,720	1,090	2,103	2,559	21,751	2,137	109	207	2.3	4.0
Latvia	na	na	na	50	279	245	379	515	303	331	400	170	250	2,670	1,138	169	72	5.6	2.2
Lithuania	na	na	na	30	31	72	152	328	921	478	375	439	395	2,826	813	108	126	3.3	3.7
Poland	0	117	284	580	542	1,134	2,741	3,041	4,966	6,348	8,171	6,502	5,000	34,426	890	211	168	5.1	3.6
Slovak Republic	24	82	100	107	236	194	199	84	374	701	2,058	1,460	4,000	5,629	1,042	381	270	10.7	7.3
Slovenia	-2	-41	113	111	131	183	188	340	250	144	110	338	553	1,847	934	55	171	0.6	1.8
Central eastern Europe and the Baltic states	*333*	*1,617*	*3,044*	*4,027*	*3,388*	*9,070*	*7,810*	*7,800*	*13,368*	*17,622*	*18,557*	*17,500*	*22,027*	*98,459*	*1,401*	*222*	*226*	*5.5*	*4.9*
Albania	na	na	20	45	65	89	97	42	45	51	141	204	153	799	259	41	66	3.8	5.0
Bulgaria	4	56	41	40	105	98	138	507	537	789	1,003	641	800	3,961	491	123	79	8.0	4.7
Bosnia and Herzegovina	na	na	na	na	0	0	0	0	100	90	150	130	200	470	109	35	30	3.4	2.9
FR Yugoslavia	na	na	na	na	na	na	0	740	113	112	25	165	300	1,155	135	3	19	0.3	1.5
FYR Macedonia	0	0	0	0	24	12	12	18	175	27	175	445	70	888	444	88	223	4.9	12.7
Romania	-18	37	73	87	341	417	415	1,267	2,079	1,025	1,051	1,154	1,200	7,928	356	47	52	2.9	3.0
South-eastern Europe	*-14*	*93*	*134*	*172*	*535*	*616*	*662*	*2,574*	*3,049*	*2,094*	*2,545*	*2,739*	*2,723*	*15,201*	*299*	*56*	*78*	*3.9*	*5.0*
Armenia	na	na	0	1	8	25	18	52	221	122	104	70	75	620	199	33	22	5.4	3.3
Azerbaijan	na	na	na	0	22	330	627	1,115	1,023	510	119	227	1,300	3,973	491	15	28	2.3	4.0
Belarus	na	na	na	18	11	15	105	350	201	443	90	84	146	1,315	132	9	8	0.7	0.7
Georgia	na	na	na	0	8	6	54	236	221	60	152	100	80	838	157	28	19	5.1	3.2
Kazakhstan	na	na	100	473	635	964	1,137	1,320	1,143	1,584	1,245	2,760	2,500	11,361	765	84	186	6.8	12.4
Kyrgyz Republic	na	na	na	na	38	96	47	83	86	38	-6	22	25	405	85	-1	5	-0.4	1.5
Moldova	na	na	17	14	18	73	23	71	88	34	128	60	100	526	146	35	17	8.9	3.8
Russia	na	na	na	na	na	1,460	1,657	1,679	1,496	1,103	-496	-137	1,000	6,762	47	-3	-1	-0.2	0.0
Tajikistan	na	na	na	9	12	10	18	18	25	21	24	9	20	155	24	4	1	2.4	0.9
Turkmenistan	na	na	na	79	103	233	108	108	62	125	126	133	150	1,077	191	23	24	5.0	4.5
Ukraine	na	na	na	na	151	257	516	581	747	489	594	769	750	4,104	84	12	16	1.9	2.0
Uzbekistan	na	na	9	48	73	-24	90	167	140	121	73	71	75	768	30	3	3	1.1	1.2
Commonwealth of Independent States	*na*	*na*	*135*	*642*	*1,079*	*3,445*	*4,400*	*5,780*	*5,453*	*4,651*	*2,152*	*4,168*	*6,221*	*31,905*	*196*	*20*	*27*	*3.2*	*3.1*
Total	**319**	**1,710**	**3,314**	**4,840**	**5,002**	**13,132**	**12,872**	**16,153**	**21,871**	**24,367**	**23,254**	**24,407**	**30,971**	**145,565**	**603**	**91**	**99**	**4.1**	**4.1**

(in US$ millions)

Sources: IMF, central banks and EBRD estimates.
Note: For most countries, figures cover only investment in equity capital and, in some cases, contributions-in-kind.

For those countries where net investment into equity capital was not easily available (e.g. Azerbaijan, Estonia, Kazakhstan and Slovak Republic), more recent data include reinvested earnings as well as inter-company debt transactions.

Gross inflows of FDI are in some cases considerably higher than net inflows on account of increasing intra-regional investment flows.

Table A.3.10

GDP growth forecasts for 2002

(in per cent)

	Average[1]	Range[2]	EBRD (Sep 2002)	European Union (Apr 2002)	OECD (Jun 2002)	IMF (Sep 2002)	Davidson Institute[4] (Sep 2002)	Economist Intelligence Unit (Aug 2002)	DRI-WEFA[5] (Jul 2002)	IWH[6] (Jul 2002)	Kopint-Datorg[7] (Jun 2002)	WIIW[8] (Jun 2002)	CSFB[9] (Aug 2002)	JP Morgan (Jul 2002)	Dun & Bradstreet (Aug 2002)
Central eastern Europe and the Baltic states															
Croatia	3.4	1.3	3.5	na	na	3.5	na	3.0	4.3	na	3.0	3.0	3.7	na	3.5
Czech Republic	3.1	1.3	2.5	3.4	3.0	2.7	3.0	3.3	3.2	3.0	3.7	3.0	3.8	2.8	3.3
Estonia	4.4	1.0	4.0	4.0	na	4.5	4.4	4.4	5.0	4.0	4.7	na	na	na	4.7
Hungary	3.5	0.9	4.0	3.5	3.5	3.5	3.2	3.4	3.6	3.5	3.7	3.3	3.9	na	3.1
Latvia	4.9	1.2	4.0	5.0	na	5.0	4.9	5.0	5.2	5.0	5.1	na	na	na	4.9
Lithuania	4.5	1.5	5.2	4.0	na	4.4	4.2	4.8	5.1	3.7	5.2	na	na	na	4.0
Poland	1.2	1.8	1.0	1.4	1.3	1.0	1.3	1.3	1.6	1.8	1.3	na	1.5	1.0	1.5
Slovak Republic	3.7	1.7	3.5	3.6	4.0	4.0	4.0	4.0	4.1	2.4	3.5	3.5	3.7	4.0	3.3
Slovenia	3.0	1.3	2.7	3.1	na	2.5	3.2	3.0	3.8	3.0	3.1	3.0	na	na	2.9
Average	*3.5*	*1.3*	*3.4*	*3.5*	*3.0*	*3.5*	*3.5*	*3.6*	*4.0*	*3.3*	*3.7*	*2.6*	*3.3*	*2.6*	*3.5*
Weighted average[3]	*2.4*	*1.5*	*2.2*	*na*	*na*	*2.2*	*na*	*2.5*	*2.8*	*na*	*2.6*	*na*	*na*	*na*	*2.5*
South-eastern Europe															
Albania	5.9	0.6	6.0	na	na	6.0	na	6.0	6.1	na	na	na	na	na	5.5
Bosnia and Herzegovina	3.7	2.7	3.0	na	na	2.3	na	5.0	4.6	na	na	na	na	na	na
Bulgaria	3.5	1.0	4.0	4.0	na	4.0	3.0	3.0	3.6	3.0	3.5	3.5	3.5	3.5	3.9
FYR Macedonia	2.3	4.3	2.0	na	na	2.5	na	1.0	4.3	na	na	0.0	na	na	4.0
FR Yugoslavia	4.4	2.9	3.0	na	na	na	na	3.8	5.9	3.0	4.5	4.0	3.8	na	5.1
Romania	3.8	2.0	3.5	4.2	na	4.3	3.0	3.7	5.0	3.0	3.2	3.0	3.7	3.5	4.0
Average	*3.9*	*2.3*	*3.6*	*4.1*	*na*	*3.8*	*3.0*	*3.8*	*4.9*	*3.0*	*3.7*	*2.6*	*3.7*	*3.5*	*4.5*
Weighted average[3]	*3.9*	*2.0*	*3.6*	*na*	*na*	*na*	*na*	*3.7*	*4.9*	*na*	*na*	*na*	*na*	*na*	*na*
Commonwealth of Independent States															
Armenia	7.4	1.5	8.0	na	na	7.5	na	6.5	7.6	na	na	na	na	na	na
Azerbaijan	8.2	2.8	8.8	na	na	7.9	na	7.0	9.8	na	na	na	na	na	7.5
Belarus	3.2	0.5	3.0	na	na	3.5	na	3.0	3.5	na	na	na	na	na	3.0
Georgia	4.1	1.5	3.5	na	na	3.5	na	5.0	4.2	na	na	na	na	na	4.5
Kazakhstan	8.1	1.2	7.6	na	na	8.0	na	8.0	8.8	na	na	na	na	na	8.0
Kyrgyz Republic	3.1	4.0	2.0	na	na	4.4	na	1.0	3.0	na	na	na	na	na	5.0
Moldova	4.1	1.3	3.5	na	na	4.8	na	4.5	3.7	na	na	na	na	na	na
Russia	3.9	1.0	4.1	na	3.5	4.4	4.1	4.0	4.1	3.8	3.9	3.4	3.7	4.0	4.0
Tajikistan	7.6	1.6	7.0	na	na	7.0	na	7.0	8.6	na	na	na	na	na	8.5
Turkmenistan	12.2	9.0	13.5	na	na	na	na	16.0	12.2	na	na	na	na	na	7.0
Ukraine	4.4	1.0	4.5	na	na	4.8	4.4	4.5	5.0	na	4.0	4.0	4.0	na	na
Uzbekistan	2.6	1.1	2.5	na	na	2.7	na	2.5	3.1	na	na	na	na	na	2.0
Average	*5.7*	*2.2*	*5.7*	*na*	*3.5*	*5.3*	*4.3*	*5.8*	*6.1*	*3.8*	*4.0*	*3.7*	*3.9*	*4.0*	*5.5*
Weighted average[3]	*4.3*	*1.1*	*4.4*	*na*	*na*	*na*	*na*	*4.4*	*4.6*	*na*	*na*	*na*	*na*	*na*	*na*
Central and eastern Europe and the CIS															
Average	*4.6*	*1.9*	*4.4*	*3.6*	*3.1*	*4.3*	*3.6*	*4.6*	*5.1*	*3.3*	*3.7*	*2.8*	*3.5*	*3.1*	*4.5*
Weighted average[3]	*3.4*	*1.4*	*3.4*	*na*	*na*	*na*	*na*	*3.5*	*3.8*	*na*	*na*	*na*	*na*	*na*	*na*

Note: All forecasts quoted were published or reported to the EBRD between April and September 2002. The dates in brackets indicate the months in which the forecasts were reported or published by each institution. There may in some instances be substantial lags between preparation and publication of forecasts.

1 The number at the bottom of this column is calculated as the mean of all the average forecasts shown in this column.
2 Data show the difference between the highest and the lowest of the forecasts.
3 Weighted average based on EBRD estimates of nominal US dollar GDP in each country in 2000.
4 William Davidson Institute at the University of Michigan Business School.
5 Data Resource Inc (DRI) and Wharton Econometric Forecasting Associates (WEFA).
6 Institute for Economic Research, Halle, Germany.
7 Kopint-Datorg is the Institute for Economic and Market Research Information, Hungary.
8 Vienna Institute for International Economic Studies.
9 Credit Suisse First Boston.

Table A.3.11

GDP growth forecasts for 2003

(in per cent)

	Average[1]	Range[2]	EBRD (Sep 2002)	European Union (Apr 2002)	OECD (Jun 2002)	IMF (Sep 2002)	Davidson Institute[4] (Sep 2002)	Economist Intelligence Unit (Aug 2002)	DRI-WEFA[5] (Jul 2002)	IWH[6] (Jul 2002)	Kopint-Datorg[7] (Jun 2002)	WIIW[8] (Jun 2002)	CSFB[9] (Aug 2002)	JP Morgan (Jul 2002)	Dun & Bradstreet (Aug 2002)
Central eastern Europe and the Baltic states															
Croatia	3.9	0.6	4.0	na	na	4.0	na	3.6	4.0	na	3.5	4.0	4.0	na	4.1
Czech Republic	3.8	1.3	3.5	3.9	3.7	3.2	4.3	4.2	4.2	3.5	4.1	4.0	4.5	3.3	3.6
Estonia	5.3	1.5	4.5	5.3	na	5.0	5.2	6.0	5.3	5.0	5.5	na	na	na	5.7
Hungary	4.3	2.1	5.5	4.5	4.3	4.0	3.8	4.4	4.3	4.0	4.6	4.0	4.5	na	3.4
Latvia	5.5	1.7	4.5	6.0	na	6.0	5.4	5.5	5.4	5.5	5.2	na	na	na	6.2
Lithuania	4.9	1.7	4.5	5.0	na	4.8	4.8	5.0	5.4	4.0	5.7	na	na	2.5	5.3
Poland	2.7	3.0	3.0	3.2	2.7	3.0	1.8	2.9	3.2	3.0	3.0	1.0	4.0	3.9	2.0
Slovak Republic	4.0	1.4	4.0	4.2	4.1	3.7	4.5	4.2	4.9	3.5	3.8	4.0	3.9	na	3.6
Slovenia	4.0	1.6	4.0	4.0	na	3.2	4.5	4.0	4.8	3.5	4.4	4.0	na	na	3.8
Average	*4.3*	*1.7*	*4.2*	*4.5*	*3.7*	*4.1*	*4.3*	*4.4*	*4.6*	*4.0*	*4.4*	*3.5*	*4.2*	*3.2*	*4.2*
Weighted average[3]	*3.5*	*2.2*	*3.7*	*na*	*na*	*3.4*	*na*	*3.6*	*3.9*	*na*	*3.7*	*na*	*na*	*na*	*3.0*
South-eastern Europe															
Albania	6.3	1.0	6.0	na	na	7.0	na	6.0	6.0	na	na	na	na	na	6.5
Bosnia and Herzegovina	4.9	2.0	4.0	na	na	4.1	na	6.0	5.5	na	na	na	na	na	na
Bulgaria	4.3	1.6	4.0	5.0	na	5.0	4.0	4.2	5.1	3.5	4.0	4.0	4.0	4.6	4.5
FYR Macedonia	3.9	3.9	3.0	na	na	4.0	na	4.0	5.9	na	na	2.0	na	na	4.5
FR Yugoslavia	5.5	2.9	4.0	na	na	na	na	6.0	6.9	na	6.0	4.0	4.0	na	6.0
Romania	4.4	1.2	4.0	4.9	na	4.9	4.0	4.4	5.1	4.0	3.9	4.0	4.0	na	4.9
Average	*4.9*	*2.1*	*4.2*	*5.0*	*na*	*5.0*	*4.0*	*5.1*	*5.8*	*3.8*	*4.6*	*3.5*	*4.0*	*4.6*	*5.3*
Weighted average[3]	*4.7*	*1.7*	*4.1*	*na*	*na*	*na*	*na*	*4.8*	*5.5*	*na*	*na*	*na*	*na*	*na*	*na*
Commonwealth of Independent States															
Armenia	6.2	1.1	7.0	na	na	6.0	na	6.0	5.9	na	na	na	na	na	7.5
Azerbaijan	7.9	2.9	8.0	na	na	7.3	na	7.0	9.9	na	na	na	na	na	2.7
Belarus	2.8	1.7	2.5	na	na	3.8	na	3.0	2.1	na	na	na	na	na	4.5
Georgia	4.7	2.5	4.0	na	na	4.0	na	6.5	4.5	na	na	na	na	na	6.5
Kazakhstan	6.8	1.3	6.2	na	na	7.0	na	7.0	7.5	na	na	na	na	na	6.0
Kyrgyz Republic	4.2	3.0	4.0	na	na	3.8	na	3.0	4.3	na	na	na	na	na	na
Moldova	4.8	1.3	4.0	na	na	5.0	na	5.0	5.3	na	na	na	na	na	3.8
Russia	4.2	1.2	3.8	na	4.0	4.9	4.5	4.0	4.3	5.0	4.1	3.8	4.2	4.2	6.0
Tajikistan	6.4	2.5	5.0	na	na	6.0	na	7.5	7.5	na	na	na	na	na	8.5
Turkmenistan	8.1	6.0	5.0	na	na	na	na	10.0	9.7	na	na	na	na	na	na
Ukraine	4.7	1.0	4.5	na	na	5.0	5.0	5.0	4.6	na	4.0	5.0	4.7	na	2.0
Uzbekistan	2.7	1.1	2.5	na	na	3.0	na	3.0	3.1	na	na	na	na	na	na
Average	*5.3*	*2.1*	*4.6*	*na*	*4.0*	*5.1*	*4.8*	*5.6*	*5.7*	*5.0*	*4.1*	*4.4*	*4.5*	*4.2*	*5.3*
Weighted average[3]	*4.4*	*1.3*	*4.0*	*na*	*na*	*na*	*na*	*4.3*	*4.6*	*na*	*na*	*na*	*na*	*na*	*na*
Central and eastern Europe and the CIS															
Average	*4.9*	*2.0*	*4.4*	*4.6*	*3.8*	*4.7*	*4.3*	*5.1*	*5.4*	*4.0*	*4.4*	*3.7*	*4.2*	*3.7*	*4.9*
Weighted average[3]	*4.0*	*1.7*	*3.9*	*na*	*na*	*na*	*na*	*4.1*	*4.3*	*na*	*na*	*na*	*na*	*na*	*na*

Note: All forecasts quoted were published or reported to the EBRD between April and September 2002. The dates in brackets indicate the months in which the forecasts were reported or published by each institution. There may in some instances be substantial lags between preparation and publication of forecasts.

1 The number at the bottom of this column is calculated as the mean of all the average forecasts shown in this column.

2 Data show the difference between the highest and the lowest of the forecasts.

3 Weighted average based on EBRD estimates of nominal US dollar GDP in each country in 2000.

4 William Davidson Institute at the University of Michigan Business School.

5 Data Resource Inc (DRI) and Wharton Econometric Forecasting Associates (WEFA).

6 Institute for Economic Research, Halle, Germany.

7 Kopint-Datorg is the Institute for Economic and Market Research Information, Hungary.

8 Vienna Institute for International Economic Studies.

9 Credit Suisse First Boston.

Table A.3.12

Average annual inflation forecasts for 2002

(change in the average consumer price level, in per cent)

	Average[1]	Range[2]	EBRD (Sep 2002)	European Union (Apr 2002)	OECD (Jun 2002)	IMF (Sep 2002)	Davidson Institute[3] (Sep 2002)	Economist Intelligence Unit (Aug 2002)	DRI-WEFA[4] (Jul 2002)	IWH[5] (Jul 2002)	Kopint-Datorg[6] (Jun 2002)	WIIW[7] (Jun 2002)	CSFB[8] (Aug 2002)	JP Morgan (Jul 2002)	Dun & Bradstreet (Aug 2002)
Central eastern Europe and the Baltic states															
Croatia	3.2	2.9	2.3	na	na	3.5	na	4.8	1.9	na	4.0	3.0	3.0	na	na
Czech Republic	2.8	2.2	2.3	3.9	3.2	2.7	2.0	2.2	2.4	4.2	3.4	3.0	2.3	2.0	na
Estonia	4.3	2.5	3.8	4.1	na	3.7	4.4	4.1	5.8	5.0	3.3	na	5.7	na	na
Hungary	5.6	1.6	4.9	5.2	5.5	5.5	5.2	5.6	6.1	6.5	5.9	5.7	na	na	na
Latvia	2.5	1.0	2.3	3.0	na	3.0	2.4	2.2	2.4	2.0	2.8	na	na	na	2.8
Lithuania	1.6	1.9	0.9	2.7	na	1.1	1.0	1.4	1.3	1.0	2.3	3.0	2.5	na	na
Poland	3.0	2.5	2.1	4.0	3.5	2.1	2.0	2.8	2.7	4.5	4.1	3.0	2.5	2.4	2.8
Slovak Republic	4.2	3.4	3.1	4.1	5.5	4.2	3.4	3.9	3.3	6.5	5.0	4.0	3.2	3.6	4.5
Slovenia	7.3	0.7	7.4	7.5	na	7.7	7.1	7.1	7.6	7.5	7.0	7.0	na	na	na
Average	*3.8*	*2.1*	*3.2*	*4.3*	*4.4*	*3.7*	*3.4*	*3.8*	*3.7*	*4.7*	*4.2*	*4.3*	*3.3*	*2.7*	*3.7*
South-eastern Europe															
Albania	5.3	0.6	5.3	na	na	5.3	na	5.0	5.6	na	na	na	na	na	na
Bosnia and Herzegovina	3.2	2.6	3.0	na	na	2.3	na	2.5	4.9	na	na	na	na	na	na
Bulgaria	7.0	4.8	6.1	7.5	na	6.4	5.7	7.5	8.8	4.0	7.3	7.0	8.4	8.4	7.0
FR Yugoslavia	22.4	8.0	21.5	na	na	na	na	18.0	20.0	na	24.0	25.0	na	na	26.0
FYR Macedonia	3.7	2.0	3.6	na	na	3.5	na	4.0	5.0	na	3.0	3.0	na	na	3.0
Romania	24.4	3.3	22.7	26.0	na	24.2	na	24.0	23.8	25.0	24.0	25.0	24.8	na	na
Average	*11.0*	*3.6*	*10.4*	*16.8*	*na*	*8.3*	*5.7*	*10.2*	*11.4*	*14.5*	*18.4*	*15.0*	*16.6*	*8.4*	*12.0*
Commonwealth of Independent States															
Armenia	2.9	2.6	1.4	na	na	2.8	na	4.0	3.3	na	na	na	na	na	na
Azerbaijan	2.7	0.4	2.8	na	na	2.4	na	2.8	2.7	na	na	na	na	na	na
Belarus	46.1	8.6	41.4	na	na	43.1	na	50.0	49.7	na	na	na	na	na	na
Georgia	5.8	0.5	5.5	na	na	5.9	na	6.0	5.9	na	na	na	na	na	na
Kazakhstan	5.8	1.1	6.0	na	na	5.8	na	6.2	5.1	na	na	na	na	na	na
Kyrgyz Republic	2.9	1.6	2.5	na	na	4.1	na	2.5	2.6	na	na	na	na	na	na
Moldova	7.9	4.8	9.0	na	na	6.6	na	5.5	10.3	na	na	na	na	na	na
Russia	16.4	4.0	16.3	na	15.0	15.8	15.9	16.0	16.3	16.5	17.0	19.0	15.9	16.4	na
Tajikistan	11.4	2.1	12.8	na	na	10.7	na	11.0	11.2	na	na	na	na	na	na
Turkmenistan	9.8	1.8	9.6	na	na	na	na	9.0	10.8	na	na	na	na	na	na
Ukraine	4.8	9.8	1.6	na	na	5.1	1.5	4.0	4.2	na	11.0	10.0	1.2	na	na
Uzbekistan	29.9	22.2	22.8	na	na	23.2	na	25.0	33.3	na	na	na	na	na	45.0
Average	*12.2*	*5.0*	*11.0*	*na*	*15.0*	*11.4*	*8.7*	*11.8*	*13.0*	*16.5*	*14.0*	*14.5*	*8.6*	*16.4*	*45.0*
Central and eastern Europe and the CIS															
Average	*9.1*	*3.7*	*8.3*	*6.8*	*6.5*	*8.0*	*4.6*	*8.8*	*9.5*	*7.5*	*8.7*	*9.6*	*7.4*	*6.6*	*14.7*

Note: All forecasts quoted were published or reported to the EBRD between April and September 2002. The dates in brackets indicate the months in which the forecasts were reported or published by each institution. There may in some instances be substantial lags between preparation and publication of forecasts.

1 The number at the bottom of this column is calculated as the mean of all the average forecasts shown in this column.
2 Data show the difference between the highest and the lowest of the forecasts.
3 William Davidson Institute at the University of Michigan Business School.
4 Data Resource Inc (DRI) and Wharton Econometric Forecasting Associates (WEFA).
5 Institute for Economic Research, Halle, Germany.
6 Kopint-Datorg is the Institute for Economic and Market Research Information, Hungary.
7 Vienna Institute for International Economic Studies.
8 Credit Suisse First Boston.

Table A.3.13

Average annual inflation forecasts for 2003

(change in the average consumer price level, in per cent)

	Average[1]	Range[2]	EBRD (Sep 2002)	European Union (Apr 2002)	OECD (Jun 2002)	IMF (Sep 2002)	Davidson Institute[3] (Sep 2002)	Economist Intelligence Unit (Aug 2002)	DRI-WEFA[4] (Jul 2002)	IWH[5] (Jul 2002)	Kopint-Datorg[6] (Jun 2002)	WIIW[7] (Jun 2002)	CSFB[8] (Aug 2002)	JP Morgan (Jul 2002)	Dun & Bradstreet (Aug 2002)
Central eastern Europe and the Baltic states															
Croatia	3.4	2.0	3.0	na	na	3.5	na	4.5	3.6	na	3.5	2.5	3.5	na	na
Czech Republic	3.0	2.0	2.1	3.5	3.3	3.0	2.6	1.9	3.0	3.8	3.9	3.5	3.1	1.9	na
Estonia	3.8	1.6	3.9	4.4	na	3.0	4.0	3.8	4.4	4.0	2.8	na	na	na	na
Hungary	5.0	1.8	4.5	4.2	5.1	5.2	4.5	5.3	4.6	6.0	5.2	4.5	5.6	na	na
Latvia	3.0	2.1	4.1	3.0	na	3.0	3.5	2.5	2.8	2.0	2.8	na	na	na	na
Lithuania	2.2	1.8	2.4	2.5	na	2.5	1.8	2.0	2.8	1.0	2.5	na	na	na	2.2
Poland	3.4	2.2	4.0	4.5	3.6	2.3	2.5	3.3	3.4	4.0	3.3	4.0	2.5	3.0	na
Slovak Republic	5.7	3.3	4.0	6.8	7.0	7.1	4.6	6.3	3.8	6.0	4.6	7.0	4.1	6.0	6.5
Slovenia	5.8	2.6	5.5	6.7	na	5.5	5.8	4.1	6.7	6.5	6.0	5.5	na	na	na
Average	*3.9*	*2.2*	*3.7*	*4.5*	*4.8*	*3.9*	*3.7*	*3.7*	*3.9*	*4.2*	*3.8*	*4.5*	*3.8*	*3.6*	*4.4*
South-eastern Europe															
Albania	3.5	3.4	3.5	na	na	3.0	na	2.0	5.4	na	na	na	na	na	na
Bosnia and Herzegovina	3.0	3.3	3.0	na	na	1.8	na	2.1	5.1	na	na	na	na	na	na
Bulgaria	5.0	4.5	3.8	5.0	na	4.3	4.6	4.7	7.5	3.0	6.0	5.0	4.8	5.1	6.0
FR Yugoslavia	13.4	10.0	11.0	na	na	na	na	12.0	12.2	na	10.0	15.0	na	na	20.0
FYR Macedonia	3.5	2.0	3.0	na	na	3.0	na	3.0	4.2	na	na	5.0	na	na	3.0
Romania	19.9	10.6	14.4	18.1	na	19.1	na	20.0	19.8	25.0	20.0	20.0	23.0	na	na
Average	*8.0*	*5.6*	*6.5*	*11.6*	*na*	*6.2*	*4.6*	*7.3*	*9.0*	*14.0*	*12.0*	*11.3*	*13.9*	*5.1*	*9.7*
Commonwealth of Independent States															
Armenia	4.2	2.7	3.8	na	na	2.8	na	4.5	5.5	na	na	na	na	na	na
Azerbaijan	3.5	1.8	3.0	na	na	3.3	na	3.0	4.8	na	na	na	na	na	na
Belarus	44.4	65.7	14.3	na	na	22.5	na	80.0	60.8	na	na	na	na	na	na
Georgia	5.5	1.5	5.0	na	na	5.0	na	5.5	6.5	na	na	na	na	na	na
Kazakhstan	5.9	1.8	5.9	na	na	6.2	na	6.6	4.8	na	na	na	na	na	na
Kyrgyz Republic	5.1	1.0	5.0	na	na	4.5	na	5.5	5.3	na	na	na	na	na	na
Moldova	9.2	3.5	9.0	na	na	8.4	na	8.0	11.5	na	na	na	na	na	na
Russia	13.4	6.0	11.5	na	10.0	11.0	13.7	14.0	14.7	13.0	16.0	16.0	13.7	13.9	na
Tajikistan	10.9	6.4	11.2	na	na	7.6	na	14.0	10.7	na	na	na	na	na	na
Turkmenistan	13.0	2.1	13.0	na	na	na	na	14.0	11.9	na	na	na	na	na	na
Ukraine	8.8	6.4	8.0	na	na	9.1	6.5	10.0	8.8	na	12.0	10.0	5.6	na	na
Uzbekistan	30.3	36.5	24.0	na	na	13.5	na	24.0	40.2	na	na	na	na	na	50.0
Average	*12.8*	*11.3*	*9.5*	*na*	*10.0*	*8.5*	*10.1*	*15.8*	*15.5*	*13.0*	*14.0*	*13.0*	*9.7*	*13.9*	*50.0*
Central and eastern Europe and the CIS															
Average	*8.8*	*7.0*	*6.9*	*5.9*	*5.8*	*6.4*	*4.9*	*9.9*	*10.2*	*6.8*	*7.0*	*8.2*	*7.3*	*6.0*	*14.6*

Note: All forecasts quoted were published or reported to the EBRD between April and September 2002. The dates in brackets indicate the months in which the forecasts were reported or published by each institution. There may in some instances be substantial lags between preparation and publication of forecasts.

[1] The number at the bottom of this column is calculated as the mean of all the average forecasts shown in this column.
[2] Data show the difference between the highest and the lowest of the forecasts.
[3] William Davidson Institute at the University of Michigan Business School.
[4] Data Resource Inc (DRI) and Wharton Econometric Forecasting Associates (WEFA).
[5] Institute for Economic Research, Halle, Germany.
[6] Kopint-Datorg is the Institute for Economic and Market Research Information, Hungary.
[7] Vienna Institute for International Economic Studies.
[8] Credit Suisse First Boston.

Agriculture and rural transition

Chapter 4

Agriculture

Chapter 5

Rural transition

Agriculture

4

Agriculture has fared poorly in the transition. Most of the transition countries have experienced significant declines in output and these declines have been persistent. Only a few have seen agricultural output grow or stabilise at pre-1990 levels. The declines have varied widely from between 15-30 per cent in central Europe to more than 50 per cent in some of the Baltic and CIS states. Even in central Europe where GDP has recovered or exceeded pre-transition levels, with the exception of Slovenia, agricultural output still remains significantly below pre-1990 levels.

This chapter examines the reasons behind the relatively poor performance of agriculture in the transition. It finds that the distortions imposed by the centrally planned economy pre-1990 – not least with respect to ownership and management of land – have continued to weigh heavily. Policies to eliminate those distortions have been implemented at a slow pace, often because of opposition by vested interests and groups fearful of the loss of employment and access to subsidised resources. This has resulted in limited improvements to output and productivity.

It is also evident that progress in general economic reform has been strongly associated with progress in agricultural sector reform. Such progress has in turn been closely associated with more democratic and competitive political systems. The more successful agricultural sector reformers have been located therefore in central Europe. By contrast, in much of the CIS major institutional and policy hurdles to increasing the performance of the sector still have to be overcome. Improving the performance of the agricultural sector requires the adoption of policies that can boost productivity through restructuring and investment. This will require greater clarity concerning title to land and the creation of a more efficient land and agricultural inputs market. In many cases, it will also involve overcoming significant political opposition to such reform from rural voters and their political

backers. Improved performance also requires growth in trading opportunities. In this respect, there have been a number of promising developments. The establishment of new markets for trade other than the transition economies has proceeded rapidly as trade relationships have responded to market signals. However, most transition countries continue to record significant agricultural trade deficits. Part of this is due to their trading partners imposing restrictions on market access but an underlying problem remains the low competitiveness of many of the transition economies.

This chapter accounts for differences in performance caused by both economic and political reasons. Section 4.1 describes the initial conditions and the reforms that have been implemented since the start of transition. Section 4.2 accounts for the differing performance of the agricultural sector across countries in terms of both output and productivity. This is achieved by identifying the relative importance of initial conditions, policy reforms and other factors explaining the differences. Section 4.3 broadens the discussion to include the impact of political institutions and voting behaviour on the performance of the sector. Section 4.4 examines the international dimension, in particular the role of trade and market access, not least in the context of EU accession.

4.1 Performance of agriculture

Chart 4.1 shows that the majority of transition economies have experienced substantial declines in agricultural output since 1990. While there has been significant variation in the scale of decline, the trend has been common across all regions. It is particularly striking how large the decline has been in the CIS countries. Chart 4.1 also shows that in central eastern Europe and the Baltic states (CEB) there has been a clear improvement in labour productivity in agriculture resulting from underlying structural reform. But in the CIS and south-eastern

Europe (SEE) agricultural labour productivity has declined substantially and in most CIS countries agricultural employment has actually increased. This is due both to a lack of restructuring in the sector and the reallocation of labour away from failing firms in the manufacturing sector. In short, the agricultural sector has significantly under-performed when compared with other sectors. To some extent, this can be explained by the fact that the agricultural sector has provided a social safety net during the restructuring process, and therefore facilitated the restructuring of the overall economy.

The transition countries started with high shares of agriculture in national income. For example, agriculture accounted for around 13-15 per cent of GDP in Hungary and Poland in the 1980s, levels significantly higher than in western Europe. In the Caucasus and Central Asia these shares ranged between 20 and 30 per cent. It seems reasonable to suppose that part of the subsequent decline – by 2001 those shares in Hungary and Poland had, for example, fallen below 5 per cent – may be due to an inflated agricultural share under socialism, so that any subsequent decline should not only have been expected but also welcomed.

This can be understood by comparing the agricultural share of output across a range of countries with comparable income levels. At the start of transition, all regions had relatively high agriculture shares (see Chart 4.2). By 1999 this was still true for the SEE group, as the share was still 50 per cent higher than the average for middle-income countries. The decline in the CIS has been so substantial that the share now lies significantly below the levels recorded by countries with comparable income levels. In the case of the CEB group, the share has fallen significantly, but it was still somewhat higher than the EU average at the end of the period. In short, part of the decline is due to the sector responding to the needs of the market.

Chart 4.1

Changes in agricultural output and productivity, 1990-99

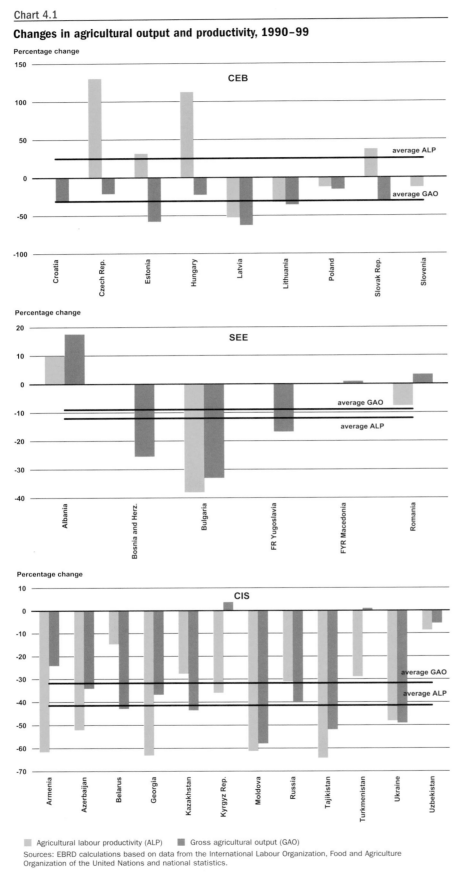

Percentage change

CEB

Croatia, Czech Rep., Estonia, Hungary, Latvia, Lithuania, Poland, Slovak Rep., Slovenia

average ALP

average GAO

Percentage change

SEE

Albania, Bosnia and Herz., Bulgaria, FR Yugoslavia, FYR Macedonia, Romania

average GAO

average ALP

Percentage change

CIS

Armenia, Azerbaijan, Belarus, Georgia, Kazakhstan, Kyrgyz Rep., Moldova, Russia, Tajikistan, Turkmenistan, Ukraine, Uzbekistan

average GAO

average ALP

■ Agricultural labour productivity (ALP)   ■ Gross agricultural output (GAO)

Sources: EBRD calculations based on data from the International Labour Organization, Food and Agriculture Organization of the United Nations and national statistics.

However, there has been much variation between regions. Explanations for these differences must take account of not only differences in conditions at the start of reform but also the differing pace and nature of the reform process. Some of the most relevant reforms for agriculture have included price and trade liberalisation, land reform and changes to ownership of land, privatisation of supply industries and agro-processing, and changes to rural finance, particularly with respect to rural banks.

Table 4.1 summarises progress in agricultural sector reform across the transition countries since 1997. Progress in reform is measured on five counts. It is clear that progress has varied widely across countries but a number of patterns emerge. There is a strong connection between progress in general economic reform and agricultural sector reform. Consequently, the more advanced reformers have mostly been in CEB. In most of CEB and SEE, agricultural prices were liberalised early, often causing the prices for agricultural outputs relative to the prices for inputs – the agricultural terms of trade – to decline dramatically. This had a negative impact on output. Over time this effect has weakened while other complementary reforms – including land ownership – have been put in place. In the CIS, price liberalisation has proceeded more slowly but has generally been implemented, except in Belarus, Turkmenistan and Uzbekistan. Among the intermediate and late reformers there have been differences in implementation across the range of reforms. For example, in Kazakhstan, Russia and Ukraine implementation of land reform and institutional change has clearly lagged behind other reforms.

Table 4.1 also indicates that there have been major differences across countries in the ways that land ownership has been changed. Where land was collectively owned prior to reform, restitution to former owners has been the most common privatisation strategy.[1] Typically the reform laws have specified that land had to be returned to former owners using historical boundaries, if possible. Otherwise former owners have been entitled to a plot of land of comparable size and quality. In the former Soviet Union, land was returned only in the

[1] See Swinnen (1999).

Chart 4.2

Agriculture shares in GDP 1990-99

Share of agriculture as a percentage of GDP

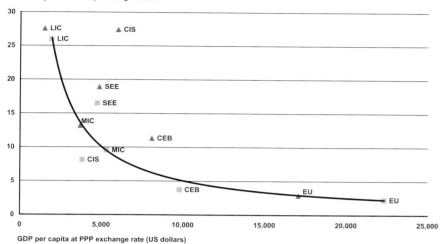

GDP per capita at PPP exchange rate (US dollars)

▲ 1990   ■ 1999

Sources: World Development Indicators and the EBRD.

Note: LIC = Low-income countries   MIC = Middle-income countries   EU = European Union

three Baltic states (Estonia, Latvia and Lithuania). Most other countries, including Russia and Ukraine, distributed collective and state farmland equally among collective farm members or state farm employees in the form of paper shares or certificates.[2] In Tajikistan and Uzbekistan private ownership of land has not yet been recognised while in Belarus and Kazakhstan only private ownership of household plots has been permitted. Physical distribution of farmland on an equal per capita basis to farm workers or rural households occurred in Albania, Armenia, Georgia and, partly, in Hungary and Romania.[3] This variation in the implementation of land reform is largely due to initial conditions, such as the length of time since nationalisation of land, and the ethnicity and equality of pre-collectivisation land ownership. Ethnic and political factors have therefore affected the way in which restitution has proceeded in the Baltic states while in the rest of the CIS claims for restitution were made only in those countries where collectivisation was imposed after the Second World War.[4]

The ability to transfer land has also varied substantially. In the advanced reformers, rights to buy and sell, as well as leasing, have been universally implemented. Nevertheless, there remains – even within this group – significant variation in the share of land held by individuals. The break-up of collective farms into individual farms has occurred in very different ways. In Albania, for example, there was a complete break-up of the collective farms while in other countries, such as Kazakhstan, the Slovak Republic, Tajikistan and Turkmenistan, the share of land used by individual farms remains small. The transition countries now commonly have a mix of farm organisations, such as private cooperative farms, joint-stock companies, family farms and part-time farmers.[5]

4.2 Explaining the differences in performance

A number of factors can help to explain the differences in agricultural performance. In the first place, the transition countries differed widely in their initial

conditions. The extent of distortions inherited from the communist regimes and the degree of development, measured by the level of GDP per capita and other social indicators, have proven to be significant factors determining GDP growth.[6] They may have also therefore affected the economic performance in the agricultural sector. Indeed, an earlier study has found that differences in initial conditions helped to explain the cumulative change in agricultural output in central and eastern Europe in the early years of transition but had a smaller impact on the change in agricultural labour productivity.[7]

Second, progress in economic and structural reforms – as measured by the EBRD indicators in Chapter 2 – can tell us how rapidly and effectively these countries have overcome their initial distortions. Earlier work has found that reforms, such as privatisation and price liberalisation, appear to have had a strong effect on productivity but not on agricultural output. Others have found a strong association between growth in agricultural production and individual land holding.[8]

Third, general macroeconomic conditions, and in particular the successful stabilisation of the domestic economy, have proven to be necessary conditions for economic growth and are likely to be strongly associated with output and productivity growth in the agricultural sector. In addition to these general differences, there are a series of sector-specific factors that should be taken into account. These include price distortions, land privatisation and reform, access to credit, access to foreign markets and shocks to the agricultural terms of trade.

To understand the relative weight of these different factors in explaining agricultural performance, the experience of a sample of 14 transition countries[9] with comparable data on the agricultural sector for a

---

[2] This is the most important method of land reform in these countries. In addition, outsiders who were not entitled to land shares could receive land for private farming from a special state reserve established for this purpose (15-20 per cent of total agricultural land) (Lerman, 1997).

[3] See, for example, Cungu and Swinnen (1999) and Lerman (2001) among others.

[4] See Swinnen (1999).

[5] See, for example, Rizov and Swinnen (2001) among others.

[6] See Berg et al. (1999), de Melo et al. (2001), Falcetti et al. (2002), Fischer and Sahay (2000), and Heybey and Murrell (1999) among others.

[7] See Macours and Swinnen (2000b).

[8] See Lerman (2000).

[9] The sample countries are: Albania, Belarus, Bulgaria, Czech Republic, Estonia, Hungary, Kazakhstan, Lithuania, Poland, Romania, Russia, Slovak Republic, Slovenia and Ukraine.

Table 4.1

Indicators of reform in agriculture

	World Bank Index 2001[1]						Potential private land ownership	Privatisation strategy[2]	Allocation strategy	Transferability	Farm organisation[3]	Percentage of rural land in individual use[4]
	Price & market	Land reform	Agro-processing	Rural finance	Insti-tutional	Total score						
Advanced												
Bulgaria	9	8	8	7	8	8.0	All	Restitution	Plots	Buy-and-sell, leasing	Individual, corporate, associations	56 (1999)
Czech Republic	9	9	10	9	9	9.2	All	Restitution	Plots	Buy-and-sell, leasing	Individual, corporate	26
Estonia	9	9	9	9	9	9.0	All	Restitution	Plots	Buy-and-sell, leasing	Individual, corporate	61
Hungary	9	9	10	9	9	9.2	All	Both	Plots	Buy-and-sell, leasing	Individual, corporate	51
Latvia	9	9	9	9	9	9.0	All	Restitution	Plots	Buy-and-sell, leasing	Individual, corporate	91
Lithuania	7	9	8	7	9	8.0	All	Restitution	Plots	Buy-and-sell, leasing	Individual, corporate	87
Poland	8	8	9	7	8	8.0	All	Indiv pre-1990	na	Buy-and-sell, leasing	Individual, corporate	84
Slovak Republic	8	8	9	8	8	8.2	All	Restitution	Plots	Buy-and-sell, leasing	Individual, corporate	9
Slovenia	9	9	10	8	10	9.2	All	Indiv pre-1990	na	Buy-and-sell, leasing	Individual, corporate	94
Intermediate												
Albania	8	8	8	7	7	7.6	All	Distribution	Plots	Buy-and-sell, leasing	Individual	95 (1996)
Armenia	8	8	8	7	6	7.4	All	Distribution	Plots	Buy-and-sell, leasing	Individual	90 (1998)
Azerbaijan	8	8	6	6	5	6.6	All	Distribution	Plots/shares	Buy-and-sell, leasing	Corporate, individual	5 (1995)
Bosnia & Herz.	7	7	6	6	5	6.2	All	Indiv pre-1990	na	Buy-and-sell, leasing	Individual, corporate	94[5] (1991)
Croatia	7	7	7	6	8	7.0	All	Indiv pre-1990	na	Buy-and-sell, leasing	Individual, corporate	66
FYR Macedonia	8	7	6	5	7	6.6	All	Indiv pre-1990	na	Buy-and-sell, leasing	Individual, corporate	80[5] (1997)
Georgia	9	7	5	7	5	6.6	All	Distribution	Plots	Buy-and-sell, leasing	Individual	44 (1998)
Kazakhstan	6	5	7	6	5	5.8	Household plots only	Distribution	Shares	Use rights transferable; buy-and-sell of private plots problematic	Corporate-renamed collectives, individual	24 (1998)
Kyrgyz Republic	7	7	6	6	5	6.2	All	Distribution	Shares	5-year moratorium on land transactions	Corporate, individual	37 (1998)
Moldova	7	7	6	6	4	6.0	All	Distribution	Plots/shares	Buy-and-sell, leasing	Corporate, individual	20 (1998)
Romania	7	8	8	7	7	7.4	All	Both	Plots	Buy-and-sell, leasing	Individual, corporate, associations	85
Russia	6	5	8	5	5	5.8	All	Distribution	Shares	Leasing, buy-and-sell problematic	Corporate-renamed collectives, individual	13 (1998)
Ukraine	7	6	7	6	4	6.0	All	Distribution	Shares	Leasing, buy-and-sell problematic	Corporate-renamed collectives, individual	17 (1998)
Belarus	2	2	2	2	1	1.8	Household plots only	Distribution	None	Use rights non-transferable; buy-and-sell of private plots problematic	Collective	14
Early												
FR Yugoslavia	6	5	5	2	5	4.8	All	Indiv pre-1990	na	Buy-and-sell, leasing	Individual, corporate	na
Tajikistan	6	6	5	3	4	4.8	None	Distribution	Shares	Use rights transferable	Collective	9 (1998)
Turkmenistan	2	3	2	1	2	2.0	All	Distribution	Leasehold	Use rights non-transferable	Collective, individual	8 (1998)
Uzbekistan	4	4	4	2	3	3.4	None	Distribution	Leasehold	Use rights non-transferable	Collective	14 (1998)

1   A scale of 1 to 10 has been used, with 1 indicating little reform from central planning and collective ownership and 10 indicating implementation of full market conditions.

2   The various privatisation strategies can be explained as follows: "Restitution" refers to the return of farmland to pre-communist owners; "Distribution" involves the allocation of farmland to either collective farm workers or the whole population; "Both" indicates that a combination of the restitution and distribution strategies have been implemented; and "Indiv pre-1990" signifies that farmland was individually held prior to the collapse of the communist regime and where privatisation was, therefore, not required.

3   The type of farm organisation is listed in order of dominance.

4   Percentage in 2000, unless stated otherwise.

5   Percentage of total arable land shown.

minimum of ten years is examined.[10] Economic performance in agriculture is measured by gross agricultural output and agricultural labour productivity. Cross-country differences are explained in terms of the initial conditions facing the economies, the type and scope of subsequent economy-wide reforms, as well as factors specific to the agricultural sector. To assess the relative importance of each of these factors, regression analysis has been used.[11]

The analysis leads to a number of firm conclusions. Table 4.2 describes the effect of the main explanatory factors on both growth and productivity. The conclusions can be summarised as follows.

▌ The initial conditions have strongly influenced the direction and outcome of economic reform. Countries that started the transition period with better initial conditions have reformed the most and benefited from higher growth in agricultural output.

▌ General reforms have helped bring about gains in agricultural labour productivity but have not significantly influenced agricultural output. Liberalising and privatising quickly has had a positive pay-off in terms of higher productivity.

▌ Changes in relative prices have been important. Reforms involved a sharp decrease in price subsidies. This led to a dramatic drop in output and productivity in the advanced reform countries. Subsequent improvements in agricultural terms of trade have exerted a positive and direct effect on changes in agricultural output and productivity.

▌ Growth in output and productivity has increased in line with the growing share of private land in individual farms. This is consistent with the results from wider research concerning the productivity effects of individual ownership and farm organisation.

▌ Agricultural labour productivity gains in transition countries have been influenced by the choice of the land reform method. Countries that followed the restitution principle seem to have

Table 4.2

Impact of specific factors on growth and productivity

Variables	Output growth	Productivity growth
Initial conditions - inherited distortions	+*	+
Initial conditions - economic development	+	-
General economic reforms	+	+**
Terms of trade	+**	+**
Individual land holding share	+*	+**
Restitution of land	+	+**

Source: EBRD.
Note: + or – indicates positive or negative growth and ** and * show that the regression coefficient is significant at the 5 and 10 per cent level respectively.

The above table details the final results of a three-step regression analysis. Initial conditions were measured by two indices: a measure of inherited distortions (including repressed inflation, the black market exchange rate premium, trade dependence on the Council for Mutual Economic Assistance, the number of years spent under central planning and the initial urbanisation rate); and a measure of the degree of the country's economic development (initial level of GDP per capita, the average pre-transition growth rate, life expectancy at birth, an indicator for countries rich in natural resources and geographical distance to Brussels).

Progress in general economic reforms is measured by the average EBRD transition score for price and trade liberalisation and small-scale privatisation.

There are three agriculture-specific factors: the measure of agricultural terms of trade (defined as the ratio between producer and input prices in the agricultural sector); the share of land in individual farms (individual land holding share); and the preferred method for land reform (restitution or distribution through paper shares).

enjoyed higher productivity compared with those that have chosen land distribution by paper shares. A possible explanation is that restitution has provided owners with more clearly defined and secure property rights. It is also possible that restitution has rewarded those with superior resources or abilities.

The findings from this cross-country analysis reinforce the view that not only has progress in agricultural sector reform been closely linked to progress in general economic reform but that the benefits from implementing reforms have been substantial. In particular, in CEB there have been strong improvements in productivity. However, the results also signal the importance not only of changing land ownership but the way in which those changes have been carried out. Differences across countries reflect a variety of factors, not least the importance of political considerations. The next section takes up these questions in more depth.

4.3 Political aspects of agricultural reform

Table 4.1 has grouped countries in terms of their progress in agricultural sector reform. It is immediately evident that these groups tend to share a number

of important political characteristics. The advanced agricultural reformers are mostly located in CEB and are all stable democracies with high levels of political competition, active democratic societies and strong political liberties. They are also candidates for the first wave of accession to the European Union – in part because of these political attributes.

An intermediate reform group includes most of SEE (Albania, Bosnia and Herzegovina, Croatia, FYR Macedonia and Romania) and the CIS (Armenia, Azerbaijan, Georgia, Kazakhstan, Kyrgyz Republic, Moldova, Russia and Ukraine). All of the countries in this group are "partially consolidated" democracies, with many of the attributes normally associated with democratic systems of governance. These include regular elections, political parties and a nominally free press. However, these countries are often deficient in political competition and effective checks and balances on the elected government and lack strong non-governmental organisations and the rule of law necessary to further advance democracy. A group of slow reformers – Belarus, Tajikistan, Turkmenistan and Uzbekistan – remain autocratic regimes with weak or non-existent public involvement in decision-making, frail democratic

---

[10] The main data sources are from National Statistical Offices, the Food and Agriculture Association of the United Nations (FAO), OECD, the EBRD and the World Bank. Zvi Lerman, Karen Macours and Johan Swinnen have provided access to their datasets, for which we are grateful.

[11] For a more detailed description of the econometric procedures and results, see Bevan et al. (2002).

Chart 4.3

Democracy and agricultural reform

Agricultural reform: World Bank Europe and Central Asia index 2001

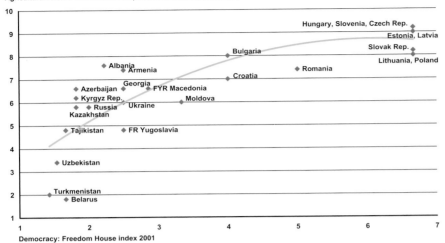

Sources: EBRD calculations based on data from the World Bank and Freedom House.

Note: The agricultural reform index is a scale of 1-10. A score of 1 indicates little reform from central planning and collective ownership, while 10 indicates implementation of full market conditions. The Freedom House index has a scale of 1-7 for both civil liberties and political rights. Normally on the Freedom House scale, 1 indicates the most free and 7 the least free. However, for the purposes of this chart the scale has been inverted with 7 representing the most free and 1 the least free. Data for Bosnia and Herzegovina were not available.

Chart 4.4

Political coalitions and agricultural reform

Agricultural reform index (World Bank, 2000)

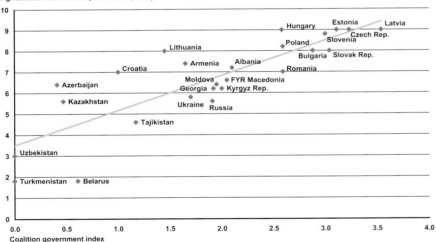

Sources: EBRD calculations based on data from the World Bank and the Polity IV database.

Note: The coalition government index is calculated as follows:

0 = non-competitive political system

1 = one-party government or presidential system without majority support in parliament

2 = two-party government or presidential system without majority support in parliament

3 = three or more party coalition

4 = minority government

See Chart 4.3 for an explanation of the agricultural reform index. Data for Bosnia and Herzegovina and FR Yugoslavia were not available.

institutions and highly centralised political power.[12] Countries in this group are characterised by strong presidential systems and very low levels of political competition.

Earlier studies of the transition countries demonstrated a positive link between democratic systems of governance and overall economic reform, involving stabili-sation, structural and institutional reform.[13] This can be attributed to the fact that democratic systems are charac-terised by a greater degree of political openness and a larger number of checks on government power by local representa-tive organisations.

Apart from the presence of regular elec-tions and political competition, stable democracies also tend to promote the rule of law, free speech and other civil and political rights. This makes them more likely to be resistant to "capture" by special interest groups that seek to maximise their private benefits. Research suggests that democracies are also better at protecting private prop-erty rights and enforcing contracts, provid-ing farmers with additional incentives to invest in their land and improve agricultural productivity.[14]

As Chart 4.3 shows, reform in agriculture follows this pattern, with a strong link between the degree of reform in the sector and the level of democracy. More specifically, Chart 4.4 shows that broad-based, multi-party coalitions have gener-ally been the most successful in imple-menting and sustaining reform in the agri-culture sector. This is in contrast with much of the conventional wisdom, which has held that successful reform has normally been associated with strong executives insulated from the constraints of political competition and the compro-mises often required to sustain coalition governments.[15]

---

[12] Although FR Yugoslavia is ranked as a slow reformer according to the World Bank, it is not a natural fit with this group since developments after 2000 have led to rapid and continuing political and economic change.

[13] See EBRD (1999).

[14] See Olson (2000), de Soto (2000), Conning and Robinson (2001).

[15] See, for example, Przeworski (1991), and Mainwaring and Shugart (2002).

Chart 4.5

Share of agricultural labour and agricultural reform

Agricultural reform index (World Bank, 2000)

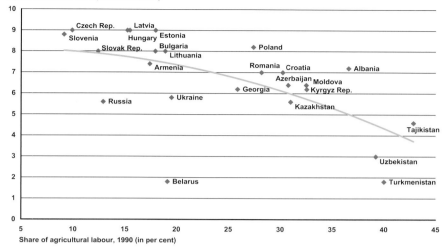

Sources: EBRD calculations based on data from the International Labour Organization, the World Bank and national statistics.

Note: See Chart 4.3 for an explanation of the agricultural reform index. Data for Bosnia and Herzegovina, FR Yugoslavia and FYR Macedonia were not available.

In addition, voting behaviour depends on the characteristics and preferences of the electorate. Rural voters, for example, tend to be more conservative. Chart 4.5 shows that a high share of rural voters has been associated with slower progress in reform, while countries with a lower share of the labour force in agriculture at the start of transition have achieved a greater degree of reform in the sector. In Russia, for example, this also applies at a regional level. Where there has been a higher share of agriculture in the labour force, regional governments have tended to be more conservative. Indeed, regions dominated politically by either communists or nationalists have had rural population shares over ten percentage points higher than in more reform-oriented regions. The share of public spending devoted to agriculture has also been significantly higher in regions with more conservative governments, particularly in communist-dominated regions.

Politics of the land

At the heart of agricultural sector reform is the issue of land ownership. It is here that the interplay of politics and economics is at its starkest. The critical reform decision has been whether to pursue restitution of land to previous owners or distribution to collective farm workers. This policy choice has been in part driven by factors such as the history of private land ownership, concentration of ownership prior to collectivisation, and the number of years under communism. Private land ownership was a well-established institution in the CEB region, and legal ownership rights remained in force even during the communist period. For these countries, the question was not whether to return land to legal owners, but how, since the political cost of not returning land and property was higher than the cost involved in breaking up the cooperative farms.[16] In countries where land ownership was not widespread before collectivisation, the choice involved deciding between considerations of historical justice and current fairness. Moreover, privatisation – either through restitution, redistribution, or a combination of the two – could be used to rebalance land holdings among different social groups (for example, between different ethnic groups). Finally, in countries where communist attitudes towards the land had taken root over several generations, the demand for private land ownership was weaker, and this contributed to the choice of share distribution and/or limited use rights rather than distribution of land plots.

Choices about how to implement land reform in the early stages of transition have had other consequences. Privatisation through land share issues – as in Kazakhstan, the Kyrgyz Republic, Russia and Ukraine – has tended to strengthen vested interest groups opposed to further land reform. Uncertainties over title and the high transactions costs associated with starting independent farms have reduced incentives for rural entrepreneurs to leave collective farms. In the absence of enforceable ownership rights and a law on mortgages, credit has been largely unavailable for independent farmers. This has in turn led to maintaining under-priced access to the raw materials, technology and social services provided by the collective farm system.[17] As a result, land markets have emerged slowly in countries that issued land shares. For example, in four countries – Albania, Armenia, Georgia and Romania – which allocated plots of land, the share of land in individual private farms increased by almost 70 per cent between 1989 and 2000. In four other countries – Kazakhstan, the Kyrgyz Republic, Russia and Ukraine – that pursued allocation by land shares, on the other hand, the comparable figure is only 15 per cent.

Resistance to reform can be traced to a variety of factors. In Russia there is evidence that some regional authorities not only resisted reforms because they would have reduced the level of subsidy to the sector but also resisted the restructuring of former collectives as they comprised a significant part of their regional power base. Regional authorities were used to providing collective farms with subsidies and preferential loans as a means of consolidating support while agricultural producers preferred the status quo for fear of jeopardising their access to subsidies.[18] Indeed, defensive motives on the part of incumbents have been an important factor. With few outside opportunities and uncertainty regarding future access to land and agricultural inputs, collective farm workers and managers have generally opposed reform.

[16] See Swinnen (1999).

[17] See Leonard (2000) and Wegren (1998).

[18] See Amelina (2000).

The Russian case also points to the additional complications that federal systems have imposed on the implementation of reform. Where legal and budgetary authority has remained unclear, individual regions have been able to pursue their own agendas in contravention of federal legislation and decrees, often without the realistic threat of sanction by the federal centre. For example, although some regional governments within Russia, such as Nizhny Novgorod and Samara, followed federal statutes, many others refused to implement the federal laws, insisting on constitutional grounds that questions regarding ownership, use and disposition of land must be decided jointly by federal and regional authorities.

In Ukraine, agriculture throughout most of the 1990s has been dominated by collective farm interests whose main objective has been to take advantage of price differences between official and market prices. They were also strong opponents to privatisation of agricultural land, which would have created more competition.[19] Access to high levels of government and strength in the parliament allowed this influential lobby to stall significant reform in agriculture.

Similarly, in Kazakhstan, largely as a result of effective lobbying by collective farm managers throughout the 1990s, former state and collective farms were able to preserve state-financed preferential loans, which weakened incentives for change in ownership and management. Although this involved low state-controlled prices for agricultural produce – and therefore low food prices for consumers – collective farm managers were won over through the provision of subsidised credits and tax breaks. Major creditors to the farm sector were largely state-controlled institutions, including the budget and extra-budgetary social funds.[20] Inevitably, this approach led to the substantial and increasing indebtedness of the agricultural sector.

Although such political obstacles to agricultural reform have proven formidable in some countries, they have not been insurmountable. For example, land ownership and demographic patterns in Poland suggest that the Polish electorate would be highly resistant to agricultural reform. However, according to the World Bank's indicators, Poland is an advanced agricultural reformer. This apparent anomaly is explained primarily by the significant reform advances made in the early years of transition, and second by the significant external policy anchor provided by accession to the EU, which has served to constrain government policy options in relation to further increasing sectoral protectionism and agricultural subsidies.

Recent progress in reform in Bulgaria, Kazakhstan, Romania and Russia illustrates how shifts in government to more reform-oriented parties, fiscal crisis and external pressure can affect policy. For example, in 1998 when faced with mounting problems in the farming sector, Kazakhstan saw a significant policy shift in farm restructuring. Repeated write-offs of public sector debt, the widespread use of barter and a severe drought had combined to bring Kazakhstan's farm sector to the brink of collapse. The government launched a new programme of farm restructuring based on the need for extensive application of bankruptcy law. In Bulgaria an acute financial crisis in 1996 led to a loss of power by the successor communist party (BSP) and the advent of a new government that was able to implement wide-ranging agricultural reforms. In Russia the combination of strong presidential leadership and a shift in the balance of power in the Russian State Duma have combined to overcome political opposition to the 2002 Land Law. This new legislation significantly strengthens the right to ownership of agricultural land and paves the way for the emergence of a land market.

Romania has also made dramatic progress in agricultural reform since 1998, particularly in improving the public institutions that support the agriculture sector and in privatising state-owned agro-processing companies. These reforms have partly been prompted by the need to fulfil requirements set out in the EU's *acquis communautaire* in order to qualify for the second round of EU accession. This factor has been important in a number of the advanced reformers in CEB, which have managed to achieve reforms despite the persistence of a conservative rural base.[21]

Finally, there is the case of the slow reformers. All are characterised by strong presidential systems, little change of government and the dominance of communist parties and vested interests. Most still prohibit private land ownership, with usage rights being controlled by the state and non-transferable between parties. The prices of agricultural produce commonly remain controlled – sometimes alongside forced deliveries – as with cotton in Uzbekistan – and these policies have greatly limited farmers' incentives to improve productivity. The suppression of opposition parties and limited external pressure for reform has allowed these highly inefficient agricultural practices to continue. This has resulted in poor output and productivity performance. Effective change has yet to begin.

4.4 Trade dimension

The transition process has brought about the collapse of earlier trade relations. This in turn has opened up new market opportunities for the transition countries and the prospect of an improvement in the performance of the agricultural sector. This section examines changes in trading patterns in agricultural goods since the start of transition and assesses the impact of trade policies and barriers on performance in the sector.

Although the transition economies still play a relatively small role in global agricultural trade, accounting for only 2 per cent of total agricultural imports by OECD countries,[22] agricultural trade remains quite important for their domestic economies. Table 4.3 shows that for most of these countries agricultural trade accounts for around 5-10 per cent of both their total trade and GDP. The majority of the transition countries are net agricultural importers but there are a number

[19] See Åslund and de Menil (2000).

[20] See Gray (2000).

[21] See Sharman (2002).

[22] See OECD (2000).

Table 4.3

Agricultural trade for selected transition economies

Country	Net agricultural trade in 2000 (US$ million)	Net agricultural trade with EU (US$ million)		Share of agricultural trade in total trade[1] (per cent)	Share of agricultural trade in GDP[1] (per cent)
		1993	2000		
Albania	-221.0	-126.2[2]	-157.0[3]	29.6	10.5
Armenia	-183.8	na	-64.0	na	na
Azerbaijan	-164.9	na	-6.5	na	na
Belarus	-602.8	na	-170.1	8.7	10.1
Bulgaria	139.0	-14.3	18.0	7.8	6.7
Croatia	-288.0	-48.2	-228.9[3]	8.4	5.5
Czech Republic	-676.0	-113.3	-621.5[3]	4.9	5.9
Estonia	-199.0	-31.8	-184.3	11.1	16.3
Georgia	-69.3	na	6.1	na	na
Hungary	1153.0	621.5	530.4	6.0	6.9
Kazakhstan	138.2	na	-21.1	7.0	6.3
Latvia	-297.0	-7.9	-163.4	9.9	7.2
Lithuania	-106.0	3.3[2]	-124.0	10.9	8.9
Moldova	179.3	na	-28.0	na	na
Poland	-533.0	-254.6	-324.8	8.4	3.7
Romania	-593.0	-332.9	-135.5	5.7	3.5
Russia	-5689.0	na	-1611.4	6.0	3.5
Slovak Republic	-382.0	-77.5	-192.9[3]	5.0	6.4
Slovenia	-361.0	-82.6	-237.1	6.5	6.7
Ukraine	442.0	na	6.7	9.3	9.1

Sources: OECD, Eurostat and the EBRD.
[1] Data for 2000.
[2] Data for 1994.
[3] Data for 1999.

of major exporters, including Bulgaria, Hungary, Kazakhstan, Moldova and Ukraine.

During the transition the net trade position of the CIS has improved while the net trade position for CEB and SEE countries has deteriorated considerably. The transition countries have tended to run significant trade deficits with their OECD trading counterparts.[23]

Among OECD countries, the European Union is by far the largest trade partner of the CEB/SEE region. The EU has significantly increased its net trade surplus with the ten CEB accession countries since the start of the transition (see Table 4.3); agricultural imports from the CEB countries have increased by about 10 per cent since 1994 while exports to CEB have increased by 30 per cent. Bulgaria and Romania are exceptions because they have substantially reduced food exports to CEB and the CIS and redirected them to the EU and the rest of

the world,[24] and this has been accompanied by a decline in the share of EU imports. By contrast, in most of the CIS, trade between CIS countries has continued to dominate agricultural trade. Russia is the one CIS country that had a higher proportion of food export trade with the OECD than with other CIS countries in 2001.

The increase in total exports from CEB to the EU has occurred across all products but the increase in total exports from the EU to CEB has been concentrated in higher-value processed products. This is due to the combination of more competitive food marketing, processing and retailing industries in the EU and a more developed institutional framework for agricultural trade, together with greater EU support in the form of export subsidies.[25] Quality differences between food products produced in CEB and the EU have restricted the ability of CEB countries to penetrate the EU market with their processed products. At the same time CEB countries have not been able to

divert their trade to alternative markets, partly reflecting earlier over-reliance on trade with other transition economies as well as the impact of the 1998 Russia crisis.

In general, CIS food imports tend to be predominately processed products. In 2000 the majority of these processed products were imported from OECD member states, with two exceptions – Belarus and Kazakhstan – which sourced around 70 and 75 per cent of their total processed imports respectively from other CIS countries. Surprisingly a high proportion of food exports from the CIS in 2000 was in the form of processed products, with the exception of Azerbaijan, Kazakhstan and Russia. Nonetheless, the vast majority of these processed exports were traded with other CIS countries.

In short, trade patterns have differed across the region. Nevertheless, some common features have emerged. A significant proportion of exports continues to be destined for other transition economies while an increasing share of imports has come from the OECD and the EU. For most transition countries their net trade deficits with the OECD and the EU have grown. One reason for this has been that the transition countries have been growing quite rapidly and are absorbing more imports. However, the transition countries have made limited progress in increasing their exports to OECD/EU agricultural markets. Moreover, the transition countries trade primarily in "temperate zone" products, such as grains, milk, butter and livestock, which tend to be the most protected commodities in global trade.

Agricultural protection

Market access is critical for the transition countries. In the OECD/EU, agricultural protection levels have been reduced to some extent in recent years in response to the 1993 World Trade Organization (WTO) Uruguay Round Agreement on Agriculture.[26] This round tackled:
(i) domestic support for agriculture by capping the most distortionary policies,

---

[23] Of course, four transition countries – the Czech Republic, Hungary, Poland and the Slovak Republic – are also OECD countries.

[24] Around 54 per cent of Romania's total agro-food export trade was with the EU in 2001.

[25] See Swinnen (2001).

[26] Of the 27 transition countries, 15 are WTO members and 11 hold observer status. Turkmenistan has yet to apply for observer status.

Table 4.4

Producer Support Estimates and Nominal Protection Coefficients, 1993-2000

Country / institution	Producer Support Estimate (PSE)[1] (per cent)		Nominal Protection Coefficient (NPC)[2] (per cent)	
	1993	2000	1993	2000
Bulgaria	-4.0	2.0	1.0	1.1
Czech Republic	27.0	16.0	1.4	1.1
Estonia	-32.0	10.0	0.7	1.0
Hungary	22.0	20.0	1.3	1.1
Latvia	-40.0	18.0	0.8	1.3
Lithuania	-37.0	9.0	0.8	1.3
Poland	12.0	7.0	1.1	1.1
Romania	16.0	11.0	1.4	1.3
Russia	-24.0	3.0	0.7	1.1
Slovak Republic	30.0	3.0	1.2	1.1
Slovenia	28.0	43.0	1.5	1.6
EU	42.0	34.0	1.6	1.3
OECD	37.0	32.0	1.5	1.3

Source: OECD.
[1] PSE measures the annual monetary value of gross transfers from consumers and taxpayers to support agricultural producers, measured at the farm gate level.
[2] NPC is the nominal rate of protection to producers measuring the ratio between the average price received by producers and the border price, measured at the farm gate.

Table 4.5

Producer Support Estimates (PSE)[1] for selected commodities in 2001

Country / institution	Agricultural commodities (per cent)						
	Wheat	Oil seeds	Sugar	Milk	Beef	Pork	Poultry
Czech Republic	5	15	21	19	31	7	35
Hungary	10	-2	20	31	26	-13	23
Poland	26	29	51	11	-80	1	20
Russia[2]	0	-62	37	12	-41	1	50
EU	44	40	46	40	91	20	46
OECD	36	28	45	45	36	16	16

Source: OECD.
[1] PSE measures the annual monetary value of gross transfers from consumers and taxpayers to support agricultural producers, measured at the farm gate level.
[2] Data for Russia are for 2000.

particularly market price support policies; (ii) export subsidies, which were capped in both volume and value; and (iii) market access issues, such as the reduction of tariff and non-tariff barriers.

However, Table 4.4 shows that the OECD/ EU continues to apply substantial levels of agricultural trade protection. In 2000 the total value of support provided to agriculture in OECD countries was estimated at 1.3 per cent of OECD GDP. Support for OECD agricultural producers translated into a Producer Support Estimate (PSE)[27] amounting to 32 per cent of total farm revenue. This support has mainly been in

the form of maintaining a minimum Market Price Support for particular products and has significantly distorted production and trade.[28]

As a consequence, prices received by OECD farmers have been over 30 per cent above world market prices on average.[29] In the case of the EU around 60 per cent of the total protection given to EU producers in 2001 was in the form of support for market prices. Consequently, EU farmers benefit from domestic prices that are around 33 per cent above world market prices. Moreover, OECD/EU agricultural support remains

skewed towards temperate products, such as sugar, dairy, beef and grains, that are important for the transition economies.

Aside from providing substantial support for producers, many OECD countries also apply high import tariffs. Recent estimates show that while average agricultural tariffs are in the region of 60 per cent, industrial tariffs tend to be far lower.[30] Once again very high tariffs are applied to temperate zone products. In short, the transition economies seem to face major barriers to raising their export levels with the OECD/EU.

However, on closer inspection, the picture is more complex. In the transition economies, it is true that average percentage PSEs are much lower than in OECD/EU economies. Direct income support has been more restricted than price support as a result of much lower budgetary capacity in the transition economies. Price support has mainly been applied through customs protection rather than through export subsidies. The difference between domestic and world market prices – with the exception of Slovenia – has been consistently smaller in the transition countries than in the OECD and EU. However, for a number of product categories the PSEs in many of the transition countries are already close to EU levels. As in the OECD/EU, transition country farmers have generally obtained most support for the production of sugar, milk, butter and poultry.

As a very crude measure of potential competitiveness, the inverse of the PSEs in Table 4.5 show that at current levels of support, only cereals and oilseeds in the Czech Republic, Hungary, Poland and Russia are likely to be competitive. These countries appear clearly uncompetitive in the production of poultry. In addition, quality differences (for example, in the case of pork) and other non-price handicaps resulting from the fragmentation of production and slow restructuring in the food industry probably make the remaining products uncompetitive.[31]

---

[27] The PSE measures the annual monetary value of gross transfers from consumers and taxpayers to support agricultural producers, measured at the farm gate level, OECD (2002).

[28] Market Price Support is an indicator of the annual monetary value of gross transfers from consumers and taxpayers to agricultural producers.

[29] As measured by the Nominal Protection Coefficient (NPC). The NPC measures the ratio between the average price received by producers at the farm gate and the border price also measured at the farm gate.

[30] See OECD (2002).

[31] See Pouliquen (2001).

Box 4.1

Likely impact of EU accession

Ten transition countries are candidates for accession to the EU. On accession, they would be subject to the Common Agricultural Policy (CAP). Accession will involve the removal of remaining intra-EU trade barriers, which should lead to an intensification of agricultural trade between current and new member states. However, according to some commentators, application of the CAP in the candidate countries could be expected to result in an increase in agricultural prices, stimulating output and exports and leading to a further redirection of trade away from non-EU countries.[1] Clearly, the key issue concerns the level of CAP support to accession countries. On 30 January 2002 the European Commission proposed that farm aid to the accession countries would initially be set at 25 per cent of the current EU level and only reach the full level in 2013.[2] If this proves to be the actual support level that is adopted, the likely impact on prices and output will be relatively small. Furthermore, the prices of many agricultural commodities in the transition economies have already converged with EU levels (and in some cases even exceed them).[3]

While it is estimated by the Commission that accession may lead to significant price increases in beef, sugar, milk products, and coarse grains,[4] increases in sugar and milk production are likely to be constrained by supply quotas. However, it should be noted that negotiations are proceeding concerning the appropriate periods for determining quota levels. Currently, beef production is below EU standards, so quality adjustments are likely to offset part of the production effects with price increases. Moreover, further reform of the support regimes – as

envisaged under the July 2002 'mid-term review' of the CAP, whereby subsidies would be gradually shifted away from direct aid for production towards rural development programmes – would further limit the impact on prices and production. If these reforms are carried out, it is likely that the only main CAP intervention commodity where significant growth in production and net exports can be expected is coarse grain, such as barley and rye.

With lower support levels, output will primarily be driven by improvements in productivity and quality. In these two respects, the accession countries still lag behind their EU counterparts to a notable extent, particularly Poland and Romania. For example, crop output and livestock production per hectare only averaged between 9 and 35 per cent of the EU average by 1999,[5] while quality standards still remain inferior. Of course, the CAP continues to impose large costs. With protection levels high in both the EU and the accession countries, both sides could gain from further trade liberalisation. Such changes are likely to be linked to the outcome of the next WTO Millennium Round of trade negotiations.

[1] See Tangermann and Banse (2000).

[2] See EU Commission (2002a).

[3] See Swinnen (2002) and Pouliquen (2001).

[4] See Munch (2002).

[5] See Pouliquen (2001).

Table 4.6

Main customs duties reciprocally applied between three transition countries and the EU in 2000 [1,2]

Country / institution	Agricultural commodities (percentage equivalent to proportion of tax)							
	Wheat	Oil seeds	Sugar	Butter	SMP [3]	Beef	Pork	Poultry
Czech Republic	76	27	172	166	108	182	64	99
Hungary	32	0	68	102	51	72	52	39
Poland	21	60	60	68	37	34	39	43
EU	46	0	169	136	70	108	38	25

Source: Pouliquen (2001).

[1] Table shows full duties applied above the reduced duty quotas.

[2] Ceilings subscribed to the WTO in 2000.

[3] Skimmed milk powder.

Furthermore, average tariff protection on agricultural products in transition countries is often not much lower than that applied by OECD and EU countries. Indeed, in 1997-98 the transition economies on average actually applied import tariffs that were higher than the OECD average on imports of rapeseed, sunflowers, cane sugar and pork while tariffs applied by OECD countries greatly exceeded transition country tariffs on barley, milk, butter and poultry imports.[32] However, the average tariffs for the transition economies are misleading. Some transition countries, such as Albania,

Belarus, Estonia, Kazakhstan, Russia and Slovenia, apply very limited tariff protection. Table 4.6 shows that in three CEB countries at the forefront of the EU accession process – the Czech Republic, Hungary and Poland – there are surprisingly high tariffs, excluding preferential quotas, applied to the import of staple products. As a result, it appears that these CEB countries have relatively low levels of EU exports reaching their domestic markets for some of these staple products to some extent because of customs protection in CEB rather than these countries' effective competitiveness. The low

competitiveness of CEB products compared with EU products is also reflected in the fact that exports to the EU have often remained far below permitted quotas at reduced duty rates under the Europe Agreements. Of course much of this reflects the difference in quality and other non-tariff barriers between CEB and EU products that limit the ability of the transition countries to penetrate the EU market.[33]

In conclusion, although the overall level of support is generally lower in transition countries than in OECD/EU countries, in some product categories the levels have approached or even exceeded EU levels. In some cases EU exports of bulk commodities that benefit from export subsidies are at the same time subject to import tariffs in recipient countries so that the net effect on trade is unclear. In a few cases, tariffs applied in OECD countries may also be reinforced by export restrictions in transition countries, again making the overall net effect unclear. Consequently, both the transition and OECD economies have significant scope for further trade liberalisation.

[32] See OECD (2000).

[33] It is difficult to assess the extent to which these qualitative barriers reflect reasonable restrictions on transition countries' exports to the EU, as opposed to being quality-based non-tariff barriers.

4.5 Conclusion

The performance of the agricultural sector in the transition has varied widely but in general the sector has under-performed. Difficult policy choices – in particular, regarding land ownership and control rights – have been slow in being implemented and in the bulk of countries – especially in the CIS – they have held back improvements in output and productivity. Consequently, the reform agenda remains wide open, with substantial areas – including market infrastructure and financing – to be adequately addressed.

This chapter has provided an analysis of the factors explaining the variation in performance. What emerges is that countries that started the transition with better initial conditions are those that have subsequently reformed the most. In addition, these are the countries that have benefited most from higher growth in agricultural output. Other reforms not specific to the sector have also generally had a positive effect, particularly with respect to productivity. This suggests that policies favouring liberalisation and privatisation of the economy as a whole have had positive consequences for the agricultural sector. However, such changes can also bring about temporary and adverse consequences for agriculture, principally through changes in relative prices or the agricultural terms of trade. This can explain the sharp falls in output near the start of transition.

In the longer run, it is clear that changes in land ownership and control – particularly the extent to which farms are held by individuals or households – have been a major factor in accounting for differences in performance. In short, the higher the share of farmland in individual hands, the higher the level of growth in output and productivity. Moreover, the method for implementing the privatisation of land has had a clear impact on productivity. Countries that followed land distribution policies have performed the worst.

Understanding agricultural reform requires an analysis of political decision-making. What has emerged from the analysis in this chapter is that not only have the most committed reformers been democracies but the least effective reformers have been characterised by a lack of democracy and weak checks on the executive branch of government. Nevertheless, there is now evidence that countries with incomplete reform – such as Kazakhstan and Russia – have begun to move forward and to break down the resistance of vested interests. A small group of laggards have yet to adopt serious reforms.

Finally, the place of agriculture in the domestic economy is only one element of the problem. This chapter has also focused on what role trade has played – and can play – in taking the transition countries forward. This is particularly relevant in the context of WTO and EU accession. Although the transition economies play a minor role in global trade, agricultural trade is important for some of these countries.

In all of the transition economies, there have been major changes in their agricultural trading patterns. Imports from OECD trade partners have risen faster than exports to such partners and this has led to burgeoning agricultural trade deficits. Part of this is due to measures taken by the OECD countries to impede or block trade access but this is only one factor. In fact, support for agricultural producers in a number of transition countries is close to, or in excess of, EU levels. In essence, the problem of low agricultural productivity – caused by incomplete reforms – remains a major factor limiting the extent of trade integration with the rest of the world.

References

M. Amelina (2000), "Why is the Russian peasant still a Kolkhoznik?", *Post-Soviet Geography and Economics*, Vol.41, No.7, pp.483-511.

A. Åslund and G. de Menil, (eds.) (2000), "Economic reform in Ukraine: The unfinished agenda", Carnegie Endowment for International Peace, New York.

A. Berg, E. Borensztein, R. Sahay and J. Zettelmeyer (1999), "The evolution of output in transition economies: Explaining the differences", IMF Working Paper WP/99/73, Washington D.C.

A. Bevan, E. Falcetti, M. Rizov and A. Taci (2002), "Ten years of transition in agriculture. Explaining differences in performance", EBRD Working Paper, forthcoming.

J. Conning and J. Robinson (2001), "Land reform and the political organization of agriculture", Williams College Working Paper (April).

A. Cungu and J. Swinnen (1999), "Albania's radical agrarian reform", *Economic Development and Cultural Change*, Vol.47, No.3, pp.605-19.

M. de Melo, C. Denizer, A. Gelb and S. Tenev (2001), "Circumstances and choice: the role of initial conditions and policies in transition economies", *World Bank Economic Review*, Vol.15, No.1, pp.1-31.

H. de Soto (2000), *The Mystery of Capital: Why Capitalism Triumphs in the West and Fails Everywhere Else*, Basic Books, New York.

EBRD (1999), *Transition Report 1999*, London.

EU Commission, DG for Agriculture (2002), "Enlargement and agriculture: Successfully integrating the new member states into the CAP", January 2002, Brussels.

EU Commission, DG for Agriculture (2002), "Analysis of the impact on agricultural markets and incomes of EU enlargement to the CEECs", March 2002, Brussels.

E. Falcetti, M. Raiser and P. Sanfey (2002), "Defying the odds: Initial conditions, reforms and growth in the first decade of transition", *Journal of Comparative Economics*, Vol.30, pp.229-50.

S. Fischer and R. Sahay (2000), "The transition economies after ten years", IMF Working Paper WP/00/30, Washington D.C.

J. Gray (2000), "Kazakhstan: A review of farm restructuring", World Bank Technical Paper No.458.

B. Heybey and P. Murrell (1999), "The relationship between economic growth and the speed of liberalization during transition", *Journal of Policy Reform*, Vol.3, No.2, pp.121-37.

C. Leonard (2000), "Rational resistance to land privatisation in Russia: Modelling the behaviour of rural producers in response to agrarian reforms, 1861-2000", St Antony's College, mimeo, Oxford (July).

Z. Lerman (2000), "From common heritage to divergence: Why the transition countries are drifting apart by measures of agricultural performance", *American Journal of Agricultural Economics*, Vol.82, No.5, pp.1140-48.

Z. Lerman (2001), "Agriculture in transition economies: From common heritage to divergence", *Agricultural Economics*, Vol.26, No.2, pp.95-114.

Z. Lerman (1997), "Experience with land reform and farm restructuring in the former Soviet Union", J. Swinnen, A. Buckwell and E. Mathijs (eds.) *Agricultural Privatization, Land Reform and Farm Restructuring in Central and Eastern Europe*, Ashgate, Aldershot.

K. Macours and J. Swinnen (2000a), "Causes of output decline in economic transition: The case of central and eastern European agriculture", *Journal of Comparative Economics*, Vol.28, pp.172-206.

K. Macours and J. Swinnen (2000b), "Impact of initial conditions and reform policies on agricultural performance in central and eastern Europe, the former Soviet Union, and East Asia", *American Journal of Agricultural Economics*, Vol.82, No.5, pp.1149-55.

S. Mainwaring and M. Shugart (2002), "Juan Linz, presidentialism, and democracy: A critical appraisal", *Comparative Politics.*, Vol.29, No.4 (July).

W. Munch (2002), *Effects of EU Enlargement to the Central European Countries on Agricultural Markets*, P.L. Verlag.

OECD (2000), *Agricultural Policies in Emerging and Transition Economies*, Paris, 2001.

OECD (2002), *Agricultural Policies in OECD Countries: Monitoring and Evaluation*, Paris, 2002.

M. Olson (2000), *Power and Prosperity: Outgrowing Communist and Capitalist Dictatorships*, Basic Books, New York.

A. Pouliquen (2001), *Competitiveness and Farm Incomes in the CEEC Agri-Food Sectors: Implications before and after Accession for EU Market Policies*, European Commission, Brussels, October 2001.

A. Przeworski (1991), *Democracy and the Market: Political and Economic Reforms in Eastern Europe and Latin America*, Cambridge University Press, Cambridge.

M. Rizov and J. Swinnen (2001), "Agricultural production organization in transition economies and the role of human capital: Evidence from Romania", PRG Working Paper, No.22, Katholieke Universiteit Leuven.

J. C. Sharman (2002), "Agrarian politics in eastern Europe in the shadow of EU accession", presented at the International Council of Europeanists, Chicago (March).

J. Swinnen (1999), "Political economy of land reform choices in central and eastern Europe", *Economics of Transition*, Vol.7, No.3, pp.637-64.

J. Swinnen (2001), "A Fischler reform of the Common Agricultural Policy?", Centre for European Policy Studies (CEPS), Working Document No.173, September 2001.

J. Swinnen (2002), "Transition and integration in Europe: Implications for agricultural and food markets, policy and trade agreements", *The World Economy*, Vol.25, No.4, pp.481-501.

S. Tangermann and M. Banse (eds.) (2000), *Central and Eastern European Agriculture in an Expanding European Union*, CABI Publishing, Oxford.

S. Wegren (1998), *Agriculture and the State in Soviet and Post-Soviet Russia*, University of Pittsburgh Press, Pittsburgh.

World Bank (2001), *Agrarian Economies of Central-Eastern Europe and the CIS*, World Bank, Washington D.C.

Rural transition

5

Rural development is a challenge world wide, and the transition countries of central and eastern Europe and the Commonwealth of Independent States are no exception.[1] Some of the issues faced by the region, such as the need to reform agriculture and preserve the rural environment, are also faced by developed countries. Other issues, such as the levels of rural poverty and poor basic services, are similar to those in developing countries, albeit less pronounced. Yet others are an inheritance of pre-1990 central planning. Although central planning assigned considerable resources to rural areas (for infrastructure, general education and medical services), its disregard for transport costs and resource constraints has left many rural regions with production patterns that are not viable in a market environment.

In addition, much of the political power of the young democracies in the region has proved to be biased towards urban areas. The main political force in transition has tended to be the urban elite, while the key rural economic players – usually large landowners or collective farm managers – were lukewarm towards agricultural and land reform and as such ineffective advocates of rural transition. In a number of countries, land reform was designed and implemented with social objectives in mind, rather than to improve agricultural productivity. As a consequence, rural reforms have not featured as prominently on the political agenda as they should have. In fact, some countries are only now starting to devise rural development strategies. These delays – together with inherent disadvantages, such as heavy reliance on agriculture and dispersed economic activity – have compounded the transition problems of rural areas.

Using household and enterprise surveys, this chapter examines the main actors in the rural economies – rural households,

farms and non-farm enterprises. The chapter explores how rural households differ from urban households, in terms of income, poverty and unemployment. It argues that the high incidence of rural poverty and unemployment is closely linked to the heavy reliance of rural areas on an unproductive agricultural sector. Increasing agricultural productivity and promoting economic diversification are therefore key aspects of rural transition. This will require substantial new investment as well as an attractive business environment. The chapter examines to what extent the rural investment climate differs from the urban investment climate, briefly compares the performance of enterprises in rural and urban areas, and identifies the main obstacles to rural enterprise development.

The final part of the chapter discusses the key challenges of rural transition. To restructure the existing economic base (both farm and non-farm enterprises), attract private capital and diversify economic activity, progress is needed on many fronts. Rural transition goes beyond the need for agricultural sector reform that was discussed in Chapter 4. Rural areas also have to enhance the quality of their infrastructure – both physical and institutional – improve access to credit and strengthen market linkages between firms. Market economies are characterised by a complex web of economic relationships of two broad types: "horizontal linkages" through which the value added in one firm is transmitted to the rest of the economy, and "vertical linkages" that connect firms with their business clients and suppliers. In many rural areas these market linkages have not yet fully matured. As a consequence, economic activity is held back and the benefits of new investment – in terms of the development of skills, increased productivity and income and employment creation – are not transmitted sufficiently into rural economies.

5.1 Rural households

Just over a third of the population of the region, or a total of 134 million people, live in rural areas. In urbanised countries, such as the Czech Republic and Russia, around a quarter of the population are rural households. In the more rural countries of Central Asia the fraction can be two-thirds or more (see Chart 5.1). The rural areas of the region differ from urban areas in their age structure and skill base, and they are characterised by a high incidence of poverty and unemployment. Incomes in rural areas are still dependent to a large extent on agriculture and the processing of food products but non-farm income and subsidies from the public budget are also significant. Overall, there are clear differences in socio-economic conditions between rural and urban households.

Demographic profile

Despite migration to the cities, the rural areas do not appear particularly disadvantaged in terms of the breakdown of the population. While rural households have higher fertility rates than urban families, rural areas tend to have a slightly higher share of people close to retirement and a smaller working age population. However, the differences are relatively small. For example, in Poland the proportion of rural people of working age is only two percentage points lower than the national average, and in Ukraine it is 1.5 percentage points lower. The differences between rural areas and the rest of the economy in the working age population close to retirement (defined as people over 45 years old) are also modest – for example, less than four percentage points in Poland.[2]

The pattern of education is more complex. In central eastern Europe and the Baltic states (CEB) there is a clear disparity in rural and urban skill levels, with rural areas having a much higher

---

[1] There are different definitions of "rural areas". The most common definitions are based either on population density or the number of people in a particular settlement. Most of the data used in this chapter are based on national definitions of rural areas, which can vary greatly. The term rural firms is used for all non-farm enterprises located in rural areas.

[2] Data from the Polish Statistical Office.

Chart 5.1

Rural population as a share of the total population

Per cent

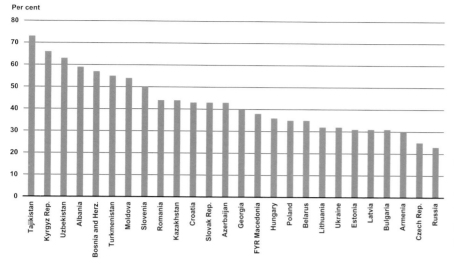

Source: World Development Indicators.

Note: Data for FR Yugoslavia were not available.

Chart 5.2

Education levels in selected countries

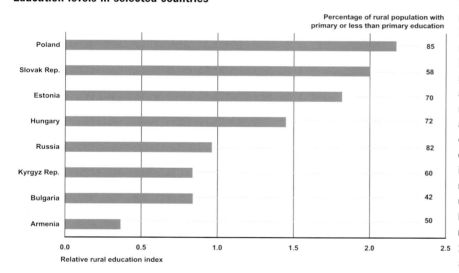

Country	Percentage of rural population with primary or less than primary education
Poland	85
Slovak Rep.	58
Estonia	70
Hungary	72
Russia	82
Kyrgyz Rep.	60
Bulgaria	42
Armenia	50

Relative rural education index

Source: World Bank household surveys. These data often show lower levels of education than reported in official national statistics.

Note: The relative rural education index shows the share of rural household heads with only a primary education, relative to the share of urban household heads with the same level of education. An index equal to one indicates that rural and urban education levels are equal. An index greater than one indicates a rural disadvantage (lower rural education levels) and the reverse for an index less than one.

share of low-educated people (see Chart 5.2). There is less evidence of an educational disadvantage in the rural areas in less advanced transition countries, particularly the Commonwealth of Independent States (CIS). In fact, in the four less advanced transition countries in Chart 5.2, the share of household heads with only a primary education is lower in rural than in urban areas. The most likely explanation for this pattern is migration. In advanced transition countries there is generally a more buoyant demand for higher skilled labour in the cities.[3] This makes migration to the cities an attractive prospect for the educated rural population

of CEB, but less so for their counterparts in south-eastern Europe (SEE) and the CIS.

Unemployment

The differences in demographic profile have direct repercussions on rural employment. While pockets of high unemployment exist both in rural and urban areas, most countries for which data are available have considerably higher rural than urban unemployment (see Chart 5.3). The difference is especially dramatic in Russia and the Slovak Republic, where the rural unemployment rate is two and three times higher respectively than the rate in urban areas. The only exceptions are the Czech Republic, with its high unemployment in urban and semi-urban industrial areas, and Romania, where forced urbanisation during communism has aggravated urban problems.

The extent of rural unemployment, and its impact on rural communities, is probably understated in official statistics. Subsistence farming is often the last resort of the rural unemployed, particularly in countries without an effective social welfare system (but also in Poland and the Slovak Republic). In addition, rural subsidies and household benefits are often linked to farm employment or ownership, particularly in CEB, and this creates a powerful incentive to remain in (or move into) agriculture. For both reasons, there can be substantial hidden unemployment in the agriculture sector. In Poland, hidden agricultural unemployment has been estimated at between 1 and 1.5 million people, which is equivalent to 15–30 per cent of the rural labour force.[4] If this estimate of hidden unemployment were included in the official statistics, Poland's rural unemployment rate would increase to 30–45 per cent, compared with the 15 per cent reported officially at the end of 2000.

However, hidden unemployment may be partly offset by hidden migration. Migration from rural to urban areas has been an important factor in lowering rural unemployment but much of it has been temporary and, therefore, not recorded in official statistics. The population of

[3] See *Transition Report* 2000.

[4] See *Transition Report* 2000.

Chart 5.3

Rural unemployment in selected countries

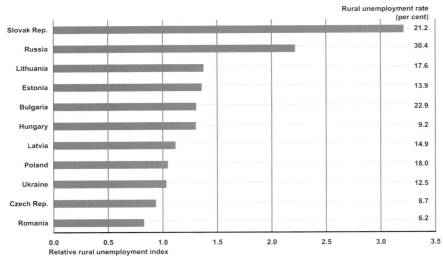

	Rural unemployment rate (per cent)
Slovak Rep.	21.2
Russia	30.4
Lithuania	17.6
Estonia	13.9
Bulgaria	22.9
Hungary	9.2
Latvia	14.9
Poland	18.0
Ukraine	12.5
Czech Rep.	8.7
Romania	6.2

Relative rural unemployment index

Sources: Eurostat: Czech Republic, Poland, Romania, Slovak Republic. National statistics: Bulgaria, Hungary, the Baltic states, Russia and Ukraine.

Note: The relative rural unemployment index shows the rate of rural unemployment, relative to urban unemployment. An index of one indicates rural and urban unemployment rates are equal. An index greater than one indicates a rural disadvantage (higher rural unemployment) and the reverse for an index less than one.

Table 5.1

Income from state benefits and home consumption

Country	Percentage of rural income			Percentage of urban income		
	Home consumption	State benefits	Other income	Home consumption	State benefits	Other income
Armenia	42.7	3.4	53.9	0.0	13.7	86.3
Bulgaria	20.7	31.9	47.4	2.3	23.9	73.9
Estonia	12.8	33.5	53.7	6.5	27.7	65.9
Hungary	0.0	52.9	47.1	0.0	45.8	54.3
Kyrgyz Republic	30.2	15.8	54.0	8.0	20.9	71.1
Poland	8.9	41.9	49.2	0.6	39.2	60.3
Russia	20.0	41.6	38.4	7.1	29.7	63.3
Slovak Republic	6.7	23.9	69.4	1.7	23.4	75.0

Source: World Bank household surveys.

Tirana, the capital of Albania, has more than doubled over the last ten years as a result of rural-urban migration.[5] In Poland there has been little permanent migration, mostly due to the lack of appropriate housing, but more than a quarter of a million people (about 4 per cent of the rural labour force) have moved to urban areas temporarily. Inter-regional migration is also a significant phenomenon in Hungary, where people move from rural regions in eastern Hungary to Budapest and the industrial centres in western Hungary. Some of the moves are again temporary, and thus hidden from official statistics.

Income

Employment is only one factor in rural income. Equally important are the productivity of, and hence wages from, employment and the presence of complementary income sources. Agriculture still makes up a significant part of rural employment, and remains a central source of rural income. The share of the rural population engaged in agriculture in CEB, either full time or part time, varies between 20 per cent in the Czech Republic and 60 per cent in Poland, but agricultural income is increasingly supplemented by non-farm income. Between 5 and 65 per cent of agricultural households also engage in

non-farm activities, and these activities account for 30-50 per cent of the agricultural household income. This is a significant fraction, and is in line with the share of non-farm income in total household income in regions such as Latin America (40 per cent), Africa (45 per cent) and Asia (35 per cent).[6]

Earned income from farm and non-farm activities is supplemented by home consumption (that is, goods and services produced for domestic consumption) and benefits from the state, such as unemployment benefits, social assistance and pensions (see Table 5.1). In EU accession countries, state benefits to rural households range from a quarter of total incomes in the Slovak Republic to over 50 per cent of total income in Hungary. In Poland over 20 per cent of the rural population living on farms is supported by either retirement or disability benefits, and state benefits make up over 40 per cent of rural incomes. State benefits are also crucial in Russia but account for only 16 per cent of rural income in the Kyrgyz Republic and less than 4 per cent in Armenia. In both Armenia and the Kyrgyz Republic the importance of state benefits is much lower for rural incomes than it is for urban incomes, which suggests an urban bias in the social assistance programmes of these two countries.

State benefits play an important role in reducing poverty among rural households. According to a World Bank estimate,[7] the removal of social welfare payments would increase the incidence of rural poverty in the Slovak Republic by about a third. By comparison, the removal of the same benefits would increase the urban poverty rate by only about a quarter. The absence of state benefits in poorer transition countries, therefore, may be an important factor in explaining the higher incidence of rural poverty in these countries. Support from the state budget to farmers' social security systems is seen both as a way of mitigating poverty and, when combined with early retirement schemes, as a way of contributing to agricultural restructuring.

[5] See Konica (1999).

[6] See Davis and Pearce (2001) and Reardon et al. (2001).

[7] See Csaki et al. (2002).

Chart 5.4

Level of rural poverty in selected countries

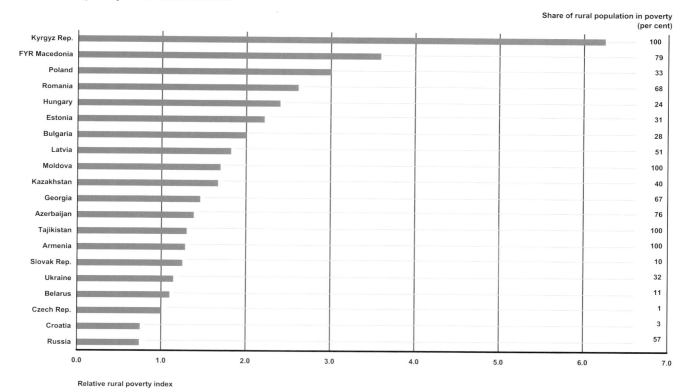

Sources: World Bank and the EBRD.

Note: The relative rural poverty index shows the share of rural people in poverty, relative to the share of urban people in poverty. An index of one indicates that the incidence of rural and urban poverty is equal. An index greater than one indicates a rural disadvantage (higher rural poverty) and the reverse for an index less than one. Data were derived using an absolute poverty line for national poverty and a relative poverty line for the contribution of rural poverty in total poverty. This may lead to an overestimate of the share of rural population in poverty.

Rural poverty

Rural poverty sharply increased during the transition and to date almost half of the rural population in the region lives in poverty – 19 per cent in CEB, 58 per cent in SEE and 71 per cent in the CIS (see Chart 5.4). Again, there are signs of a rural disadvantage. The incidence of poverty in rural areas is higher than in urban areas in all transition countries, except Croatia and Russia, by an average of 14 per cent.

Poverty is more prevalent in rural areas than in urban areas not only in poor transition countries with limited market reforms, such as the Kyrgyz Republic, but also in more well-off and advanced countries, such as Poland, where the incidence of rural poverty exceeds urban poverty by a factor of three. Nevertheless, studies have found that poverty is linked to the extent of market reform and this result extends to rural poverty.[8] However, the reduction in urban poverty levels has

[8] See World Bank (2002) and Milanovic (1998).

been more pronounced than in rural areas, and as a consequence more advanced transition countries typically have a higher incidence of rural poverty, compared with urban poverty, than slow reformers (see Chart 5.5). This is true across the range of countries but the poverty-transition relationship in CEB countries is different from the rest of the region.

Taking into account the level of reform, relative rural poverty is smaller in CEB countries than in SEE and the CIS. In other words, the CEB countries have managed to keep the extent of rural poverty at a lower level than their stage of transition would have indicated. This may be due to different initial conditions at the start of transition and the fact that CEB countries have greater resources for, and perhaps are more efficient at, providing social benefits.

The gap between rural and urban poverty is probably due, at least partially, to the neglect of rural issues during the early

years of transition. As a result, the rural population remains trapped in the unproductive agricultural sector in many parts of the region, with few alternative job opportunities. The incidence of rural poverty is closely linked to the share of rural employment in the agricultural sector (see Chart 5.6).

In order to reduce rural poverty, agricultural productivity has to increase (see Chapter 4) and there needs to be a wider range of economic activities in rural areas. This will create outside options for farm workers and ease the restructuring of the agricultural sector. However, for these changes to occur, governments will have to create a more attractive environment for investment in rural areas and combine country-level reform with dedicated rural policies.

5.2 Rural investment climate

An attractive investment climate is important both for the performance of existing firms and for the attraction of new firms

Chart 5.5

Rural poverty and transition progress in selected countries

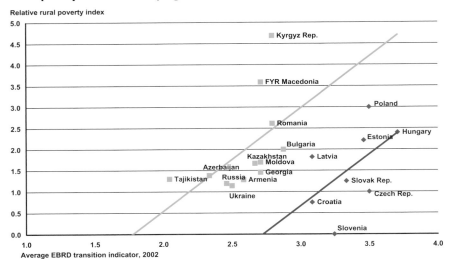

Relative rural poverty index

Average EBRD transition indicator, 2002

■ CIS and SEE   ◆ CEB

Source: EBRD.

Note: The linear regression lines were estimated by ordinary least squares using a dummy for CEB. This relationship also holds in a regression that includes per capita GDP. Data were derived using an absolute poverty line for national poverty and a relative poverty line for the contribution of rural poverty to total poverty. This may lead to an overestimate of the share of rural population in poverty. A definition of the relative rural poverty index is given in Chart 5.4.

Chart 5.6

Rural poverty and share of rural population in agriculture

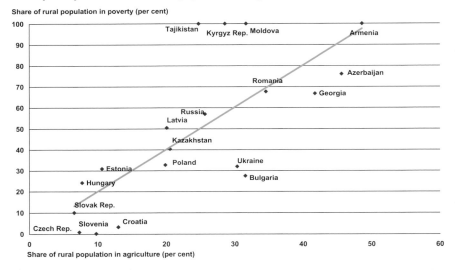

Share of rural population in poverty (per cent)

Share of rural population in agriculture (per cent)

Source: EBRD.

Note: Data were derived using an absolute poverty line for national poverty and a relative poverty line for the contribution of rural poverty in total poverty. This may lead to an overestimate of the share of rural population in poverty. Data for the following countries were not available: Albania, Belarus, Bosnia and Herzegovina, FR Yugoslavia, FYR Macedonia, Lithuania, Turkmenistan and Uzbekistan.

into rural areas. A large number of farms and enterprises have been surveyed to shed light on the extent to which rural enterprises face a different investment climate than their urban counterparts. These surveys suggest that rural areas face substantial obstacles to business development, but overall the differences

to urban areas are smaller than expected. Nevertheless, for specific countries and obstacles the rural-urban differences can be significant.

Obstacles to rural enterprise development

Evidence of the barriers faced by rural non-farm enterprises is available from the Business Environment Enterprise Performance Survey (BEEPS), conducted by the EBRD and the World Bank in 1999 and 2002.[9] The main obstacles identified in this survey can be grouped under three broad categories: physical infrastructure, finance and state governance (including corruption).[10] Chart 5.7 presents comparisons between rural and urban firms in each of these areas, based on the 2002 BEEPS and averaged across all of the transition countries. In terms of infrastructure, Chart 5.7 shows that rural enterprises are more severely affected by inadequate electric power supply than are firms in urban areas. On average there is relatively little difference for transport infrastructure, although for countries such as Uzbekistan, Romania and the Czech Republic the survey shows a significant rural disadvantage. The 1999 BEEPS identified access to adequate water supply as a significantly more important obstacle for rural than for urban firms, similar in magnitude to the differences in electric power supply, but this information was not available in the 2002 survey.

Inferior communication networks were identified as a constraint in the 1999 BEEPS, but according to the 2002 survey the gap has been substantially closed, probably because of the wider availability of mobile telephony. Similar evidence is available for households, where key problems include lack of access to water supplies, inferior communication networks and a poor local road network. For example, in many transition countries, fewer than half of rural households have access to adequate water supplies as compared with more than 75 per cent of urban households.[11]

[9] The 1999 survey covered more than 4,000 non-farm enterprises in 25 transition countries, while the 2002 survey covered close to 6,000 firms in 26 countries. The 1999 data are now available on the World Bank Web site. For details, see Hellman et al. (2000) and Annex 2.3.

[10] For this discussion an enterprise is treated as rural if it is in the countryside or a city with a population of less than 50,000. The analysis is based on multivariate regression analysis of the scores reported for each obstacle by firms in the survey. The control variables include three categories of firm size (small, medium and large), dummy variable for manufacturing versus service sectors, three types of ownership status (start-up, privatised and state), and fixed country effects.

[11] See Csaki and Tuck (2000).

Chart 5.7

Investment climate

Average score across EBRD countries of operations

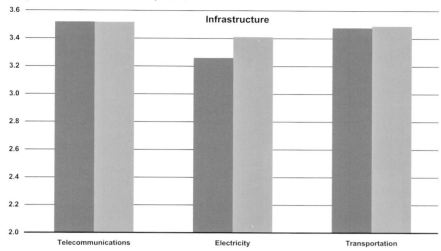

Average score across EBRD countries of operations

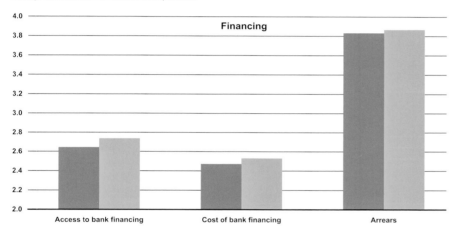

Average score across EBRD countries of operations

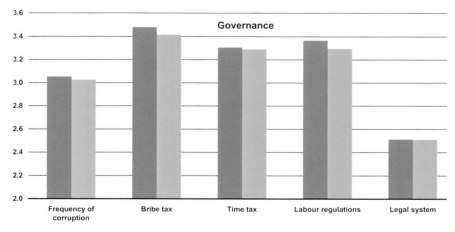

■ Rural   ■ Urban

Source: Business Environment and Enterprise Performance Survey, 2002.

Note: Scores range from 1 to 4, where 4 indicates no obstacles in the investment climate and 1 indicates major obstacles. Bribe tax is the percentage of revenues paid in bribes. Time tax is the amount of time spent dealing with government bureaucrats.

There are also differences in many aspects of access to finance (see Chart 5.7). Rural firms report that they face severe obstacles in obtaining finance, especially long-term credit, as a result of collateral requirements, high interest rates and shortage of bank funds. All of this points to the relative under-development of rural financial services. The financing constraints of rural firms do not appear to be offset by larger arrears to utilities, suppliers, workers and government taxes, as compared with firms in urban areas, which suggests that lack of finance is a binding constraint to enterprise development.

Interestingly, however, rural enterprises on the whole do not report significantly worse experience with governance and overall corruption than urban firms (see Chart 5.7). The reported frequency of corruption is somewhat lower in rural areas, and the percentage of revenues paid in bribes (bribe tax) and the percentage of time spent dealing with government bureaucrats (time tax) are also lower. However, the 1999 BEEPS showed that lower bribe payments were accompanied by more inter-vention by government bureaucrats in enterprise decision-making.[12] There are also significant differences between countries, with many of them actually reporting a higher incidence of bribery in rural areas. There are no reported differences in the obstacles posed by the legal system and in terms of labour market regulation, which urban firms describe as more stringent or at least more stringently enforced.

The location of a firm – rural versus urban – is as important to the business environment as the size of the firm. Chart 5.8 presents the probability that a firm will report that finance obstacles are either moderately or very severe. These proba-bilities are calculated for three types of firms: a large, urban privatised firm; a small, urban start-up firm; and a small, rural start-up firm.[13] The left-hand side of the graph shows the rural-urban differ-ence according to the 1999 survey. The (estimated) probability that a large priva-tised firm in an urban area will report finance as a major obstacle is about

---

[12] This evidence is consistent with the argument that firms can trade-off the level of bribery and government interference within any given regulatory environment. See Hellman and Schankerman (2000).

[13] Using ordered probit regression, the probability is computed for each component of finance shown in Chart 5.7 (except arrears) and each country, and then averaged over both dimensions.

Chart 5.8

Probability of major obstacles in financing

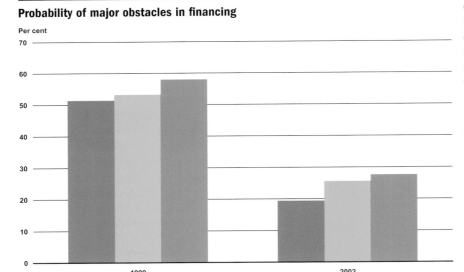

Per cent

Source: Business Environment and Enterprise Performance Survey, 1999 and 2002.

Note: Results are obtained from ordered probit estimation. Probabilities are averaged across the EBRD's countries of operations and across the two components of the financing climate (i.e. access to bank financing and cost of bank financing).

Table 5.2

Average enterprise growth

(in per cent)

Central eastern Europe and the Baltic states	1997-99		1999-2002	
	Rural	Urban	Rural	Urban
Sales	13.6	27.7	23.1	18.0
Investment	15.4	27.6	29.8	23.0
Export	2.7	7.3	8.2	6.2

South-eastern Europe	1997-99		1999-2002	
	Rural	Urban	Rural	Urban
Sales	-2.8	10.5	18.5	19.2
Investment	10.3	15.4	22.1	20.7
Export	-0.3	2.4	3.5	3.9

Commonwealth of Independent States	1997-99		1999-2002	
	Rural	Urban	Rural	Urban
Sales	2.7	13.7	27.9	31.8
Investment	2.3	10.4	20.9	23.7
Export	-1.4	0.0	4.0	4.8

Sources: Business Environment and Enterprise Performance Survey, 1999 for 1997-99 estimates.
Business Environment and Enterprise Performance Survey, 2002 for 1999-2002 estimates.

51 per cent, averaged across all the transition countries. For a small start-up in an urban area, the probability is slightly higher at 53 per cent, but for a small start-up in a rural area, it is 58 per cent. These differences are statistically significant.

The importance of location, relative to size, is somewhat smaller in the 2002 survey. However, the more striking feature is the extent to which complaints about access to finance have declined for all

types of firms, reflecting improvements in this area. The probability that a small rural firm will report financing to be a major obstacle declined from 58 per cent in 1999 to 28 per cent in 2002.

In short, the disadvantages of being a rural firm rather than an urban one are of a similar magnitude as the disadvantages of being a small firm rather than a large one. This is true both for finance and for other aspects of the investment climate,

in particular infrastructure. The well-documented disadvantages of small firms regarding access to finance are often cited as justification for public policies in support of small firms. There may be a similar case for targeted policies to improve the rural investment climate, including the development of rural infrastructure and dedicated, commercially oriented finance institutions.

The relative disadvantage faced by rural enterprises varies depending on the level of market reform. Charts 5.9 and 5.10 illustrate the difficulties presented by poor electricity infrastructure and lack of access to finance, and the gap between rural and urban firms in various transition countries, based on the 2002 BEEPS.[14] The quality of finance and power supply is typically higher in the more advanced transition countries, although the differences are small and there is substantial variation, particularly among less advanced countries. The gap between rural and urban firms does not appear to vary systematically across countries at different stages of transition. The gap in power infrastructure is particularly large in Azerbaijan and Central Asia, while the rural-urban gap in finance is especially large in the Czech Republic, one of the more advanced transition countries, and in Azerbaijan, Ukraine and Uzbekistan.

The inferior investment climate facing rural firms has important economic consequences in terms of their performance. Table 5.2 presents the average growth rate in sales, investment and exports over two periods, 1997-99 and 1999-2002, based on the two BEEPS surveys. On average, rural firms throughout the region had much slower growth than urban firms during the first period. After 1999, rural enterprises began to catch up in CEB countries and in fact reported higher growth than urban firms. In SEE countries, rural and urban firms grew at roughly the same rate, but rural enterprises continue to lag behind in the CIS. Average growth rates for enterprises were much higher during 1999-2002 than in the first period in all three sub-regions.

Rural enterprises have been slower in undertaking "deep restructuring" to become more cost efficient, consumer

[14] These findings are confirmed by multivariate regression analysis.

Chart 5.9

Quality of electricity infrastructure in rural areas

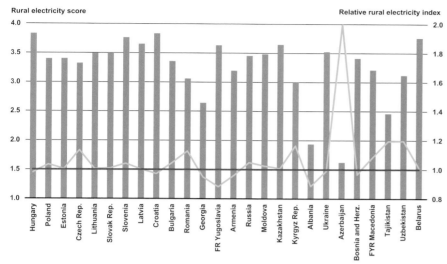

Rural electricity score

Relative rural electricity index

■ Rural electricity score — Relative rural electricity index

Source: Business Environment and Enterprise Performance Survey, 2002.

Note: The countries are listed in order of their average EBRD Transition Index. Scores range from 1 to 4, where 4 indicates that the electricity supply represents no obstacle to business operation and growth and 1 indicates major obstacles. The relative rural electricity index is calculated as a ratio of the urban score to the rural score. An index above 1 indicates a rural disadvantage. The rural sample sizes are small for small countries. Data for Turkmenistan were not available.

Chart 5.10

Access to and cost of financing in rural areas

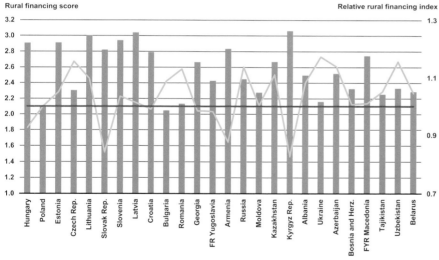

Rural financing score

Relative rural financing index

■ Rural financing score — Relative rural financing index

Source: Business Environment and Enterprise Performance Survey, 2002.

Note: The countries are listed in order of their average EBRD Transition Index. The financing score is calculated as the average of access to financing and cost of financing scores. Scores range from 1 to 4, where 4 indicates no obstacles and 1 indicates major obstacles. The relative rural financing index is calculated as a ratio of the urban score to the rural score. An index above 1 indicates a rural disadvantage. The rural sample sizes are small for small countries. Data for Turkmenistan were not available.

oriented and competitive. Table 5.3 summarises information about three types of deep restructuring, based on the two BEEPS surveys. It shows that

between 1997 and 1999 fewer rural firms upgraded existing products or introduced major new products. Rural firms still lagged behind for the period 1999 to

2002, but the gap was much smaller. The table also shows that over the entire six-year period rural firms achieved less organisational change, an important part of enterprise reform. Nearly two-thirds of rural enterprises report that they had not changed their organisational structure until 1999, and almost half of them had still not done so by 2002.[15]

Obstacles to farm development

Farm surveys undertaken during the past ten years reveal that farmers face somewhat different but equally serious problems in their business environment. Chart 5.11 shows the main obstacles faced by Czech and Slovak farmers, according to a 1999 survey. The most important issues raised are the deficiency of "market infrastructure", which includes financing constraints (limited retained earnings and access to credit for investment), and the functioning of input-output markets (horizontal and vertical linkages). Many farmers also see the underdeveloped state of land markets as an important obstacle but access to market information is not a commonly cited problem. These results are similar to those from earlier studies by the World Bank.[16]

Following privatisation and the removal of price subsidies in the agribusiness sector, the traditional communist structure of state-controlled marketing and supply monopolies has undergone major changes throughout the region. New market relations have developed, with many private suppliers and traders emerging in a new input-output network. In the countries more advanced in transition, the composition and levels of output as well as trade patterns have adjusted relatively well to the new market conditions. However, elsewhere in the region well-functioning, competitive (not state monopolised) markets for farm supplies and products have not yet fully emerged.

In response to disruption in the existing supply and output markets, many small farmers have withdrawn from the market. Nearly 40 per cent of farmers interviewed in the Czech and Slovak surveys

---

[15] These conclusions, both about enterprise performance and restructuring, also hold in multivariate regressions that control for other firm characteristics including size, sector, ownership type and country.

[16] World Bank studies from 1992 include Albania, Bulgaria, the Czech Republic, Hungary, Poland, Romania and the Slovak Republic. Later studies cover Russia (1992 and 1994), Armenia (1997), Moldova (1997), Ukraine (1997-98), Belarus (1998) and Turkmenistan (1998). See Dries and Swinnen (2001).

Table 5.3

Average enterprise restructuring

	1997-99 (per cent)		1999-2002 (per cent)	
	Rural	Urban	Rural	Urban
Product development:				
Successfully developed new product line	24.6	28.1	36.0	39.9
Upgraded existing product line	29.8	36.2	50.5	52.8
Organisational change:				
No reorganisation	63.0	48.5	47.2	40.7
Small reorganisation	20.0	28.1	25.1	29.7
Major or complete reorganisation	17.0	23.3	27.7	29.6

Sources: Business Environment and Enterprise Performance Survey, 1999 for 1997-99 estimates.
Business Environment and Enterprise Performance Survey, 2002 for 1999-2002 estimates.

Chart 5.11

Main obstacles to farm development

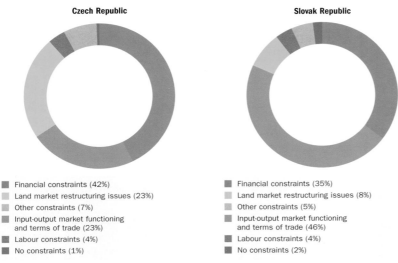

Czech Republic

Slovak Republic

Czech Republic:
- ■ Financial constraints (42%)
- ■ Land market restructuring issues (23%)
- ■ Other constraints (7%)
- ■ Input-output market functioning and terms of trade (23%)
- ■ Labour constraints (4%)
- ■ No constraints (1%)

Slovak Republic:
- ■ Financial constraints (35%)
- ■ Land market restructuring issues (8%)
- ■ Other constraints (5%)
- ■ Input-output market functioning and terms of trade (46%)
- ■ Labour constraints (4%)
- ■ No constraints (2%)

Sources: Research Group on Food Policy, Transition and Development, Katholieke Universiteit Leuven and EBRD calculations.
Note: Data show percentage of survey respondents which identified a particular obstacle as the main impediment to farm development.

consumed their entire output. A similar trend was observed among dairy farmers in the north-east of Poland, where, faced with changes in market conditions, many farmers stopped delivering milk to the dairy and continued to produce for their own consumption only, if at all.[17]

Poorly functioning output markets for agricultural products appear to be a larger impediment than inefficiencies in the supply markets. To some extent, the past experience with collective farming has prevented farmers from joining cooperatives, which could have helped to overcome constraints in the marketing of output.

The dominant complaint about low prices for farm products may in some countries be a consequence of monopolies in marketing and processing that artificially depress producer prices. In Belarus, Turkmenistan and Uzbekistan most commercial sales are still channelled through state procurement organisations and state-controlled processors, and procurement prices are fixed below market level. Even in more advanced countries some private agents exercise control over agricultural input and output markets, although the level of government interference is lower. However, complaints about low prices for agricultural products in

these countries also reflect the generally low profitability of agriculture and insufficient agricultural productivity.

Farm surveys identify shortage of capital and unavailability of rural credit as major reasons for the lack of agricultural development. Only a small percentage of farmers surveyed have access to official lending from a commercial bank or other credit institution, with relatives being the main source of funds. This problem is not limited to countries at relatively early stages of transition. Access to finance was also identified as a major obstacle in the Czech and Slovak farm surveys. Only 9.4 per cent of Czech and 4.6 per cent of Slovak farmers receive loans from a bank or other credit institution.

Financing constraints are caused by a number of problems for both the providers of finance and those who require it.[18] The main issues for the providers of finance include the high transaction costs involved in reaching small farmers and information barriers, which are aggravated by inexperience with agricultural lending. Other issues include the perceived high risk and seasonality of agricultural production, insufficient income levels of farm households, and the lack of suitable collateral. On the demand side, low education levels, uncertainty and low profitability deter farmers from applying for loans. In addition, inter-enterprise arrears have become a serious problem in some countries and sub-sectors (such as sugar processing).

Farm surveys confirm that the lack of suitable collateral is one of the most significant problems for farmers, both for obtaining working capital and for making long-term investments. According to the 1999 farm surveys in the Czech and Slovak Republics, only 1 per cent of agricultural borrowers in the Czech Republic and 10 per cent in the Slovak Republic used agricultural land as collateral. The asset most commonly used as collateral is residential property. Surveys in other transition countries show a similar picture.

---

[17] See Dries and Swinnen (2001).

[18] See Davis and Hare (1997), Davis et al. (1998), Heidhues et al. (1997), Swinnen and Gow (1999) and farm survey results.

This outcome reflects two distinct factors. The first is the reluctance of farmers to offer their agricultural land as collateral, which they view as essential for their long-term economic security, especially in view of the limited job opportunities elsewhere. The second, more important factor is the underdeveloped state of land markets, which makes banks reluctant to accept agricultural land as collateral. Transaction costs are much higher and the value of such collateral is more uncertain than the value of residential property or other assets, such as machinery. Well-functioning and competitive land markets, including the purchase, leasing and mortgaging of land, are necessary to promote access to finance. But these markets can only function effectively if farmers have well-defined and enforceable property rights.

As in the case of non-farm rural enterprises, the shortcomings in the rural investment climate have had a noticeable effect on the performance of farms although they are not the only factors holding back farm development. The productivity of the agricultural sector has remained low, restructuring of farms has been slow and growth has been negligible. In many cases, performance has deteriorated (see Chapter 4).

5.3 Reform challenges

The previous sections showed that there are significant differences between the economic prospects of rural and urban households and the investment climate for rural and urban enterprises. Several factors impede the development of rural economies, including a less well-educated population, poor infrastructure, under-developed financial services, insufficient input-output linkages and lack of reform, particularly in agriculture.

Improving this situation will require changes on many fronts. General country-level reforms, as discussed in Chapter 2, benefit rural and urban economies alike. These include price and trade liberalisation, better legal frameworks and reforms in the enterprise, infrastructure and banking sectors. They have to be complemented by the agriculture-specific structural reforms discussed in Chapter 4.

In addition, rural transition can be advanced by: (i) using the market linkages among rural enterprises and between rural and urban enterprises as a way to promote enterprise-level reform; (ii) improving rural physical and institutional infrastructure; and (iii) improving access to rural finance. Governments and the private sector have an important role to play in achieving these objectives, as examples in this section will illustrate. They also have responsibility for ensuring that these objectives are pursued in a manner that is consistent with the notion of sustainable development, which involves the development and preservation of adequate human, social and environmental capital (see Chapter 1).[19]

Strengthening vertical linkages among enterprises

Perhaps the most important challenge for rural economies is the restructuring of existing enterprises to increase their productivity and the quality of their output. This will require substantial new investment and access to know-how about international business practices, production technologies and management techniques. Small rural businesses are unlikely to attract these resources directly.

The region has so far attracted limited foreign investment, particularly the CIS, and most of the investment that has occurred has gone to urban areas. Typically, the capital cities receive over 50 per cent of foreign direct investment while rural regions account for less than a fifth. However, rural firms may gain indirect access through links with their more sophisticated business partners. An important way to promote rural transition is by supporting companies with particularly close links to the rural economy, such as food processors, supermarket chains and the suppliers of machinery and other goods.

Such vertical linkages work through several channels. Firms can assist their rural partners by facilitating the adoption of new technologies, providing working capital and imposing higher standards for the supplied product.[20] These links can also help to improve the environmental, health and safety performance of rural enterprises. Strengthening the rural sector in this way has benefits for other companies that have business links with rural enterprises.

Furthermore, a sustained increase in the demand for rural products will encourage new entrants into the rural market. This will intensify pressure on existing firms to reduce inefficiency and improve output quality. This "competition effect" is an important way of bringing about productivity gains, which can occur only if entry barriers for new enterprises are low. Public policies to maintain low barriers to market entry are therefore an essential element in any rural development strategy.

Studies in transition countries have found that foreign companies' investments in food producers have a particularly strong impact on the rural economy.[21] Food producers in transition countries often lack specialised materials and equipment, and foreign investors have established ways of transferring this technology. They have done this by introducing programmes for providing technology and for encouraging investment, and by developing new technical support and extension programmes. The impact of these programmes – combined with the important practice of paying farms on time – was substantial. Production and yields of farmers under contract with the foreign investor dramatically increased.

A good example of the importance of vertical linkages among enterprises was observed after the foreign take-over of a Slovak sugar producer, Juhocuker, in 1993.[22] To encourage farms to invest in high-quality beet production and deliver their produce to the company, the foreign investor introduced new contractual

[19] For a discussion of human capital in rural areas, see Swinnen et al. (2001).

[20] See Dunning (1993), Hobday (1995), Lall (1980), Markusen and Venables (1999), and Matouschek and Venables (1999).

[21] See Gow et al. (2000), and Dries and Swinnen (2001). Their findings were corroborated by a study on developing countries by Key and Runsten (1999).

[22] See Gow et al. (2000).

Box 5.1

Dnipropetrovsk Oil Extraction Plant

Located in the middle of Ukraine's sunflower growing area, the Dnipropetrovsk Oil Extraction Plant (DOEP) was the first fully integrated edible oil plant in the CIS. The company was privatised in 1994, and after a series of ownership changes Eridania Beghin-Say (EBS), Europe's leading producer of edible oils, became the main sponsor in February 1998 through its wholly owned division, Cereol Holding. The EBRD has supported the company through a number of equity and working capital investments totalling US$ 63.5 million. At the time of the EBRD's original investment, there was no other manufacturer of bottled refined oil in Ukraine and no foreign investors had entered the sector. In 1999, DOEP had a crushing capacity of 260,000 tonnes of seeds per year, which represented around a fifth of the country's total crushing capacity.

The main benefit that was originally expected from the investment was an increase in the quality and yields of local growers through the introduction of new financing schemes (working capital and cash-based payments for supplies). The provision of working capital was attempted in 1997 and 1998, when the company advanced fuel, sowing seeds and herbicides to farmers in the spring for autumn delivery. However, as other companies engaged in this activity in Ukraine had already experienced, the incidence of default was very high. Since that period, only very limited pre-financing (of no more than 5,000 tonnes per year) has taken place at DOEP. Therefore, compared with the Polish dairy sector, where banks and processors were successful in setting up financing schemes that promoted investments by farmers, the investments in Ukraine, if they occurred, were financed without bank loans or help from the processors. As a result, the opportunity to improve yields (for example, by introducing new and better yielding hybrids, or by supplying other materials) was limited and yields continue to be erratic. For effective pre-financing to take place, institutional, legal and attitude changes are still necessary.

However, the DOEP case study shows that a market of buyers with clearly defined contracts and on-time payments are essential for promoting increased production. In fact, the main impact of the DOEP investment resulted from the payment in cash for seeds, which eliminated previous barter and tolling transactions. Before the investment, approximately 45 per cent of the seeds were paid for by tolling arrangements, whereby the supplier was paid with part of the crude oil produced. In addition, at the time of harvest, many suppliers were paid with fuel (pure barter).

Now, suppliers are paid in cash within two days of receiving the warehouse receipt from the silo, which documents the transfer of ownership. If delivery is to the plant, farmers are paid in cash two days after delivery. In the rest of Ukraine barter and tolling has also been reduced substantially although there are still a few crushers, most of them domestically owned, which use such arrangements because of the chronic lack of financing in the sector.

As foreign investments in other crushers in Ukraine have also shown, turning to a cash-based financing scheme has helped farms to overcome their own cash-flow problems, improve their financial security and encouraged them to grow sunflower seeds on a larger scale. While the impact on yields is inconclusive, the overall production of sunflower seeds in the Dnipropetrovsk area has increased dramatically since 1995 (as well as for Ukraine as a whole). This points to the fact that the presence of well-funded buyers able to pay in time and in cash make sunflower seed production more attractive.

Sources: LMC International (2002) and the EBRD.

Change in seed production

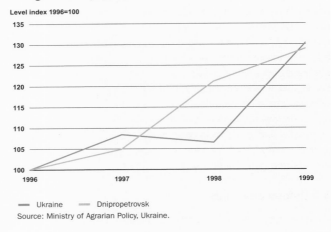

Level index 1996=100

— Ukraine — Dnipropetrovsk

Source: Ministry of Agrarian Policy, Ukraine.

---

arrangements along with a range of schemes to assist farmers in purchasing necessary fertiliser and machinery. These schemes reduced the growers' risk of a contract breach by the sugar company since the growers would not have to pay for the fertiliser and machinery in that event. In addition, an investment programme was developed in cooperation with an agricultural bank to facilitate investments by contract growers.

The impact of these programmes was dramatic. Hectares under contract more than doubled over a four-year period. As a result of these schemes, farm yields increased from 32.5 tonnes per hectare to 45 tonnes per hectare and the extractable sugar content increased from 14 per cent to 16 per cent on average.

Another example of the importance of vertical linkages among enterprises is foreign investment in the dairy sector in Warminsko-Mazurskie in the north-east of Poland.[23] Dairy companies assisted their small suppliers in improving milk quality through advice and investment support, and in upgrading their equipment and cattle stock through leasing and credit assistance. The foreign investors introduced credit programmes to enable farmers to upgrade their cooling and milking equipment. They also provided improved access to materials such as feed/seeds and fertilisers for feed production. Furthermore, the companies sent out agents to assist farmers with crop production, animal nutrition and health issues as well as the purchase of high-yield cattle. The programmes

resulted in a dramatic increase in the quality of delivered milk. The share of milk of EU quality standards increased from below 50 per cent of total deliveries in 1995 to more than 80 per cent in 2000.

A further example of the benefits of vertical links between enterprises is the EBRD investment in the Dnipropetrovsk Oil Extraction Plant, which resulted in significant increases in seed production (see Box 5.1). However, the example illustrates that institutional and legal changes are still necessary in some countries to fully exploit vertical linkages.

Farm restructuring is also promoted through linkages with large food retailers. Recent studies in Latin America and

---

[23] See Dries and Swinnen (2001).

industrialised countries have shown that supermarkets have a large impact on local suppliers, both farms and food processors, by improving contractual arrangements and market institutions. These include developing supply networks and distribution centres, imposing higher standards for product quality and designing transparent and timely purchasing arrangements.[24]

These developments can increase the incentive for investment by farmers and stimulate the adoption of new management techniques, technology and commercial practices. However, these benefits need to be underpinned by safeguards to prevent the abuse of any market power by large supermarkets – for example, by keeping barriers to market entry low.

Experience has shown that investments to promote vertical linkages among enterprises require careful structuring.[25] Most importantly, they require strong investors that are able to promote good corporate governance and are committed to restructuring activities in more market-oriented ways. Second, they require careful due diligence of the input, supply, cost competitiveness and industry risks. Lastly, in order to maximise the linkages, investments in fixed assets should be complemented by investments in managerial and technological know-how and quality improvements.

Strengthening horizontal linkages among enterprises

Another essential element of an effective rural development strategy involves strengthening the horizontal linkages among firms. These linkages occur when growth in one sector, and the subsequent improvement in income and wages, increase the demand for consumption goods and thereby create growth in the rest of the (rural) economy. These links can exist among firms in the same industrial sector (intrasectoral links) or between firms in different sectors (intersectoral links). Horizontal linkages are key to spreading the benefits of reform throughout the economy.[26]

There is evidence that reforms in the agricultural sector have generally had a positive influence on the development of the non-farm sector.[27] Farm restructuring leads to a rise in productivity, which makes resources available for redeployment. It also leads to increases in income and stimulates demand in the non-farm sector.

There are also benefits in the reverse direction, with investments in non-farm activities having positive effects on farm income and productivity. In the absence of effective credit markets, non-farm income is one of the key sources of finance for the agricultural sector.[28] The availability of non-farm income helps to overcome lack of credit and assists the purchase of costly materials. Furthermore, the availability of alternative sources of income may encourage farmers to adopt more lucrative but also riskier production methods.

Perhaps the most important horizontal effect is on rural unemployment (both hidden and direct). Employment creation in the non-farm rural economy will tighten agricultural labour markets and help to absorb under-utilised resources.[29] The construction of a float glass plant by Pilkington (with the support of the EBRD) in Sandomierz, in south-east Poland, is a good example. The project is located in a region burdened with high hidden unemployment in the agriculture sector. The new production facility provided new job opportunities in the non-farm sector but also stimulated the creation of new service companies to meet the increased demands, such as new computer and truck servicing companies.[30]

Horizontal linkages among enterprises are also potentially important for disseminating new technical, management and corporate governance standards. This can occur through various channels, including firms imitating the practices of successful competitors, the transfer of skills through the movement of workers between jobs, and the demand by innovating firms for the provision of complementary services (such as accounting or consultancy firms), which then become generally available.

Supporting evidence of such spill-overs is not conclusive. However, there is reason to believe that they may be important in transition countries, which have less experience of innovation and fewer developed channels for the transfer of technology and knowledge.[31] The study on the Slovak sugar market mentioned above found that the success of a foreign investor using new contracts led to competing domestic firms adopting similar contractual arrangements within one or two years. Similarly, when Polish dairies in the Warminsko-Mazurskie region learned about the milk quality improvement programmes implemented by a foreign investor, they started copying these practices and there has been a clear improvement in milk quality throughout the region as a result.[32]

Improving infrastructure

As the survey evidence showed, poor infrastructure is a serious obstacle for both rural households and firms, impeding new business start-ups and the expansion of existing rural enterprises. This concerns physical infrastructure, such as inadequate roads and telecommunications links as well as institutional infrastructure, such as underdeveloped distribution networks and complementary services for rural businesses.

Centrally funded efforts have tended to focus on the main cities while changes in the fiscal relation between the central

[24] See Reardon and Berdegué (2002).

[25] See EBRD (2002).

[26] The study of horizontal linkages goes back to the 1940s and 1950s when researchers explored the ideas of "balanced growth" and "big push" industrialisation (Rosenstein-Rodan, 1943; Nurkse, 1953; Scivotsky, 1954; Fleming, 1955). A more recent analysis is Murphy et al. (1989).

[27] See Lanjouw and Lanjouw (2001), Davis and Pearce (2001), and Greif (1997).

[28] See Reardon et al. (1994), and Lanjouw (1999).

[29] See Lanjouw and Lanjouw (2001).

[30] See Matouschek and Venables (1999).

[31] See Blalock and Gertler (2002), Dyker (1999) and Lall (1980).

[32] See Gow et al. (2000), and Dries and Swinnen (2001).

government budget and the regional budgets have adversely affected regional resources, with repercussions for the maintenance and expansion of rural infrastructure.

Yet the economic benefits from improving infrastructure in rural areas can be substantial. A World Bank programme to improve 975 km of rural roads in Albania and to provide better access to 125,000 hectares of land reportedly yielded an economic rate of return of around 35 per cent, taking into account only the reduced vehicle operating costs and travelling times.[33]

Beyond these direct benefits, better infrastructure generates important indirect benefits in terms of competitive "market selection".[34] Better access and lower costs encourage new firms to enter the market, increase competition and force inefficient firms either to improve or exit. Easier access to the rural areas exposes local firms to more products from outside, which further intensifies competition. An improved infrastructure is also necessary if enterprises are to break their dependence on local market demand.[35]

Better institutional infrastructure can generate similar benefits. While government institutions are not viewed as significantly worse by rural enterprises than by urban enterprises (according to the survey evidence), rural development is impeded by poor market institutions and business support networks. Similarly, inadequate institutions are often at the heart of rural environmental problems (see Annex 5.1).

A good example of such institutional infrastructure is the construction of market-oriented distribution channels. The breakdown of pre-1990 command economy distribution systems created an institutional vacuum and left producers and retailers with the difficult challenge of finding satisfactory outlets and adequate sources of good-quality supplies.

Several countries have sought to overcome a part of this problem by establishing wholesale markets for agricultural products. For example, in Warsaw a new wholesale market started operating in 1999 (with support from the EBRD). The new market reduced an important bottleneck in the distribution of local produce, particularly of fruit and vegetables. By concentrating supply and demand in one well-defined area, it led to increased competition, more transparent price setting, quality improvements and better hygiene standards. The daily trading volumes at the market increased from zero to about US$ 1 million, with around 5,000 vehicles entering the market on a daily basis.

The success of the Warsaw market is partly due to the (forced) closure of private open-air markets and the restriction of direct, out-of-van sales. The market also introduced international standards for the handling, grading and hygienic classification of fresh produce, which stimulated farms to improve their own quality standards. This kind of standardisation was absent in the open-air markets, which suffered from congestion and unhygienic conditions.

However, other wholesale markets in transition countries have been less successful, not least because important reforms were blocked by vested interests and corrupt practices. In many instances the new wholesale markets lacked the commitment and financial support of the municipalities in which they were created. For example, the EBRD withdrew from an investment into a wholesale market in Yerevan, Armenia, because the municipality refused to stop illegal informal street trading, which undermined the operation of the more transparent wholesale market.

Improving access to finance

As shown earlier, rural areas suffer from limited access to finance. This affects both rural households and enterprises but is probably most difficult to resolve for farmers. Insufficient reforms, the uncertainty of climatic conditions, the instability of market prices, the relatively small size of most farms and their low equity levels resulting from lack of land markets all imply greater risks and higher transaction costs in farm lending, compared with other sectors of the economy.

To improve access to finance, rural areas still have to restructure much of their existing banking system. Under central planning, specialised agricultural banks and cooperatives were used to provide preferential loans to large, commercially non-viable state farms. This practice continued during the first years of transition, and burdened the banks with a growing portfolio of bad assets.

Some of these banks are still in operation, such as the agricultural banks of Tajikistan and Uzbekistan, which continue to bankroll the state-controlled cotton sector. Remnants of the old agricultural banks also remain in Poland, Romania and Russia, among other countries. In Poland the agriculture and agribusiness loans of the main agriculture bank, Bank Gospodarki Zywnosciowej (BGZ), still represented over 50 per cent of the total corporate loan portfolio in 2001 although there are plans to transform the bank into a universal bank. In Romania, Banca Agricola underwent a major reduction in branches and staff as well as a freeze in lending before its privatisation in 2001. In Russia, Agroprombank was merged with a private bank, SBS, to form SBS-AGRO but the state retains a blocking minority and the sector orientation of the bank has not changed.

In all of these cases the low quality of the loan portfolio has meant that the banks can ill-afford continued lending to the agricultural sector at non-commercial rates and should instead restructure to become more market-oriented. This would probably entail a reduction in lending to the agricultural sector.

Elsewhere in the region the specialised agriculture banks were mainly liquidated and donor-supported agricultural development banks (funds) were sometimes established instead. In most CEB countries the specialised banks were either closed down or restructured into universal banks and sold to strategic investors. The restructured banks were forced to streamline their operations, and this often meant reduced lending to the agricultural sector and the closure of costly branches in rural areas.

[33] See World Bank (2000).

[34] See Aghion and Schankerman (2000).

[35] See Mead (1984).

Box 5.2

EBRD lending to rural micro and small enterprises

The EBRD is supporting lending to micro and small enterprises in both rural and urban areas either by working with existing banks or by establishing dedicated micro-finance institutions. The objective of the micro and small enterprise lending programme is to promote the development of a competitive, commercially viable and sustainable micro-finance sector in transition countries. This means developing institutions that provide tailored financial services to micro and small enterprises with extensive regional coverage, that focus on the smallest companies, and that cater for enterprises with no previous experience with the formal financial sector. Three principles lie at the heart of the EBRD's activities in the sector:

■ Financial sector orientation: The EBRD does not provide financial services directly to micro enterprises but seeks to support or create financial institutions that are both able and keen to cater for the target group.

■ A commercial approach: Only a profitable institution can hope to remain in existence and be able to provide lasting benefits to its clients. The essential elements of a commercial approach are that the institution: (a) focuses on keeping its costs under control; and (b) charges interest rates and fees that are in keeping with its total costs.

■ Institution-building focus: Offering credit is not enough. Products need to be tailored to the needs of clients, and they have to be professionally delivered and monitored. This makes the training and developing of specialised credit staff essential.

To date, the EBRD has collaborated with 36 banks and micro-finance institutions in 14 countries (see table). Banks typically have an average of ten branches, and 100 of them, or about 28 per cent of the total, are in rural areas. The rural branches have extended significantly fewer and smaller loans than urban branches. As a consequence, rural loans account for only 19 per cent of the portfolio in terms of loan numbers and 8 per cent in terms of loan amounts.

EBRD experience in micro-lending

	Rural	Total
Participating countries	-	14
Number of partner banks	-	36
Number of branches / lending outlets	100	353
Number of loans disbursed	40,000	210,616
Amount of loans disbursed (US$ million)	120	1,500
Number of loans outstanding	16,800	84,445
Amount of loans outstanding (US$ million)	42	426

Source: Group for Small Business, EBRD.

This has left a major vacuum in the provision of rural finance in almost all transition countries. Filling this gap does not only require the expansion of universal banks into rural areas but also the establishment of financial institutions that specifically target micro and small enterprises. The financial needs of individual farmers and non-farm rural enterprises are relatively small, and rural financial institutions have to pay particular attention to this segment of the market. However, the development of commercially viable micro-lending is difficult and requires specialised lending skills.

To reduce the high costs associated with smaller loans – administration costs are not proportionate to loan size – banks engaging in micro-finance have to develop standardised loan products and lending procedures. International financial institutions can play an important role in building this capacity, and they can also provide the seed capital to kick-start the market.

Experience shows that the establishment of dedicated micro-finance banks and the long-term cooperation with local banks to build up the necessary expertise and

capacity can unlock a substantial lending potential and lead to the development of a sustainable micro-finance market (see Box 5.2).

Rural finance also requires modifications in standard lending techniques, which are mostly tailored to urban customers and do not take into account the seasonal nature of cash flows in the agricultural sector. Farms often require access to financing during the pre-harvest season to buy materials such as seeds and fertilisers, which they can only repay after the harvest. Whereas urban micro-borrowers are mainly engaged in trade and services that have high turnover and generate smooth cash flows, the cash flows of farms tend to be much more uneven. This requires repayment in less frequent instalments, which in turn increases risks for lenders and the need for monitoring.

There is also the important issue of correlated risks when lending to farms – all borrowers are affected by some of the same risks, such as low market prices and reduced yields. Micro-lenders in the rural areas therefore have to diversify their portfolio to cover farm and non-farm activities.

Perhaps the most important obstacle that needs to be addressed to improve access to finance is the issue of collateral. A number of legal and institutional issues need to be overcome before banks can take as security rural assets, such as land, land user rights and farm equipment. In particular, the legal basis for using land – the main asset for farm borrowers – as collateral is often insufficient or non-existent (see Chapter 4).

In this situation, warehouse receipts – certificates issued by licensed warehouses in exchange for agricultural commodities that are stored at the warehouse – can be an alternative form of security to finance working capital (see Box 5.3).

However, financing based on warehouse receipts can be effective only if certain institutional arrangements are in place. These include an appropriate legal environment that ensures effective enforceability of the underlying collateral, reliable and well-functioning warehouses, and adequate licensing, inspection and monitoring of warehouses.

Also needed are an indemnity fund or performance guarantees that cover potential fraud or negligent behaviour

Box 5.3

Warehouse Receipts Programme

Insufficient access to working capital is one of the key problems in the agricultural sector in transition countries. The use of warehouse receipts as a form of collateral has proven to be a simple and cost-effective way to overcome this problem and to provide financing to the agribusiness and farm sector. The basic mechanism of warehouse receipt based financing is described below (see chart).

At the time of harvest, farmers store their crop at a licensed warehouse, receiving a Certificate of Title (CT) and a Certificate of Pledge (CP). The warehouse will only release the crop to the owner of both documents except when the loan is defaulted. A national indemnity fund and regular inspections reduce the risk of damage or fraud while the crop is stored in the silo.

When farmers borrow against the crop, the bank keeps the CP as security and the CT for safekeeping. Before the maturity of the loan (typically up to nine months) the farmer sells the crop to a processor (or to a trader) by "selling" the CT following consultation with the bank. At maturity of the loan or when it needs the crop, the processor redeems the CP from the bank by repaying the loan. The processor, now owner of both CT and CP, can collect the crop from the silo.

There are several advantages to financing based on warehouse receipts. The farmers can choose when to sell without being forced to sell at the time of harvest when prices are generally low. Their access to finance improves, which enables them to secure the supply of materials throughout the year. The risk of lending for banks is reduced by the availability of collateral that is relatively easy to liquidate, and this lowers the cost of financing available to the agricultural sector. Price fluctuations during the year are also generally reduced. The general condition of the storage sector can be expected to improve as the implementation of warehouse receipts requires tight regulation and inspections to reduce post-harvest losses of grain in the warehouses. Finally, government interference in the sector, such as price fixing, may be reduced as the system allows for more transparency and commercial financing. Ultimately, the system may lead to the development of commodity exchanges, including commodity futures, to further increase market transparency.

Since 1998, the EBRD has provided the equivalent of €87.5 million of working capital financing collateralised by warehouse receipts in Bulgaria, Kazakhstan and the Slovak Republic, which has the most extensive warehouse receipts programme in the region. The Slovak authorities passed a Warehouse Receipts Act in 1998 and soon after its adoption the EBRD, together with a local bank, started to provide financing backed by warehouse receipts. Between 1998 and 2001 the EBRD co-financed 340 sub-loans worth €16.5 million. Other Slovak commercial banks soon began to lend against warehouse receipts as well, enhancing both price transparency and competition in the agricultural sector. Competition in the storage sector also increased as quality control of grain inventories improved and warehouses were licensed. However, the lack of an indemnity fund and the continued provision of state subsidies to primary producers raise questions about the commercial sustainability and long-term future of the instrument.

Sources: Martin and Bryde (1999) and EBRD.

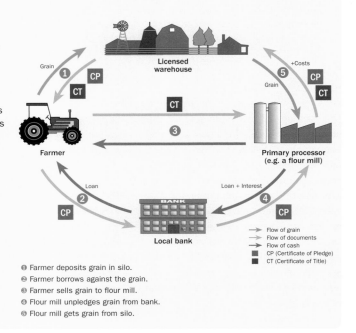

① Farmer deposits grain in silo.
② Farmer borrows against the grain.
③ Farmer sells grain to flour mill.
④ Flour mill unpledges grain from bank.
⑤ Flour mill gets grain from silo.

by the licensed warehouses, and agricultural commodity prices that are determined by the market.[36]

The development of farm equipment leasing is another useful way to provide long-term capital expenditure financing to farmers. But again, this requires an adequate institutional framework, in particular the legal enforceability of leasing contracts and developed secondary markets for farm equipment.

5.4 Conclusion

Over a third of the population of the region live in rural areas. Yet rural areas have not featured prominently on the reform agenda during the first decade of transition. In Russia, for example, serious rural land reform started only in 2002, with the passage of a new Land Code that will gradually liberalise the market for agricultural land. In CEB the formulation of rural development plans has been driven as much by the demands of EU accession as by internal pressure for rural reform. This is in stark contrast

to China, where rural areas are central to the economy and hence at the centre of the reform process.

Because of this lack of attention, rural areas typically lag behind urban areas in terms of a number of transition and development indicators. The incidence of rural poverty and unemployment are significantly higher than the urban equivalents, in some countries by a factor of two or more, and the rural investment climate is less business-friendly in several important respects. Rural non-farm enterprises are constrained more severely than urban

[36] See Martin and Bryde (1999).

firms by poor physical and market infrastructure and lack of access to finance. The magnitude of the rural disadvantage is relatively modest on average, but it can be large for specific countries and obstacles, and is often of similar importance as the disadvantage associated with the small size of a firm. The shortcomings in the investment climate have had a noticeable impact on the performance of rural enterprises, which have grown less, invested less and restructured more slowly than urban firms.

There are no signs that the rural-urban gap is narrowing during the transition process. While the overall investment climate is better in countries at more advanced stages of transition, the gap between the rural and urban investment climate does not vary systematically with the stage of transition. However, in the case of rural poverty and unemployment, the rural-urban gap is largest in advanced transition countries. This suggests that, while reforms have resulted in some improvements in the rural business environment, they were not sufficient to trigger substantial new investment and job creation.

Given the dominance of the farm sector, reforming agriculture, increasing farm productivity and promoting land reform remain the dominant rural transition issues (see Chapter 4). But an effective farm sector is only one element of balanced rural development. Rural areas also need to promote non-farm activities to diversify their economic activities.

A key requirement for both farm and non-farm development is the attraction of outside investment and skills. But as long as differences in the investment climate remain significant, large-scale investment will be difficult to attract. In this situation, the best way to reach rural enterprises may be through policies that strengthen vertical linkages with their business clients and suppliers. There is evidence that links between rural firms and their clients and suppliers can be an effective way of bringing about enterprise reform, developing skills and providing working capital. This is particularly the case if the contact is with leading international firms. Horizontal linkages between firms are equally important to spread the benefits of new investment across rural economies. They also help to disseminate skills among enterprises and to diversify rural economies from farm into non-farm activities. Another important link is between rural firms and finance institutions, which provide access to credit that is not available from other sources. The credit needs and available collateral of rural borrowers are often particular to the rural economy, especially in the farming sector. Transition countries are still in the process of reforming their rural banking sector and developing the legal and institutional framework, such as new land codes, leasing laws, grain laws and secured warehouses, that would allow banks to take adequate security and to develop lending skills for the rural market.

For horizontal and vertical links to function effectively, the market system needs to be strengthened. Rural authorities have to put in place the physical and institutional infrastructure that both rural households and enterprises need for their long-term future. This includes safeguards – in the form of regulation, incentives and transfers – to protect the less well-off and to guide economic activity in a direction that preserves the social structure and environmental quality of rural areas.

References

P. Aghion and M. Schankerman (2000), "A model of market enhancing infrastructure", CEPR Discussion Paper 2462.

G. Blalock and P. Gertler (2002), "Technology diffusion from foreign direct investment through supply chains", Working Paper, Department of Applied Economics and Management, Cornell University.

C. Csaki, A. Nucifora, Z. Lerman, T. Herzfeld and G. Blaas (2002), *Food and Agriculture in the Slovak Republic: The Challenges of EU Accession*, World Bank, Washington D.C.

C. Csaki and L. Tuck (2000), "Rural development strategy. Eastern Europe and Central Asia", World Bank Technical Paper No.484, World Bank, Washington D.C.

J.R. Davis, A. Gaburici and P.G. Hare (1998), "What's wrong with Romanian rural finance? Understanding the determinants of private farmers' access to credit", CERT Discussion Paper, CERT – Centre for Economic Reform and Transformation, Heriot-Watt University, Edinburgh.

J.R. Davis and P.G. Hare (1997), "Reforming the systems of rural finance provision in Romania: Some options for privatisation and change", CERT Discussion Paper No.97/13, CERT – Centre for Economic Reform and Transformation, Heriot-Watt University, Edinburgh.

J. Davis and D. Pearce (2001), "The non-agricultural rural sector in Central and Eastern Europe", in C. Csaki and Z. Lerman (eds.), *The Challenge of Rural Development in the EU Accession Countries*, World Bank, Washington D.C.

L. Dries and J.F.M. Swinnen (2001), "The impact of globalization, transition and EU accession on the Polish Dairy Sector", paper presented in the organised symposium on Globalization, Regional Integration and Rural Development at the American Agricultural Economics Association meeting in Chicago, 5-8 August 2001.

J. Dunning (1993), *Multinational Enterprises and the Global Economy*, Addison-Wesley Publishing Co, Reading.

D.A. Dyker (1999), "Foreign direct investment in the former communist world: A key vehicle for technological upgrading?", *Innovation: The European Journal of Social Sciences*, Vol.12, No.3, pp.345-53.

EBRD (2000), *Transition Report* 2000, London.

EBRD (2002), Agribusiness Operations Policy, London.

M.J. Fleming (1955), "External economies and the doctrine of balanced growth", *Economic Journal*, Vol.65, pp.241-56.

H.R. Gow, D.H. Streeter and J.F.M. Swinnen (2000), "How private contract enforcement mechanisms can succeed where public institutions fail: The case of Juhocukor a.s.", *Agricultural Economics*, Vol.23, pp.253-65.

F. Greif (1997), "Off-farm income sources and uses in transition countries", unpublished manuscript.

F. Heidhues, J.R. Davis and G. Schrieder (1997), "Agricultural transformation and implications for designing rural financial policies in Romania", CERT Discussion Paper, CERT – Centre for Economic Reform and Transformation, Heriot-Watt University, Edinburgh.

J. Hellman and M. Schankerman (2000), "Intervention, corruption and capture: the nexus between enterprises and the state" *Economics of Transition*, Vol.8, No.3, pp.545-76.

J. Hellman, G. Jones, D. Kaufmann and M. Schankerman (2000), "Measuring governance and state capture: The role of bureaucrats and firms in shaping the business environment", World Bank Working Paper No.2312.

M. Hobday (1995), *Innovation in East Asia: The Challenge to Japan*, Aldershot, London.

N. Key and D. Runsten (1999), "Contract farming, smallholders, and rural development in Latin America: The organization of agro-processing firms and the scale of outgrower production", *World Development*, Vol.27, No.2, pp.381-401.

N. Konica (1999), "The emigration experience and its impact on the Albanian economy", PhD dissertation, CERGE, Prague.

S. Lall (1980), "Vertical interfirm linkages in LDCs: An empirical study", *Oxford Bulletin of Economics and Statistics*, Vol.42, pp.203-26.

J.O. Lanjouw and P. Lanjouw (2001), "The rural non-farm sector: Issues and evidence from developing countries", *Agricultural-Economics*, Vol.26, No.1, pp.1-23.

P. Lanjouw (1999), "Rural nonagricultural employment and poverty in Ecuador", *Economic Development and Cultural Change*, Vol.48, No.1, pp.91-122.

J.R. Markusen and A.J. Venables (1999), "Foreign direct investment as a catalyst for industrial development", *European Economic Review*, Vol.43, pp.335-56.

E. Martin and P. Bryde (1999) "Grain receipts in economies in transition: An introduction to financing of warehouse receipts", in *Agricultural Finance and Credit Infrastructure in Transition Economies: Proceedings of OECD Expert Meeting*, Moscow, February 1999, OECD, Paris and Washington D.C.

N. Matouschek and A.J. Venables (1999), "Evaluating investment projects in the presence of sectoral linkages: Theory and application to transition economies", unpublished manuscript.

D.C. Mead (1984), "Of contracts and sub-contracts: Small firms in vertically dis-integrated production-distribution systems in LDCs", *World Development*, Vol.12, Nos.11-12, pp.1095-106.

B. Milanovic (1998), *Income, Inequality, and Poverty during the Transition from Planned to Market Economy*, World Bank, Washington D.C.

K.M. Murphy, A. Shleifer and R.W. Vishny (1989), "Industrialization and the big push", *Journal of Political Economy*, Vol.97, No.5, pp.1003-26.

R. Nurkse (1953), *Problems of Capital Formation in Underdeveloped Countries*, Oxford University Press, New York.

T. Reardon and J.A. Berdegué (2002), "The rapid rise of supermarkets in Latin America: Challenges and opportunities for development", *Development Policy Review*, Vol.20, No.4, pp.371-88.

T. Reardon, J. Berdegué and G. Escobar (2001), "Rural nonfarm employment and incomes in Latin America: Overview and policy implications", *World Development*, Vol.29, No.3, pp.395-409.

T. Reardon, E. Crawford and V. Kelly (1994), "Links between nonfarm income and farm investment in African households: Adding the capital market perspective", *American Journal of Agricultural Economics*, Vol.76, pp.1172-76.

P. Rosenstein-Rodan (1943), "Problems of industrialisation of eastern and south-eastern Europe", *Economic Journal*, Vol.53, pp.202-11.

T. Scivotsky (1954), "Two concepts of external economies", *Journal of Political Economy*, Vol.62, pp.143-51.

J.F.M. Swinnen and H.R. Gow (1999), "Agricultural credit problems and policies during the transition to a market economy in central and eastern Europe", *Food Policy*, Vol.24, No.1, pp.21-47.

J.F.M. Swinnen, L. Dries and E. Mathijs (2001), "Critical constraints to rural development in central and eastern Europe", in C. Csaki and Z. Lerman (eds.), *The Challenge of Rural Development in the EU Accession Countries*, World Bank, Washington D.C.

World Bank (2001), Albania Rural Roads Project. Implementation Completion Report No.22071, Washington D.C.

World Bank (2002), *Transition: The First Ten Years. Analysis and Lessons for Eastern Europe and the Former Soviet Union*, Washington D.C.

Country assessments

Since 1994, the EBRD has charted the transition progress of each of its countries of operations in the *Transition Report*. The Bank's annual assessments have highlighted key developments and issues central to transition in a wide range of areas, including liberalisation, macroeconomic stabilisation, privatisation, enterprise, infrastructure, financial and social sector reform. The key challenges facing each country are summarised at the beginning of the text. The assessment is complemented by a timeline of important historical events in the transition process.

To provide a quantitative foundation for analysing progress in transition, each country assessment includes a table of structural and institutional indicators. The data in this table are grouped into the same categories as the text of the transition assessment, except for macroeconomic stabilisation. This aspect is covered by a separate table on macroeconomic indicators.

At the top of the structural indicators table are a set of "snapshots" to provide an overview of selected institutional and legal arrangements as of September 2002. The table itself provides indicators of progress in structural change within each category. These data help to describe the process of transition in a particular country, but they are not intended to be comprehensive. Given the inherent difficulties of measuring structural and institutional change, they cannot give a complete account or precise measurement of progress in transition. Moreover, some entries, such as the exchange rate regime and the privatisation methods, are useful only for information and carry no normative content. Other variables may have normative content, but their evaluation may vary depending on the specific country context.

The data should be interpreted with caution also because their quality varies across countries and categories. The data are based on a wide variety of sources, including national authorities, EBRD staff estimates, and other international organisations. To strengthen the degree of cross-country comparability, some of the data were collected through standardised EBRD surveys of national authorities. The technical notes at the end of this section provide definitions of the variables, along with country specific qualifications.

Albania

Key reform challenges

- Improving physical infrastructure, strengthening law enforcement and renewing efforts to combat corruption are all essential for encouraging private sector development and attracting more foreign investment.

- Implementation of the strategic action plan for reforming the energy sector is central to resolving the immediate energy crisis and to preparing for comprehensive reform.

- A successful sale of the last remaining state-owned bank will eliminate a captive source of finance for the government and improve access to banking services for businesses and households.

Liberalisation

Negotiations on a Stabilisation and Association Agreement delayed.

Albania was due to begin formal negotiations with the EU on a Stabilisation and Association Agreement (SAA) in spring 2002, but political uncertainty and a change of government caused a postponement. However, the negotiations are expected to start before the end of the year. The main focus of the SAA will be to improve standards of governance and to strengthen state institutions and the legal framework. In March 2002, the Albanian government and the EU signed a financial agreement under the EU's Community Assistance for Reconstruction, Development and Stabilisation (CARDS) programme. This programme will provide assistance of around €145 million for the period 2002–04 to assist with Albania's integration into European structures.

Progress made in signing bilateral Free Trade Agreements.

Albania concluded a Free Trade Agreement (FTA) with FYR Macedonia in March 2002. An agreement with Croatia is expected to be signed shortly. Negotiations on FTAs with Bulgaria, Bosnia and Herzegovina, FR Yugoslavia and Romania are under way and the target for completion is the end of 2002. The agreements are being negotiated under the framework of the Memorandum on Trade Liberalisation signed by the seven countries of south-eastern Europe in June 2001.

Stabilisation

Further reforms in tax and customs administration introduced.

Tax revenue collection failed to reach the government's target for the year 2001, due in part to the significant scale of the informal economy. This has led to renewed efforts by the government to improve tax and customs administration. During the first half of 2002, regional directorates for customs administration were established. Cooperation between the EU-financed customs assistance mission (CAM-Albania) and the tax directorate has been enhanced in order to improve the valuation of imports and to detect under-invoicing. At the same time, a performance-based reward scheme was also introduced

for tax department staff and an independent taxpayer appeal commission has been set up. The government expects that by stepping up enforcement efforts, the tax base for registered payers of corporate tax will rise and the extent of the informal economy will decline.

Privatisation

Large-scale privatisation in oil and mining sectors prepared.

Both the continued low level of foreign investor interest and the recent increase in political uncertainty have contributed to delays in the large-scale privatisation programme. However, the government has prepared plans for selling state assets in the oil and mining sectors. Privatisation in the oil sector is planned to start with the sale of the oil service company Servcom by the end of 2002. The Albanian Petroleum Company (Albpetrol, oil and natural gas extraction) and Albanian Refining and Marketing Oil (ARMO, refining) will also be prepared for privatisation by international tender during 2002. The process is to be completed by June 2003. The government has also prepared a privatisation strategy for the mining sector, allowing investors to use mining assets and granting them various concessions. During 2001, the government granted two 30-year concessions on chromium mining to the Italian company DARFO, as well as providing concessions to the Turkish copper mining company Ber Oner. DARFO has already re-started operations in two chromium mines in the south-western part of Albania, but investments under the second concession in the north have been delayed due to the energy crisis.

Enterprise reform

Further efforts made to remove obstacles to private sector development.

Despite some improvements in the investment climate, private enterprises still encounter many obstacles to their development, including inadequacies in the legal framework and corruption. In late 2001, the government adopted a strategy for small and medium-sized enterprises (SMEs). As part of the strategy, a draft law on processing SME financing and credit is to be passed and

an SME promotion agency is to be established by the end of 2002. In July 2002, the government reached an agreement with the Foreign Investment Advisory Service (FIAS) to undertake a study on administrative barriers to entry, such as lengthy and complex registration and licensing requirements. A law for the establishment of an Investment

Enterprises, infrastructure, finance and social reforms

1992
Apr   Two-tier banking system established

1993
Jul   First foreign-owned bank opened
Jul   Enterprise restructuring agency established

1995
Jul   Competition law enacted
Oct   Bankruptcy law enacted

1996
Mar   Securities and exchange commission established
May   Stock exchange established
Jul   First large enterprise liquidated
Dec   First pyramid scheme collapsed

1997
Jul   Law on transparency adopted
Nov   Pyramids placed under international administration

1998
Mar   State-owned Rural Commercial Bank closed
Jul   Banking law amended

1999
May   Capital adequacy ratio raised to 12 per cent
Nov   Credit ceilings lifted for private banks

2000
Jan   Secured transaction law enacted
Jun   National Commercial Bank sold to foreign investor
Jul   Mobile telecommunications company sold to foreign investor

2001
Feb   Second mobile licence awarded to foreign investor

2002
Mar   Deposit insurance law enacted
Oct   Bankruptcy law enacted

Promotion Agency that will provide "one-stop-shop" facilities for foreign investors and support an increase in non-privatisation FDI was approved in March 2002. A mediation centre with the aim of improving relations with the business community by providing alternative forms of conflict resolution will also be established during 2002. In addition, a new bankruptcy law was enacted in October 2002.

Infrastructure

Urgent reforms of the electric power sector initiated ...

The Albanian Electric Corporation (KESH), the main energy supplier in the country, continues to suffer from a long period of neglect and under-investment, as well as from energy loss and theft. The energy crisis, which became particularly acute during winter 2001–02, adversely affected industrial production, especially metallurgy and textiles, which slowed down in the last quarter of 2001. In response, the government, in consultation with the World Bank, put in place in January 2002 a new two-year energy sector action plan. The goals of this plan are to improve the financial situation of KESH, reduce energy losses and budgetary subsidies, increase generation capacity and diversify energy supply sources. However, implementation of the plan has been incomplete, with the targets for reducing losses being missed in the first half of 2002. In order to manage more effectively the use of electric energy for heating purposes, energy prices were doubled in January 2002 to USc 5.7 per kWh. In addition, the Prosecutors Office has been asked to prosecute cases of electricity theft submitted to their attention by KESH.

... while plans for its comprehensive restructuring are prepared.

The government is preparing to take the first steps in restructuring KESH, with a view towards its future privatisation. KESH is to be divided into production, transmission and distribution divisions by the beginning of 2003. Albania's energy regulatory body ERE will coordinate the sale and purchasing prices of electricity between the divisions. From January 2003, the different divisions of KESH are to maintain separate financial accounts.

Privatisation of the state-owned fixed-line telecommunication monopoly delayed.

The tender for the privatisation of the state-owned fixed-line telecommunication company, Albtelecom, announced in January 2002, failed to attract any interest. This reflects not only the weakening of the global telecommunication sector but also a number of company-specific impediments, such as unresolved financial and legal disputes, that were revealed during the tender process.

Financial institutions

Sale of the last state-owned bank fails for a second time.

The privatisation of the Savings Bank, the largest bank in Albania and the last one still in state hands, was postponed from the end of 2001 due to a lack of investor interest. The completion of the sale by the end of the first half of 2002 failed again for the same reason. A major factor deterring foreign investors is the Savings Bank's role in

financing the government deficit, covering 80 per cent of the Treasury bill market. In other developments, a law on deposit insurance was approved in March 2002. A Deposit Insurance Agency will be established to guarantee deposits of up to US$ 5,000, thus covering almost 60 per cent of current depositors. The large state insurance company INSIG is also to be prepared for privatisation by end-2002. Under the government's privatisation bill for INSIG, 51 per cent of the company's capital will be sold to a strategic investor and a maximum of 40 per cent will go to international financial institutions.

Social reform

Health and education reforms progress.

While Albania has one of the highest incidences of poverty in the region, health and education are the main priorities under the government's Poverty Reduction and Growth Strategy (PRGS), adopted in November 2001. The government's expenditure allocation for health and education between 2002 and 2004 is to increase by about 30 per cent and 20 per cent respectively, in real terms, to reach 3.2 per cent of GDP and 3.7 per cent of GDP respectively. In 2002, salaries of employees in the heath care and education sectors increased by 12 per cent, compared with an 8 per cent increase for total budgetary salaries. The aim is to retain and attract skilled employees in these sectors.

Comprehensive reform of pension system developed.

Pension reform is being developed, in cooperation with the World Bank, to reduce budgetary transfers and to improve the long-term financial viability of the pension system. As of February 2002, the contribution ceiling was raised from three to five times the minimum wage and the retirement age was increased to 65 years for men and to 60 for women (from the current ages of 60 and 55 respectively). At the same time, pensions were increased by 10 per cent in the cities and by 25 per cent for former members of agricultural cooperatives. As part of the pension reform, per capita contributions in the rural scheme were raised in January 2002 from US$ 7 to about US$ 16.8 to finance the planned increase in rural pension benefits.

Liberalisation	Privatisation	Infrastructure	Social reform
Current account convertibility – **full**	Primary privatisation method – **MEBOs**	Independent telecoms regulator – **yes**[1]	Share of the population in poverty –
Interest rate liberalisation – **full**	Secondary privatisation method – **vouchers**	Separation of railway accounts – **no**	**46.6 per cent**[2]
Wage regulation – **no**	Tradability of land – **limited de facto**	Independent electricity regulator – **yes**[1]	Private pension funds – **yes**

Stabilisation	Enterprises and markets	Financial sector	
Share of general government tax revenue in GDP – **15.9 per cent**	Competition Office – **yes**	Capital adequacy ratio – **12 per cent**	
		Deposit insurance system – **yes**	
Exchange rate regime – **managed float**		Secured transactions law – **yes**	
		Securities commission – **yes**	

	1993	1994	1995	1996	1997	1998	1999	2000	2001
Liberalisation									
Share of administered prices in CPI (in per cent)	na	na	na	na	na	na	na	na	na
Number of goods with administered prices in EBRD-15 basket	10.0	10.0	10.0	10.0	10.0	10.0	10.0	na	na
Share of trade with non-transition countries (in per cent)	na	na	na	na	na	95.6	96.3	95.2	91.2
Share of trade in GDP (in per cent)	60.1	38.4	35.8	42.9	37.3	33.8	38.1	35.3	39.9
Tariff revenues (in per cent of imports)	5.7	10.9	9.9	8.0	8.7	10.1	7.4	9.1	7.1
EBRD index of price liberalisation	3.0	3.0	3.0	3.0	3.0	3.0	3.0	3.0	3.0
EBRD index of forex and trade liberalisation	4.0	4.0	4.0	4.0	4.0	4.0	4.0	4.3	4.3
Privatisation									
Privatisation revenues (cumulative, in per cent of GDP)	1.8	3.0	3.1	3.3	3.6	3.6	3.9	7.0	8.7
Private sector share in GDP (in per cent)	40.0	50.0	60.0	75.0	75.0	75.0	75.0	75.0	75.0
Private sector share in employment (in per cent)	58.5	69.8	74.1	78.6	79.6	80.4	81.1	82.2	82.1
EBRD index of small-scale privatisation	3.0	3.0	4.0	4.0	4.0	4.0	4.0	4.0	4.0
EBRD index of large-scale privatisation	1.0	1.0	2.0	2.0	2.0	2.0	2.0	2.0	3.0
Enterprises									
Budgetary subsidies and current transfers (in per cent of GDP)	1.9	1.2	0.6	0.4	0.5	0.5	0.5	0.5	0.9
Effective statutory social security tax (in per cent)	na	na	na	na	37.3	na	na	32.5	na
Share of industry in total employment (in per cent)	na	10.2	8.3	7.6	8.0	7.8	5.7	5.5	5.2
Change in labour productivity in industry (in per cent)	na	na	23.8	26.5	-8.8	9.0	na	9.7	na
Investment rate/GDP (in per cent)	13.2	17.9	18.0	15.5	16.0	16.0	16.8	18.6	19.4
EBRD index of enterprise reform	1.0	2.0	2.0	2.0	2.0	2.0	2.0	2.0	2.3
EBRD index of competition policy	1.0	1.0	1.0	1.7	1.7	1.7	1.7	1.7	1.0
Infrastructure									
Main telephone lines per 100 inhabitants	1.2	1.2	1.2	1.7	2.3	3.1	3.7	3.9	6.0
Railway labour productivity (1989=100)	33.7	33.6	33.3	35.8	21.4	28.5	32.1	34.9	38.3
Electricity tariffs, USc kWh (collection rate in per cent)	na	na	4.8 (na)	4.3 (na)	3.0 (72)	3.2 (70)	3.5 (58)	2.8 (60)	2.9 (85)
GDP per unit of energy use (PPP in US dollars per kgoe)	6.8	7.2	8.5	8.5	9.5	9.1	10.4	na	na
EBRD index of infrastructure reform	1.0	1.0	1.3	1.3	1.3	1.3	1.3	2.0	2.0
Financial institutions									
Number of banks (foreign owned)[3]	na	6 (3)	6 (3)	8 (3)	9 (3)	10 (8)	13 (11)	13 (12)	13 (12)
Asset share of state-owned banks (in per cent)	na	97.8	94.5	93.7	89.9	85.6	81.1	64.8	59.2
Non-performing loans (in per cent of total loans)[4]	na	na	34.9	40.1	91.3	35.4	32.7	42.6	6.9
Domestic credit to private sector (in per cent of GDP)	na	3.9	3.6	3.9	3.8	0.6	2.0	3.0	4.0
Stock market capitalisation (in per cent of GDP)	na	na	na	na	na	na	na	na	na
EBRD index of banking sector reform	1.3	2.0	2.0	2.0	2.0	2.0	2.0	2.3	2.3
EBRD index of reform of non-banking financial institutions	1.0	1.0	1.0	1.7	1.7	1.7	1.7	1.7	2.0
Legal environment									
EBRD rating of legal extensiveness (company law)	na	na	na	na	2.0	2.0	2.0	3.3	2.7
EBRD rating of legal effectiveness (company law)	na	na	na	na	2.0	2.0	1.7	1.7	2.0
Social sector									
Expenditures on health and education (in per cent of GDP)	na	na	na	na	na	na	5.1	6.1	6.5
Life expectancy at birth, total (years)	71.3	72.5	71.3	71.7	71.7	na	74.0	74.0	na
Basic school enrolment ratio (in per cent)	95.3	96.6	96.8	96.1	94.6	92.6	89.8	87.3	na
Earnings inequality (GINI-coefficient)	na	na	na	na	na	na	na	na	na

[1] Independent regulators are in place but most regulatory functions are still carried out by the government.
[2] Percentage of population living on less than US$ 2 per day.
[3] Includes branches of foreign banks.
[4] Includes loans of banks under forced administration.

	1994	1995	1996	1997	1998	1999	2000	2001 Estimate	2002 Projection
Output and expenditure					*(Percentage change in real terms)*				
GDP	8.3	13.3	9.1	-7.0	8.0	7.3	7.8	6.5	6.0
Private consumption	na	na	na	na	na	na	na	na	na
Public consumption	na	na	na	na	na	na	na	na	na
Gross fixed investment	na	na	na	na	na	na	na	na	na
Exports of goods and services	na	na	na	na	na	na	na	na	na
Imports of goods and services	na	na	na	na	na	na	na	na	na
Industrial gross output	-2.0	6.0	13.6	-5.6	4.1	6.4	5.0	6.5	na
Agricultural gross output	8.3	13.2	3.0	1.0	5.0	3.7	4.5	1.4	na
Employment					*(Percentage change)*				
Labour force (end-year)	1.3	1.8	1.8	-23.6	1.5	-1.1	-1.8	-2.7	na
Employment (end-year)	9.7	5.7	-2.5	-0.8	-2.0	-0.4	-1.3	-0.2	na
					(In per cent of labour force)				
Unemployment (end-year) [1]	16.1	13.9	9.3	14.9	17.8	18.0	16.8	14.6	na
Prices and wages					*(Percentage change)*				
Consumer prices (annual average)	22.6	7.8	12.7	33.2	20.6	0.4	0.1	3.1	5.3
Consumer prices (end-year)	15.8	6.0	17.4	42.1	8.7	-1.0	4.2	3.5	4.0
Producer prices (annual average)	na	na	na	na	na	na	na	na	na
Producer prices (end-year)	na	na	na	na	na	na	na	na	na
Gross average monthly earnings in economy (annual average)	46.9	25.6	20.0	0.0	26.1	-0.3	14.3	13.0	na
Government sector [2]					*(In per cent of GDP)*				
General government balance	-12.6	-10.1	-12.1	-12.6	-10.4	-11.4	-9.1	-8.5	-8.0
General government expenditure	36.4	33.4	30.3	29.4	30.7	32.7	31.4	31.5	na
General government debt	na	na	na	68.9	60.1	62.2	71.5	72.6	na
Monetary sector					*(Percentage change)*				
Broad money (M2, end-year)	40.6	51.8	43.8	28.5	20.6	22.3	12.1	11.8	na
Domestic credit (end-year)	17.8	-10.0	48.1	43.0	13.2	12.3	39.0	32.0	na
					(In per cent of GDP)				
Broad money (M2, end-year)	38.4	46.8	55.0	58.1	52.0	57.9	60.9	62.1	na
Interest and exchange rates					*(In per cent per annum, end-year)*				
Refinancing rate	25.0	20.5	24.0	32.0	22.9	17.8	10.8	10.2	na
Treasury bill rate (3-month maturity)	10.0	14.7	21.1	35.3	19.9	14.8	7.8	8.0	na
Deposit rate (1 year) [3]	16.5	13.7	19.1	28.5	16.5	9.1	7.7	7.7	na
Lending rate (1 year) [4]	20.0	21.0	28.8	43.0	25.0	25.8	23.7	24.0	na
					(Leks per US dollar)				
Exchange rate (end-year)	95.0	94.5	103.7	149.8	141.4	135.2	142.6	136.6	na
Exchange rate (annual average)	95.4	93.0	104.8	149.6	151.2	138.1	143.7	143.8	na
External sector					*(In millions of US dollars)*				
Current account	-279	-177	-245	-276	-186	-265	-260	-258	-372
Trade balance	-460	-475	-692	-518	-621	-846	-814	-1,027	-1,072
Merchandise exports	141	205	229	167	205	275	256	305	342
Merchandise imports	601	680	921	685	826	1,121	1,070	1,332	1,414
Foreign direct investment, net	65	89	97	42	45	51	141	204	153
Gross reserves (end-year), excluding gold	204	240	275	306	384	485	608	680	na
External debt stock	1,074	756	811	841	970	1,068	1,130	1,157	na
					(In months of imports of goods and services)				
Gross reserves (end-year), excluding gold	2.9	2.7	4.0	3.8	4.2	4.9	4.4	4.6	na
					(In per cent of exports of goods and services)				
Debt service	19.7	2.5	6.0	6.1	6.2	2.8	3.3	4.7	na
Memorandum items					*(Denominations as indicated)*				
Population (annual average, millions)	3.2	3.2	3.3	3.4	3.4	3.4	3.4	3.1	na
GDP (in millions of leks)	184,393	229,793	280,998	341,716	460,631	506,200	539,210	590,237	658,811
GDP per capita (in US dollars)	604	761	817	681	903	1,078	1,094	1,330	na
Share of industry in GDP (in per cent)	12.5	11.7	12.2	12.4	11.9	11.9	11.5	27.3	na
Share of agriculture in GDP (in per cent)	54.6	54.6	51.5	56.0	54.4	52.6	51.0	49.1	na
Current account/GDP (in per cent)	-14.4	-7.2	-9.1	-12.1	-6.1	-7.2	-6.9	-6.3	-6.0
External debt - reserves, in US$ millions	870	516	536	535	586	583	522	477	na
External debt/GDP (in per cent)	55.6	30.6	30.2	36.8	31.8	29.1	30.1	28.2	na
External debt/exports of goods (in per cent)	487.3	248.9	226.4	364.4	332.7	196.2	160.5	137.7	na

[1] Figures do not include emigrant workers abroad who accounted
    for an estimated 18 per cent of the total labour force in 1995.
[2] General government includes the state, municipalities and extra-budgetary funds.
    Budget balance on a commitment basis.

[3] Until 1995, the figures show the floor of the band set by the Central Bank.
    Thereafter, data refer to weighted average interest rates on new one-year
    deposits in commercial banks.
[4] Until 1995, data refer to the guideline rate announced by the Central Bank.
    Thereafter, data refer to weighted average interest rates for one-year loans by
    commercial banks.

Armenia

Key reform challenges

- The government must advance its efforts to improve the investment climate and encourage enterprise restructuring, thereby broadening economic growth and spreading the benefits more widely.

- Poor integration in regional markets is currently holding back export-led growth. Improvements to the trade infrastructure and the removal of political trade restrictions are needed to boost exports and allow enterprises to exploit economies of scale.

- Fiscal discipline, including consistent revenue collection and measures to cut quasi-fiscal expenditures, is key to preserving macroeconomic stability, clearing past arrears and maintaining external debt at a sustainable level.

Liberalisation

Non-tariff barriers hold back regional trade.

Armenia has one of the most open trade regimes in the CIS, with its trade policies essentially consistent with the WTO rules. The government is committed to complete the WTO accession process as soon as possible. However, trade is being held back by a weak transport infrastructure, insufficient communication links and poor customs administration. The main impediment to regional trade is the lack of official trade relations with neighbouring Turkey and Azerbaijan, a remnant of the 1994 Nagorno-Karabakh conflict. Armenia recognises that the resolution of this issue is crucial to strengthen its regional integration. According to one estimate, the re-establishment of trade relations with Turkey and Azerbaijan would boost Armenian exports by up to 30 per cent. However, little progress has been made this year in the ongoing negotiations.

Stabilisation

Low government revenues remain a concern.

While the Central Bank has established a good track record on monetary policy, fiscal policy continues to pose challenges. The main problem is the low level of revenues, which forces the government to keep a tight grip on expenditures. In 2001, total revenue and grants amounted to 17.1 per cent of GDP and total revenues to 15.5 per cent of GDP. The quasi-fiscal support to the irrigation and energy sectors further constrains the government's ability to provide an adequate level of public services and reduce the stock of arrears accumulated mostly in 1999–2000. Revenue collection has improved in the first part of 2002, but public finance remains vulnerable and reliant on external official sources of finance.

External deficit and debt still high.

Substantial transfers from its diaspora allow Armenia to run a large current account deficit that would not otherwise be sustainable. Nevertheless, both external imbalances and debt must be reduced to more sustainable

levels and over the past year Armenia has made progress in this regard. In 2001, the current account deficit fell to 9.5 per cent of GDP, compared with 14.6 per cent the year before. The improvement was due mainly to increased exports, which grew by 20.8 per cent. Export growth has continued in 2002, increasing by as much as 40 per cent in the first eight months, but there are structural issues that limit the scope for further growth. At the same time, a proposed debt-for-equity swap with Russia, the main bilateral creditor, would further improve the external debt profile. The deal, on which political agreement has apparently been reached, is to be implemented in early 2003.

Privatisation

Last stage of the privatisation programme begins.

The final stage of the Armenian privatisation programme, approved in 2001, foresees the sale (or liquidation) of more than 900 enterprises, practically the entire portfolio of remaining state-owned enterprises, over a period of three years. Implementation of the programme is moving ahead slowly. Privatisation revenues in 2001 were half the expected level, with only 37 enterprises being sold between January and May 2002. In mid-2002, the government agreed to sell the large Nairit chemical plant to the British trading group that had assumed management control a few months earlier. An agreement has also been reached with a South American diaspora investor on Zvartnots airport. With little interest being shown from large Western sponsors, most firms have been sold to Russian investors or entrepreneurs connected to the diaspora.

Enterprise reform

Modest progress on key investment climate issues ...

Armenia's difficult investment climate is one of the main obstacles to start-ups and foreign investment. The business community remains concerned about the lack of transparency in the regulatory system, burdensome administrative procedures and the uneven application of laws. Reform efforts

are under way in the regulatory, legal and judicial systems, including streamlining the business regulations (e.g. governing construction and land development), the drafting of a new bankruptcy law and training for lawyers and judges. However, despite increased training efforts, the capacity of the judiciary to deal with commercial cases remains limited. Frequent changes in laws and delays in their implementation contribute to uncer-

Enterprises, infrastructure, finance and social reforms

1992
Dec   Central Bank law adopted

1993
May   Stock exchange established

1995
May   Bankruptcy law adopted
Jun   Foreign bank ownership allowed
Sep   Banking crisis peaked

1996
Mar   First foreign-owned bank opened
Jun   Banking law amended
Jul   IAS audit of banking system conducted

1997
Jan   Bankruptcy law enacted
Jun   Energy Regulatory Commission established
Jun   Energy law adopted
Jul   Financial rehabilitation plan for the energy sector adopted
Dec   National telecommunications operator privatised

1998
Feb   Telecommunications law adopted
Feb   Transport law adopted
Mar   IAS accounting for banks introduced
May   Law on accountancy adopted
Nov   Securities and Exchange Commission established

1999
Jan   New poverty benefits system introduced
Jan   New civil code introduced
Jan   Energy tariffs increased
Apr   New reserve requirements for commercial banks established

2000
Jun   New securities market law adopted
Jul   Yerevan water utility transferred to private management
Dec   New competition law adopted

2001
Mar   New energy law adopted
Jul   Bank capital requirements raised

2002
Jul   Bank capital requirements raised further

---

tainty among both civil servants and the private sector as to the latest status and the interpretation of laws in practice.

... and in the fight against corruption.
Bureaucratic corruption is still seen as endemic by many investors and making "facilitation payments" remains a widely accepted way of doing business. The problem is recognised by the government, which has declared improvements in governance and implementation of an anti-corruption programme a top priority. The civil service law, introduced in 2001, set limits on the participation of state officials in business enterprises and the 2001 financial disclosure law aims to increase transparency by requiring all highly placed officials to fully declare their property and income.

Industrial growth picks up, but its base is narrow.
After a period of relative stagnation, industrial growth has begun to accelerate. Industrial output rose by 11 per cent in the first five months of 2002, outperforming the rest of the economy for the first time in several years. However, the recovery remains narrow and is based on growth in a relatively small number of firms. One of the main engines of growth remains the diamond sector, where a handful of enterprises generate close to a third of Armenia's exports. In other sectors, growth can similarly be traced back to changes in relatively few firms. The reasons for this narrow output base are the small size of the domestic market, which does not allow firms to exploit economies of scale, the difficult investment climate, which is holding back start-ups, and the slow progress in enterprise restructuring, which means much of the existing capacity remains idle. Privatisation has mostly led to a consolidation of control by incumbent managers, with little injection of new capital and know-how.

Infrastructure

Electricity distribution companies sold.
Two attempts to privatise the country's four power distribution utilities failed in 2001 owing to a lack of interest by leading international power companies. Following the second tender, the government merged the four utilities into a single company and in August 2002 announced the sale of an 80 per cent stake in the new company to a UK-based investor. Plans for further divestitures focus on generation. As part of a debt-for-equity swap between Russia and Armenia, ownership over the Hrazdan power generation complex will be transferred to the Russian government, with management entrusted to RAO UES.

Financial institutions

Weaknesses in the banking sector persist despite tighter regulation.
The Central Bank has continued its policy to strengthen banking regulation and encourage consolidation. The minimum capital requirement for existing banks has been further increased to US$ 1.65 million, in accordance with a schedule that should see the standard rise to US$ 5 million by 2005. The US$ 5 million level already applies to new banks. Nevertheless, the banking system remains small, with assets equivalent to about 25 per cent of GDP, and populated by a large number of relatively weak banks with average capital of US$ 2-3 million. Total capital fell from US$ 60 million in 2001 to US$ 36 million in February 2002, as a result of significant losses suffered by a number of banks. About a quarter of Armenia's banks are currently under temporary external administration and a similar fraction are reported to be in financial difficulties. The government has agreed to begin liquidating these banks as part of their IMF programme.

Social reform

Census exposes the scale of emigration ...
A census carried out in autumn 2001 has revealed that between 1991 and 2001 Armenia's population has fallen from 3.7 million to 3.0 million. The census provides a quantitative appraisal of Armenia's emigration problem, of which the authorities have long been aware but which had not been reflected in official population statistics. Taking into account domestic developments, the figures suggest that as many as 900,000 people, or a quarter of the population, may have left the country since independence. The majority of emigrants are young and educated and their departure contributes to an erosion of the skill base on which the local economy relies. The government intends to use the census results to restructure government policies in core social sectors, including for improvement of poverty monitoring and alleviation.

... in response to widespread poverty.
Much of the emigration is motivated by economic factors. Despite eight consecutive years of economic growth, poverty is still widespread. Social assistance programmes such as the poverty family benefit have helped to alleviate extreme poverty, but over half the families and 80 per cent of children remain below the national poverty line, according to a Ministry of Health estimate. Like other low-income countries, Armenia has embarked on a comprehensive review of its poverty reduction strategy, in collaboration with the World Bank, the IMF and the donor community. The new strategy should be finalised by the end of 2002.

Liberalisation

Current account convertibility – **full**

Interest rate liberalisation – **full**

Wage regulation – **no**

Stabilisation

Share of general government tax revenue
 in GDP – **17.1 per cent**

Exchange rate regime – **floating** [1]

Privatisation

Primary privatisation method – **direct sales**

Secondary privatisation method – **MEBOs**

Tradability of land – **full except foreigners**

Enterprises and markets

Competition Office – **yes**

Infrastructure

Independent telecoms regulator – **no**

Separation of railway accounts – **no**

Independent electricity regulator – **yes**

Financial sector

Capital adequacy ratio – **12 per cent**

Deposit insurance system – **no**

Secured transactions law – **yes**

Securities commission – **yes**

Social reform

Share of the population in poverty –
 86.2 per cent [2]

Private pension funds – **no**

	1993	1994	1995	1996	1997	1998	1999	2000	2001
Liberalisation									
Share of administered prices in CPI (in per cent)	8.9	12.8	6.2	7.7	7.0	8.0	9.3	5.4	5.4
Number of goods with administered prices in EBRD-15 basket	3.0	2.0	2.0	1.0	1.0	1.0	1.0	1.0	1.0
Share of trade with non-transition countries (in per cent)	na	34.3	52.4	55.5	55.4	60.0	62.0	78.4	79.8
Share of trade in GDP (in per cent)	87.7	94.0	73.4	65.8	62.7	54.7	52.5	56.7	53.2
Tariff revenues (in per cent of imports)	6.1	0.7	1.0	1.9	2.7	2.8	2.1	2.1	na
EBRD index of price liberalisation	3.0	3.0	3.0	3.0	3.0	3.0	3.0	3.0	3.0
EBRD index of forex and trade liberalisation	2.0	2.0	3.0	4.0	4.0	4.0	4.0	4.0	4.0
Privatisation									
Privatisation revenues (cumulative, in per cent of GDP)	3.3	3.4	3.4	3.4	3.4	5.6	6.7	8.8	na
Private sector share in GDP (in per cent)	40.0	40.0	45.0	50.0	55.0	60.0	60.0	60.0	60.0
Private sector share in employment (in per cent)	43.6	46.6	48.8	59.9	61.7	68.5	71.7	72.9	na
EBRD index of small-scale privatisation	2.0	2.3	2.7	3.0	3.0	3.3	3.3	3.3	3.7
EBRD index of large-scale privatisation	1.0	1.0	2.0	3.0	3.0	3.0	3.0	3.0	3.0
Enterprises									
Budgetary subsidies and current transfers (in per cent of GDP)	na	12.8	0.9	0.1	0.6	0.1	1.4	0.7	na
Effective statutory social security tax (in per cent)	na	12.9	19.1	19.3	na	na	na	na	na
Share of industry in total employment (in per cent)	23.5	23.9	20.5	17.8	16.7	15.7	15.0	14.3	na
Change in labour productivity in industry (in per cent)	0.3	7.5	19.0	20.4	12.4	6.6	12.9	13.2	na
Investment rate/GDP (in per cent)	12.5	20.2	16.2	17.9	16.2	19.1	18.4	19.2	na
EBRD index of enterprise reform	1.0	1.0	2.0	2.0	2.0	2.0	2.0	2.0	2.0
EBRD index of competition policy	1.0	1.0	1.0	1.0	1.0	1.0	1.0	1.0	2.0
Infrastructure									
Main telephone lines per 100 inhabitants	15.4	15.7	15.5	15.4	15.0	15.7	15.5	15.2	14.0
Railway labour productivity (1989=100)	28.8	26.3	20.3	16.9	19.9	20.1	16.2	15.2	17.2
Electricity tariffs, USc kWh (collection rate in per cent)	na	0.4 (na)	1.5 (na)	2.2 (76)	3.3 (80)	4.9 (87)	4.7 (88)	4.6 (80)	4.4 (87)
GDP per unit of energy use (PPP in US dollars per kgoe)	3.0	4.7	4.4	4.4	4.3	4.4	4.9	na	na
EBRD index of infrastructure reform	1.0	1.3	1.7	1.7	2.0	2.0	2.3	2.3	2.3
Financial institutions									
Number of banks (foreign owned)	na	41 (1)	35 (3)	33 (4)	30 (4)	31 (10)	32 (11)	31 (11)	30 (13)
Asset share of state-owned banks (in per cent)	na	1.9	2.4	3.2	3.4	3.7	2.4	0.3	na
Non-performing loans (in per cent of total loans)	na	34.0	36.1	22.6	7.9	10.4	4.3	6.2	6.0
Domestic credit to private sector (in per cent of GDP)	na	na	na	na	na	na	5.9	7.5	6.3
Stock market capitalisation (in per cent of GDP)	na	na	na	0.2	1.0	1.0	1.3	1.3	1.2
EBRD index of banking sector reform	1.0	1.0	2.0	2.0	2.3	2.3	2.3	2.3	2.3
EBRD index of reform of non-banking financial institutions	1.0	1.0	1.0	1.0	1.0	2.0	2.0	2.0	2.0
Legal environment									
EBRD rating of legal extensiveness (company law)	na	na	na	na	3.0	4.0	3.7	3.7	2.7
EBRD rating of legal effectiveness (company law)	na	na	na	na	3.0	3.0	2.0	2.0	2.0
Social sector									
Expenditures on health and education (in per cent of GDP)	7.8	3.4	5.1	3.5	3.4	4.5	3.7	4.2	na
Life expectancy at birth, total (years)	71.1	71.4	72.3	72.7	73.7	74.4	73.0	73.6	na
Basic school enrolment ratio (in per cent)	86.4	82.2	81.4	82.8	82.9	82.6	81.6	79.5	na
Earnings inequality (GINI-coefficient)	36.6	32.1	38.1	na	na	na	na	48.6	na

[1] Rare interventions but no explicit exchange rate target.

[2] Based on the international poverty line. The poverty rate based on the
 national poverty line is 55 per cent.

	1994	1995	1996	1997	1998	1999	2000	2001	2002
								Estimate	*Projection*
Output and expenditure	*(Percentage change in real terms)*								
GDP	5.4	6.9	5.9	3.3	7.3	3.3	6.0	9.6	8.0
Private consumption	5.2	9.0	3.8	7.3	5.3	1.4	5.9	15.2	na
Public consumption	-3.2	0.2	-2.4	-2.3	-2.2	1.3	-0.3	na	na
Gross fixed investment	44.9	-17.3	10.3	2.1	12.0	0.6	8.7	24.8	na
Exports of goods and services	na	-7.8	-9.7	28.9	8.9	6.5	16.6	20.8	na
Imports of good and services	na	-10.3	-5.5	24.4	5.0	-8.1	5.1	1.2	na
Industrial gross output	5.3	1.5	1.4	0.9	-2.5	5.2	6.4	3.8	na
Agricultural gross output	3.2	4.7	1.8	-5.9	13.1	1.3	-2.3	11.6	na
Employment	*(Percentage change)*								
Labour force (end-year)	-2.2	-0.8	0.1	-2.8	-4.0	-0.9	-0.7	-1.3	na
Employment (end-year)	-3.6	-0.8	-2.8	-4.4	-2.5	-2.9	-1.2	0.2	na
	(In per cent of labour force)								
Unemployment (annual average) [1]	6.6	6.7	9.3	10.8	9.4	11.2	11.7	9.6	na
Prices and wages	*(Percentage change)*								
Consumer prices (annual average)	4,962.0	175.8	18.7	14.0	8.7	0.7	-0.8	3.2	3.0
Consumer prices (end-year)	1,761.0	32.2	5.8	21.8	-1.3	2.1	0.4	3.0	3.0
Producer prices (annual average)	4,714.2	275.4	22.4	19.0	13.4	2.3	0.8	-0.4	na
Producer prices (end-year)	2,272.2	38.3	9.6	12.4	8.2	3.8	0.4	-4.3	na
Gross average monthly earnings in economy (annual average)	2,726.9	243.6	45.7	37.8	31.0	19.2	22.5	5.4	na
Government sector [2]	*(In per cent of GDP)*								
General government balance	-16.5	-9.0	-8.5	-5.8	-4.9	-7.4	-6.3	-3.8	-3.2
General government expenditure	44.1	28.9	26.1	25.5	25.6	30.1	25.9	23.9	na
General government debt	na	na	na	na	na	na	na	na	na
Monetary sector	*(Percentage change)*								
Broad money (M2, end-year)	na	na	na	8.7	23.3	-2.2	36.3	10.8	na
Domestic credit (end-year)	1,510.6	68.0	27.8	6.3	60.8	7.7	22.2	-3.9	na
	(In per cent of GDP)								
Broad money (M2, end-year)	na	na	6.5	5.8	6.0	5.7	7.4	7.2	na
Interest and exchange rates	*(In per cent per annum, end-year)*								
Refinancing rate	210.0	52.0	60.0	54.0	39.0	43.0	25.0	15.0	na
Money market rate [3]	na	na	48.6	36.4	27.8	23.7	18.6	19.4	na
Deposit rate [4]	na	63.2	32.2	26.1	24.9	27.4	18.1	14.9	na
Lending rate [4]	na	111.9	66.4	54.2	48.5	38.9	31.6	26.7	na
	(Drams per US dollar)								
Exchange rate (end-year)	405.5	402.0	435.1	495.0	522.0	523.8	552.2	561.8	na
Exchange rate (annual average)	288.7	405.9	414.0	490.8	504.9	535.1	539.5	555.1	na
External sector	*(In millions of US dollars)*								
Current account	-104	-218	-291	-295	-403	-307	-278	-201	-199
Trade balance	-178	-403	-469	-559	-577	-474	-464	-420	-389
Merchandise exports	215	271	290	234	229	247	310	353	458
Merchandise imports	394	674	760	793	806	721	773	773	847
Foreign direct investment, net	8	25	18	52	221	122	104	70	75
Gross reserves (end-year), excluding gold	32	100	171	243	298	305	314	329	na
External debt stock	200	387	533	679	787	855	862	905	na
	(In months of imports of goods and services)								
Gross reserves (end-year), excluding gold	0.9	1.5	2.1	2.9	3.9	3.8	3.8	3.7	na
	(In per cent of exports of goods and services)								
Debt service	3.4	20.9	20.3	14.2	19.0	14.3	10.7	9.7	na
Memorandum items	*(Denominations as indicated)*								
Population (end-year, millions) [5]	3.2	3.1	3.2	3.1	3.1	3.1	3.1	3.1	na
GDP (in billions of drams)	187.1	522.3	661.2	804.3	955.4	987.1	1,031.0	1,175.0	1,286.3
GDP per capita (in US dollars)	205.1	408.9	507.0	522.2	605.1	589.6	614.0	678.5	na
Share of industry in GDP (in per cent)	29.1	24.2	23.8	23.9	21.6	21.5	22.0	20.2	na
Share of agriculture in GDP (in per cent)	43.5	40.7	33.0	30.4	30.8	25.4	22.5	25.5	na
Current account/GDP (in per cent)	-16.0	-17.0	-18.2	-18.0	-21.3	-16.6	-14.6	-9.5	-8.9
External debt - reserves, in US$ millions	168.1	287.4	362.3	435.5	489.0	550.0	548.0	576.2	na
External debt/GDP (in per cent)	30.9	30.1	33.4	41.4	41.6	46.3	45.1	42.8	na
External debt/exports of goods and services (in per cent)	87.5	129.2	144.9	205.5	218.6	223.2	192.8	167.6	na

[1] Registered unemployed. Unofficial estimates indicate substantially higher unemployment.
[2] Consolidated accounts of the Republican government and the local authorities.
[3] Average of one to three month Treasury bills.
[4] Weighted average rate for maturities of 15 days to less than one year.
[5] Official figures. Based on 2001 census.

Azerbaijan

Liberalisation

Foreign exchange and trade liberalised further.

In June 2002, the National Bank of Azerbaijan issued new rules which further liberalise foreign currency transactions. The new regulations include an increase in the permissible level of advance payments for imports from US$ 10,000 to US$ 25,000. They remove all restrictions on residents withdrawing cash from banks in foreign currency and permit individuals to carry out foreign currency transactions through authorised banks without having to open an account. The authorities have also informed the IMF of their intention to accept some of the obligations of Article VIII of the IMF's Articles of Agreement (Sections 2, 3 and 4), although some issues still have to be resolved. At the same time, a comprehensive Customs Committee reform programme was adopted in January 2002 to improve the efficiency and accountability of the customs administration.

Stabilisation

Energy sector reform puts some pressure on inflation and the measured fiscal deficit.

The authorities have agreed with the IMF on a somewhat higher inflation target of 3 per cent for 2002. The new target takes into account the likely inflationary impact of increased energy prices, following the replacement of preferential tariffs with explicit subsidies for some customer groups including refugees, internally displaced people and pensioners. During the first half of 2002, inflation had already reached 2.3 per cent. While the consolidated government budget recorded a surplus of 0.9 per cent of GDP in 2001 (a 2.9 per cent deficit excluding the Oil Fund), measures to bring energy subsidies on budget are likely to result in a small deficit in 2002.

Poverty alleviation and broad-based growth remain the key challenges.

Key development challenges remain poverty alleviation and diversification away from hydrocarbon-related activities. A comprehensive series of measures will be included in the government's poverty reduction strategy and their implementation will require significant financing from external and domestic sources. A significant source of potential funding is the national Oil Fund, which had assets in excess of US$ 600 million by mid-August. Reform priorities include strengthening the financial sector, improving governance, reforming the judiciary and implementing the second privatisation programme to support growth in the non-oil sector.

Privatisation

Some privatisation progress achieved, but large-scale privatisation remains slow.

By the end of 2001, the authorities had made substantial progress in small-scale privatisation, with more than 29,000 small enterprises privatised. The corporatisation and privatisation of medium-sized companies has also advanced, but privatisation of large-scale companies remains slow. The most noteworthy success over the last year was the privatisation of the electricity distribution company in Baku. In addition, tenders have been conducted for the sale of the remaining electricity distribution companies and negotiations with preferred bidders are to be finalised shortly. The privatisation of gas and water utilities and the necessary changes in the regulatory framework are under preparation with assistance from the World Bank. However, proposed large-scale privatisations in the telecommunications, banking, transport, chemical and manufacturing sectors have yet to materialise.

Enterprise reform

New measures adopted to improve governance and to level the playing field.

The authorities have implemented several significant measures to improve governance under the terms of the Poverty Reduction and Growth Facility (PRGF) with the IMF. Recent measures include the adoption of an improved public procurement law, the transparent management and external audit of the Oil Fund and improvements in tax and customs administration. In December 2001, parliament passed the first reading of the anti-corruption legislation and revised the law on the Chamber of Accounts to increase the

Enterprises, infrastructure, finance and social reforms

1994
Jul	Bankruptcy law adopted
Jul	Bank consolidation begins
Sep	First international oil PSA signed
Nov	Law on joint-stock companies adopted

1995
Jun	Law on unfair competition adopted
Aug	Railway law adopted

1996
Jun	Banking law adopted
Aug	Law on natural monopolies adopted
Sep	Bank restructuring commences

1997
Feb	Law on competitive government procurement adopted
Jun	BIS capital adequacy enacted
Jun	Amended bankruptcy law adopted
Jul	Telecommunications law adopted
Dec	Northern pipeline to Novorossiisk opened

1998
Apr	Electricity law adopted
Aug	Pledge law adopted
Sep	New securities law adopted
Nov	Tender for privatisation of International Bank authorised
Dec	Western pipeline to Georgia opened

1999
Oct	Water law adopted
Dec	Decree on Oil Fund issued

2000
Mar	Baku-Ceyhan pipeline agreement ratified

2001
Mar	Shakh Deniz gas purchase agreements with Turkey signed
May	Agroprom's banking licence revoked
Dec	Revised Law on Chamber of Accounts passed

2002
Mar	Energy sector reform plan passed by President
Jul	Minimum capital requirements increased by National Bank
Aug	Minister of Transport appointed

Chamber's supervisory powers and independence. The IMF has agreed that the 2002 budget contains adequate funding for the Chamber, which has the authority to audit and publicly disclose its findings on all government agencies and extra-budgetary funds. Tax administration was improved further with the strengthening of the large taxpayer unit and the approval and publication of all regulations necessary for the implementation of the new tax code. All legal entities (other than SOCAR) will now be required to pay tax according to their legal liabilities, whereas large state enterprises were previously permitted to negotiate their tax liabilities.

Infrastructure

Energy sector reform plan progresses.
A comprehensive energy sector reform programme was adopted by presidential decree in March 2002. The plan aims to address low collection rates and poorly directed subsidies, which have led to substantial quasi-fiscal deficits and have discouraged industrial restructuring. Measures include the clarification of subsidies and their explicit inclusion in the government budget, the privatisation of electricity and gas distribution companies, the restructuring of Azerenerji and Azerigaz, the creation of a tariff board, and the gradual reduction of the domestic-export price differential for oil, oil products and natural gas. The plan also aims to separate SOCAR's services, transport and social functions, and either privatise the separated enterprises or transfer ownership to alternative institutions. Progress is likely to be slow, however, given the complexity of the task and the final restructuring programme is not expected for some time.

A Ministry of Transport has been created.
The long-awaited creation of the Ministry of Transport has been completed with the appointment of a Minister of Transport in August 2002. The establishment of the Ministry paves the way for the separation of policy and regulatory functions from commercial activities and privatisation within the sector.

Financial institutions

Banking sector consolidation continues.
The Ministry of Finance re-capitalised United Universal Bank in February 2002 by issuing it with state debentures to the value of AZM 30 billion (US$ 7.1 million). The Ministry also fully paid-in United Universal's share capital at International Bank of Azerbaijan (IBA) in the first half of 2002. The National Bank has also terminated the licences of nine banks, thereby reducing the number of active banks in Azerbaijan to 45 and further consolidating the sector. In July 2002, the managements of Promtekbank and Mbank announced their intention to merge later in the year, pending agreement of their shareholders at a meeting scheduled for September. Other mergers are expected to follow. However, the deposit base of the sector continues to be dominated by IBA. Prospects for the long-awaited privatisation of this bank have improved with the IMF requesting a memorandum of understanding on its privatisation, prior to the Fund releasing the third tranche of the PRGF programme. The government seems likely to agree to the privatisation by 2004.

Prudential regulation strengthened, but enforcement is key.
In July 2002, the National Bank increased the minimum capital requirement for local banks from US$ 2 million to US$ 2.5 million, and announced its intention to increase the requirement to US$ 5 million by the end of 2005. The strict enforcement of the prudential standards is, however, key to ensure a level playing field and to encourage further consolidation of the sector. The National Bank also increased the ceiling on the foreign share of banking sector capital from 30 to 50 per cent, in an attempt to increase competition in the sector. However, the announced withdrawal of the main foreign-owned bank, HSBC, in March 2002 is a significant setback to the development of, and competition in, the banking sector.

Social reform

Oil Fund reserves to fund immediate priorities of the poverty reduction strategy.
Following the national workshops in early July 2002, the draft poverty reduction strategy was distributed for final comment at the beginning of August. The strategy is expected to receive government approval at the beginning of September and its implementation should be officially launched at a National Conference at the end of October. The World Bank is also providing technical assistance for the creation of an adequate social safety net and the government has allocated US$ 75 million from the Oil Fund to improve the living conditions of the refugees and internally displaced people currently living in camps in the Bilasuvar region.

Liberalisation

Current account convertibility – **limited**

Interest rate liberalisation – **full**

Wage regulation – **no**

Stabilisation

Share of general government tax revenue
in GDP – **22.4 per cent**

Exchange rate regime – **managed float**

Privatisation

Primary privatisation method –
cash auctions

Secondary privatisation method – **vouchers**

Tradability of land – **limited de jure**

Enterprises and markets

Competition Office – **yes**

Infrastructure

Independent telecoms regulator – **no**

Separation of railway accounts – **no**

Independent electricity regulator – **no**

Financial sector

Capital adequacy ratio – **8 per cent**

Deposit insurance system – **no**

Secured transactions law – **restricted**

Securities commission – **yes**

Social reform

Share of the population in poverty –
64.2 per cent [1]

Private pension funds – **no**

	1993	1994	1995	1996	1997	1998	1999	2000	2001
Liberalisation									
Share of administered prices in CPI (in per cent)	na	8.0	8.0	8.0	6.0	6.0	na	na	na
Number of goods with administered prices in EBRD-15 basket	na	12.0	12.0	4.0	3.0	3.0	1.0	1.0	na
Share of trade with non-transition countries (in per cent)	na	58.4	58.3	53.1	43.8	43.7	59.2	78.2	79.3
Share of trade in GDP (in per cent)	115.8	116.8	67.7	66.9	55.1	54.0	53.7	64.4	62.0
Tariff revenues (in per cent of imports)	1.2	1.1	1.6	1.9	5.5	4.4	5.4	7.2	7.0
EBRD index of price liberalisation	3.0	3.0	3.0	3.0	3.0	3.0	3.0	3.0	3.0
EBRD index of forex and trade liberalisation	1.0	1.0	2.0	2.0	2.3	3.0	3.3	3.3	3.3
Privatisation									
Privatisation revenues (cumulative, in per cent of GDP)	0.0	0.0	0.0	0.1	0.3	0.9	1.5	1.7	1.9
Private sector share in GDP (in per cent)	10.0	20.0	25.0	25.0	40.0	45.0	45.0	45.0	60.0
Private sector share in employment (in per cent)	35.5	37.6	42.8	48.5	53.6	57.9	63.7	na	na
EBRD index of small-scale privatisation	1.0	1.0	1.0	2.0	3.0	3.3	3.3	3.3	3.3
EBRD index of large-scale privatisation	1.0	1.0	1.0	1.0	2.0	2.0	1.7	1.7	2.0
Enterprises									
Budgetary subsidies and current transfers (in per cent of GDP)	4.6	5.4	2.2	2.1	0.7	0.1	0.1	0.2	0.4
Effective statutory social security tax (in per cent)	62.7	54.7	33.9	62.1	63.0	76.3	82.0	na	na
Share of industry in total employment (in per cent)	10.5	10.3	9.7	7.7	6.6	6.8	7.0	6.7	6.8
Change in labour productivity in industry (in per cent)	-12.0	-21.0	-16.6	-66.2	17.5	-1.5	1.0	10.7	3.9
Investment rate/GDP (in per cent)	19.0	26.3	15.6	29.1	38.0	40.6	40.0	26.0	na
EBRD index of enterprise reform	1.0	1.0	1.7	1.7	1.7	1.7	1.7	2.0	2.0
EBRD index of competition policy	1.0	1.0	2.0	2.0	2.0	2.0	2.0	2.0	2.0
Infrastructure									
Main telephone lines per 100 inhabitants	8.4	9.3	9.4	8.5	8.6	8.9	9.5	10.4	11.1
Railway labour productivity (1989=100)	28.3	19.2	8.5	9.2	11.7	16.4	17.5	23.7	25.4
Electricity tariffs, USc kWh (collection rate in per cent)	na	0.67 (na)	1.98 (na)	2.48 (na)	2.7 (na)	na	na	1.3 (15)	2.1 (30)
GDP per unit of energy use (PPP in US dollars per kgoe)	1.2	1.0	1.1	1.3	1.4	1.5	1.6	na	na
EBRD index of infrastructure reform	1.0	1.0	1.0	1.3	1.3	1.3	1.3	1.7	1.7
Financial institutions									
Number of banks (foreign owned)	164 (1)	210 (2)	180 (5)	136 (6)	99 (6)	79 (4)	70 (5)	59 (5)	53 (5)
Asset share of state-owned banks (in per cent)	80.4	77.6	80.5	77.6	80.9	65.5	82.5	60.4	na
Non-performing loans (in per cent of total loans)	26.6	15.7	22.3	20.2	19.9	19.6	37.2	na	na
Domestic credit to private sector (in per cent of GDP)	na	na	na	na	na	na	na	na	na
Stock market capitalisation (in per cent of GDP)	na	na	na	na	0.0	0.1	0.1	0.1	0.1
EBRD index of banking sector reform	1.0	1.0	2.0	2.0	2.0	2.0	2.0	2.0	2.3
EBRD index of reform of non-banking financial institutions	1.0	1.0	1.0	1.0	1.0	1.7	1.7	1.7	1.7
Legal environment									
EBRD rating of legal extensiveness (company law)	na	na	na	na	2.3	3.0	3.3	3.0	3.0
EBRD rating of legal effectiveness (company law)	na	na	na	na	1.0	2.0	2.0	2.0	2.0
Social sector									
Expenditures on health and education (in per cent of GDP)	10.9	6.8	4.9	5.2	4.8	4.2	5.2	4.7	4.3
Life expectancy at birth, total (years)	69.4	69.4	69.0	70.0	70.9	71.4	71.5	71.7	na
Basic school enrolment ratio (in per cent)	89.1	90.3	91.2	90.6	91.5	86.1	85.5	89.6	na
Earnings inequality (GINI-coefficient)	na	42.8	45.9	45.8	46.2	46.2	na	50.6	na

[1] The State Statistics Committee reports 49 per cent of the population were
in poverty in 2001. Poverty is defined as households with a budget of
less than AZM 120,000 (US$ 25) per month.

	1994	1995	1996	1997	1998	1999	2000	2001	2002
								Estimate	Projection
Output and expenditure				*(Percentage change in real terms)*					
GDP	-19.7	-11.8	1.3	5.8	10.0	7.4	11.1	9.9	8.8
Private consumption	na	na	na	na	na	na	na	na	na
Public consumption	na	na	na	na	na	na	na	na	na
Gross fixed investment	na	na	na	na	na	na	na	na	na
Exports of goods and services	na	na	na	na	na	na	na	na	na
Imports of goods and services	na	na	na	na	na	na	na	na	na
Industrial gross output [1]	-24.7	-21.4	-6.7	0.5	2.2	4.2	6.9	4.7	na
Agricultural gross output	-13.0	-6.8	3.0	6.1	6.2	7.0	12.1	9.7	na
Employment [2]				*(Percentage change)*					
Labour force (end-year)	-1.4	1.0	2.5	-11.0	0.3	0.1	0.0	0.1	na
Employment (end year)	-2.3	-0.5	2.0	0.2	0.2	0.0	0.0	0.0	na
				(In per cent of labour force)					
Unemployment (end-year)	0.6	0.7	0.8	1.0	1.1	1.2	1.2	1.2	na
Prices and wages				*(Percentage change)*					
Consumer prices (annual average)	1,664.0	412.0	19.7	3.5	-0.8	-8.5	1.8	1.5	2.8
Consumer prices (end-year)	1,788.0	85.0	6.5	0.4	-7.6	-0.5	2.2	1.5	2.6
Producer prices (annual average)	na	1,734.0	122.7	29.8	0.0	-6.1	27.4	na	na
Producer prices (end-year)	na	na	87.2	2.2	-21.5	17.9	14.5	-4.4	na
Gross average monthly earnings in economy (annual average)	601.5	307.6	43.1	58.5	18.9	9.5	20.2	15.7	na
Government sector				*(In per cent of GDP)*					
General government balance [3]	-12.1	-4.9	-2.8	-1.6	-3.9	-4.7	-0.6	1.4	-0.1
General government expenditure [3]	45.9	22.5	20.3	20.8	23.7	23.6	20.8	19.9	na
General government debt	25.7	19.6	14.1	13.5	14.9	24.2	25.7	29.4	na
Monetary sector				*(Percentage change)*					
Broad money (M2, end-year)	na	na	25.7	29.2	-21.7	15.2	18.3	-3.4	na
Domestic credit (end-year)	841.0	61.0	33.2	11.1	13.0	-15.2	17.6	-13.5	na
				(In per cent of GDP)					
Broad money (M2, end-year)	na	9.0	8.8	9.9	7.1	7.4	7.0	6.0	na
Interest and exchange rates				*(In per cent per annum, end-year)*					
Refinance rate (6 months)	na	80.0	20.0	12.0	14.0	10.0	10.0	10.0	na
Inter-bank interest rate (3 months) [4]	na	na	36.0	22.9	23.2	20.5	22.5	19.8	na
Deposit rate [5]	406.0	90.0	13.0	11.5	10.9	9.9	12.2	12.0	na
Lending rate [5]	406.0	107.0	33.0	21.5	27.7	27.5	27.2	28.1	na
				(Manats per US dollar)					
Exchange rate (end-year)	4,330.0	4,440.0	4,098.0	3,888.0	3,890.0	4,378.0	4,565.0	4,775.0	na
Exchange rate (annual average)	1,433.0	4,417.0	4,300.0	3,983.0	3,869.0	4,120.0	4,472.0	4,656.6	na
External sector				*(In millions of US dollars)*					
Current account	-123	-318	-821	-915	-1,364	-600	-168	-51	-1,365
Trade balance	-163	-275	-549	-567	-1,046	-408	319	614	-462
Merchandise exports	682	680	789	808	678	1,025	1,858	2,079	1,593
Merchandise imports	845	955	1,338	1,375	1,724	1,433	1,539	1,465	2,055
Foreign direct investment, net	22	330	627	1,115	1,023	510	119	227	1,300
Gross reserves (end-year), excluding gold [6]	2	119	214	467	447	673	680	897	na
External debt stock	239	425	521	602	717	1,034	1,259	1,402	na
				(In months of imports of goods and services)					
Gross reserves (end-year), excluding gold [6]	0.0	1.1	1.5	2.7	2.2	4.2	4.0	5.1	na
				(In per cent of exports of goods and services)					
Debt service	0.4	5.2	7.4	7.3	4.7	4.8	4.5	5.7	na
Memorandum items				*(Denominations as indicated)*					
Population (end-year, millions)	7.6	7.7	7.8	7.9	8.0	8.0	8.1	8.1	na
GDP (in millions of manats)	1,873,400	10,669,000	13,663,200	15,791,400	17,203,000	18,875,000	23,591,000	26,619,000	29,772,709
GDP per capita (in US dollars) [7]	171	313	407	503	559	572	653	706	na
Share of industry in GDP (in per cent)	20.4	27.3	25.8	25.2	22.0	28.2	32.0	0.2	na
Share of agriculture in GDP (in per cent)	32.2	25.1	24.7	20.0	17.9	18.4	18.1	0.1	na
Current account/GDP (in per cent)	-9.4	-13.2	-25.8	-23.1	-30.7	-13.1	-3.2	-0.9	-22.4
External debt - reserves, in US$ millions	237	306	307	135	270	361	579	505	na
External debt/GDP (in per cent)	18.3	17.6	16.4	15.2	16.1	22.6	23.9	24.5	na
External debt/exports of goods and services (in per cent)	29.2	49.9	55.5	52.3	71.0	80.7	59.4	59.2	na

[1] Industrial output excludes crude oil production.

[2] Employment and labour force estimates differ from official statistics. Labour force data are correct for the working age population outside the labour force. Unemployment is based on survey data. Less than 5 per cent of all unemployed are registered.

[3] General government consolidates all levels of government except for municipalities and SOEs, and includes the Oil Fund and other extra-budgetary funds.

[4] 90 day inter-bank offer rate in manats, nominal.

[5] 1994-95: minimum rate for household time deposits, minimum lending rate for private enterprises respectively. From 1996, three-month deposit and lending rates to "bank-clients".

[6] By mid-August 2002, there were additional foreign exchange assets of around US$ 600 million in the account of the state Oil Fund.

[7] The manat became official legal tender in January 1994. An improved method of calculating value-added in the oil sector has led to a sharp upward revision in nominal GDP and related variables for 2000 and beyond relative to previous estimates.

Belarus

Key reform challenges

- Liberalisation initiated as part of the 2001 IMF Staff Monitored Programme should continue, including the abolition of administered prices and interference in wage setting.

- Declining competitiveness of the enterprise sector points to macroeconomic structural weakness. This must be addressed by structural reform if macroeconomic growth is to be sustained.

- Following tentative steps towards corporatisation of state-owned enterprises, improvements in the investment climate and implementation of large-scale privatisation are needed to increase the pace of restructuring.

Liberalisation

Liberalisation progresses, but restrictive controls remain in place.

Progress in liberalisation of the foreign exchange market, initiated as part of an IMF Staff Monitored Programme, enabled Belarus to accept some of the obligations of Article VIII of the IMF's Articles of Agreement (Sections 2, 3 and 4) in November 2001. However, many other restrictive practices remain in place, including administrative price controls and a surrender requirement on foreign currency transactions, which remains at 30 per cent but does not apply to all exports. Although the National Bank has expressed its intention to remove the surrender requirements on Russian rouble transactions in 2002, there are no plans to remove requirements on other foreign exchange at present. The Belarussian authorities have continued to express their interest in reaching agreement with the IMF on a credit arrangement. However, the Fund had stated that it would only be prepared to consider a request for a Stand-By Arrangement following a demonstrated track record of successful policy implementation. As the first Staff Monitored Programme (SMP) in 2001 was not fully successful, the Fund favours agreement on and implementation of a second SMP. However, the Belarussian authorities appear to be reluctant to enter into a second SMP and have so far not presented an alternative mode of demonstrating a successful reform track record.

Stabilisation

Output increases, but so does stock building.

According to official statistics, GDP grew by 4.7 per cent in the first half of 2002, compared with 3 per cent over the same period last year and 4.1 per cent for the whole of 2001. This is slightly below the government's target of 4.9 per cent growth for the first half of 2002, established under the terms of its social and economic development programme. However, while output has increased, so have unsold stocks, with 75 per cent of enterprises' monthly output in June being stockpiled. In addition, around 40 per cent of enterprises were reported to be unprofitable in the first half of the year. Although the government met eight of its 16 socio-economic development targets in the first half of the year, there is still no consistent macroeconomic policy framework for reducing macroeconomic imbalances and for achieving sustainable growth.

Inflationary pressures persist.

While the government is targeting inflation of 27 per cent in 2002, down from 46 per cent in 2001, the cumulative increase in consumer prices amounted to 20.2 per cent in the first half of the year. Given current trends it seems unlikely that inflation will fall below 40 per cent for the year as a whole. Government directed wage increases in excess of productivity gains appear to have been a key factor in sustaining these inflationary pressures, as well as the continued financing of the budget deficit by the National Bank (NBB).

Privatisation

Steps taken towards corporatisation, but privatisation remains stalled.

While privatisation remains essentially stalled, the government has made some progress on corporatisation. This is particularly evident in the petrochemicals sector where the Ministry of Economy has drafted resolutions on the incorporation of several companies and has stated its intent to partially privatise them. However, no date has been set and a series of restrictions on potential buyers (including requirements on the retention of workers, wage increases and remittances to the state) are likely to reduce the attractiveness of companies made available for privatisation. Moreover, the government has recently stated that it intends to retain a controlling interest in certain, as yet undefined, strategic enterprises, although it has committed to releasing full ownership of other enterprises. Although discussions have continued with Russia's Baltika over the privatisation of the Krynitsa brewery, the authorities have announced that the release of equity tranches to Baltika will be partly conditional on its fulfilment of set production targets.

Enterprises, infrastructure, finance and social reforms

1991
May   Bankruptcy law adopted

1992
Dec   Competition law adopted

1993
Mar   Stock exchange established

1995
Apr   Investment funds' licences suspended

1996
Feb   All enterprises required to re-register
May   State share in commercial banks increased

1997
Dec   Energy regulation transferred to Ministry of Economy

1998
Jan   Golden share rights for state in private companies introduced
Jul   Belarus stock exchange nationalised
Sep   Registration of new private businesses suspended

1999
Jan   Railway law adopted
Jan   New civil code adopted
Jan   New land code adopted
Mar   New (unfavourable) business registration procedures adopted

2001
Apr   Directed credits eliminated
Apr   Staff Monitored Programme with IMF initiated
Jun   New World Bank programme introduced

2002
Jan   Minimum banking capital requirements increased to €10 million
May   New National Bank programme agreed by President

Enterprise reform

Some improvements to investment climate, but it remains poor.
There have been two notable legislative measures to improve the business climate. A new investment code was adopted in October 2001, which provides governmental support and guarantees for investors. This was followed by the mid-November 2001 repeal of Presidential Decree No.40, which empowered the state to confiscate property of individuals and legal entities that caused (undefined) damage to the state. The arrests of several senior business figures in early 2002 – mainly on charges of corruption or mismanagement – are, however, seen as a setback to the investment climate, with some commentators feeling the arrests were politically motivated. The investment climate has also been further weakened by the authorities introducing "golden shares" into enterprises that have already been privatised. In May 2002, the government passed a programme to boost foreign investment, largely by reducing licensing and registration requirements and simplifying tax regulations. The programme aims to attract US$ 400 million of foreign direct investment in 2002 (US$ 300 million of which is expected from the privatisation of six petrochemicals companies), US$ 1 billion in 2003 and a planned total of US$ 8–13.5 billion by 2010. Russia is the most likely source of the foreign investment, but a dramatic improvement in the investment climate will be required if the government is to meet these targets. This was exemplified by the August 2002 withdrawal of IKEA from a potential US$ 25 million investment in a sawmill, after failing to agree terms with the authorities following lengthy discussions.

Infrastructure

Energy debt increased.
During the first five months of the year, debts to Russian gas companies Itera and Gazprom increased to US$ 28.7 million and US$ 220 million respectively. The increase is mainly due to the deterioration of collection rates from domestic users, with Beltransgaz collecting only 78 per cent of tariffs due. As a consequence, Itera, which supplies around 40 per cent of Belarussian gas, cut supplies to Beltransgaz by 50 per cent in mid-June, before restoring full supply in early July, once Beltransgaz had partially repaid its debt which stood at US$ 24.5 million in August.

Russian gas tariff increases not being passed on fully to local enterprises.
Under an interstate treaty, gas and transport prices are to be equalled for Russian and Belarussian consumers. Russia increased gas prices by 15 per cent in July, but the increase is unlikely to stimulate demand and trigger energy efficiency improvements, following a resolution passed by the Belarussian parliament that reduces gas tariffs charged to certain, as yet undefined, companies.

Financial institutions

New programme to strengthen the banking sector prepared.
The National Bank (NBB) has prepared a programme to increase the strength of the banking sector in Belarus. This has been submitted to the Council of Ministers, following agreement with the President in May 2002. Under the terms of the programme, the NBB will cease to grant credits to the government from 2004, will no longer purchase government securities at time of issuance, and will increase its supervision of banking sector regulations. However, the National Bank remains reluctant to increase the foreign capital limit in the banking sector beyond the current 25 per cent level, following the increase of the minimum capital requirement for banks that take household deposits to €10 million in January 2002. As a result of this requirement, one bank has had its licence revoked and another five have had their licences suspended. At least a further five banks are reported to be in violation of the new requirement, but the NBB is believed to have softened its stance by looking favourably upon banks making an effort to increase their capital base. Another factor weakening the banking sector is a presidential decree instructing commercial banks to provide new loans to specific agricultural processing enterprises. This decree, announced in mid-2002, goes against the IMF SMP which eliminated directed lending.

Social reform

Untargeted support is of doubtful sustainability.
Following promises to increase the average monthly state sector wage to US$ 100 during last year's presidential election, President Lukashenka has stated that wages should increase by a further 8 per cent in 2002 and reach US$ 250 by 2005. Wage arrears have, however, increased and reached BLR 27 billion (US$ 14.4 million) by the end of April. The government has recently stated that it intends to undertake a review of the social sphere and believes it can save BLR 50 billion (US$ 27.5 million) in social expenditure by limiting free of charge medicines. In August 2001, the World Bank announced its intention to provide a US$ 17 million loan for the prevention of AIDS and tuberculosis, but there has yet to be an agreement with the government on the terms of the programme.

Liberalisation

Current account convertibility – **limited**

Interest rate liberalisation –
  limited de facto

Wage regulation – **yes**

Stabilisation

Share of general government tax revenue
  in GDP – **41.3 per cent**

Exchange rate regime – **crawling peg
  with band to Russian rouble**

Privatisation

Primary privatisation method – **MEBOs**

Secondary privatisation method – **vouchers**

Tradability of land – **limited de jure**

Enterprises and markets

Competition Office – **no**

Infrastructure

Independent telecoms regulator – **no**

Separation of railway accounts – **no**

Independent electricity regulator – **no**

Financial sector

Capital adequacy ratio – **10 per cent**

Deposit insurance system – **yes**

Secured transactions law – **restricted**

Securities commission – **no**

Social reform

Share of the population in poverty –
  10.4 per cent

Private pension funds – **no**

	1993	1994	1995	1996	1997	1998	1999	2000	2001
Liberalisation									
Share of administered prices in CPI (in per cent)	70.0	60.0	45.0	30.0	27.0	na	na	na	na
Number of goods with administered prices in EBRD-15 basket [1]	6.0	6.0	6.0	6.0	6.0	6.0	6.0	6.0	6.0
Share of trade with non-transition countries (in per cent)	na	28.5	20.5	19.0	19.3	17.3	22.6	22.9	45.7
Share of trade in GDP (in per cent)	121.9	113.4	98.8	88.6	108.8	91.6	98.8	116.4	123.3
Tariff revenues (in per cent of imports) [2]	3.7	5.4	3.2	3.4	4.1	4.3	3.8	2.5	1.9
EBRD index of price liberalisation	2.0	2.0	3.0	3.0	3.0	2.0	1.7	1.7	2.0
EBRD index of forex and trade liberalisation	1.0	1.0	2.0	2.0	1.0	1.0	1.0	1.7	2.0
Privatisation									
Privatisation revenues (cumulative, in per cent of GDP)	0.1	0.4	0.5	0.7	0.8	1.0	1.1	na	na
Private sector share in GDP (in per cent)	10.0	15.0	15.0	15.0	20.0	20.0	20.0	20.0	20.0
Private sector share in employment (in per cent)	na	na	6.8	9.3	12.0	16.4	18.6	na	na
EBRD index of small-scale privatisation	2.0	2.0	2.0	2.0	2.0	2.0	2.0	2.0	2.0
EBRD index of large-scale privatisation	1.7	1.7	1.7	1.0	1.0	1.0	1.0	1.0	1.0
Enterprises									
Budgetary subsidies and current transfers (in per cent of GDP)	na	na	na	15.6	17.1	17.2	18.6	18.8	13.8
Effective statutory social security tax (in per cent)	65.2	67.5	80.4	82.1	86.8	81.9	84.9	na	na
Share of industry in total employment (in per cent)	29.6	29.0	27.6	27.5	27.6	27.6	27.7	27.6	na
Change in labour productivity in industry (in per cent)	-5.7	-10.7	-0.9	29.4	18.6	10.9	9.4	8.4	na
Investment rate/GDP (in per cent)	33.9	33.2	25.0	22.0	24.7	26.0	24.0	23.0	na
EBRD index of enterprise reform	1.0	1.0	1.7	1.7	1.0	1.0	1.0	1.0	1.0
EBRD index of competition policy	2.0	2.0	2.0	2.0	2.0	2.0	2.0	2.0	2.0
Infrastructure									
Main telephone lines per 100 inhabitants	17.8	18.6	19.2	20.8	22.6	24.3	25.7	26.9	27.9
Railway labour productivity (1989=100)	46.5	33.6	29.9	28.8	32.6	32.2	35.9	37.5	35.2
Electricity tariffs, USc kWh (collection rate in per cent)	na	na	na	1.5 (na)	1.1 (na)	0.8 (na)	0.4 (na)	1.4 (50)	1.3 (na)
GDP per unit of energy use (PPP in US dollars per kgoe)	2.0	2.2	2.2	2.2	2.4	2.7	2.9	na	na
EBRD index of infrastructure reform	1.0	1.0	1.0	1.0	1.0	1.0	1.3	1.3	1.3
Financial institutions									
Number of banks (foreign owned)	na	48 (na)	42 (1)	38 (2)	38 (2)	37 (2)	36 (4)	31 (6)	29 (9)
Asset share of state-owned banks (in per cent)	na	69.2	62.3	54.1	55.2	59.5	66.6	66.0	53.2
Non-performing loans (in per cent of total loans)	na	8.4	11.8	14.1	12.5	16.5	13.1	15.2	11.9
Domestic credit to private sector (in per cent of GDP)	na	17.6	6.2	6.5	8.3	16.2	9.4	na	na
Stock market capitalisation (in per cent of GDP)	na	na	na	na	4.4	3.5	3.4	4.1	3.0
EBRD index of banking sector reform	1.0	1.0	2.0	1.0	1.0	1.0	1.0	1.0	1.0
EBRD index of reform of non-banking financial institutions	2.0	2.0	2.0	2.0	2.0	2.0	2.0	2.0	2.0
Legal environment									
EBRD rating of legal extensiveness (company law)	na	na	na	na	2.0	2.0	2.0	1.0	3.0
EBRD rating of legal effectiveness (company law)	na	na	na	na	2.0	2.0	2.0	2.3	3.0
Social sector									
Expenditures on health and education (in per cent of GDP)	15.1	12.9	10.4	10.8	12.6	11.4	11.0	10.8	7.7
Life expectancy at birth, total (years)	69.0	68.8	68.5	68.6	68.5	68.4	67.9	68.1	na
Basic school enrolment ratio (in per cent)	94.1	94.0	94.6	94.3	94.9	94.6	94.8	95.4	na
Earnings inequality (GINI-coefficient)	39.9	na	37.3	35.6	35.4	35.1	33.7	33.7	na

[1] Data on price controls for coal, wood, rents and inter-city bus services were not available.
   Adding these to the number of controlled prices would bring the total up to 9.

[2] Refers to taxes on international trade.

	1994	1995	1996	1997	1998	1999	2000	2001	2002 Estimate
Output and expenditure					*(Percentage change in real terms)*				
GDP [1]	-12.6	-10.4	2.8	11.4	8.4	3.4	5.8	4.1	3.0
Private consumption	-14.5	-12.3	4.5	11.4	14.1	9.5	8.0	8.3	na
Public consumption	-5.6	-2.6	-1.0	6.8	6.3	5.5	6.8	0.5	na
Gross fixed investment	-17.2	-28.7	7.2	15.9	6.9	-16.0	5.5	na	na
Exports	28.1	90.8	27.1	23.9	-3.4	-2.3	na	na	na
Imports	21.4	79.8	26.5	24.9	-1.2	-8.6	na	na	na
Industrial gross output	-14.8	-11.7	3.5	18.8	12.4	10.3	8.0	na	na
Agricultural gross output	-14.4	-4.7	2.4	-4.9	-0.7	-8.3	9.3	5.0	na
Employment					*(Percentage change)*				
Labour force (end-year)	-2.4	-5.7	0.1	-2.5	-1.1	-0.4	-0.1	0.0	na
Employment (end-year)	-2.6	-6.2	-1.0	0.1	1.1	0.6	0.0	-0.1	na
					(In per cent of labour force)				
Unemployment (end-year) [2]	2.1	2.7	3.9	2.8	2.3	2.2	2.1	2.2	na
Prices and wages					*(Percentage change)*				
Consumer prices (annual average)	2,221.0	709.3	52.7	63.8	73.2	293.8	168.9	61.4	41.4
Consumer prices (end-year)	1,959.9	244.2	39.3	63.4	181.7	251.3	107.5	46.3	27.8
Producer prices (annual average)	2,171.0	462.0	33.6	88.0	72.0	355.0	185.6	72.0	na
Producer prices (end-year)	1,866.7	122.0	31.3	89.0	200.5	245.0	168.0	na	na
Gross average monthly earnings in economy (annual average)	60.4	668.9	60.5	87.3	104.2	322.4	200.9	112.0	na
Government sector [3]					*(In per cent of GDP)*				
General government balance	-3.5	-2.7	-1.8	-1.2	-0.5	-1.8	0.3	-0.4	-0.7
General government expenditure	47.3	43.0	41.2	44.8	43.9	46.4	44.3	31.3	na
General government debt	na	na	3.9	4.0	4.8	na	na	na	na
Monetary sector					*(Percentage change)*				
Broad money (M2, end-year)	3,269.0	158.4	52.4	111.4	276.0	132.7	219.3	58.9	na
Domestic credit (end-year)	2,030.9	226.5	58.8	115.1	300.5	141.3	190.8	65.4	na
					(In per cent of GDP)				
Broad money (M2, end-year)	39.0	15.0	14.3	15.7	31.0	16.9	17.7	15.2	na
Interest and exchange rates					*(In per cent per annum, end-year)*				
Refinancing rate	300.0	66.0	35.0	40.0	48.0	120.0	90.0	61.0	na
Treasury bill rate (3-month maturity)	320.0	70.0	37.0	38.4	43.2	80.0	na	na	na
Deposit rate (1 year)	89.6	100.8	32.3	15.6	14.3	23.8	37.6	34.2	na
Lending rate (1 year)	148.5	175.0	62.3	31.8	27.0	51.0	67.7	47.0	na
					(Belarussian roubles per US dollar)				
Official exchange rate (end-year) [4]	10.6	11.5	15.5	30.7	107.0	320.0	1,180.0	1,580.0	na
Official exchange rate (annual average) [4]	3.7	11.5	13.3	26.2	46.4	248.8	717.0	1,390.0	na
External sector					*(In millions of US dollars)*				
Current account	-444	-458	-516	-859	-1,017	-194	-270	91	-53
Trade balance	-490	-666	-1,149	-1,407	-1,501	-570	-838	-380	-672
Merchandise exports	2,510	4,803	5,790	6,919	6,172	5,646	6,987	7,314	7,525
Merchandise imports	3,000	5,469	6,939	8,326	7,673	6,216	7,825	7,694	8,197
Foreign direct investment, net	11	15	105	350	201	443	90	84	146
Gross reserves (end-year), excluding gold	101	377	469	394	703	294	350	391	na
External debt stock [5]	1,251	1,527	950	976	1,011	886	903	930	na
					(In months of imports of goods and services)				
Gross reserves (end-year), excluding gold	0.4	0.8	0.8	0.5	1.0	0.5	0.5	0.5	na
					(In per cent of exports of goods and services)				
Debt service [6]	4.3	2.9	2.3	2.0	1.8	3.1	1.7	2.5	na
Memorandum items					*(Denominations as indicated)*				
Population (end-year, millions)	10.3	10.3	10.3	10.2	10.2	10.0	10.0	10.0	na
GDP (in millions of Belarussian roubles)	17,815	119,813	190,886	366,859	701,020	2,987,779	9,125,976	16,913,000	22,234,671
GDP per capita (in US dollars)	471	1,009	1,399	1,368	1,481	1,195	1,274	1,217	na
Share of industry in GDP (in per cent) [7]	26.7	31.4	34.6	34.3	33.4	31.9	30.1	34.0	na
Share of agriculture in GDP (in per cent) [7]	15.0	17.7	16.0	15.4	13.9	14.6	15.3	6.5	na
Current account/GDP (in per cent)	-9.1	-4.4	-3.6	-6.1	-6.7	-1.6	-2.1	0.8	-0.4
External debt - reserves, in US$ millions	1,150	1,150	481	582	308	592	552	540	na
External debt/GDP (in per cent)	25.7	14.7	6.6	7.0	6.7	7.4	7.1	7.6	na
External debt/exports of goods and services (in per cent)	45.3	29.0	14.2	12.5	14.2	13.8	11.3	11.1	na

[1] The Belarussian national accounts are believed to overstate real GDP growth by 1-2 per cent.

[2] Officially registered unemployed.

[3] General government includes the state budget, social funds and extra-budgetary funds, excluding inter-budgetary transfers.

[4] A significant parallel market premium, peaking at around 300 per cent in December 1999, existed until unification of the exchange rate in September 2000. Hence, there was no end-of-period premium in 2000 although the annual average premium was around 140 per cent.

[5] Medium and long-term public and publicly guaranteed debt. From 1994, the debt stock includes short-term external debt.

[6] Amortisation of public and publicly guaranteed debt and total interest payments.

[7] Figures are based on current prices. Variations in the shares thus reflect changes in relative prices.

Bosnia and Herzegovina[1]

Key reform challenges

- Economic cooperation between the two Entities is improving but inter-entity capital and labour mobility is limited. New laws at both state and entity level are needed to develop further the single economic space.

- To reverse the recent decline in growth and kick-start the economy, large-scale privatisation, which is moving slowly and marred by lack of transparency and extensive insider control, should be reformed and accelerated.

- The anticipated decline in external grants and loans means that government spending must be reduced over the medium term and the pace of reform accelerated to ensure fiscal sustainability.

Liberalisation

Tax harmonisation contributes to the development of a single economic space ...

There has been some progress in inter-entity unification of indirect taxes. The scope of sales taxes and sales tax rates on goods and services have been harmonised over the past year. In July 2002, an agreement was signed by the two Entities and the District of Brčko to ensure that the previous system of double taxation on inter-entity (or entity-Brčko) trade is removed and excise taxes are collected only once in the place of final consumption.

... but the passage of new laws is an urgent priority.

A number of laws that would help promote the development of a normal functioning market economy have been held up repeatedly, both at state and entity level. At the end of June 2002, the Office of the High Representative identified 12 laws that require urgent passage to promote the single economic space. These laws are essential to facilitate greater flows of exports and foreign investment and to allow the operation of well regulated and efficient public utilities.

Progress on the EU road map accelerates.

Progress on the "road map" towards formal negotiation of a Stabilisation and Association Agreement (SAA) with the EU has accelerated in recent months. By September 2002, Bosnia and Herzegovina had satisfied most of the 18 steps required by the EU. Once the process is complete, the EU will begin a feasibility study to determine the preparedness of the country for an SAA. In addition, Free Trade Agreements have been signed this year with FR Yugoslavia and FYR Macedonia and WTO accession is now expected for 2003.

Stabilisation

Fiscal imbalances threaten medium term growth and sustainability.

Under the Central Bank's currency board arrangement, macroeconomic stability has been preserved and annual inflation in both Entities is low. In the short term, macroeconomic stability will be underpinned by a 15-month Stand-By Arrangement with the IMF, approved in August 2002. However, government spending as a percentage of GDP, at more than 60 per cent, is one of the highest in the region, reflecting the country's multi-layered structure of government. The associated large fiscal deficits of the consolidated general government (6.3 per cent of GDP in 2001, on a commitment basis) are a threat to medium-term fiscal sustainability. The high level of public spending reflects, among other things, a bloated state bureaucracy, generous veterans' benefits and excessive military expenditure.

Privatisation

Privatisation continues in both Entities ...

Privatisation is proceeding slowly in both Entities. In the Federation, small-scale privatisation was about two-thirds complete by mid-2002, with 214 companies sold out of 322. Sales of large-scale companies have been sluggish, however, with less than 200 sold out of 1,034 identified for sale. The rate of progress in the RS has been similar, with proportionally fewer small enterprises sold (119 out of 276 offered for sale) and more large enterprises (154 out of 648) fully privatised by end-June. In both Entities, the programme is behind schedule and targets set for end-2002 are unlikely to be met. Sales have been made mostly to the public through vouchers and to management-employee buy-out teams.

... but sales of strategic enterprises continue to lag behind.

In the Federation, the list of 86 strategic companies identified for sale, with the assistance of the International Advisory Group on Privatisation (IAGP), was reduced to 56 following the withdrawal of donor support for the remaining 30. By the end of June 2002, 13 companies had been privatised with a number of other companies being prepared for privatisation later in the year. In the RS, only four companies out of 52 had been sold by end-June 2002. Two high-profile tenders in the RS – the Fruktona enterprise and the Banja Luka brewery –

Liberalisation, stabilisation, privatisation

1992
Mar   Independence from Yugoslavia declared

1995
Dec   Civil war ends

1996
Oct   Law on privatisation agencies in the Federation enacted

1997
Aug   Currency board established
Aug   Central Bank of Bosnia and Herzegovina established
Dec   Federation law on privatisation enacted

1998
Jun   Enterprise privatisation law adopted in RS
Jun   Konvertible Marka bank notes introduced
Jul   State umbrella law on privatisation adopted
Aug   VAT introduced in RS

1999
Apr   Markas becomes convertible abroad
May   Preferential trade regime with Croatia and FR Yugoslavia abolished
Jun   Small-scale privatisation begins

2000
Mar   Excise taxes between Entities harmonised
May   Framework privatisation law amended

2002
Jul   Double taxation on inter-entity trade ended

failed earlier in 2002 due to disagreements between the potential buyers (both foreign companies) and the government over interpretation of the privatisation law. Several privatisations in the Federation that involved foreign buyers have also been problematic.

Enterprise reform

Action plan to remove investment barriers prepared.

Two surveys carried out in 2001, in cooperation with the World Bank, identified a number of administrative barriers to investment. These barriers include the absence of: a harmonised legal environment; clear administrative procedures for new investments (including labour and tax regulations); and an efficient judicial system. Corruption was also identified as a major barrier to investment. In response to these concerns, the governments at state and entity level have developed jointly a concrete Action Plan, launched in February 2002. Implementation

Enterprises, infrastructure, finance and social reforms

1996

Jan	Federation banking agency established

1998

Mar	RS banking agency established
Apr	Bank privatisation law enacted in the Federation
Jun	New company law adopted
Jun	Federation bank privatisation agency established
Jul	RS bank privatisation agency established
Sep	New telecommunications law adopted
Oct	New banking law adopted in the Federation
Dec	Joint Power Coordination Centre (JPCC) established

1999

Apr	Minimum bank capital requirements increased
Apr	Securities Commission in the Federation established
Apr	Banking law adopted in RS

2001

Jan	Payments bureaux closed
Feb	Deposit insurance introduced in the Federation
Jun	Minimum bank capital requirements increased further

2002

Mar	Banja Luka stock exchange opened
Mar	State electricity law approved
Apr	Sarajevo stock exchange opened
Sep	State deposit insurance agency formed

of the plan will be key to attracting foreign direct investment, which remains one of the lowest levels per capita in the region.

Infrastructure

Power sector regulatory reform lags behind investment.

A major programme of investment in the power sector, to be financed by international organisations including the EBRD, EIB and World Bank, is under way, but associated regulatory reforms have been delayed. Some progress was made in March 2002 when the state parliament passed a law on electricity transmission, regulator and system operators, providing the legal basis for the establishment of a new, independent institutional structure at state level. However, by the end of July 2002, the entity laws had not yet harmonised with state level regulations, preventing the establishment of a well regulated energy sector and hindering its eventual privatisation.

Railway and road reforms progress slowly.

The Commission for Public Corporations, established in accordance with Annex 9 of the Dayton Peace Agreement, created the BH Railways Public Corporation (RPC) and the BH Road Infrastructure Public Corporation (BRIC). The RPC is operational and is working together with the two Entities' railways operators on the implementation of a €65 million infrastructure rehabilitation project, co-financed by the EBRD, EIB, Japan, USA and Canada. The BRIC is not yet operational but it is expected to participate in the implementation of a US$ 30 million road safety and management project, financed by the World Bank, signed in 2002.

New licences granted to fixed-line telecommunications operators.

Since the end of the war in 1995, telecommunications services in Bosnia and Herzegovina have been provided along ethnic lines. There are three public fixed-line operators – BiH Telecom, Telekom Srpske and HPT Mostar. In an effort to promote cross-ethnic competition, the state-level Communications Regulatory Agency (CRA) granted licences to all three operators, in June 2002, that will allow them to provide telecommunications services throughout the country. According to a new rule on interconnection, each operator will have to connect its own network with those of its competitors.

Financial institutions

Reform of the banking sector advanced ...

In the Federation, bank privatisation is virtually complete, while in the RS recent sales have left only two banks in state hands. The deadline for privatisation has been extended to the end of 2002. In April, the largest bank in the RS, Kristal Banka, was sold to Hypo Alpe Adria Banka of Austria for the nominal amount of €1, in exchange for taking on the bank's liabilities.

... but development of the sector remains limited.

Interest rates on commercial loans have decreased to an annual rate of around 10 to 12 per cent, but bank lending to the private sector remains limited. As at the end of 2001, bank claims on commercial enterprises were KM 2.41 billion (€1.23 billion), down slightly on the end-2000 figure of KM 2.59 billion (€1.32 billion). Consolidation in the sector is a priority and should be encouraged by the new minimum capital requirement, effective from 1 January 2003, of KM 15 million (€7.5 million). In addition, a state level deposit insurance agency will be introduced later in 2002, following passage of the appropriate legislation in July 2002.

New stock markets opened in both Entities.

New stock exchanges have opened during 2002 in both Entities. The Banja Luka stock exchange started trading on 14 March 2002 and the Sarajevo exchange opened on 12 April 2002. Market capitalisation of both exchanges is small and the impact on the economy is likely to be minimal for the foreseeable future.

Social reform

Pension reform has advanced, but social spending must be better targeted.

The authorities in both Entities have made significant advances in improving the financial performance and transparency of the pension systems. However, significant arrears remain from the year 2000 – 3.3 months of total payments in the Federation and 4.5 months in the RS. A new indexation system links monthly payments more closely to revenues and is designed to avoid the accumulation of new arrears. A key medium-term challenge is to reduce the overall level of social spending, while targeting available funds more effectively. The problem is exacerbated by the existence of parallel systems in each Entity and the lack of transparency in spending on items such as defence and veterans' benefits. Reform of social spending will be a central element of the government's Poverty Reduction Strategy Paper, which is to be completed by the end of 2002 or early 2003 following a period of public consultation.

---

[1] The territorial constitutional entities distinguished in this assessment include the State of Bosnia and Herzegovina (BH), the Federation of Bosnia and Herzegovina (FBH), the Republika Srpska (RS) and the cantons of the Federation. The FBH and the RS are referred to as the "Entities". The District of Brčko enjoys a special status based on an Arbitration Award in accordance with the Dayton Peace Agreement.

Liberalisation

Current account convertibility – **full**

Interest rate liberalisation – **full**

Wage regulation – **no**

Stabilisation

Share of general government tax revenue
in GDP – **55 per cent**

Exchange rate regime – **currency board
pegged to euro**

Privatisation

Primary privatisation method – **vouchers**

Secondary privatisation method –
direct sales

Tradability of land – **limited de jure**

Enterprises and markets

Competition Office – **no**

Infrastructure

Independent telecoms regulator – **no**

Separation of railway accounts – **no**

Independent electricity regulator – **yes**

Financial sector

Capital adequacy ratio – **8 per cent**

Deposit insurance system – **yes**

Secured transactions law – **no**

Securities commission – **yes in
the Federation**

Social reform

Share of the population in poverty – **na**

Private pension funds – **no**

	1993	1994	1995	1996	1997	1998	1999	2000	2001
Liberalisation									
Share of administered prices in CPI (in per cent)	na	na	na	na	na	na	na	na	na
Number of goods with administered prices in EBRD-15 basket	na	na	na	na	na	na	na	na	na
Share of trade with non-transition countries (in per cent)	na	58.3	67.3	57.2	53.9	59.0	67.4	75.5	52.8
Share of trade in GDP (in per cent)	na	78.5	66.1	80.9	85.0	78.8	70.1	78.0	80.9
Tariff revenues (in per cent of imports)	na	na	na	10.5	7.8	9.1	10.5	na	na
EBRD index of price liberalisation	1.0	1.0	1.0	2.0	2.0	3.0	3.0	3.0	3.0
EBRD index of forex and trade liberalisation	2.0	1.0	1.0	1.0	3.0	3.0	3.0	3.0	3.0
Privatisation									
Privatisation revenues (cumulative, in per cent of GDP)	na	na	na	na	na	0.0	0.7	1.3	1.0
Private sector share in GDP (in per cent)	na	na	na	na	na	35.0	35.0	35.0	40.0
Private sector share in employment (in per cent)	na	na	na	na	na	na	na	na	na
EBRD index of small-scale privatisation	2.0	2.0	2.0	2.0	2.0	2.0	2.0	2.3	2.7
EBRD index of large-scale privatisation	1.0	1.0	1.0	1.0	1.0	2.0	2.0	2.0	2.3
Enterprises									
Budgetary subsidies and current transfers (in per cent of GDP)	na	na	na	1.1	0.1	0.4	0.5	0.8	0.5
Effective statutory social security tax (in per cent)	na	na	na	na	na	na	na	na	na
Share of industry in total employment (in per cent)	na	na	na	na	na	na	na	na	na
Change in labour productivity in industry (in per cent)	na	na	na	na	na	na	na	na	na
Investment rate/GDP (in per cent)	na	na	na	na	na	na	na	na	na
EBRD index of enterprise reform	1.0	1.0	1.0	1.0	1.0	1.7	1.7	1.7	1.7
EBRD index of competition policy	1.0	1.0	1.0	1.0	1.0	1.0	1.0	1.0	1.0
Infrastructure									
Main telephone lines per 100 inhabitants	14.6	7.1	5.4	9.0	8.0	9.1	9.6	10.3	11.1
Railway labour productivity (1996=100)	na	na	na	100.0	85.5	111.3	153.7	177.2	245.9
Electricity tariffs, USc kWh (collection rate in per cent)	na	na	na	4.4 (60)	3.6 (60)	3.5 (86)	5.1 (94)	4.3 (75)	5.6 (95)
GDP per unit of energy use (PPP in US dollars per kgoe)	na	na	na	na	na	na	na	na	na
EBRD index of infrastructure reform	1.0	1.0	1.0	1.3	1.3	1.3	1.3	2.0	2.0
Financial institutions									
Number of banks (foreign owned)	na	na	na	na	na	na	na	56 (14)	na
Asset share of state-owned banks (in per cent)	na	na	na	na	na	na	75.9	55.4	8.9
Non-performing loans (in per cent of total loans)	na	na	na	na	na	na	58.7	15.8	7.0
Domestic credit to private sector (in per cent of GDP)	na	na	na	na	na	na	8.9	7.5	2.2
Stock market capitalisation (in per cent of GDP)	na	na	na	na	na	na	na	na	na
EBRD index of banking sector reform	1.0	1.0	1.0	1.0	1.0	2.3	2.3	2.3	2.3
EBRD index of reform of non-banking financial institutions	1.0	1.0	1.0	1.0	1.0	1.0	1.0	1.0	1.0
Legal environment									
EBRD rating of legal extensiveness (company law)	na	na	na	na	na	2.0	2.0	3.0	1.3
EBRD rating of legal effectiveness (company law)	na	na	na	na	na	1.0	1.0	1.0	2.0
Social sector									
Expenditures on health and education (in per cent of GDP)	na	na	na	na	na	na	na	na	na
Life expectancy at birth, total (years)	na	na	na	na	73.1	73.3	73.0	73.3	na
Basic school enrolment ratio (in per cent)	na	na	97.6	103.6	101.4	na	na	na	na
Earnings inequality (GINI-coefficient)	na	na	na	na	na	na	na	na	na

	1994	1995	1996	1997	1998	1999	2000	2001	2002
								Estimate	Projection
Output and expenditure				*(Percentage change in real terms)*					
GDP	-40.0	20.8	86.0	37.0	9.9	10.6	4.5	2.3	3.0
Total consumption	na	4.8	52.5	15.0	7.6	na	na	na	na
Gross fixed investment	na	67.1	175.1	61.3	5.2	na	na	na	na
Industrial gross output	na	33.0	38.1	33.0	24.0	8.0	9.0	4.0	na
Agricultural gross output	na	-9.7	28.4	22.8	8.6	na	na	na	na
Employment				*(Percentage change)*					
Labour force (end-year)	-12.5	-12.5	-12.5	4.1	-2.7	1.3	-0.2	-1.9	na
Employment (end-year) [1]	na	na	na	na	0.0	0.6	-0.9	-1.4	na
				(In per cent of labour force)					
Unemployment (end-year)	na	na	na	na	38.0	38.5	39.6	40.4	na
Prices and wages				*(Percentage change)*					
Consumer prices (annual average) [2]									
Federation (KM based)	780.0	-4.4	-24.5	14.0	5.1	-0.3	1.9	3.3	2.0
Republika Srpska (KM based)	1,061.0	12.9	16.9	-7.3	2.0	14.0	14.7	11.0	5.0
Consumer prices (end-year)									
Federation (KM based)	na	na	7.7	13.6	1.8	-1.0	4.0	2.4	2.0
Republika Srpska (KM based)	na	na	-17.7	-10.0	5.6	14.0	16.0	6.2	5.0
Gross average monthly earnings in economy (annual average)									
Federation	na	na	289.5	66.6	6.3	17.2	8.3	-12.9	na
Republika Srpska	na	na	41.7	62.4	52.2	60.0	39.9	32.7	na
Government sector				*(In per cent of GDP)*					
General government balance	na	-0.3	-4.4	-0.5	-8.0	-9.1	-10.1	-6.3	-5.5
General government expenditure	na	39.3	52.7	39.7	65.3	69.5	66.4	61.3	
Monetary sector				*(Percentage change)*					
Broad money (M2, end-year)	na	8.5	96.2	52.0	31.3	39.9	13.9	89.3	na
Domestic credit (end-year)	na	-9.0	4.3	-17.5	16.2	-1.3	10.0	-1.6	na
				(In per cent of GDP)					
Broad money (M2, end-year)	17.9	14.8	18.8	19.3	21.1	25.2	26.2	47.0	na
Exchange rates				*(Dinar/KM per DM)*					
Exchange rate (annual average) [3]	na	1.0	1.0	1.0	1.0	1.0	1.0	1.0	na
External sector				*(In millions of US dollars)*					
Current account	-177	-193	-748	-1,060	-712	-971	-948	-1,050	-1,017
Trade balance	-803	-930	-1,546	-1,758	-1,881	-1,852	-1,655	-1,668	-1,599
Merchandise exports	91	152	336	575	702	744	903	1,002	1,165
Merchandise imports	894	1,082	1,882	2,333	2,583	2,542	2,558	2,670	2,764
Foreign direct investment, net [4]	0	0	0	0	100	90	150	130	200
Gross reserves (end-year), excluding gold	na	na	235	80	175	455	488	1,253	na
External debt stock	na	3,361	3,620	4,076	2,985	3,095	2,969	2,609	na
				(In months of imports of goods and services)					
Gross reserves (end-year), excluding gold	0.6	0.6	1.2	0.4	0.8	2.0	2.1	5.2	na
				(In per cent of exports of goods and services)					
Debt service	na	134.6	87.1	38.4	10.4	12.3	11.4	12.2	na
Memorandum items				*(Denominations as indicated)*					
Population (end-year, millions) [5]	4.2	4.2	4.1	4.2	4.2	4.3	4.3	4.3	na
GDP (in millions of markas)	2,035	2,676	4,125	6,116	7,336	8,604	9,433	9,940	10,400
GDP per capita (in US dollars)	299	445	669	815	993	1,090	1,031	1,056	na
Share of industry in GDP (in per cent)	na	23.9	21.4	22.6	22.5	na	na	na	na
Share of agriculture in GDP (in per cent)	na	24.6	20.5	17.5	16.0	na	na	na	na
Current account/GDP (in per cent)	-14.1	-10.3	-27.3	-31.0	-17.1	-20.7	-21.4	-23.1	-20.3
External debt - reserves, in US$ millions	na	3,154	3,162	3,996	2,810	2,640	2,481	1,356	na
External debt/GDP (in per cent)	na	180.0	132.1	119.1	71.6	66.0	66.9	57.5	na
External debt/exports of goods and services (in per cent)	na	882.2	550.2	406.8	236.0	238.8	217.8	183.0	na

[1] Bosniak-majority area prior to September 1996, state thereafter.
Before September 1996, data include personnel who were not actually working but for whom contributions (pension, health) were paid.

[2] Before 1995, retail price index (RPI) is used. From 1995, consumer price index (CPI) is used.

[3] Pre-1997 refers to Bosnian dinar in units of 100. Since August 1997, Bosnia and Herzegovina has a common Central Bank. The new currency, the Konvertible Marka (KM), is pegged to the Deutschmark at 1:1 under currency board rules (1.95 per euro).

[4] Excludes capital transfers for reconstruction.

[5] Includes refugees abroad.

Bulgaria

Key reform challenges

- The successful finalisation of the large-scale privatisations re-launched this year, including that of the dominant telecommunications operator, would be a crucial achievement and would lead to further investment and growth in these sectors.

- Implementation of proposed changes to the Energy Act, in line with the recent adoption of a new national energy strategy, should speed up liberalisation and enhance the performance of the power sector.

- Further structural reforms are needed to rationalise public expenditures and secure the long-term viability of the social security programme.

Liberalisation

EU and NATO accession negotiations accelerated.

Over the last year, Bulgaria has made significant progress in both EU and NATO accession negotiations. By the end of September 2002, the country had provisionally closed 22 of the 30 chapters of the *acquis communautaire*. This compares favourably to the same time last year, when 11 chapters of the accession negotiations had been provisionally closed. Bulgaria's application to join NATO is scheduled for consideration at the Prague Summit in November 2002. In June 2002, the government launched an army reform plan, to bring it in line with NATO requirements, which will see the reduction of military personnel by about 7,000 (or 11 per cent) by 2004.

Stabilisation

Active debt management policy contributes to decline in debt burden.

In November 2001, Bulgaria accessed the international capital markets with a €250 million Eurobond issue. The issue, which was substantially oversubscribed, allowed the Ministry of Finance (MoF) to establish a benchmark for Bulgarian bonds and embark on its strategy of gradually shifting the currency composition of external debt from US dollars to euros. Further supporting this strategy, the MoF completed a Brady swap in March 2002, exchanging US$ 1.3 billion of Brady bonds for US$ 1.2 billion of new dollar and euro-denominated bonds. In September 2002, the MoF announced a further US$ 800 million swap of Brady bonds for dollar-denominated Eurobonds, maturing in 2015. The combination of a more active debt management policy and the recent appreciation of the leva has reduced the ratio of external public debt to 61.3 per cent of GDP, as at June 2002.

New National Revenue Agency expected to boost tax collection.

In July 2002, the Council of Ministers approved the creation of a National Revenue Agency (NRA), which will administer the collection of all public receivables such as taxes, excise duties, social and pension insurance contributions, and state and municipal fees. The parliament adopted this plan at first reading in September. The NRA, to be funded by a US$ 36 million loan from the World Bank and US$ 24 million from the government, will be subordinated to the Finance Minister and is expected to be fully functional in 2005. Current tax revenue is less than 30 per cent of GDP and the creation of this new institution is expected to improve tax collection rates and enhance public expenditure management.

Privatisation

Parliament passes new Privatisation Act.

In March 2002, a new Privatisation Act aimed at greater transparency and compliance with sale contracts was passed by the parliament. The bill prohibits privatisations based on bilateral negotiations with potential investors (without open tendering), which had been a potential source of corruption in the past. It paves the way for the privatisation of about 440 majority state-owned companies, including the tobacco monopoly, Bulgartabac Holding, the Telecommunications Company (BTC), the Sea Fleet and River Shipping, the Vazov Group arms plants, and a number of district heating companies. At the end of July 2002, four final offers, ranging from US$ 64-110 million, were submitted to the Bulgarian Privatisation Agency for the 80 per cent state stake in Bulgartabac. The government, which will maintain a golden share in the company, have selected the consortium formed by the local Tobacco Capital Partners and a Dutch firm, Clar Innis, as the preferred buyer.

Enterprise reform

The investment climate improves, but further efforts are required.

During October 2001, in an effort to improve the country's investment climate, the government adopted a national anti-corruption strategy and appointed the British Crown Agents as consultants on custom administration reform. However, despite significant progress in building a supportive legislative framework for the private sector, there are still a number of administrative obstacles affecting enterprise start ups, as well as bankruptcy procedures, that require elimination. In February 2002, an inter-departmental

Liberalisation, stabilisation, privatisation

1991
Feb	Most consumer prices liberalised
Feb	Import controls removed
Feb	Interest rates liberalised
Feb	Unified exchange rate introduced
Jul	Treasury bills market initiated

1992
Feb	Restitution law enacted
Apr	Privatisation law adopted

1993
Jan	Small-scale privatisation law adopted
Feb	Large-scale privatisation begins
Jul	EFTA membership granted

1994
Mar	Currency crisis ensues
Apr	VAT introduced
Nov	Debt-equity swaps added to privatisation

1995
Jan	EU Association Agreement signed
Oct	Price controls reinstalled

1996
Oct	First voucher privatisation round begins
Dec	WTO membership granted

1997
Feb	Macroeconomic crisis peaks
Jul	Currency board introduced
Oct	New Foreign Investment Act adopted

1998
Jan	Comprehensive tax reform begins
Mar	Privatisation law amended
May	First company privatised through the stock exchange
Sep	Full current account convertibility introduced

1999
Jan	CEFTA membership granted
Jan	Second voucher privatisation round begins
May	First municipal Eurobond issued
Jul	Currency re-denominated

2000
Jan	Extra-budgetary funds closed
Jan	Export tax abolished
Mar	EU accession negotiations begin

2001
Nov	First government Eurobond issue

2002
Jan	VAT introduced on drugs, alcohol and coffee
Jul	Electricity and heat tariffs increase

	1994	1995	1996	1997	1998	1999	2000	2001	2002
								Estimate	*Projection*
Output and expenditure					*(Percentage change in real terms)*				
GDP	5.9	6.8	6.0	6.5	2.5	-0.9	2.9	3.8	3.5
Private consumption	na	na	na	na	-0.6	-2.9	4.2	4.6	na
Public consumption	na	na	na	na	2.3	2.8	-1.5	-4.3	na
Gross fixed investment	na	na	na	na	2.5	-3.9	-3.8	9.7	na
Exports of goods and services	na	na	na	na	3.9	0.7	12.0	8.7	na
Imports of goods and services	na	na	na	na	-4.9	-3.5	3.7	9.3	na
Industrial gross output	-2.7	0.3	3.1	6.8	3.7	-1.4	1.7	6.0	na
Agricultural gross output	-0.3	0.7	1.3	4.0	10.2	-3.5	2.8	8.5	na
Employment [1]					*(Percentage change)*				
Labour force (end-year)	-1.0	-1.3	0.9	3.4	-1.5	-1.0	7.2	-5.6	na
Employment (end-year) [1]	-4.2	-3.3	-1.4	3.4	-3.1	-3.4	4.1	-5.4	na
					(In per cent of labour force)				
Unemployment (end-year)	14.5	14.5	10.0	9.9	11.4	13.6	16.1	15.8	na
Prices and wages					*(Percentage change)*				
Retail prices (annual average)	97.6	2.0	3.5	3.6	5.7	4.2	6.2	4.9	2.3
Retail prices (end-year)	-3.0	3.8	3.4	3.8	5.4	4.4	7.4	2.6	2.7
Producer prices (annual average)	77.6	0.7	1.4	2.3	-1.2	2.6	9.7	3.6	na
Producer prices (end-year)	-5.5	1.6	1.5	1.6	-2.1	5.9	11.2	-3.1	na
Gross average monthly earnings in economy (annual average) [2]	na	34.0	12.3	13.1	12.6	10.2	7.0	3.9	na
Government sector [3]					*(In per cent of GDP)*				
General government balance	1.2	-1.4	-1.0	-1.9	-1.0	-6.5	-7.1	-5.8	-4.6
General government expenditure	40.6	44.9	45.3	44.4	46.7	49.7	48.8	46.0	na
General government debt	22.2	19.3	29.2	29.3	34.6	43.0	50.1	53.2	na
Monetary sector					*(Percentage change)*				
Broad money (M4, end-year)	75.7	39.3	49.1	38.3	13.0	-1.2	28.9	45.2	na
Domestic credit (end-year)	36.3	18.6	3.1	44.4	22.4	-6.5	8.9	23.0	na
					(In per cent of GDP)				
Broad money (M4, end-year)	20.2	25.0	34.0	41.0	41.7	40.0	47.9	65.1	na
Interest and exchange rates					*(In per cent per annum, end-year)*				
Refinancing rate (3 months)	14.0	27.0	9.5	9.0	10.5	11.6	7.0	4.3	na
Inter-bank interest rate (daily)	17.8	27.2	10.4	9.4	15.8	12.7	4.5	2.7	na
Deposit rate [4]	5.0	6.1	4.2	4.4	4.1	4.3	3.4	2.8	na
Lending rate [4]	15.4	22.3	18.5	14.1	16.1	13.5	10.5	9.5	na
					(Kuna per US dollar)				
Exchange rate (end-year)	5.6	5.3	5.5	6.3	6.2	7.6	8.8	8.4	na
Exchange rate (annual average)	6.0	5.2	5.4	6.2	6.4	7.1	8.3	8.3	na
External sector					*(In millions of US dollars)*				
Current account	854	-1,442	-1,091	-2,325	-1,530	-1,391	-433	-642	-753
Trade balance	-1,142	-3,259	-3,624	-5,196	-4,147	-3,299	-3,204	-4,012	-4,545
Merchandise exports	4,260	4,633	4,546	4,210	4,605	4,395	4,567	4,752	4,657
Merchandise imports	5,402	7,892	8,169	9,407	8,752	7,693	7,771	8,764	9,202
Foreign direct investment, net	110	109	486	347	835	1,445	1,086	1,325	970
Gross reserves (end-year), excluding gold	1,405	1,895	2,314	2,539	2,816	3,025	3,525	4,697	na
External debt stock	3,020	3,809	5,308	7,452	9,586	9,872	11,002	11,189	na
					(In months of imports of goods and services)				
Gross reserves (end-year), excluding gold	2.5	2.4	2.8	2.7	3.2	3.7	4.4	5.3	na
					(In per cent of exports of goods and services)				
Debt service	8.9	9.6	8.9	10.4	12.9	21.8	22.1	18.8	na
Memorandum items					*(Denominations as indicated)*				
Population (mid-year, millions)	4.6	4.7	4.5	4.6	4.5	4.6	4.4	4.5	na
GDP (in millions of kuna)	87,441	98,382	107,981	123,811	137,604	141,579	152,519	162,909	172,506
GDP per capita (in US dollars)	3,137	4,029	4,422	4,398	4,805	4,371	4,206	4,385	na
Share of industry in GDP (in per cent)	na	22.8	21.6	21.9	21.1	21.1	20.7	20.7	na
Share of agriculture, in GDP (in per cent) [5]	na	8.6	8.4	7.8	7.9	8.1	7.4	7.1	na
Current account/GDP (in per cent)	5.9	-7.7	-5.5	-11.6	-7.1	-7.0	-2.3	-3.3	-3.5
External debt - reserves, in US$ millions	1,615	1,914	2,994	4,913	6,771	6,848	7,477	6,492	na
External debt/GDP (in per cent)	20.7	20.2	26.7	37.1	44.3	49.6	59.7	57.3	na
External debt/exports of goods and services (in per cent)	42.4	53.7	67.7	90.7	111.9	121.6	127.0	116.2	na

[1] Employment service and enterprise data until 1996. From 1997, based on labour force surveys.
[2] Until 1994 net wages, gross wages thereafter.
[3] Consolidated central government. Government expenditures include net lending.
[4] Weighted average over all maturities.
[5] Includes hunting, forestry and fishing.

Czech Republic

Liberalisation, stabilisation, privatisation

1990
Jul   First Czechoslovak Eurobond issued

1991
Jan   Exchange rate unified
Jan   Fixed exchange rate regime adopted
Jan   Most prices liberalised
Jan   Most foreign trade controls lifted
Jan   Small-scale privatisation begins
Feb   Restitution law adopted
Mar   Skoda Auto sold to Volkswagen

1992
Feb   Treasury bills market initiated
May   First wave of voucher privatisation begins
Jul   EFTA agreement signed

1993
Jan   Czechoslovakia splits into Czech and Slovak Republics
Jan   VAT introduced
Jan   Income tax law adopted
Feb   New currency (koruna) introduced
Mar   First Czech Eurobond issued
Mar   CEFTA membership granted

1994
Mar   Second wave of voucher privatisation begins

1995
Jan   WTO membership granted
Oct   Full current account convertibility introduced
Dec   OECD membership granted

1996
Feb   Exchange rate band widened

1997
Apr   Austerity package announced
May   Currency crisis ensues
May   Managed float exchange rate regime adopted
May   Second austerity package announced

1998
Mar   EU accession negotiations commence
Apr   Investment incentives adopted

Stabilisation

Large fiscal deficits increase the public debt.

The general government deficit has increased in recent years and is expected to exceed 5 per cent of GDP in 2002, excluding bank restructuring costs and privatisation revenues. This is mostly due to high social transfers, large investments in infrastructure and housing, and lower revenues. In addition, the floods of August 2002 are tentatively estimated to cost both the public and private sector about CZK 60–90 billion, or 2.6 to 4.0 per cent of GDP. About a quarter of this is expected to be met by the state. According to projections of the new government, formed in July 2002, the fiscal deficit will exceed 7 per cent of GDP by 2004 and fall to about 5 per cent in 2006. This could result in the delayed adoption of the euro, with the Czech Republic unable to satisfy the Maastricht criteria due to the size of its fiscal deficits. It will also lead to an increase in the public debt from the current level of below 20 per cent of GDP to over 30 per cent by 2006.

Central Bank to target price stability.

An amendment to the Central Bank law was enacted in August 2001, changing the main goal of monetary policy from currency stability to price stability, while a further amendment in May 2002 brought the law in line with EU requirements. The new law otherwise left the Central Bank's independence to conduct monetary policy unchanged.

Privatisation

Steel sector privatisation has progressed.

At the end of May 2002, the government approved the sale of troubled steelworks Nova Hut (NH) to LNM Holdings, a large international steel company. LNM will pay US$ 20 million for a 67 per cent stake in NH and pay its debts to the state. LNM will restructure US$ 250 million of the company's bank debts, inject US$ 32 million in capital, provide a US$ 33 million loan for working capital and carry out investments worth US$ 243 million over 10 years. It has also guaranteed to keep 8,860 of NH's current 12,000 workers. The government has also granted LNM a six month exclusive period

for negotiating the purchase of majority state-owned Vitkovice steelworks and OKD, the country's largest mining group, in which the state has only a minority stake. The successful privatisation of Vitkovice to a strategic investor, following on from the sale of NH, would be a crucial step towards restructuring the steel sector.

Planned sale of dominant petrochemical company collapses.

In December 2001, the government agreed to sell a 63 per cent share in the already partly privatised petrochemical conglomerate Unipetrol to local agrochemical company Agrofert Holding for €361 million. Although a foreign bidder, British Roch Energy, had offered €444 million, substantially more than the winning bid, the government quoted its lack of sector experience and recent problems in financing a similar deal in Poland as reasons for rejecting the bid. However, in September 2002, the sale was cancelled by the buyer. A consortium of Agip, Royal Dutch Shell and Conoco already holds a 49 per cent stake in the Unipetrol refinery and may be interested in increasing its stake into a majority in due course.

Enterprise reform

Complex business regulations and arbitrary procurement practices persist ...

Small and medium-sized enterprises continue to be adversely affected by complex legislation and inefficient state administration, particularly in the areas of commercial registration, judiciary and bankruptcy. In addition, a large number of exemptions and a high degree of discretion in the public procurement process have contributed to lower standards of business conduct.

... but foreign direct investment is boosted by special incentives.

As a result of a transparent and generous set of incentives for large investors, Toyota Motor Corp and PSA Peugeot Citroen decided in December 2001 to build a €1.5 billion greenfield car assembly plant in the Central Bohemian town of Kolin. The plant, which will produce 300,000 small cars annually, is the

largest greenfield investment in the country so far and emphasises the dominance of the automotive sector in Czech manufacturing. Following the success of this project, the authorities are now keen to diversify the economic base with the public investment promotion agency, Czech Invest, recently developing investment incentives targeting hi-tech services.

Enterprises, infrastructure, finance and social reforms

1992
Mar	Telecommunications law amended
Apr	Investment companies law enacted
May	First bank privatised
May	Insurance law adopted
Nov	Securities law adopted

1993
Apr	Stock exchange begins trading
Apr	Bankruptcy law amended

1994
Sep	First pension fund obtains licence
Nov	First corporate Eurobond issued

1995
Jan	Bad loan provisioning regulation adopted
Jan	Energy law adopted
Jun	Telecommunications privatisation begins
Jul	Mortgage banking law adopted

1996
Jan	BIS capital adequacy regulation enacted
Jul	Securities law amended
Oct	Largest private bank forced into administration
Nov	Competition agency established

1997
Oct	First large power company sold

1998
Jan	Bankruptcy law amended
Apr	Independent securities regulator established
Jun	Law on investment funds adopted
Jul	Utility prices increased significantly
Sep	Banking law amended

1999
May	Enterprise restructuring agency established

2000
Mar	Largest savings bank privatised
May	New bankruptcy law adopted
May	New telecommunications law adopted
Jun	IPB, major Czech bank, forced into administration

2001
Jan	New capital market legislation adopted
Feb	First package of Consolidation Bank's bad loans sold
Jun	Bank privatisation completed

2002
Apr	Gas sector privatisation completed
May	Central Bank law amended
Jun	Major steel company privatised
Jul	Telecommunications liberalisation completed
Aug	Telecommunications privatisation completed

Infrastructure

Privatisation in the telecommunications sector close to completion as liberalisation advances.

In August 2002, the government decided to sell its 51 per cent stake in Cesky Telecom to a consortium of Deutsche Bank and Danish telecommunications company TDC for €1.8 billion. The sale will complete the privatisation of the telecommunications sector. The final formal barriers to the liberalisation of the sector were removed at the beginning of July 2002, allowing competitors to offer fixed-line services. In the mobile telecommunications sector, only two out of three local mobile operators bid for the third generation licences in December 2001. The sale of these licences generated only CZK 7.4 billion (approximately €220 million) for the government.

Privatisation of the gas sector completed ...

The state-owned stakes in the gas sector were sold off in April 2002. The German gas company RWE paid €4.1 billion for a 97 per cent stake in gas transit company Transgas and 46 to 58 per cent stakes in each of the eight regional gas distributors. RWE agreed not to take control of the gas company Moravske Naftove Doly Hodonin (MND), which is now its only competitor in the Czech market and in which Transgas holds a 21.5 per cent stake. RWE also agreed not to use its stake in MND to interfere in its business strategy or buy stakes in any power and heating utilities before completion of the privatisation of CEZ, the dominant power generating company.

... but electric power privatisation has been postponed.

The government has had to postpone the sale of its stakes in power sector companies, including the dominant power generating company CEZ and several distribution companies, as all the potential bidders failed to match the minimum price of CZK 200 billion (almost €7 billion). The government is now focusing on transforming the energy sector structure, including changing the ownership links among power generation, transmission and distribution. The privatisation of CEZ has been complicated by its ownership of Temelin, a controversial nuclear power plant built according to Soviet design and equipped with US technology, since a number of potential investors do not want to operate a nuclear facility.

Financial institutions

Anti-money laundering measures introduced.

An amendment to the banking law has banned anonymous bank accounts, thereby combating money laundering and increasing the transparency of financial transactions.

At the end of 2001, there were still 7 million anonymous bank accounts, mostly in the dominant savings bank Ceska Sporitelna, with total deposits of CZK 130 billion (€4 billion).

Banking sector stabilised.

Following the privatisation of the large state banks, the banking sector has now stabilised and bad loans as a share of the total are below 15 per cent following transfers of non-performing assets from commercial banks to the specialised Consolidation Agency. This agency is now in charge of working out CZK 300 billion of impaired assets, equivalent to €10 billion or almost 20 per cent of GDP.

Social reform

Poverty low, but social expenditures remain high.

The share of public spending on health, education, housing, social security and welfare in the Czech Republic is one of the highest among the OECD countries at approximately 70 per cent of total government expenditure. Given the low level of poverty, it is likely that a reform of social spending could be achieved without adverse social consequences while it would substantially improve fiscal performance and macroeconomic stability. In particular, pension reform is becoming urgent as total pension transfers increased from 7.5 per cent of GDP in 1993 to 9.3 per cent in 2001. In the absence of reform, the current combination of demographic trends and levels of i) pension contributions, ii) retirement age and iii) pension entitlements, is likely to lead to unsustainable pension system deficits in the medium term.

Liberalisation

Current account convertibility – **full**

Interest rate liberalisation – **full**

Wage regulation – **no**

Stabilisation

Share of general government tax revenue
in GDP – **36.2 per cent**

Exchange rate regime – **managed float**

Privatisation

Primary privatisation method – **vouchers**

Secondary privatisation method –
direct sales

Tradability of land – **full except foreigners**

Enterprises and markets

Competition Office – **yes**

Infrastructure

Independent telecoms regulator – **yes**

Separation of railway accounts – **no**

Independent electricity regulator – **yes**

Financial sector

Capital adequacy ratio – **8 per cent**

Deposit insurance system – **yes**

Secured transactions law – **yes**

Securities commission – **yes**

Social reform

Share of the population in poverty –
0.8 per cent

Private pension funds – **yes**

	1993	1994	1995	1996	1997	1998	1999	2000	2001
Liberalisation									
Share of administered prices in CPI (in per cent)	17.9	18.1	17.4	17.4	13.3	13.3	13.3	13.3	12.4
Number of goods with administered prices in EBRD-15 basket	4.0	4.0	4.0	4.0	2.0	2.0	2.0	2.0	2.0
Share of trade with non-transition countries (in per cent)	na	68.6	68.1	71.3	72.1	74.3	73.9	76.8	79.9
Share of trade in GDP (in per cent)	82.8	80.9	89.4	85.9	93.6	95.3	99.0	119.2	123.1
Tariff revenues (in per cent of imports)	3.5	3.5	2.6	2.6	1.7	1.5	1.2	1.1	0.7
EBRD index of price liberalisation	3.0	3.0	3.0	3.0	3.0	3.0	3.0	3.0	3.0
EBRD index of forex and trade liberalisation	4.0	4.0	4.0	4.3	4.3	4.3	4.3	4.3	4.3
Privatisation									
Privatisation revenues (cumulative, in per cent of GDP)	na	2.7	4.6	6.3	7.1	7.9	9.3	10.3	12.9
Private sector share in GDP (in per cent)	45.0	65.0	70.0	75.0	75.0	75.0	80.0	80.0	80.0
Private sector share in employment (in per cent)	47.1	53.0	57.2	58.9	59.7	60.6	65.0	65.0	70.0
EBRD index of small-scale privatisation	4.0	4.0	4.0	4.3	4.3	4.3	4.3	4.3	4.3
EBRD index of large-scale privatisation	3.0	4.0	4.0	4.0	4.0	4.0	4.0	4.0	4.0
Enterprises									
Budgetary subsidies and current transfers (in per cent of GDP) [1]	6.4	7.1	8.3	8.0	7.8	7.7	7.4	9.8	8.3
Effective statutory social security tax (in per cent)	88.2	91.9	91.7	90.8	93.7	93.2	92.5	na	na
Share of industry in total employment (in per cent)	33.5	32.2	32.1	31.6	32.9	33.4	34.7	33.5	32.8
Change in labour productivity in industry (in per cent)	-1.0	8.7	11.2	12.0	0.7	3.4	-2.5	8.0	9.3
Investment rate/GDP (in per cent)	26.6	29.5	34.0	36.6	35.1	33.6	32.6	33.5	35.0
EBRD index of enterprise reform	3.0	3.0	3.0	3.0	3.0	3.0	3.0	3.3	3.3
EBRD index of competition policy	2.7	2.7	2.7	3.0	3.0	3.0	3.0	3.0	3.0
Infrastructure									
Main telephone lines per 100 inhabitants	19.2	21.2	23.6	27.3	31.8	36.4	37.1	37.8	37.4
Railway labour productivity (1989=100)	76.8	80.0	84.0	83.2	80.2	73.0	69.2	74.1	71.9
Electricity tariffs, USc kWh (collection rate in per cent)	na	3.23 (95)	3.73 (95)	3.83 (95)	3.69 (95)	4.96 (na)	5.12 (na)	4.5 (na)	6.0 (na)
GDP per unit of energy use (PPP in US dollars per kgoe)	2.7	2.9	3.1	3.2	3.2	3.3	3.5	na	na
EBRD index of infrastructure reform	2.0	2.3	2.3	2.3	2.7	2.7	2.7	2.7	3.0
Financial institutions									
Number of banks (foreign owned)	52 (18)	55 (21)	55 (23)	53 (23)	50 (24)	45 (25)	42 (27)	40 (26)	38 (26)
Asset share of state-owned banks (in per cent)	11.9	17.9	17.6	16.6	17.5	18.6	23.1	28.2	3.8
Non-performing loans (in per cent of total loans) [2]	na	na	26.6	21.8	19.9	20.3	21.5	19.3	13.7
Domestic credit to private sector (in per cent of GDP)	51.0	50.3	46.7	47.2	54.3	47.0	42.3	36.6	24.5
Stock market capitalisation (in per cent of GDP)	na	14.2	30.2	31.4	26.4	19.7	22.3	20.9	15.4
EBRD index of banking sector reform	3.0	3.0	3.0	3.0	3.0	3.0	3.3	3.3	3.7
EBRD index of reform of non-banking financial institutions	2.0	2.7	2.7	2.7	2.7	3.0	3.0	3.0	3.0
Legal environment									
EBRD rating of legal extensiveness (company law)	na	na	na	na	4.0	4.0	3.3	3.0	3.0
EBRD rating of legal effectiveness (company law)	na	na	na	na	4.0	4.0	2.7	3.3	3.0
Social sector									
Expenditures on health and education (in per cent of GDP)	12.6	11.9	11.8	11.7	11.1	10.6	9.7	9.6	9.9
Life expectancy at birth, total (years)	72.7	73.0	73.4	73.8	73.9	74.5	74.7	74.8	na
Basic school enrolment ratio (in per cent)	100.6	100.0	99.6	97.3	97.6	97.6	97.7	98.4	na
Earnings inequality (GINI-coefficient)	25.8	26.0	28.2	25.4	25.9	25.8	25.7	27.0	na

[1] Subsidies to enterprises and financial institutions, including Konsolidacni Banka Agency.

[2] Excludes loans on the books of Kosolidacni Banka Agency, banks in receivership and the loan of CSOB to Slovenska Inkasni. Changes in non-performing loans compared with previous *Transition Reports* are due to the change of loan categories included in non-performing loans (see definitions).

	1994	1995	1996	1997	1998	1999	2000	2001	2002
								Estimate	Projection
Output and expenditure					*(Percentage change in real terms)*				
GDP [1]	2.2	5.9	4.3	-0.8	-1.0	0.5	3.3	3.3	2.5
Private consumption	6.9	5.9	7.9	2.4	-1.6	1.7	2.5	3.9	na
Public consumption	0.2	-4.3	3.6	-4.4	-4.4	2.3	-1.0	0.3	na
Gross fixed investment	9.1	19.8	8.2	-2.9	0.7	-1.0	5.3	7.2	na
Exports of goods and services	1.7	16.7	8.2	9.2	10.0	6.1	17.0	12.3	na
Imports of goods and services	14.7	21.2	13.4	8.1	6.6	5.4	17.0	13.6	na
Industrial gross output	2.9	11.8	11.1	0.1	2.8	-0.4	5.1	6.8	na
Agricultural gross output	-6.6	3.2	2.5	-1.5	-1.8	2.3	-2.0	1.8	na
Employment					*(Percentage change)*				
Labour force (end-year)	-1.1	0.8	0.7	0.1	0.5	0.4	0.2	0.0	na
Employment (end-year)	0.7	2.8	1.2	-1.7	-2.5	-1.7	0.9	-0.2	na
					(In per cent of labour force)				
Unemployment (end-year)	3.2	2.9	3.5	5.2	7.5	9.4	8.8	8.9	na
Prices and wages					*(Percentage change)*				
Consumer prices (annual average)	9.9	9.1	8.8	8.5	10.7	2.1	3.9	4.7	2.3
Consumer prices (end-year)	9.7	7.9	8.6	10.0	6.8	2.5	4.0	4.1	2.1
Producer prices (annual average)	5.3	7.6	4.8	4.9	4.9	1.0	4.9	2.9	na
Producer prices (end-year)	5.6	7.2	4.4	5.7	2.2	3.4	5.0	0.8	na
Gross average monthly earnings in economy (annual average)	18.5	18.5	18.4	10.5	9.4	8.2	7.0	8.6	na
Government sector					*(In per cent of GDP)*				
General government balance [2]	-1.9	-1.6	-1.9	-2.0	-2.4	-2.0	-4.2	-5.2	-9.3
General government expenditure [2]	45.8	44.1	42.9	42.3	41.6	43.0	44.2	45.2	na
General government debt [3]	17.6	15.3	13.2	12.9	13.0	14.5	16.7	18.7	na
Monetary sector					*(Percentage change)*				
Broad money (M2, end-year)	20.8	19.4	7.8	8.7	5.2	8.1	6.8	13.0	na
Domestic credit (end-year)	16.0	12.2	12.0	8.6	3.4	0.9	-2.6	16.0	na
					(In per cent of GDP)				
Broad money (M2, end-year)	73.6	75.3	71.5	72.5	69.6	72.8	74.5	76.9	na
Interest and exchange rates					*(In per cent per annum, end-year)*				
2-week repo rate	na	11.3	12.4	14.8	9.5	5.3	5.3	4.8	na
3-month PRIBOR	12.7	10.9	12.7	17.5	10.1	5.6	5.4	4.7	na
Deposit rate [4]	7.1	7.0	6.8	7.7	8.1	4.5	3.4	3.0	na
Lending rate [4]	13.1	12.8	12.5	13.2	12.9	8.7	7.1	7.0	na
					(Korunas per US dollar)				
Exchange rate (end-year)	28.2	26.7	27.3	34.7	30.0	35.7	38.8	36.5	na
Exchange rate (annual average)	28.8	26.5	27.1	31.7	32.3	34.6	38.6	38.0	na
External sector					*(In millions of US dollars)*				
Current account	-787	-1,369	-4,121	-3,564	-1,255	-1,462	-2,718	-2,625	-2,500
Trade balance [5]	-1,381	-3,678	-5,706	-4,893	-2,603	-1,903	-3,131	-3,068	-3,500
Merchandise exports [5]	15,929	21,463	21,947	22,359	25,853	26,265	29,052	33,378	35,000
Merchandise imports [5]	17,310	25,140	27,654	27,252	28,456	28,167	32,183	36,446	38,500
Foreign direct investment, net	749	2,526	1,276	1,275	3,591	6,234	4,943	4,820	8,000
Gross reserves (end-year), excluding gold	6,243	14,023	12,435	9,774	12,617	12,825	13,139	14,464	na
External debt stock	10,694	16,549	20,845	21,352	24,047	22,615	21,372	21,696	na
					(In months of imports of goods and services)				
Gross reserves (end-year), excluding gold	3.4	5.6	4.4	3.6	4.4	4.5	4.2	4.1	na
					(In per cent of current account revenues, excluding transfers)				
Debt service	11.3	8.9	10.4	15.2	14.6	14.2	9.6	6.4	na
Memorandum items					*(Denominations as indicated)*				
Population (end-year, millions)	10.3	10.3	10.3	10.3	10.3	10.3	10.3	10.3	na
GDP (in millions of korunas)	1,182,784	1,381,049	1,566,968	1,679,921	1,839,088	1,902,293	1,984,833	2,157,828	2,261,907
GDP per capita (in US dollars)	3,977	5,049	5,601	5,143	5,535	5,332	4,984	5,503	na
Share of industry in GDP (in per cent)	33.6	33.3	33.8	35.9	36.9	35.5	36.0	37.3	na
Share of agriculture in GDP (in per cent)	4.9	4.7	4.9	5.0	4.8	3.9	3.9	3.8	na
Current account/GDP (in per cent)	-1.9	-2.6	-7.1	-6.7	-2.2	-2.7	-5.3	-4.6	-3.6
External debt - reserves, in US$ millions	4,451	2,526	8,409	11,578	11,430	9,790	8,233	7,232	na
External debt/GDP (in per cent)	26.0	31.8	36.1	40.3	42.2	41.1	41.6	38.2	na
External debt/current acc. revenues, excl. transfers (in per cent)	48.9	56.3	66.6	69.0	68.3	64.3	56.4	50.9	na

[1] GDP and GDP component data in 1995 constant prices.

[2] General government excludes privatisation revenues.

[3] Consolidated outstanding debt including state budget, health insurance, extra-budgetary funds and local governments, but excluding the indirect debt of special state financial institutions (Konsolidacni Agency) and publicly guaranteed debt.

[4] Weighted average over all maturities.

[5] Break in series in 1995 due to a change in the reporting system.

Estonia

Stabilisation

Budgetary planning improved, but municipalities need further consolidation.

Over the past year, the government has improved overall budget planning and control over local governments' borrowing through the introduction of tighter borrowing limits and stiffer penalties for exceeding these limits. However, despite plans to reduce the number of municipal governments from 247 at the end of 2001, there have only been a small number of mergers so far. Around half of local municipalities govern populations of less than 2,000 residents, while more than two-thirds have populations of less than 3,000. The Ministry of Internal Affairs devised a "Strategy of Local Government Administrative Reform" in January 2001, which included a specific timetable for implementing reforms by the end of 2001. The initiative has been delayed on several occasions partly as a result of political resistance. However, the amended organic budget law should be adopted shortly, which will reinforce the high degree of fiscal transparency.

First Eurobond issued.

After several delays due to legislative disputes in parliament, Estonia issued its first ever Eurobond in June 2002. The five-year €100 million issue was 2.7 times oversubscribed. Over half of the bonds were subscribed for by German investors. The bond issue will be used to refinance 13 foreign loans and to finance the Defence Ministry's purchase of a long-distance surveillance radar system, interior ministry border guard sea surveillance radars and other special equipment. The international ratings agencies Standard & Poors and Fitch both assigned an A– rating to the issue, which will serve as a benchmark for other Estonian issuers.

Enterprise reform

A new Competition Act in place, but court capacity remains weak.

Recent efforts to improve the investment climate include the introduction of a new Competition Act in October 2001. The Act sets out merger control and contains amended anti-trust rules, which are applied and enforced by the Competition Office. The 2001 Regular Report by the EU Commission also noted that the enforcement of laws and the administrative capacity of local courts needs to be improved, in particular the independence of courts, the backlog of cases, the quality of decisions at the lowest level and the effective enforcement of laws. For example, the close administration of courts by the Ministry of Justice and their limited financial autonomy is seen as a threat to judicial independence.

Infrastructure

The privatisation of the monopoly power producer cancelled ...

In January 2002, the previous government cancelled an agreement, signed in August 2000, with the US company NRG Energy for the sale of a 49 per cent stake in Narva Elektrijaamad. Narva Elektrijaamad owns the country's two power plants and a 51 per cent stake in the state-owned oil shale company. NRG was to pay US$ 71 million for the 49 per cent stake, but a final deadline of end December 2001 passed without NRG gaining approval for a US$ 285 million loan. This was due, in part, to the events surrounding September 11 and the Enron scandal. The new government subsequently announced that privatisation was no longer an option in the foreseeable future. In August 2002, NRG filed a lawsuit against Eesti Energia claiming EEK 2.4 billion (€153 million) for the failed acquisition. Meanwhile, the company is still continuing with renovations, which form a key part of the reforms necessary to satisfy EU requirements relating to energy and environment. A new restructuring plan is to be submitted to parliament in September 2002. Part of the costs of the restructuring are to be covered by the debut issue of a €200 million seven-year Eurobond in July 2002. Eesti Energia is rated A– by Standard & Poor's and Baa1 by Moody's, although the issue received an A3 rating from the latter and was almost two times oversubscribed. In addition, despite uncertain market conditions, Eesti Energia signed an agreement for a €150 million loan for 15 years in June 2002 (without any government guarantees).

Enterprises, infrastructure, finance and social reforms

1993
Apr — Banking regulations adopted
Jun — Securities markets law adopted
Jun — Securities Commission established
Jun — Competition law passed
Oct — Competition agency established
Dec — Law on electricity sector regulation approved

1994
Sep — BIS capital adequacy requirements introduced

1995
Jan — IAS introduced
Feb — First state-owned bank privatised
Feb — Commercial code adopted

1996
May — Stock exchange established
May — Electric power pricing reformed
May — Money laundering regulations adopted
Jun — Trade in fully listed shares begins
Nov — Energy law approved
Dec — Insolvency law amended

1998
Apr — Utility prices adjusted
Jun — Pension reform law adopted
Jul — Third pension tier introduced
Oct — Deposit insurance law adopted
Oct — EU compatible competition law adopted

1999
Jan — First pension tier becomes operational
Feb — First Estonian Eurobond issued by Uhispank
Feb — Eesti Telekom floated
Feb — Telecommunications law amended
Feb — Banking law amended

2000
Jun — Last state-owned bank privatised

2001
Jan — Telecommunications market liberalised
May — Law on unified financial sector supervisory agency passed
Aug — Railways privatised
Sep — New act on contractual and extra-contractual obligations passed
Sep — Legislation for second pension pillar passed
Oct — New Competition Act adopted
Oct — New Securities Market Act adopted

2002
Jan — Integrated financial sector supervisory agency established
Jan — New unemployment insurance scheme adopted
Feb — Merger of the Tallinn Stock Exchange with Helsinki Exchange completed
Jul — First Eurobond issued by Eesti Energia

... but important reforms in the energy sector are still necessary.

EU accession will require eventual competition in the generation and supply of electricity, regulated third-party access to the network and an independent regulator for transmission and distribution. In July 2002, the government agreed with the EU a transition period for the step-by-step opening of its electricity market by 2012. According to the government's 2001 "National Programme for Adopting the *Acquis*" liberalisation of the electricity and gas market was scheduled for 2002. However, the preparation of legislation has been slow and the end-2002 target is unlikely to be met. In addition, the independence of the regulator, the Energy Market Inspectorate, has been called into question. Although there have been significant tariff increases in recent years, the government has requested a reduction in tariff increases agreed between Eesti Energia and the Inspectorate in September 2001. In April 2002, electricity tariffs were increased but the size of the increase was less than previously announced. Eesti Energia decided to lower the monthly electricity fee from the intended 20 kroons to 5 kroons, but to make no changes in the new tariffs per kilowatt-hour.

Financial institutions

Financial sector supervision has strengthened.

An integrated financial supervisory authority for banking, securities and insurance started operations in January 2002 with operational and financial independence according to international best practice. Following the adoption by parliament of the law on obligations and the Securities Market Act at the end of 2001, Estonian legislation in the field of payment and settlements are now in full compliance with the EU *acquis communautaire*. The former law enhances consumer protections, while the latter enhances investor protection and regulates the topics related to the provision of investment services and securities settlement. An inter-bank payment system was launched at the beginning of 2002. However, one distortion that remains in the sector is the tax exempt status of income earned on bank deposits.

Stock exchange consolidation with the Helsinki Exchange completed.

In May 2001, the owner of the Helsinki Stock Exchange, HEX Group, acquired a majority holding in the Tallinn Stock Exchange. The integration was completed in February 2002, with the creation of a common trading environment for securities listed on the Helsinki and Tallinn bourses. The new Securities Market Act, which was passed in October 2001 and came into force in January 2002, regulates Estonia's investment services and securities settlements.

The Act enforces prudential requirements for investment firms that are non-credit institutions, prohibits market manipulations and regulates the issues of securities.

Social reform

Legislation passed to establish the second pension pillar.

In response to the build-up of unfunded pension liabilities, the authorities are moving from the pay-as-you-go pension system to a three-tier partially funded scheme. The first pillar, or state pension reformed in 1998, involves the gradual raising of the pension age for men and women to 63 and the index-ation of pensions, which became effective from April 2002. The third tier (introduced in July 1998) consists of voluntary contributions administered by private pension funds and insurance companies. The fully-funded second tier will offer additional pension coverage financed by mandatory individual contributions. Legislation for the second pillar was approved by parliament in September 2001, making participation mandatory for new entrants to the labour market, but voluntary (although irreversible) for existing workers. Employees who are members of the second pillar pension scheme contribute an additional 2 per cent of their gross wages to the mandatory (second pillar) pension funds. This is topped by an additional 4 per cent, deducted from the employee's social tax contribution, paid by the employer. The first round of switching took place in May 2002. The collection of contributions from those who joined before 1 June, started on 1 July 2002. A second round of switching will last until 1 November, and these contributions will start on 1 January 2003. The actual number of people who have already joined the funded pension pillar was 92,000 at the end of September 2002, indicating that public interest towards the new system is very high.

New unemployment insurance scheme becomes effective.

In January 2002, a new unemployment insurance scheme became effective. Insurance is paid in the case of redundancy, termination of collective agreements and employer insolvency. According to the scheme, employees and employers pay 1 per cent and 0.5 per cent respectively of wage income into an unemployment insurance fund administered by the Ministry of Finance. The first payments from the fund will, however, not be paid for another year, given the eligibility requirements. The scheme, together with the 2 per cent contribution of wage income to the second pension pillar, substantially increases the already high level of payroll taxation.

Liberalisation
Current account convertibility – **full**
Interest rate liberalisation – **full**
Wage regulation – **no**

Stabilisation
Share of general government tax revenue
in GDP – **34.5 per cent**
Exchange rate regime – **currency board**

Privatisation
Primary privatisation method – **direct sales**
Secondary privatisation method – **vouchers**
Tradability of land – **full**

Enterprises and markets
Competition Office – **yes**

Infrastructure
Independent telecoms regulator – **yes**
Separation of railway accounts – **yes**
Independent electricity regulator – **yes**

Financial sector
Capital adequacy ratio – **10 per cent**
Deposit insurance system – **yes**
Secured transactions law – **yes**
Securities commission – **yes**

Social reform
Share of the population in poverty –
19.3 per cent
Private pension funds – **yes**

	1993	1994	1995	1996	1997	1998	1999	2000	2001
Liberalisation									
Share of administered prices in CPI (in per cent)	na	21.1	18.0	24.0	24.0	25.6	25.6	25.6	28.9
Number of goods with administered prices in EBRD-15 basket	na	3.0	3.0	3.0	3.0	2.0	2.0	2.0	2.0
Share of trade with non-transition countries (in per cent)	54.8	54.5	61.6	59.5	73.1	64.3	76.3	84.7	74.3
Share of trade in GDP (in per cent)	107.2	122.0	113.8	106.6	123.8	124.3	112.5	143.6	136.5
Tariff revenues (in per cent of imports) [1]	0.0	0.9	0.2	0.0	0.0	0.0	0.0	0.1	0.1
EBRD index of price liberalisation	3.0	3.0	3.0	3.0	3.0	3.0	3.0	3.0	3.0
EBRD index of forex and trade liberalisation	3.0	4.0	4.0	4.0	4.0	4.0	4.0	4.3	4.3
Privatisation									
Privatisation revenues (cumulative, in per cent of GDP)	na	0.0	0.0	0.0	0.2	0.3	4.2	5.2	7.2
Private sector share in GDP (in per cent)	40.0	55.0	65.0	70.0	70.0	70.0	75.0	75.0	75.0
Private sector share in employment (in per cent)	na	na	na	na	na	na	na	na	na
EBRD index of small-scale privatisation	3.0	4.0	4.0	4.3	4.3	4.3	4.3	4.3	4.3
EBRD index of large-scale privatisation	2.0	3.0	4.0	4.0	4.0	4.0	4.0	4.0	4.0
Enterprises									
Budgetary subsidies and current transfers (in per cent of GDP)	na	0.9	0.5	0.4	0.3	0.9	0.9	0.8	0.8
Effective statutory social security tax (in per cent)	84.3	81.2	76.6	81.6	82.9	86.7	76.4	na	na
Share of industry in total employment (in per cent)	25.9	25.3	28.8	27.9	25.9	25.7	25.3	26.3	26.1
Change in labour productivity in industry (in per cent)	na	4.0	4.2	7.1	18.2	5.2	1.9	11.5	7.1
Investment rate/GDP (in per cent)	24.4	27.0	26.0	27.8	30.9	29.3	24.5	27.8	27.7
EBRD index of enterprise reform	3.0	3.0	3.0	3.0	3.0	3.0	3.0	3.0	3.3
EBRD index of competition policy	2.0	2.0	2.0	2.0	2.0	2.0	2.7	2.7	2.7
Infrastructure									
Main telephone lines per 100 inhabitants	23.1	25.2	27.7	29.9	32.1	34.4	35.7	36.3	35.2
Railway labour productivity (1989=100)	55.0	47.7	50.8	55.0	74.2	98.6	124.6	148.7	172.2
Electricity tariffs, USc kWh (collection rate in per cent)	na	1.6 (99)	3.0 (100)	3.2 (98)	3.4 (97)	4.1 (99)	4.1 (na)	4.1 (na)	4.9 (97)
GDP per unit of energy use (PPP in US dollars per kgoe)	1.8	1.8	2.0	1.9	2.2	2.4	2.6	na	na
EBRD index of infrastructure reform	2.0	2.0	2.3	2.3	2.3	3.0	3.0	3.3	3.3
Financial institutions									
Number of banks (foreign owned) [2]	21 (1)	22 (2)	19 (5)	15 (4)	12 (4)	6 (3)	7 (3)	7 (4)	7 (4)
Asset share of state-owned banks (in per cent) [3]	25.7	28.1	9.7	6.6	0.0	7.8	7.9	0.0	0.0
Non-performing loans (in per cent of total loans) [4]	na	3.5	2.4	2.0	2.1	4.0	2.9	1.6	1.5
Domestic credit to private sector (in per cent of GDP)	10.6	13.3	14.0	18.1	25.6	25.9	26.0	25.5	27.8
Stock market capitalisation (in per cent of GDP)	na	na	na	na	24.7	9.4	36.6	34.5	27.0
EBRD index of banking sector reform	3.0	3.0	3.0	3.0	3.3	3.3	3.7	3.7	3.7
EBRD index of reform of non-banking financial institutions	1.7	1.7	1.7	2.0	3.0	3.0	3.0	3.0	3.0
Legal environment									
EBRD rating of legal extensiveness (company law)	na	na	na	na	4.0	3.0	3.3	3.7	3.3
EBRD rating of legal effectiveness (company law)	na	na	na	na	4.0	4.0	3.7	3.3	4.0
Social sector									
Expenditures on health and education (in per cent of GDP)	12.0	12.1	9.6	13.4	12.2	12.2	13.1	11.7	na
Life expectancy at birth, total (years)	68.0	67.0	67.8	69.8	70.1	69.8	70.6	70.6	na
Basic school enrolment ratio (in per cent)	91.7	91.2	92.2	92.8	93.7	95.9	97.5	102.8	na
Earnings inequality (GINI-coefficient)	na	na	na	na	33.6	38.4	40.1	na	na

[1] Excludes differential excise taxes on imports.
[2] Includes Merita-Nordbanken branch and investment banks.
[3] Increase in 1998 is due to renationalisation of Optiva Bank, following its insolvency in late 1998.
[4] Changes in non-performing loans data compared with previous *Transition Reports* are due to the change in the definition of non-performing loans (see definitions).

	1994	1995	1996	1997	1998	1999	2000	2001	2002
								Estimate	Projection
Output and expenditure				*(Percentage change in real terms)*					
GDP	-2.0	4.3	3.9	9.8	4.6	-0.6	7.1	5.0	4.0
Private consumption	0.6	3.3	9.2	7.8	4.3	-2.9	6.5	4.9	na
Public consumption	5.5	16.3	-1.0	1.8	4.5	3.8	0.1	2.1	na
Gross fixed investment	6.3	4.1	11.4	17.6	11.3	-14.8	13.3	9.1	na
Exports of goods and services	3.5	5.3	2.4	29.5	12.0	0.5	28.6	-0.2	na
Imports of goods and services	12.2	5.4	7.6	29.1	12.9	-5.4	27.9	2.1	na
Industrial gross output	-1.8	11.0	1.6	15.4	2.8	-4.2	14.6	7.0	na
Agricultural gross output	-8.4	2.6	-1.2	5.8	1.1	-2.6	0.9	-6.7	na
Employment				*(Percentage change)*					
Labour force (annual average) [1]	-2.3	-4.0	-2.0	3.8	-1.5	-1.9	0.4	-0.2	na
Employment (annual average) [1]	-3.4	-6.2	-2.2	4.0	-1.7	-4.5	-1.2	0.9	na
				(In per cent of labour force)					
Unemployment (annual average) [1]	7.6	9.7	10.0	9.6	9.8	12.2	13.6	12.6	na
Prices and wages				*(Percentage change)*					
Consumer prices (annual average)	47.7	29.0	23.1	11.2	8.1	3.3	4.0	5.8	3.8
Consumer prices (end-year)	41.7	28.9	14.8	12.5	4.2	3.8	5.0	4.2	4.1
Producer prices (annual average)	36.3	25.6	14.8	8.8	4.2	-1.2	4.9	4.4	na
Producer prices (end-year)	32.8	21.8	9.9	7.7	0.1	2.2	6.0	1.7	na
Gross average monthly earnings in economy (annual average) [2]	62.7	37.0	25.7	19.7	15.4	7.6	10.5	12.3	na
Government sector [3]				*(In per cent of GDP)*					
General government balance	1.3	-1.3	-1.5	2.2	-0.3	-4.6	-0.7	0.4	-1.0
General government expenditure	40.5	41.5	40.5	37.6	39.6	42.7	38.6	37.8	na
General government debt	na	8.6	8.0	6.7	5.8	6.5	5.0	4.8	na
Monetary sector				*(Percentage change)*					
Broad money (M2, end-year)	30.9	27.8	37.2	37.8	4.2	23.7	25.7	23.0	na
Domestic credit (end-year)	na	59.0	92.5	78.3	16.5	9.6	27.2	24.4	na
				(In per cent of GDP)					
Broad money (M2, end-year)	28.3	26.5	28.3	32.0	29.0	34.6	38.0	42.3	na
Interest and exchange rates				*(In per cent per annum, end-year)*					
Inter-bank interest rate (up to 30 days maturity)	na	na	7.9	15.8	18.5	5.1	6.1	4.0	na
Deposit rate (over 12 months) [4]	8.8	8.7	10.5	10.8	8.9	8.9	6.8	4.5	na
Lending rate (over 12 months) [5]	17.5	15.8	13.9	11.2	16.3	8.6	8.9	10.1	na
				(Kroons per US dollar)					
Exchange rate (end-year)	12.4	11.5	12.4	14.3	13.4	15.6	16.8	17.7	na
Exchange rate (annual average)	13.0	11.5	12.0	13.9	14.1	14.7	17.0	17.6	na
External sector				*(In millions of US dollars)*					
Current account	-167	-158	-398	-563	-478	-247	-294	-340	-422
Trade balance	-357	-666	-1,019	-1,125	-1,115	-822	-767	-790	-957
Merchandise exports	1,226	1,697	1,813	2,294	2,690	2,515	3,309	3,358	3,626
Merchandise imports	1,583	2,363	2,832	3,419	3,806	3,337	4,076	4,148	4,583
Foreign direct investment, net	212	199	111	130	574	222	324	343	300
Gross reserves (end-year), excluding gold	511	650	703	821	876	944	1,006	903	na
External debt stock [6]	381	626	1,534	2,562	2,924	2,879	3,011	3,279	na
				(In months of imports of goods and services)					
Gross reserves (end-year), excluding gold	3.1	2.7	2.5	2.4	2.2	2.7	2.4	2.1	na
				(In per cent of exports of goods and services)					
Debt service	1.6	1.7	2.6	4.3	7.5	7.1	6.6	7.1	na
Memorandum items				*(Denominations as indicated)*					
Population (end-year, millions)	1.4	1.4	1.4	1.4	1.4	1.4	1.4	1.4	na
GDP (in millions of kroons)	29,867	40,897	52,423	64,045	73,538	76,327	87,236	96,571	104,286
GDP per capita (in US dollars)	1,590	2,503	3,098	3,312	3,788	3,790	3,761	4,039	na
Share of industry in gross value added (in per cent)	22.7	22.0	21.1	20.3	20.3	19.1	20.0	20.3	na
Share of agriculture in gross value added (in per cent)	9.4	7.8	7.5	7.0	6.5	6.1	5.5	5.2	na
Current account/GDP (in per cent)	-7.2	-4.4	-9.2	-12.1	-9.2	-4.7	-5.7	-6.2	-6.7
External debt - reserves, in US$ millions	-130	-24	831	1,742	2,048	1,935	2,004	2,375	na
External debt/GDP (in per cent)	16.5	17.5	35.2	55.5	56.0	55.4	58.6	59.6	na
External debt/exports of goods and services (in per cent)	21.9	24.3	52.5	70.9	70.1	71.9	62.6	65.5	na

[1] New series based on ILO methodology. Population aged 15-74.

[2] Starting in 1998, the data on average monthly gross wages do not include compensations from the Health Insurance Fund.

[3] General government includes the state, municipalities and extra-budgetary funds. General government expenditure includes net lending.

[4] Weighted average annual interest rate of time deposits.

[5] Weighted average annual interest on kroon loans.

[6] The debt data from 1996 onwards are from the Bank of Estonia. The data include non-resident currency and deposits, liabilities to affiliated enterprises and liabilities to direct investors.

FR Yugoslavia[1]

Key reform challenges

- While a new privatisation programme is in place, the key challenge is to implement the process transparently and efficiently to attract much-needed local and foreign investment.

- Much of the infrastructure is in poor condition and its rehabilitation will require both investment and tariff increases, but these must be managed carefully in light of limited affordability.

- A comprehensive overhaul of the financial sector is under way and the emphasis is now on complementing achievements so far by introducing and implementing new laws and strengthening regulatory procedures to foster greater confidence and encourage financial deepening.

Liberalisation

Full current account convertibility introduced.

In May 2002, the authorities introduced full current account convertibility by abolishing all restrictions on payments and transfers for current international transactions. Some controls remain on short-term capital transactions. At the same time, a new foreign exchange law was introduced to liberalise further the market for foreign exchange. However, the new law had retained restrictive provisions that prohibited non-residents from withdrawing foreign currency from local accounts, but this provision was effectively rescinded following strong opposition. In addition, the law states that share capital can be denominated in foreign currency, while the securities law states that it must be in dinars, a conflict that has yet to be resolved.

Regional trade talks progressing.

In common with other countries in south-eastern Europe, FR Yugoslavia has committed to signing bilateral Free Trade Agreements (FTAs) with its neighbours by the end of 2002. By mid-2002, FTAs were in place with Bosnia and Herzegovina and FYR Macedonia, and negotiations with the other countries were ongoing. FR Yugoslavia has applied to join the WTO but membership is unlikely before 2004. At present, import tariffs and other trade barriers differ between the two republics. Tariffs average about 9 per cent in Serbia compared with only 3 per cent in Montenegro, where non-tariff barriers are more significant. Both republics have committed to phasing out non-tariff barriers on exports by end-2003 and on imports by end-2004.

Stabilisation

Rapid increase in foreign reserves underpins the near-pegged exchange rate policy.

Since the unification of the exchange rate at the end of 2000, the National Bank of Yugoslavia (NBY) has operated a tight monetary policy, underpinned by a near-peg of the currency to the euro. The exchange rate policy has been successful in terms of restoring confidence to the currency and reducing inflationary expectations. Foreign currency reserves at the Central Bank have risen sharply since early 2001 and by August 2002 stood at about €2 billion, covering more than four months of imports. Inflation continues to fall but remains in double figures, due partly to the effects of administered price increases.

Debt restructuring helping the return to international solvency.

FR Yugoslavia has made substantial progress in reducing and restructuring its external debt burden. The authorities have successfully concluded restructuring agreements with almost all multilateral creditors, including a re-scheduling of its outstanding US$ 1.8 billion debt to the World Bank. In November 2001, the country achieved a major write-off of outstanding debts to the Paris Club of bilateral official creditors. The Paris Club agreed to a 66 per cent reduction, to be implemented in two phases. In the first phase, 51 per cent of the US$ 4.6 billion debt would be written off upon the signing of a three-year programme with the IMF. In May 2002, the Board of the IMF approved a three-year Extended Arrangement for FR Yugoslavia, to the value of US$ 829 million. In the second phase, a further 15 per cent of the debt will be written off in three years' time provided the IMF programme has been successfully completed and payments to the Paris Club in the intervening period have been made on time. Negotiations with the London Club of commercial creditors on outstanding debts of US$ 2.2 billion are ongoing.

Privatisation

Privatisation under way in Serbia ...

A comprehensive privatisation programme is under way in Serbia, following approval of an investor-oriented law in June 2001. In December 2001, three cement plants were sold for US$ 139 million (€158 million) to foreign strategic investors following a tender launched in October 2001. Another 16 companies were offered for tender in early 2002 and a total of up to 50 may be offered for tender by the end of the year. About 4,000 small and medium enterprises are also scheduled for privatisation, mostly through auctions. The target is to have around 1,000 auctions by the end of the year, but at the

Enterprises, infrastructure, finance and social reforms

1992
Apr   Two-tier banking system established
Jun   Securities and Exchange Commission established

1993
May   BIS capital adequacy adopted

1994
Jan   Bank credit ceilings introduced

1995
Mar   Banking rehabilitation law adopted

1996
Mar   Stock exchange begins trading
Apr   Banking law adopted
Jun   Telecommunications law adopted

1997
Mar   TAT Savings House collapsed
Jul   Securities law adopted
Nov   Electricity law adopted

1998
May   New bankruptcy law adopted

1999
Dec   Competition and anti-monopoly laws adopted

2000
Mar   Pension reforms introduced
Apr   Credit ceilings on domestic banks lifted
Apr   Largest bank fully privatised
Jul   New mortgage law adopted
Jul   Law on banks adopted
Jul   Law on securities adopted
Oct   Bankruptcy law amended

2001
Apr   Minimum bank capital requirements raised
Jul   New payments system adopted

2002
Jan   Central Bank law adopted
Mar   Law on money-laundering adopted

New money laundering code in force.
In March 2002, a new law against money laundering took effect. The law allowed the creation of a new directorate within the Ministry of Finance, with responsibility for investigating suspected cases of money laundering. Under the law, individuals and legal entities, including banks and law firms, that may unintentionally be involved in money laundering are obliged to report their suspicions to this new directorate.

Infrastructure

Licence for a second mobile operator sold.
In November 2001, the Greek telecommunications company OTE won the tender to build the second mobile network in FYR Macedonia. The licence cost €28.5 million. The system is expected to be operational in late 2002. In the fixed-line sector, Macedonian Telecom continues to have the exclusive rights to provide voice telephony, telegraphy, telex, public pay phones and leased lines services, as well as to construct, own and operate fixed public telecommunications networks. Under the SAA signed with the EU, its exclusivity lasts until the end of December 2004. While considerable progress has been made in reforming the telecommunications sector, further work is necessary with respect to the implementation of the newly created regulatory framework and the functioning of the Telecommunications Agency as a fully independent regulatory authority.

Privatisation plans for the energy sector proceeding.
The government has decided to privatise the integrated monopoly, Electric Power Company of Macedonia (ESM). In February 2002, the Ministry of Economy signed a contract with Meinl Bank of Austria, which is leading the consortium acting as privatisation adviser. USAID-sponsored consultants will assist with most of the legal and regulatory issues. The sale is expected to be concluded in 2003. A successful privatisation will require unbundling of ESM into separate generation, distribution and transition companies and the setting up of an appropriate regulatory environment.

Financial institutions

Foreign investment in banks and greater competition leading to consolidation.
At the end of 2001, there were 21 commercial banks in FYR Macedonia – down from 23 at the end of 2000 – due to the net effect of one merger, two acquisitions and the establishment of a new bank, Euroswiss Banka a.d. Skopje. There were also 17 savings houses in the country. The share of privately owned bank capital had risen slightly to 84.3 per cent and eight banks were 100 per cent private. In addition, 18 banks had obtained a full licence for foreign payment operations. Overall the banking sector coped well with the crisis in 2001, but the quality of banks' loan portfolios deteriorated during the year. By the end of 2001, 38.2 per cent of the total portfolio was classified in the risk categories C, D or E, up 3.4 percentage points compared with the end of 2000. In an effort to facilitate the provision of credit to micro enterprises, the parliament adopted a law in July 2002 that defines the conditions under which specialised micro-finance banks can be established. In addition to micro-finance lending programmes among existing banks, a specialised micro-finance bank is likely to be set up in the near future and will involve the EBRD and other international investors.

Payments system reformed.
A new payments system has been in place since July 2001. For six months, the system ran concurrently with the old payments bureau (ZPP), which was closed at the end of 2001. Five new entities were created by the reform: a central registry, an inter-bank clearing system (owned and run by the banks), a securities depository, an agency dealing with 'blocked accounts' and a national payment card. To date, the new system has been running efficiently.

Social reform

Health care reform envisaged.
The new law on local self-government, approved in early 2002, envisages significant reform to health care provision. Until now, health care has been highly centralised, with the provision of medical supplies controlled by the Health Insurance Fund. Among other things, the law allows for the decentralisation of some parts of the health care system. In addition, the privatisation of some local clinics is also contemplated, but will require separate legislation.

Liberalisation
Current account convertibility – **full**
Interest rate liberalisation – **full**
Wage regulation – **no**

Stabilisation
Share of general government tax revenue
in GDP – **31.9 per cent**
Exchange rate regime – **fixed to euro**

Privatisation
Primary privatisation method – **MEBOs**
Secondary privatisation method –
 direct sales
Tradability of land – **limited de jure**

Enterprises and markets
Competition Office – **no**

Infrastructure
Independent telecoms regulator – **no**
Separation of railway accounts – **no**
Independent electricity regulator – **no**

Financial sector
Capital adequacy ratio – **8 per cent**
Deposit insurance system – **yes**
Secured transactions law – **yes**
Securities commission – **yes**

Social reform
Share of the population in poverty –
 43.9 per cent
Private pension funds – **no**

	1993	1994	1995	1996	1997	1998	1999	2000	2001
Liberalisation									
Share of administered prices in CPI (in per cent)	15.0	15.5	15.0	19.6	19.6	na	na	na	na
Number of goods with administered prices in EBRD-15 basket	3.0	2.0	2.0	2.0	2.0	na	na	na	na
Share of trade with non-transition countries (in per cent)	na	55.5	54.2	74.7	75.6	83.1	84.7	63.4	57.6
Share of trade in GDP (in per cent)	82.4	69.6	59.0	59.2	76.6	83.9	75.5	89.1	78.8
Tariff revenues (in per cent of imports)	8.5	10.5	12.6	11.4	6.8	7.3	9.2	6.3	5.7
EBRD index of price liberalisation	3.0	3.0	3.0	3.0	3.0	3.0	3.0	3.0	3.0
EBRD index of forex and trade liberalisation	3.0	4.0	4.0	4.0	4.0	4.0	4.0	4.0	4.0
Privatisation									
Privatisation revenues (cumulative, in per cent of GDP)	na	na	na	na	na	na	na	na	na
Private sector share in GDP (in per cent)	35.0	35.0	40.0	50.0	50.0	55.0	55.0	55.0	60.0
Private sector share in employment (in per cent)	na	na	na	na	na	na	na	na	na
EBRD index of small-scale privatisation	3.0	4.0	4.0	4.0	4.0	4.0	4.0	4.0	4.0
EBRD index of large-scale privatisation	2.0	2.0	2.0	3.0	3.0	3.0	3.0	3.0	3.0
Enterprises									
Budgetary subsidies and current transfers (in per cent of GDP)	na	na	na	na	1.7	1.3	1.2	1.4	1.3
Effective statutory social security tax (in per cent)	na	na	na	na	na	na	na	na	na
Share of industry in total employment (in per cent)	39.8	39.9	38.3	28.9	27.4	28.2	27.7	27.1	na
Change in labour productivity in industry (in per cent)	-9.7	-4.1	5.2	-7.8	14.0	-0.3	-2.0	5.0	na
Investment rate/GDP (in per cent)	16.8	14.4	16.5	17.4	17.5	17.9	na	na	na
EBRD index of enterprise reform	1.0	2.0	2.0	2.0	2.0	2.0	2.0	2.3	2.3
EBRD index of competition policy	1.0	1.0	1.0	1.0	1.0	1.0	1.0	2.0	2.0
Infrastructure									
Main telephone lines per 100 inhabitants	15.6	16.1	16.5	17.0	20.5	21.9	23.4	25.5	26.4
Railway labour productivity (1989=100)	56.2	21.8	24.8	47.8	50.9	68.6	66.7	89.7	78.9
Electricity tariffs, USc kWh (collection rate in per cent)	na	2.73 (90)	2.81 (90)	3.1 (90)	3.54 (90)	3.73 (88.8)	3.30 (86.5)	3.7 (60)	4.1 (80)
GDP per unit of energy use (PPP in US dollars per kgoe)	na	na	na	na	na	na	na	na	na
EBRD index of infrastructure reform	1.3	1.3	1.3	1.7	1.7	1.7	1.7	1.7	2.0
Financial institutions									
Number of banks (foreign owned)	na	6 (3)	6 (3)	22 (5)	22 (5)	24 (6)	23 (5)	22 (7)	21 (8)
Asset share of state-owned banks (in per cent) [1]	na	na	na	0.0	0.0	1.4	2.5	1.1	1.3
Non-performing loans (in per cent of total loans) [2]	na	na	na	21.7	21.1	7.8	9.4	26.9	24.7
Domestic credit to private sector (in per cent of GDP)	59.3	45.3	23.1	26.5	27.3	17.7	10.4	10.5	12.5
Stock market capitalisation (in per cent of GDP)	na	na	na	2.3	0.3	0.2	0.2	0.2	0.4
EBRD index of banking sector reform	1.3	2.0	3.0	3.0	3.0	3.0	3.0	3.0	3.0
EBRD index of reform of non-banking financial institutions	1.0	1.0	1.0	1.0	1.0	1.7	1.7	1.7	1.7
Legal environment									
EBRD rating of legal extensiveness (company law)	na	na	na	na	2.0	3.0	3.7	3.3	3.3
EBRD rating of legal effectiveness (company law)	na	na	na	na	2.0	4.0	3.7	2.3	3.7
Social sector									
Expenditures on health and education (in per cent of GDP)	14.3	14.4	13.8	10.9	na	na	na	na	na
Life expectancy at birth, total (years)	na	71.7	71.9	72.2	72.4	na	72.5	72.8	na
Basic school enrolment ratio (in per cent)	97.0	97.0	97.9	98.4	99.1	98.8	99.6	100.1	na
Earnings inequality (GINI-coefficient)	27.2	25.3	27.0	25.0	25.9	27.1	27.7	27.7	na

[1] Increase in 1998 is due to the establishment of the Macedonian Bank for Development Promotion.

[2] Includes loans of banks under forced administration.

	1994	1995	1996	1997	1998	1999	2000	2001	2002
								Estimate	Projection
Output and expenditure					*(Percentage change in real terms)*				
GDP	-1.8	-1.2	1.2	1.4	3.4	4.3	4.6	-4.1	2.0
Industrial gross output	-9.7	-8.9	5.0	2.9	4.4	-2.6	3.5	-8.7	na
Agricultural gross output	7.8	2.3	-2.9	0.0	3.9	0.3	na	na	na
Employment [1]					*(Percentage change)*				
Labour force (end-year)	-2.4	-1.5	na	1.4	2.9	-2.1	-0.6	na	na
Employment (end-year)	-6.0	-9.9	na	-4.7	5.4	1.0	0.9	8.9	na
					(In per cent of labour force)				
Unemployment (end-year) [2]	31.4	37.7	31.9	36.0	34.5	32.4	32.1	30.5	na
Prices and wages					*(Percentage change)*				
Consumer prices (annual average)	126.5	16.4	2.5	0.8	2.3	-1.3	6.5	5.3	3.6
Consumer prices (end-year)	55.0	9.0	-0.6	2.6	0.8	2.3	6.0	3.7	3.2
Producer prices (annual average)	84.6	3.9	-0.3	4.2	4.0	-0.1	8.9	-1.2	na
Producer prices (end-year)	28.5	2.2	-0.6	8.6	-0.2	4.2	7.9	-2.5	na
Gross average monthly earnings in economy (annual average)	103.8	10.4	2.7	2.8	3.7	2.9	5.5	3.0	na
Government sector [3]					*(In per cent of GDP)*				
General government balance	-2.7	-1.0	-1.4	-0.4	-1.7	0.0	2.5	-6.3	-4.4
General government expenditure	45.8	39.0	37.1	35.1	35.0	35.4	34.2	40.6	na
Monetary sector					*(Percentage change)*				
Broad money (M2, end-year)	na	na	-1.1	22.9	14.4	29.7	24.4	66.3	na
Domestic credit (end-year)	31.2	-48.8	-11.5	6.8	-31.7	12.8	-10.7	-15.0	na
					(In per cent of GDP)				
Broad money (M2, end-year)	na	11.0	10.5	12.2	13.3	16.1	17.8	29.3	na
Interest and exchange rates					*(In per cent per annum, end-year)*				
Basic rate of the National Bank [4]	66.0	16.0	11.0	15.2	18.3	11.8	8.9	11.0	na
Inter-bank interest rate	na	35.7	22.5	21.1	18.1	11.6	7.2	11.9	na
Deposit rate	117.6	24.1	12.8	11.6	11.7	11.3	10.7	10.0	na
Lending rate [5]	159.8	46.0	21.6	21.4	21.0	20.0	19.0	19.2	na
					(Denars per US dollar)				
Exchange rate (end-year)	40.6	38.0	41.4	55.4	51.8	60.0	67.8	68.4	na
Exchange rate (annual average)	43.2	38.0	40.0	49.8	54.5	56.9	65.9	68.1	na
External sector					*(In millions of US dollars)*				
Current account	-180	-222	-289	-289	-363	-124	-111	-345	-409
Trade balance	-186	-221	-317	-386	-419	-392	-556	-397	-487
Merchandise exports	1,086	1,204	1,147	1,237	1,292	1,192	1,319	1,183	1,187
Merchandise imports	1,272	1,425	1,464	1,623	1,711	1,584	1,875	1,580	1,674
Foreign direct investment, net [6]	24	12	12	18	175	27	175	445	70
Gross reserves (end-year), excluding gold	165	257	240	256	304	469	703	723	na
External debt stock	844	1,062	1,118	1,167	1,437	1,490	1,488	1,410	na
					(In months of imports of goods and services)				
Gross reserves (end-year), excluding gold	1.2	1.7	1.6	1.6	1.8	2.9	3.8	4.5	na
					(In per cent of exports of goods and services)				
Debt service	15.8	10.4	11.1	8.7	10.1	13.9	13.1	19.0	na
Memorandum items					*(Denominations as indicated)*				
Population (mid-year, millions)	1.9	2.0	2.0	2.0	2.0	2.0	2.0	2.0	na
GDP (in millions of denars)	146,409	169,521	176,444	186,019	194,981	209,101	236,211	238,570	252,174
GDP per capita (in US dollars)	1,742	2,267	2,225	1,867	1,790	1,837	1,792	1,753	na
Share of industry in GDP (in per cent)	24.3	19.6	19.5	20.7	21.8	20.7	na	na	na
Share of agriculture in GDP (in per cent)	9.1	10.6	10.7	10.7	10.0	9.2	na	na	na
Current account/GDP (in per cent)	-5.3	-5.0	-6.5	-7.7	-10.1	-3.4	-3.1	-9.8	-10.2
External debt - reserves, in US$ millions	678.6	805.0	878.5	910.8	1,133.1	1,021.4	785.3	687.0	na
External debt/GDP (in per cent)	24.9	23.8	25.3	31.3	40.1	40.5	41.5	40.2	na
External debt/exports of goods and services (in per cent)	67.1	76.5	85.9	85.5	101.0	103.5	91.7	99.3	na

[1] Figures on employment and labour force up to 1995 are based on census data and are not comparable with later years, which are based on the ILO definition of unemployed.

[2] The figures up to 1995 refer to officially registered unemployed. From 1996, they are based on a labour force survey.

[3] General government includes the state, municipalities and extra-budgetary funds.

[4] Weighted interest rate of credits sold at auction (seven days maturity). The figure for 2000 is from the October auction, the last one of the year.

[5] Minimum lending rate offered to small enterprises until 1995, mid-point rates for short-term lending to all sectors thereafter.

[6] The large increase in FDI for 2001 is mainly due to the sale of a majority stake in the fixed-line telephone company.

Georgia

Liberalisation

Ban on the export of scrap metal lifted.

A ban on the export of scrap metal was introduced in December 2001 to prevent theft. The consequences were potentially serious, given that scrap metal accounts for around 8 per cent of total exports; however, the ban was lifted by parliament in June 2002 to fulfil IMF loan conditionality. These developments followed a similar decision at the end of 2001 to remove a ban on timber exports, which was in effect during the second half of 2001 to prevent the theft of timber.

Stabilisation

The external debt position remains difficult.

The independent National Bank of Georgia has continued to implement a tight monetary policy in 2002, contributing to the stability of both inflation and the exchange rate. However, the external debt position is difficult. After allowing for the Paris Club re-scheduling of 2001, debt service in 2003 and 2004 is forecast at around 40 per cent of government revenues and 70 per cent of foreign exchange reserves. Hence, the need for further debt rescheduling cannot be ruled out. In the longer term, the sustainability of the external debt could improve with appropriate rescheduling terms and an increase in transit revenues from planned new oil and gas pipelines between the Caspian Sea and Turkey.

Tax revenue remains low.

Georgia's tax revenues, at less than 15 per cent of GDP, remain among the lowest in the region. Some tax reforms have been introduced recently, for example the abolition of corporate tax exemptions. A more comprehensive reform of the tax system, proposed by the Ministry of Finance, planned for January 2002 was, however, shelved due to the lack of support from parliament and some parts of the government. Improvement of tax collection efforts, particularly targeted at large non-payers, would enhance the budget position.

Privatisation

Large-scale privatisation continues to advance slowly.

The large-scale privatisation process has moved slowly owing to concerns over asset values, social obligations of potential investors and problems related to the investment climate. Under the current World Bank Structural Adjustment Credit, 29 large industrial companies were to be privatised by early 2001. However, by July 2002, only 14 companies had been successfully privatised, two of them to foreign investors. High profile efforts to privatise the Rustavi Metalurgical Complex have also remained unsuccessful. Nevertheless, a tender for the sale of a majority stake in a company producing electric locomotives was announced in June 2002 and a concession for the operation of Poti Port will be tendered in the fourth quarter of 2002.

Enterprise reform

Corruption continues to undermine the investment climate.

Enterprises and in particular SMEs remain vulnerable to corruption in law enforcement, tax collection and other aspects of public administration. The government has recognised the need to improve the business environment in its draft Poverty Reduction Strategy Paper, which is currently being finalised. An Anti-Corruption Committee, established in June 2000, has developed a long-term anti-corruption strategy which was approved by the government in January 2002. The strategy outlines proposals to improve the business environment by setting transparent and fair tax rules, raising salaries of government staff, reducing the number of governmental agencies, introducing a code of ethics and strengthening the judiciary through the introduction of more stringent selection and testing criteria. However, the implementation of the strategy is still uncertain.

Liberalisation, stabilisation, privatisation

1991
Apr	Independence from Soviet Union declared
Aug	Exchange rate unified
Aug	Interest rates liberalised

1992
Jan	Personal income tax and corporate profit taxes introduced
Feb	Most prices liberalised
Mar	Controls on foreign trade lifted
Mar	VAT introduced

1993
Mar	Small-scale privatisation begins

1994
Dec	Export tax to non-CIS countries abolished
Dec	Unified import tariff structure introduced

1995
Jan	Trade regulations streamlined
Jun	State order system abolished
Jun	Voucher privatisation begins
Jun	Large-scale privatisation commences
Oct	New currency (lari) introduced

1996
Mar	Tradability of land rights enacted
Jun	Voucher privatisation ends
Dec	Full current account convertibility introduced

1997
May	New privatisation law adopted
Aug	Treasury bills market initiated

1998
Dec	Freely floating exchange regime adopted

1999
Jan	Registration of agriculture land titles begins
Apr	Council of Europe membership granted
May	Privatisation law amended

2000
Jun	WTO membership granted

2001
Apr	Paris Club debt rescheduled

Infrastructure

Steps taken to raise collection rates in the power sector.

Collections by the privatised Telasi power distribution company (serving Tbilisi) stand at around 70 per cent. Collections by the Georgian United Distribution Company

Enterprises, infrastructure, finance and social reforms

1994
Jan   First foreign-owned bank opened

1995
Jun   Two-tier banking system established

1996
Jun   Competition law adopted
Jul   Basel capital adequacy requirement introduced
Aug   Loan classification and provision requirements introduced
Sep   Anti-Monopoly Office established (not independent)
Dec   First bank privatised

1997
Jan   Bankruptcy law adopted
Apr   Securities regulator established (not independent)
Jun   Electricity law adopted
Jun   Independent electricity regulator established

1998
Oct   Law on non-state pension insurance adopted
Nov   Major electricity utility privatised
Dec   Law on securities market adopted

1999
Apr   Oil pipeline Baku-Supsa completed

2000
Jan   Minimum capital requirements for banks increased
Mar   Stock exchange trading commences
May   Baku-Ceyhan pipeline agreement ratified
Jun   Independent telecommunications regulator established

2001
Feb   IAS accounts introduced for all banks

2002
Jan   Anti-corruption strategy approved by government

(serving the rest of the country) are around 15 per cent. The low overall sector collections pose a severe threat to the sustainability of the sector. Recent advances include the introduction of private sector companies to manage the wholesale market, thereby creating a financial clearing mechanism. In time this should result in higher collections from large customers billed directly from the wholesale market. Payments to the transmission company should also improve following the tendering of a management contract to a private company. The IFC is currently

providing advice on the introduction of the private sector to the remaining state-owned distribution companies.

Progress in utilities privatisation mixed ...
Progress has been made on bringing in the private sector to manage the Tbilisi water company. Five international companies have expressed an interest following the launch of the tender process in November 2001 and detailed financial and technical proposals are due in the third quarter of 2002. The sale of a 75 per cent stake in the Georgian fixed-line telecommunications operator, however, failed in November 2001 due to a lack of investor interest. A new tender is expected to be announced later this year. Negotiations with a foreign strategic investor for the sale of a majority stake in the Tbilisi gas distribution network broke down in July 2002.

... while oil and gas pipeline projects move forward.
The Baku-Tbilisi-Erzerum gas pipeline project – from the Shah Deniz gas field in the Caspian Sea to Turkey – was ratified by the Georgian parliament in November 2001. The transit fees due to Georgia – to be paid in gas rather than money – will be worth around US$ 175 million per year. The gas pipeline is expected to be in operation by 2004-05. A consortium has been formed to work on the Baku-Tbilisi-Ceyhan oil pipeline. It is forecast that this pipeline will transport one billion barrels of oil per day and provide substantial transit fee income over time.

Financial institutions

The banking sector remains weak ...
The level of financial intermediation remains low, with a ratio of deposits to GDP of around 2.5 per cent and loans to GDP of 8 per cent. Competition is limited, reflected in spreads between lending and deposit rates of around 15 per cent. Most lending (some 85 per cent) is in foreign currency. The number of banks is high relative to the size of the sector, with 23 of the 26 banks having capital of between GEL 5-10 million (US$ 2.4-4.8 million). Progress in consolidation has been limited, with just three distressed banks closed in 2001-02.

... but banking regulation has been strengthened.
Following problems in the banking sector in 2000 when some failing banks were allowed to continue operating, the National Bank has worked with donors and development institutions to strengthen banking regulation. In 2001, a new asset classification was issued, IAS accounting rules were implemented and the primacy of bank law in bank-related matters was established. In 2002, an analytical framework for resolution of distressed banks was adopted and published, and procedures were introduced for the close supervision of banks in danger

of having their licence revoked. It is envisaged that criteria on the qualification of bank managers will be developed by September 2002, together with supporting legislation. In addition, a law on money laundering is planned for adoption at the end of the year.

Social reform

Winter heating programme expanded.
Georgia has one of the lowest per capita incomes in the region. Unemployment is high and over 50 per cent of the population live below the official poverty line. Government spending on pensions, poverty benefits, refugee allowances, health care, education and food amounts to 8 per cent of GDP. However, spending in these areas is constrained by fiscal considerations and an increase would require comprehensive tax reform and higher rates of tax collection. Current spending levels are complemented by a USAID-funded winter heating programme, which provides targeted subsidies to the poor for their heating and electric power. The funding for this programme was increased in 2002 from US$ 5 million to US$ 10 million and the number of people benefiting rose by 50,000 to 150,000. Nevertheless, the programme is oversubscribed. The government has produced a draft Poverty Reduction Strategy Paper, which focuses on private sector growth as the means to alleviate poverty in the medium term and which lays out a path towards a sustainable social safety net.

Liberalisation	Privatisation	Infrastructure	Social reform
Current account convertibility – **full**	Primary privatisation method – **vouchers**	Independent telecoms regulator – **yes**	Share of the population in poverty –
Interest rate liberalisation – **full**	Secondary privatisation method –	Separation of railway accounts – **no**	**54.2 per cent**
Wage regulation – **no**	**direct sales**	Independent electricity regulator – **yes**	Private pension funds – **yes**[1]
	Tradability of land – **limited for foreigners**		
Stabilisation		**Financial sector**	
Share of general government tax revenue	**Enterprises and markets**	Capital adequacy ratio – **12 per cent**	
in GDP – **14 per cent**	Competition Office – **yes (not independent)**	Deposit insurance system – **no**	
Exchange rate regime – **floating**		Secured transactions law – **restricted**	
		Securities commission – **yes**	
		(not independent)	

	1993	1994	1995	1996	1997	1998	1999	2000	2001
Liberalisation									
Share of administered prices in CPI (in per cent)	na	13.4	13.0	13.0	8.3	3.0	3.0	na	na
Number of goods with administered prices in EBRD-15 basket	5.0	5.0	4.0	3.0	3.0	0.0	0.0	0.0	na
Share of trade with non-transition countries (in per cent)	na	33.3	33.1	27.6	35.7	58.7	70.0	72.4	68.4
Share of trade in GDP (in per cent)	154.8	90.2	37.0	39.1	43.8	39.6	53.1	48.7	45.8
Tariff revenues (in per cent of imports)	na	0.3	0.5	2.0	4.4	4.2	1.7	na	na
EBRD index of price liberalisation	3.0	3.0	3.0	3.0	3.0	3.0	3.0	3.3	3.3
EBRD index of forex and trade liberalisation	1.0	1.0	2.0	3.0	4.0	4.0	4.0	4.3	4.3
Privatisation									
Privatisation revenues (cumulative, in per cent of GDP)	10.4	14.6	19.1	19.8	20.5	21.8	22.7	23.0	na
Private sector share in GDP (in per cent)	20.0	20.0	30.0	50.0	55.0	60.0	60.0	60.0	60.0
Private sector share in employment (in per cent)	na	na	na	na	na	na	na	na	na
EBRD index of small-scale privatisation	2.0	2.0	3.0	4.0	4.0	4.0	4.0	4.0	4.0
EBRD index of large-scale privatisation	1.0	1.0	2.0	3.0	3.3	3.3	3.3	3.3	3.3
Enterprises									
Budgetary subsidies and current transfers (in per cent of GDP)	na	13.8	1.1	1.5	2.2	2.1	2.0	na	2.1
Effective statutory social security tax (in per cent)	7.6	9.1	12.8	26.1	38.2	39.8	64.3	na	na
Share of industry in total employment (in per cent)	16.9	15.8	14.5	10.4	5.1	6.9	na	na	na
Change in labour productivity in industry (in per cent)	-7.7	-34.4	-0.6	49.9	-2.5	-7.3	na	na	na
Investment rate/GDP (in per cent)	3.1	1.6	4.0	6.0	7.2	7.8	na	na	na
EBRD index of enterprise reform	1.0	1.0	2.0	2.0	2.0	2.0	2.0	2.0	2.0
EBRD index of competition policy	1.0	1.0	1.0	2.0	2.0	2.0	2.0	2.0	2.0
Infrastructure									
Main telephone lines per 100 inhabitants	10.5	9.6	10.3	10.5	11.3	11.6	12.3	13.9	15.9
Railway labour productivity (1989=100)	22.0	22.6	18.9	18.1	28.4	38.9	47.7	59.5	65.1
Electricity tariffs, USc kWh (collection rate in per cent)	na	1.6 (20)	3.5 (35)	2.8 (na)	3.1 (na)	3.5 (na)	3.0 (32)	4.4 (35)	4.2 (32)
GDP per unit of energy use (PPP in US dollars per kgoe)	2.9	3.1	6.9	5.2	5.0	4.7	4.8	na	na
EBRD index of infrastructure reform	1.0	1.0	1.0	1.0	1.7	2.0	2.3	2.3	2.3
Financial institutions									
Number of banks (foreign owned)	176 (na)	226 (1)	101 (3)	61 (6)	53 (8)	42 (9)	36 (9)	30 (8)	27 (7)
Asset share of state-owned banks (in per cent)	75.0	67.9	48.6	0.0	0.0	0.0	0.0	0.0	0.0
Non-performing loans (in per cent of total loans)[2]	10.3	23.9	33.3	6.7	6.6	6.5	4.9	7.2	8.5
Domestic credit to private sector (in per cent of GDP)	na	6.1	3.4	3.8	5.0	na	5.8	6.5	7.0
Stock market capitalisation (in per cent of GDP)	na	na	na	na	na	na	na	0.8	2.9
EBRD index of banking sector reform	1.0	1.0	2.0	2.0	2.3	2.3	2.3	2.3	2.3
EBRD index of reform of non-banking financial institutions	1.0	1.0	1.0	1.0	1.0	1.0	1.0	1.7	1.7
Legal environment									
EBRD rating of legal extensiveness (company law)	na	na	na	na	3.0	3.0	2.0	3.0	3.0
EBRD rating of legal effectiveness (company law)	na	na	na	na	2.0	3.0	2.0	2.0	3.0
Social sector									
Expenditures on health and education (in per cent of GDP)	9.7	8.3	1.7	2.8	4.1	4.0	na	na	1.0
Life expectancy at birth, total (years)	na	na	72.5	na	72.5	na	na	73.0	na
Basic school enrolment ratio (in per cent)	82.4	80.7	79.8	80.6	81.0	81.2	85.2	86.1	na
Earnings inequality (GINI-coefficient)	40.0	na	na	na	49.8	na	na	na	na

[1]   At early stages of development.

[2]   Changes in non-performing loans data compared with previous
      Transition Reports are due to the change of loan categories included in
      non-performing loans (see definitions).

	1994	1995	1996	1997	1998	1999	2000	2001	2002
								Estimate	Projection
Output and expenditure				*(Percentage change in real terms)*					
GDP	-11.4	2.4	10.5	10.8	2.9	3.0	2.0	4.5	3.5
Private consumption	na	na	na	na	na	na	na	na	na
Public consumption	na	na	na	na	na	na	na	na	na
Gross fixed investment	na	na	na	na	na	na	na	na	na
Exports of goods and services	na	na	na	na	na	na	na	na	na
Imports of goods and services	na	na	na	na	na	na	na	na	na
Industrial gross output	-40.0	-10.0	7.7	2.5	-2.7	3.4	3.2	na	na
Agricultural gross output	11.6	19.9	5.1	3.9	-6.6	6.9	-12.6	na	na
Employment [1]				*(Percentage change)*					
Labour force (end-year)	-8.0	9.9	5.0	13.5	-18.3	3.1	na	na	na
Employment (end-year)	-2.4	-1.1	0.6	28.3	-22.5	0.1	0.9	4.0	na
				(In per cent of labour force)					
Unemployment (end-year) [2]	3.6	3.1	2.8	7.7	12.3	12.7	10.3	11.1	na
Prices and wages				*(Percentage change)*					
Consumer prices (annual average)	15,606.5	162.7	39.4	7.1	3.6	19.2	4.1	4.7	5.5
Consumer prices (end-year)	6,473.9	57.4	13.7	7.3	7.2	10.9	4.6	3.4	6.0
Producer prices (annual average)	211.6	36.8	32.4	29.0	2.3	na	na	na	na
Producer prices (end-year)	na	na	na	na	3.7	15.7	na	na	na
Gross average monthly earnings in economy (annual average)	22,042.9	122.6	110.1	89.3	19.8	14.4	9.8	9.8	na
Government sector [3]				*(In per cent of GDP)*					
General government balance	-7.4	-5.3	-7.3	-6.7	-5.4	-6.7	-4.1	-2.0	-1.7
General government expenditure	23.5	12.3	21.1	21.0	19.1	22.1	19.4	18.2	na
General government debt	na	na	na	na	na	na	na	na	na
Monetary sector				*(Percentage change)*					
Broad money (M3, end-year)	2,229.0	135.1	41.9	45.6	-1.2	20.6	39.0	18.5	na
Domestic credit (end-year)	3,448.3	80.7	59.6	56.1	39.1	36.7	18.7	na	na
				(In per cent of GDP)					
Broad money (M3, end-year)	5.6	4.9	6.7	8.0	6.4	7.8	10.3	11.0	na
Interest and exchange rates				*(In per cent per annum, end-year)*					
Inter-bank credit rate (3-month) [4]	na	na	27.0	31.0	40.0	na	20.0	22.0	na
Treasury bill rate (3-month maturity) [5]	na	na	na	44.0	39.1	na	29.0	33.1	na
Deposit rate (3-month)	na	17.9	16.1	12.6	10.0	12.0	10.0	12.0	na
Lending rate (3-month)	na	69.8	53.2	45.0	38.0	35.0	31.0	35.0	na
				(Laris per US dollar)					
Exchange rate (end-year)	1.3	1.2	1.3	1.3	1.7	1.9	2.0	2.1	na
Exchange rate (annual average)	1.1	1.3	1.3	1.3	1.4	2.0	2.0	2.1	na
External sector				*(In millions of US dollars)*					
Current account	-278	-216	-275	-375	-389	-232	-165	-215	-211
Trade balance	-365	-338	-351	-559	-685	-541	-409	-458	-475
Merchandise exports	381	363	417	494	478	477	528	496	510
Merchandise imports	746	700	768	1,052	1,164	1,018	937	954	985
Foreign direct investment, net	8	6	54	236	221	60	152	100	80
Gross reserves (end-year), excluding gold	41	157	158	173	118	132	110	160	na
External debt stock	1,004	1,217	1,357	1,508	1,652	1,700	1,612	1,704	na
				(In months of imports of goods and services)					
Gross reserves (end-year), excluding gold	0.6	2.3	2.2	1.5	1.0	1.3	1.0	1.4	na
				(In per cent of current account revenues, excluding transfers)					
Debt service	na	7.2	9.2	4.7	13.4	17.4	10.2	7.4	na
Memorandum items				*(Denominations as indicated)*					
Population (end-year, millions)	5.4	5.4	5.4	5.4	5.4	5.4	5.4	5.4	na
GDP (in millions of laris)	1,373	3,694	3,847	4,679	5,741	5,665	6,016	6,655	7,264
GDP per capita (in US dollars)	232	535	563	657	771	524	562	592	na
Share of industry in GDP (in per cent)	25.4	14.0	11.4	12.5	11.9	13.0	na	na	na
Share of agriculture in GDP (in per cent)	34.2	29.8	27.0	35.5	30.9	28.0	na	na	na
Current account/GDP (in per cent)	-22.3	-7.5	-9.1	-10.6	-9.4	-8.2	-5.5	-6.8	-6.2
External debt - reserves, in US$ millions	963	1,060	1,199	1,334	1,534	1,568	1,502	1,544	na
External debt/GDP (in per cent)	80.4	63.7	44.9	42.8	39.8	60.3	53.6	53.8	na
External debt/exports of goods and services (in per cent)	208.0	251.2	265.7	228.0	229.3	229.6	154.4	343.5	na

[1] Figures from 1997 onwards are from the State Department for Statistics (SDS) Household Survey.

[2] Based on registered unemployed. This series closely matches data based on the ILO methodology.

[3] General government includes the state, municipalities and extra-budgetary funds.

[4] Determined at credit auctions at which Central Bank and commercial banks participate. The three-month credit auction was suspended from September 1998 to November 2000. Figure for 1998 relates to August. Figure for 2000 relates to December.

[5] Treasury bills were introduced in August 1997. Market was suspended from September 1998 to August 1999. The data for 1998 relate to August. The data for 2000 relate to December.

Hungary

Stabilisation

The government aims to reduce the budget deficit ...

The new government, elected in April 2002, aims to reduce budget deficits over the medium term. The goal is a reduction in the general government deficit from an estimated 5.9 per cent of GDP in 2002 (according to EU definitions) to 2 per cent of GDP in 2006. From 2003, the government also intends to bring budget accounting in line with EU norms. This would increase fiscal transparency by consolidating the extra-budgetary activities of the state privatisation and holding company APV Rt., the state-owned bank MFB Rt. and the national motorway company NA Rt. into budget accounting.

... while the forecast for inflation has been revised.

Annual inflation declined to 6.8 per cent by December 2001, partly due to lower world energy prices, and stood at 4.5 per cent in August 2002. The government has revised its inflation forecast to 5.5 per cent year-on-year in December 2002 and 4.5 per cent in December 2003, both of which are at the top end of the targeted range. For the same period, the Central Bank's forecasts are 5.1 per cent and 4.3 per cent respectively.

Privatisation

Several remaining state assets prepared for privatisation.

The state privatisation and holding company APV Rt. is preparing an asset management strategy for remaining state assets. The strategy, scheduled to be completed by autumn 2002, will be guided by the new government's determination to speed up the privatisation of most state-owned enterprises following their restructuring by APV. The remaining state assets include the power company MVM, the airline company Malev, the steel firm Dunaferr, the national broadcasting company Antenna Hungaria, the shipping firm Mahart and the agricultural company Babolna, as well as large minority stakes in MOL and Richter. Dunaferr is still receiving state subsidies, contrary to EU

regulations. By October 2002, it plans to submit to APV a restructuring plan in preparation for privatisation. Control over the Hungarian Post and Postabank will be transferred to APV, while the oversight of the state railways, MAV, will remain at the Transport Ministry. The privatisation of the pharmaceutical wholesaler company Hungaropharma was completed in early July 2002. Hungaropharma controls about 30 per cent of the Hungarian pharmaceuticals market and its yearly turnover is around HUF 80 billion (€328 million).

Privatisation of arable land negatively affects production.

In late 2001, the government introduced a framework within which it would subsidise loans issued to family farmers by the state-owned Konzumbank for the purchase of state-owned land currently leased by 350 private cooperatives. The family farm support package includes interest subsidies of between 50 and 100 per cent of the loan amounts needed to purchase the land, as well as direct support based on land size. It also created a national land fund (NFA) to manage the state land destined to be privatised. The assets of the NFA currently include 370,000 hectares of state-owned arable land, which is not subject to restitution. While sales to family farmers started in June 2002, new farms lack the funds to afford the necessary investments and have suffered from inefficient scale. The process has also been marred by the unorthodox structure of land auctions. In its negotiations with the EU on agriculture, Hungary has insisted on retaining the right to subsidise agricultural investments, even though EU regulations limit investment subsidies in areas where there is chronic over-production.

Enterprise reform

Enterprise statistics point to difficulties for small enterprises' growth prospects.

According to data from Eurostat, Hungarian SMEs have the lowest survival rate among central and east European transition countries (53.8 per cent). Moreover, while small

and large enterprises recorded positive growth during the 1996–2000 period, the medium size category shrank in the economy as a whole and only marginally increased in the manufacturing sector. Taxation features as one of the major obstacles affecting business. Data from the tax office show that, throughout the past decade, SMEs – and in particular enterprises with 0-9 employees – faced the highest average tax burden (calculated as payable tax, minus the subsidies received, minus the tax benefits enjoyed)

Enterprises, infrastructure, finance and social reforms

1990
Jan   Securities law adopted
Jun   Stock exchange established
Oct   Banking law adopted

1991
Jan   Competition law adopted
Jul   Matav transformed into joint-stock company
Sep   Bankruptcy law adopted
Dec   Electricity board transformed into joint-stock company

1992
Nov   Telecommunications law adopted

1993
Jan   BIS capital adequacy adopted
Sep   Bankruptcy law amended
Oct   Railway law enacted
Dec   First major utility partially privatised (Matav)

1994
Apr   Electricity law adopted
Apr   Independent electricity regulator established
Jul   First state bank privatised

1995
Dec   Securities and Exchange Commission established
Dec   Matav becomes majority privately owned

1996
Jan   Restructuring of MAV (national railway) begins
Dec   Financial sector supervision law adopted
Dec   IAS introduced

1997
Jan   New banking law adopted
Jan   Competition law amended
Jul   Pension reform adopted
Oct   Land Credit and Mortgage Bank established

1998
Apr   Venture capital law enacted
Aug   Health insurance fund reformed

2000
Jun   Insurance law amended
Dec   Competition act amended

2001
Jan   Capital gains tax introduced
Jun   New telecommunications law approved
Jul   New central banking act introduced
Jul   Take-over law amended

within the enterprise sector. This tax inequality was reduced in 1999, but has not yet been eliminated.

Foreign direct investment slowed.
In the first seven months of 2002, foreign direct investment in Hungary totalled €631 million, 27 per cent less than the amount for the same period in 2001. A number of factors are believed to have contributed to the decline, including a reduction in multinational firm activity, the near conclusion of the privatisation process and a perceived lack of competitiveness due to recent upward wage pressure and appreciation of the exchange rate. However, the previous government's policy of favouring domestic over foreign companies in the allocation of infrastructure contracts may also have deterred potential foreign investors. Furthermore, the privatisation of Postabank and the conflict between Canadian investors and the previous government over the cancellation of their public-private partnership for the construction and management of the Budapest Airport Terminal 2B may also have discouraged investors.

Infrastructure

Gradual reform of the railways continues.
Some steps have been taken recently in reforming the loss-making MAV – Hungary's state railway and, with 54,000 workers, the country's largest employer. MAV holds the monopoly for rail traffic on most of the network. The company continues to benefit from subsidies, which amounted to about 0.8 per cent of GDP in 2001. On 1 January 2002, the company's freight cargo branch was separated from the rest of its services, both in accounting and operational terms.

Deregulation of the electricity market still in the early stages.
In December 2001, parliament approved the further partial opening of the electricity market for industrial customers using over 6.5 GWh, of which there are 200, as of January 2003. This means that the large electricity users, accounting for 30 per cent of the market, will be allowed to choose their suppliers for 50 per cent of their electricity consumption. However, because 95 per cent of import capacity is locked into long-term contracts, this measure may not bring immediate significant improvements in competition. Full liberalisation of the market is scheduled for completion in 2010.

Financial institutions

Postabank privatisation may be revisited.
The new finance minister may re-open the Postabank's privatisation. The previous government decided to keep the bank in state hands and sold it in August 2001 to the Hungarian Post Office. The bank will likely be offered to a strategic investor in 2003. Several Hungarian banks have already

announced their intention to bid for the purchase of Postabank. The potential bidders include Hungary's largest bank, OTP Bank, Budapest Bank, the Hungarian subsidiary of Austrian Erste Bank and the Hungarian subsidiary of Bank of China, which has started operations in Hungary. Several banks have expressed an interest in purchasing the state-owned Konzumbank, which is also due to be privatised in 2003. The government has also announced the intention to sell the mortgage bank, FHB, through a public offer on the stock exchange. A successful completion of these sales would complete privatisation of the banking sector.

Social reform

Recent changes to the pension system reverse some of the advances of earlier reforms.
In November 2001, the government introduced a number of changes to the multi-pillar pension system. The decision to join the traditional pay-as-you-go system or the multi-pillar system was made voluntary, with the minimum benefit state-guarantee for privately funded pensions abolished (other components of the multiple state-guarantee system continue to be in place). The first decision, in a context of falling birth-rates and rising life expectancy, could lead to an increase in the unfunded liabilities of the pension system. Financing of the second pillar, which has so far been maintained at 6 per cent of participants' pension contributions, will be increased to 8 per cent from 1 January 2003. Also from next year, the multi-pillar system will once again be mandatory for new entrants in the labour force.

Health care reform overdue.
In order to strengthen public expenditure control and to improve delivery of quality services, health care reform should be a priority on the authorities' agenda. Hospital debt (which is already large and mounting), the current heavily subsidised drug pricing system and productivity issues (particularly in light of large recent pay increases) all need to be urgently addressed. Outdated equipment and underpaid medical staff are both accounting for deteriorating quality of medical services provision. After the adoption of a very general 10-year action plan in mid-2001, a clear reform strategy – in terms of commitments, timing and costing – has yet to be adopted.

Liberalisation

Current account convertibility – **full**

Interest rate liberalisation – **full**

Wage regulation – **no**

Stabilisation

Share of general government tax revenue
in GDP – **41.6 per cent**

Exchange rate regime – **fixed with
band to euro**

Privatisation

Primary privatisation method – **direct sales**

Secondary privatisation method – **MEBOs**

Tradability of land – **full except foreigners**

Enterprises and markets

Competition Office – **yes**

Infrastructure

Independent telecoms regulator – **yes**

Separation of railway accounts – **yes**

Independent electricity regulator – **yes**

Financial sector

Capital adequacy ratio – **8 per cent**

Deposit insurance system – **yes**

Secured transactions law – **yes**

Securities commission – **yes**

Social reform

Share of the population in poverty –
15.4 per cent

Private pension funds – **yes**

	1993	1994	1995	1996	1997	1998	1999	2000	2001
Liberalisation									
Share of administered prices in CPI (in per cent)	10.8	11.8	12.9	12.8	15.9	17.0	18.2	18.3	18.5
Number of goods with administered prices in EBRD-15 basket	2.0	2.0	2.0	2.0	2.0	2.0	2.0	2.0	2.0
Share of trade with non-transition countries (in per cent)	78.2	79.1	77.7	77.0	81.2	84.3	87.9	87.2	84.4
Share of trade in GDP (in per cent)	50.4	45.4	62.8	68.6	90.2	93.2	95.5	112.2	109.3
Tariff revenues (in per cent of imports)	12.3	12.7	13.0	9.7	4.0	2.7	2.5	1.8	1.1
EBRD index of price liberalisation	3.0	3.0	3.0	3.0	3.3	3.3	3.3	3.3	3.3
EBRD index of forex and trade liberalisation	4.0	4.3	4.3	4.3	4.3	4.3	4.3	4.3	4.3
Privatisation									
Privatisation revenues (cumulative, in per cent of GDP)	8.7	12.3	20.8	23.4	27.5	28.6	29.8	30.2	30.3
Private sector share in GDP (in per cent)	50.0	55.0	60.0	70.0	75.0	80.0	80.0	80.0	80.0
Private sector share in employment (in per cent)	na	na	71.0	76.8	83.3	81.4	na	na	na
EBRD index of small-scale privatisation	3.0	3.7	3.7	4.0	4.3	4.3	4.3	4.3	4.3
EBRD index of large-scale privatisation	3.0	3.0	4.0	4.0	4.0	4.0	4.0	4.0	4.0
Enterprises									
Budgetary subsidies and current transfers (in per cent of GDP)	5.2	5.9	4.9	5.6	4.9	5.2	4.9	na	na
Effective statutory social security tax (in per cent)	76.6	78.3	76.2	78.4	80.1	84.3	79.1	na	na
Share of industry in total employment (in per cent)	28.4	27.6	26.7	26.7	26.7	27.8	27.4	26.8	27.4
Change in labour productivity in industry (in per cent)	16.4	14.8	10.5	4.3	9.3	7.4	9.5	19.7	3.7
Investment rate/GDP (in per cent)	18.9	20.1	20.0	21.4	22.2	23.2	27.8	30.1	26.6
EBRD index of enterprise reform	3.0	3.0	3.0	3.0	3.0	3.3	3.3	3.3	3.3
EBRD index of competition policy	2.0	3.0	3.0	3.0	3.0	3.0	3.0	3.0	3.0
Infrastructure									
Main telephone lines per 100 inhabitants	14.5	17.3	21.1	26.1	30.4	33.6	37.1	37.3	37.4
Railway labour productivity (1989=100)	72.9	85.6	92.6	93.2	108.4	112.9	117.0	122.8	123.3
Electricity tariffs, USc kWh (collection rate in per cent)	na	3.99 (90)	5.85 (90)	5.96 (90)	6.75 (90)	6.97 (na)	7.26 (na)	5.9 (na)	6.8 (na)
GDP per unit of energy use (PPP in US dollars per kgoe)	3.5	3.8	3.9	3.8	4.1	4.3	4.6	na	na
EBRD index of infrastructure reform	2.3	2.7	3.0	3.0	3.0	3.3	3.7	3.7	3.7
Financial institutions [1]									
Number of banks (foreign owned)	40 (16)	43 (18)	43 (21)	42 (24)	45 (30)	44 (28)	43 (29)	42 (33)	41 (31)
Asset share of state-owned banks (in per cent)	76.3	61.5	49.0	15.3	3.5	9.8	7.8	7.7	9.0
Non-performing loans (in per cent of total loans) [2]	na	na	na	na	6.6	7.9	4.4	3.1	3.1
Domestic credit to private sector (in per cent of GDP)	26.5	24.9	22.7	21.9	24.2	24.2	25.8	29.5	30.6
Stock market capitalisation (in per cent of GDP)	2.3	4.2	5.8	12.4	35.2	29.9	36.4	25.2	18.7
EBRD index of banking sector reform	3.0	3.0	3.0	3.0	4.0	4.0	4.0	4.0	4.0
EBRD index of reform of non-banking financial institutions	2.0	2.0	3.0	3.0	3.3	3.3	3.3	3.7	3.7
Legal environment									
EBRD rating of legal extensiveness (company law)	na	na	na	na	4.0	4.0	4.0	4.0	3.7
EBRD rating of legal effectiveness (company law)	na	na	na	na	4.0	4.0	3.7	3.7	3.7
Social sector									
Expenditures on health and education (in per cent of GDP)	11.4	11.3	9.5	8.9	9.2	9.3	9.2	8.8	8.3
Life expectancy at birth, total (years)	69.0	69.4	69.8	70.3	70.6	70.6	70.6	71.2	na
Basic school enrolment ratio (in per cent)	98.1	97.9	98.5	98.2	97.9	98.0	98.7	na	na
Earnings inequality (GINI-coefficient)	32.0	32.4	na	na	35.0	na	na	na	na

[1] Entries changed compared with previous *Transition Reports* due to changes in definitions by the Hungarian authorities.

[2] Changes in non-performing loans data compared with previous *Transition Reports* are due to the change of loan categories included in non-performing loans (see definitions).

	1994	1995	1996	1997	1998	1999	2000	2001 Estimate	2002 Projection
Output and expenditure					*(Percentage change in real terms)*				
GDP	2.9	1.5	1.3	4.6	4.9	4.2	5.2	3.8	4.0
Private consumption	-0.2	-7.1	-3.4	1.7	4.9	4.6	4.1	5.1	na
Public consumption [1]	-12.7	-4.1	-4.2	5.7	-0.3	1.8	1.2	0.4	na
Gross fixed investment	12.5	-4.3	6.7	9.2	13.3	5.9	7.7	3.1	na
Exports of goods and services	13.7	13.4	8.4	26.4	16.7	13.1	21.8	9.1	na
Imports of goods and services	8.8	-0.7	6.6	24.6	10.1	12.3	21.1	6.3	na
Industrial gross output	9.6	4.6	3.4	11.1	12.4	10.4	18.3	6.4	na
Agricultural gross output	3.2	2.6	6.3	-1.8	-0.3	0.9	-7.9	8.5	na
Employment					*(Percentage change)*				
Labour force (annual average) [2]	-3.3	-2.6	-1.2	-1.3	0.4	2.1	0.4	-0.5	na
Employment (annual average) [2]	-2.0	-1.9	-0.8	0.0	1.4	3.1	1.0	0.3	na
					(In per cent of labour force)				
Unemployment (end-year) [3]	12.4	12.1	11.8	11.6	10.1	9.9	9.1	8.4	na
Prices and wages					*(Percentage change)*				
Consumer prices (annual average)	18.8	28.2	23.6	18.3	14.3	10.0	9.8	9.2	4.9
Consumer prices (end-year)	21.2	28.3	19.8	18.4	10.3	11.2	10.1	6.8	4.6
Producer prices (annual average)	11.3	28.9	21.8	20.4	11.3	5.1	11.7	5.7	na
Producer prices (end-year)	14.8	30.2	20.1	19.5	7.1	8.2	12.4	-0.6	na
Gross average monthly earnings in economy (annual average)	22.6	16.8	20.4	22.3	18.3	13.9	13.5	18.2	na
Government sector [4]					*(In per cent of GDP)*				
General government balance	-7.5	-6.7	-5.0	-4.8	-4.8	-3.4	-3.3	-4.7	-6.0
General government expenditure	59.5	52.6	48.8	49.5	50.4	44.8	46.0	43.0	na
General government debt	88.2	86.4	72.8	63.9	61.9	60.7	57.6	51.5	na
Monetary sector					*(Percentage change)*				
Broad money (M2, end-year)	13.0	18.4	40.9	19.8	15.5	15.6	12.1	16.8	na
Domestic credit (end-year) [5]	18.1	13.7	7.6	12.0	13.2	-6.4	14.8	6.2	na
					(In per cent of GDP)				
Broad money (M2, end-year)	45.5	41.9	48.1	46.5	45.5	46.6	44.3	45.6	na
Interest and exchange rates					*(In per cent per annum, end-year)*				
Refinance rate	25.0	28.0	23.0	20.5	17.0	14.5	11.0	9.8	na
Inter-bank interest rate (up to 30-day maturity)	31.3	27.8	23.2	19.7	17.3	14.5	11.9	10.0	na
Deposit rate weighted average (fixed for less than 1 year)	22.9	24.4	18.6	16.3	14.4	11.9	9.9	9.4	na
Lending rate weighted average (maturing within 1 year)	29.7	32.2	24.0	20.8	18.8	19.4	12.8	12.0	na
					(Forints per US dollar)				
Exchange rate (end-year)	110.7	139.5	164.9	203.5	219.0	252.5	284.7	279.0	na
Exchange rate (annual average)	105.1	125.7	152.6	186.8	214.5	237.3	282.3	286.5	na
External sector					*(In millions of US dollars)*				
Current account [6]	-3,912	-2,480	-1,678	-981	-2,298	-2,081	-1,325	-1,118	-1,517
Trade balance [6]	-3,635	-2,442	-2,645	-1,963	-2,353	-2,176	-1,771	-2,029	-2,635
Merchandise exports [6]	7,613	12,810	14,183	19,637	20,749	21,844	25,861	28,074	31,613
Merchandise imports [6]	11,248	15,252	16,828	21,600	23,102	24,020	27,632	30,103	34,248
Foreign direct investment, net	1,097	4,410	2,279	1,741	1,555	1,720	1,090	2,103	2,559
Gross reserves (end-year), excluding gold	8,727	11,967	9,681	8,400	9,312	10,948	11,202	10,894	na
External debt stock	28,521	31,655	27,956	24,395	27,280	29,336	30,528	33,871	na
					(In months of imports of goods and services)				
Gross reserves (end-year), excluding gold	7.5	7.6	5.7	4.0	4.1	4.6	4.0	3.7	na
					(In per cent of exports of goods and services)				
Debt service	58.8	46.1	47.9	37.6	26.8	18.4	16.8	15.4	na
Memorandum items					*(Denominations as indicated)*				
Population (end-year, millions)	10.2	10.2	10.2	10.2	10.1	10.0	10.2	10.0	na
GDP (in millions of forints)	4,364,811	5,614,042	6,893,934	8,540,669	10,087,357	11,393,508	13,452,033	15,247,826	16,633,439
GDP per capita (in US dollars)	4,052	4,359	4,425	4,495	4,641	4,757	4,745	5,228	na
Share of industry in GDP (in per cent)	21.9	23.1	23.5	25.0	25.9	26.7	28.0	na	na
Share of agriculture in GDP (in per cent)	5.9	5.9	6.1	5.8	5.4	5.3	4.6	na	na
Current account/GDP (in per cent)	-9.4	-5.6	-3.7	-2.1	-4.9	-4.3	-2.8	-2.1	-2.4
External debt - reserves, in US$ millions	19,794	19,688	18,275	15,995	17,968	16,332	19,326	22,976	na
External debt/GDP (in per cent)	68.7	70.9	61.9	53.3	58.0	56.8	64.1	63.6	na
External debt/exports of goods and services (in per cent)	267.2	176.3	138.6	96.2	102.3	106.7	94.9	94.6	na

[1] Data for public expenditure and imports in 1994 include payments for Russian military equipment. Government consumption excludes social transfers, which are included in household final consumption.

[2] Data on labour force and employment are from the Labour Force Survey.

[3] Registered unemployed. Data from the Labour Force Survey for 1994 to 2001 indicate lower rates of respectively 11.9, 10.7, 10.2, 9.9, 8.7, 7.8, 7, 6.4 and 5.7 per cent.

[4] Government sector data are official fiscal balance data. According to calculations based on ESA95 methodology, the general government deficit for 2001 amounted to 5 per cent of GDP.

[5] Changes in domestic credit adjusted to account for bank recapitalisation in 1994-95.

[6] Data from balance of payments.

Kazakhstan

Key reform challenges

- The process of economic diversification, which started in 2001, needs to accelerate through further improvements in the business environment, reform of the customs and judiciary, and prudent deepening of financial intermediation.

- Fuller disclosure of the financial interests of public officials is central to good governance and to the creation of a level playing field for private investors.

- To improve the quality of infrastructure, the government should continue with commercialisation of public services, tariff reform and the organisational restructuring of infrastructure enterprises.

Liberalisation

The WTO accession process enters into a critical phase.

Negotiations on WTO accession are gaining pace. Critical issues on the agenda include the restriction of protective measures before accession, the tariffs for agriculture, food processing and other light domestic industries, the liberalisation of domestic services to foreign entry, and the reduction of domestic subsidies, particularly for farmers. Kazakhstan continues to intervene in domestic markets in ways that are not compatible with WTO rules, for example, by imposing export bans on fuel products and more recently timber. The new procurement rules for the oil and gas sector, which require public approval of even minor purchases, may also conflict with WTO principles.

Stabilisation

Prudent fiscal policy maintained.

Kazakhstan ran a consolidated budget surplus of around 2.8 per cent of GDP in 2001, including KZT 81 billion (US$ 550 million) of taxes and royalties transferred to the national fund (NFRK). According to the audited annual accounts of the NFRK, no capital spending was recorded in 2001, although such spending is in principle possible. As of mid-2002, the total resources held by the NFRK were US$ 1.65 billion. Strong fiscal performance has been helped by the new treasury system in operation since 2000 and improved tax compliance. A new transfer pricing law came into effect in January 2002, applicable to a range of commercial transactions, including but not restricted to those between related parties. This aims to further raise tax receipts, particularly from the resources sector, but critics are concerned about the additional bureaucracy and room for discretion this creates.

Privatisation

Blue chip sales off – and on again.

The new government's privatisation policy remains unclear after the announcement to end privatisations was followed by preparations to sell stakes in four blue chip companies. All four companies are in the metallurgical sector and government stakes range from 15 to 39 per cent. The sales are intended to provide additional instruments to the domestic securities market, but the shares will probably be bought by the present majority owners. In a positive development, land reform is back on the political agenda. The new draft land code provides for private, tradable land titles, although individual holdings would initially be restricted in size and owners would not be able to resell land for five years. Foreigners would remain excluded from private land ownership.

Enterprise reform

Concerns over transparency and governance persist.

The wide-ranging business interests of public officials give rise to conflicts of interest and undermine the impartiality of the authorities in relation to private businesses. The newly created national oil company Kazmunaigas, which has resulted from the merger of Kazakhoil (production) and Kaztransoil (oil and gas transport), for instance, raises concerns over non-arm's-length transactions among its many subsidiaries. At the same time, private companies often fail to follow good international practice in terms of financial transparency and disclosure of ownership and related party interests.

Courts and customs weakest links, according to new governance survey.

A survey of 400 enterprise managers, 600 public officials and 1,000 individuals carried out on behalf of the government and the World Bank reveals widespread dissatisfaction with the quality of service provided by the courts and customs administration. Less than a third of respondents rate the quality of courts and customs services as "good" compared with over 70 per cent for financial services. About 20 per cent of enterprises and 35 per cent of public officials believe corruption in the courts is widespread.

Liberalisation, stabilisation, privatisation

1991
Dec	Independence from Soviet Union declared

1993
Nov	New currency (tenge) introduced

1994
Apr	Mass privatisation begins; first voucher auction held
Apr	First treasury bills issued
Nov	Most prices liberalised
Dec	Law on foreign investment enacted

1995
Jan	Customs union with Russia and Belarus established
Feb	Directed credits eliminated
Feb	Most foreign trade licences abolished
Apr	Central Bank law adopted
Jun	State orders in agriculture abolished
Jul	New tax code introduced
Jul	Customs code introduced
Jul	Barter trade prohibited
Aug	Foreign exchange surrender abolished
Dec	Edict on land enacted
Dec	Privatisation law adopted

1996
Jun	IMF programme agreed
Jun	Last voucher auction held
Jun	Cash sales to strategic investors begin
Jul	Full current account convertibility introduced
Dec	First sovereign Eurobond issued

1999
Jan	Temporary trade restrictions on neighbours introduced
Jan	Major budgetary reforms introduced
Apr	Export surrender requirement re-introduced temporarily
Sep	First sovereign Eurobond issued in CIS following Russian crisis

2000
Jan	Oil export quota introduced temporarily
Jul	Lifelong privileges granted to President
Aug	Minority stake in TC Oil sold to Chevron
Aug	National Fund set up

2001
Jul	Capital amnesty decreed
Jul	Simplified new tax code enacted

2002
Jan	New transfer pricing law adopted
Jun	Revised foreign investment law adopted

Enterprises, infrastructure, finance and social reforms

1993
Apr   Law on banking adopted

1994
Jan   Prudential regulations introduced
Jun   Competition agency established
Dec   New civil code enacted

1995
Apr   Presidential decree on bankruptcy issued
Apr   Bank and enterprise restructuring agency established
Apr   Anti-monopoly legislation introduced
Dec   Telecommunications law adopted

1996
Jan   Subsoil code enacted
May   First major power sector utility privatised
Nov   New accounting standards adopted

1997
Jan   New bankruptcy law enacted
Jun   Pension reform law adopted
Jul   First ADR issued
Jul   National power grid formed
Oct   Stock exchange begins trading

1998
Jan   Pension reform launched
Apr   Turan-Alem Bank privatised, largest to date
Sep   Law on natural monopolies adopted
Dec   Small business support programme approved

1999
May   New telecommunications law adopted
Jul   New energy law introduced
Jul   First municipal bond issued
Aug   First domestic corporate bond issued
Oct   Decree on inspections passed

2000
Jan   New civil service law adopted
Jun   Tractebel leaves Kazakhstani energy sector
Jul   Wholesale power trading company (KOREM) established
Dec   National Development Bank established

2001
May   Gas and oil transport companies merged, creating Kaztransneftegas
Jul   Railway law adopted

2002
Apr   National oil and gas company created
Jul   New tariff methodology for utilities adopted

The output expansion broad-based, but investment remains energy focused.

Kazakhstan has shown some encouraging signs of economic diversification. In the first half of 2002, the textiles industry grew 50 per cent, chemicals, transport equipment and furniture 30 per cent, and metal and agro-processing 9 per cent, compared with a 10 per cent rise in energy and mining output. A 13 per cent rise in real incomes has helped to support domestic expansion, but this has not been accompanied by a commensurate rise in non-oil investment. In June 2002, the government passed a new law on investment, replacing the 1994 foreign investment law. The new legislation makes investment incentives available to both domestic and foreign firms and partially abolishes the earlier protection of foreign investors against legislative changes. Major obstacles to investment, however, remain bureaucratic harassment and corruption.

Infrastructure

New tariff methodology adopted for public utilities ...

In June 2002, the government approved in principle a new tariff methodology for public utilities in the water, electricity and municipal services sectors. The price cap methodology sets forward-looking tariffs over a three- to five-year period to equate revenues with total (operating and investment) costs. Once set, the tariffs are adjusted for movements in inflation, the real exchange rate and demand, but not increases in operating cost, thus providing an incentive for efficient performance. The new method will replace the current cost-plus approach and is to be applied first in the water sector, where tariffs are expected to rise by 16 per cent in 2003. Implementation in the power sector may be more selective, partially because the funds to compensate poor consumers are not available.

... but slow progress in railways and telecommunications reform.

The railways restructuring programme has been reviewed following a change in railway management in early 2002. The July 2001 railway law called for competition and the full privatisation of freight and passenger operators, with the rail tracks and related infrastructure to remain in state hands. While the unbundling and privatisation of service companies has slowly begun, the revised plan retains a role for a state-owned operator competing with private service companies. In April 2002, the government approved a concept paper on communications, which provides for competition in fixed-line telephony, but this has so far not been implemented.

Financial institutions

Central Bank tightens supervision, as the lending boom shows signs of slowing down.

After bank lending to the private sector increased 50 per cent in 2001, recent data points to a moderation in the pace of financial deepening with lending growing around 15 per cent in the year to June. Rapid credit growth has raised concerns over increasing credit risks, particularly among second-tier banks, which are often still dominated by related party lending. Since early 2002, the National Bank of Kazakhstan (NBK) requires banks to fully disclose their ownership structure and all related party exposure. A new head of consolidated financial supervision has also been appointed. In a separate development, a 33 per cent stake in Halyk Bank, the third largest in terms of assets, was sold in late 2001 in a transaction that was widely seen as non-transparent.

Limited asset diversification and low yields put pension reform at risk.

Total pension assets grew to around US$ 1.4 billion by mid-2002, a considerable amount relative to the size of the domestic securities market (roughly US$ 2.3 billion including the two sovereign Eurobonds). The dearth of attractive assets on the domestic market will become even more pronounced after the repayment of the government's US$ 350 million Eurobond in October 2002. The government plans to relax restrictions on investments in foreign A-rated securities and introduce market valuation for pension fund portfolios to encourage diversification into foreign assets and equities. With the present concentration on a few domestic securities, pensioners face considerable risks. Other reform priorities include the introduction of a minimum state-funded pension, the introduction of a market for annuities and the merger of pension funds and asset management companies to save on administrative costs and promote competition.

Social reform

Significant reforms to social assistance under way.

In January 2002, a new social assistance law was adopted, which shifts the focus of social assistance from the support of specific vulnerable groups to means tested transfers to the poor. The new law provides the basis for cash compensation to people below the national poverty line, set at KZT 1,895 (US$ 12) per month. In 2002, 10 per cent of the population lived below the poverty line, according to a new household budget survey. By alleviating affordability concerns, the new system should in principle support the important tariff reforms for public utilities. However, there are concerns that budget allocations to local governments, responsible for social assistance, may not be sufficient to provide the required compensation.

Liberalisation
Current account convertibility – **full**
Interest rate liberalisation – **full**
Wage regulation – **yes**

Stabilisation
Share of general government tax revenue
  in GDP – **22.5 per cent**
Exchange rate regime – **managed float**

Privatisation
Primary privatisation method – **direct sales**
Secondary privatisation method – **vouchers**
Tradability of land – **limited de jure**

Enterprises and markets
Competition Office – **yes**

Infrastructure
Independent telecoms regulator – **no**
Separation of railway accounts – **no**
Independent electricity regulator – **yes**

Financial sector
Capital adequacy ratio – **12 per cent**
Deposit insurance system – **yes**
Secured transactions law – **yes**
Securities commission – **yes**

Social reform
Share of the population in poverty –
  30.9 per cent[1]
Private pension funds – **yes**

	1993	1994	1995	1996	1997	1998	1999	2000	2001
Liberalisation									
Share of administered prices in CPI (in per cent)	2.5	2.5	0.0	0.0	0.0	0.0	0.0	0.0	0.0
Number of goods with administered prices in EBRD-15 basket	3.0	3.0	0.0	0.0	0.0	0.0	0.0	0.0	0.0
Share of trade with non-transition countries (in per cent)	na	33.2	39.9	41.7	52.4	47.3	58.7	64.2	65.4
Share of trade in GDP (in per cent)	179.6	64.4	64.9	61.8	63.6	56.9	69.3	88.3	77.7
Tariff revenues (in per cent of imports)[2]	0.5	5.6	3.9	2.0	1.5	1.9	1.7	1.9	2.0
EBRD index of price liberalisation	2.0	2.0	3.0	3.0	3.0	3.0	3.0	3.0	3.0
EBRD index of forex and trade liberalisation	2.0	2.0	3.0	4.0	4.0	4.0	3.0	3.3	3.3
Privatisation									
Privatisation revenues (cumulative, in per cent of GDP)[3]	2.7	3.0	3.3	5.5	8.9	12.7	14.4	15.3	16.2
Private sector share in GDP (in per cent)	10.0	20.0	25.0	40.0	55.0	55.0	60.0	60.0	60.0
Private sector share in employment (in per cent)	na	na	na	na	na	na	na	na	na
EBRD index of small-scale privatisation	2.0	2.3	3.0	3.3	4.0	4.0	4.0	4.0	4.0
EBRD index of large-scale privatisation	2.0	2.0	2.0	3.0	3.0	3.0	3.0	3.0	3.0
Enterprises									
Budgetary subsidies and current transfers (in per cent of GDP)[4]	na	3.2	3.6	2.6	1.8	0.8	1.3	1.2	1.5
Effective statutory social security tax (in per cent)	na	39.8	55.3	56.3	51.5	na	na	na	na
Share of industry in total employment (in per cent)	21.2	20.7	20.5	20.9	22.2	24.6	26.8	26.4	26.5
Change in labour productivity in industry (in per cent)	-1.0	-22.7	-0.1	12.3	18.6	3.8	16.2	18.0	11.3
Investment rate/GDP (in per cent)	27.9	22.6	20.5	11.8	15.6	17.3	14.6	14.0	18.0
EBRD index of enterprise reform	1.0	1.0	1.0	2.0	2.0	2.0	2.0	2.0	2.0
EBRD index of competition policy	1.0	2.0	2.0	2.0	2.0	2.0	2.0	2.0	2.0
Infrastructure									
Main telephone lines per 100 inhabitants	11.7	11.7	11.8	11.6	11.0	10.9	10.8	11.3	11.3
Railway labour productivity (1989=100)	51.4	37.6	32.6	30.4	30.0	31.2	27.6	42.5	46.3
Electricity tariffs, USc kWh (collection rate in per cent)	na	4.2 (73)	3.2 (75)	3.0 (70)	3.8 (50)	4.7 (na)	3.2 (na)	2.7 (na)	2.6 (na)
GDP per unit of energy use (PPP in US dollars per kgoe)	1.3	1.3	1.4	1.6	1.8	1.8	2.1	na	na
EBRD index of infrastructure reform	1.0	1.0	1.7	2.0	2.0	2.0	2.0	2.0	2.0
Financial institutions									
Number of banks (foreign owned)	204 (5)	184 (8)	130 (8)	101 (9)	81 (22)	71 (20)	55 (18)	48 (16)	44 (15)
Asset share of state-owned banks (in per cent)[5]	na	na	24.3	28.4	44.8	23.0	19.9	1.9	3.5
Non-performing loans (in per cent of total loans)[6]	na	na	14.9	19.9	6.0	4.7	5.5	2.1	2.1
Domestic credit to private sector (in per cent of GDP)	49.3	26.6	6.1	4.3	4.3	5.4	7.4	10.6	14.9
Stock market capitalisation (in per cent of GDP)	na	na	na	na	6.1	8.2	15.5	7.5	5.5
EBRD index of banking sector reform	1.0	1.0	2.0	2.0	2.3	2.3	2.3	2.3	2.7
EBRD index of reform of non-banking financial institutions	1.0	1.7	1.7	1.7	1.7	2.0	2.0	2.3	2.3
Legal environment									
EBRD rating of legal extensiveness (company law)	na	na	na	na	2.0	2.3	3.3	4.0	4.0
EBRD rating of legal effectiveness (company law)	na	na	na	na	2.0	2.0	3.3	3.7	4.0
Social sector									
Expenditures on health and education (in per cent of GDP)	6.5	5.3	7.5	7.2	7.1	6.2	6.1	5.3	5.6
Life expectancy at birth, total (years)	66.7	65.7	64.9	64.1	64.5	64.6	65.5	65.5	na
Basic school enrolment ratio (in per cent)	93.8	94.2	94.4	94.7	94.2	94.3	94.2	99.5	na
Earnings inequality (GINI-coefficient)	na	na	na	na	na	na	na	na	na

[1] World Bank data for 1996. In 2002, the share of people in poverty had fallen to
  10 per cent according to a household suvery using a national poverty line.
[2] Refers to taxes on international trade.
[3] Excludes sale of 5 per cent stake in TCO for US$ 660 million in January 2001.
[4] Data for 1998 and 1999 refer to expenditures on the economy (fuel and energy,
  agriculture and mining).

[5] The state share of banking sector assets increased in 1997 following the
  merger of privately owned Alem Bank and a state-owned institution. In 1998,
  the merger bank was reprivatised. In December 2000, the state reduced its
  stake in the Savings Bank to less than 50 per cent.
[6] Changes in non-performing loans data compared with previous *Transition
  Reports* are due to the change of loan categories included in
  non-performing loans (see definitions).

	1994	1995	1996	1997	1998	1999	2000	2001 Estimate	2002 Projection
Output and expenditure					*(Percentage change in real terms)*				
GDP	-12.6	-8.2	0.5	1.7	-1.9	2.7	9.8	13.2	7.6
Private consumption	na	-21.5	-4.0	2.5	-0.8	0.8	1.6	4.8	na
Public consumption	na	-7.3	-13.2	-12.1	-13.8	8.0	37.0	18.9	na
Gross fixed investment	na	-41.0	-30.4	6.3	-2.9	12.1	8.1	55.0	na
Exports of goods and services	na	5.0	2.0	1.2	-11.9	12.7	32.9	-0.2	na
Imports of goods and services	na	-19.9	-17.1	7.5	-7.2	-18.3	24.2	23.0	na
Industrial gross output	-27.5	-8.6	0.3	4.1	-2.4	2.7	15.5	13.5	8.9
Agricultural gross output	-21.0	-24.4	-5.0	-0.8	-18.9	21.6	-3.2	na	5.0
Employment					*(Percentage change)*				
Labour force (end-year)	1.6	3.4	14.6	0.4	1.8	-6.1	10.2	-1.4	na
Employment (end-year)	-3.8	-7.8	-12.3	-17.1	-15.4	-19.0	-0.6	1.9	na
					(In per cent of labour force)				
Unemployment (end-year)	8.1	13.0	8.6	7.3	6.6	6.3	12.2	11.0	na
Prices and wages					*(Percentage change)*				
Consumer prices (annual average)	1,892.0	176.3	39.1	17.4	7.3	8.3	13.2	8.4	6.0
Consumer prices (end-year)	1,158.3	60.4	28.6	11.2	1.9	17.8	9.6	6.4	6.2
Producer prices (annual average)	2,920.4	231.2	24.3	15.6	0.8	18.8	38.0	0.0	na
Producer prices (end-year)	1,923.8	40.2	18.5	11.7	-5.5	57.2	19.4	-14.1	na
Gross average monthly earnings in economy (annual average)	1,248.2	177.3	42.9	24.9	13.4	13.4	30.9	20.8	15.0
Government sector [1]					*(In per cent of GDP)*				
General government balance [2]	-7.7	-3.4	-5.3	-7.0	-8.0	-5.2	-1.0	-1.1	-2.0
General government expenditure [3]	18.4	20.8	18.6	20.4	26.1	23.1	22.8	22.4	23.0
General government debt	na	14.6	13.9	17.1	22.4	27.9	26.1	19.9	na
Monetary sector					*(Percentage change)*				
Broad money (M2, end-year)	576.1	108.2	20.9	8.2	-21.3	73.4	14.7	14.3	na
Domestic credit (end-year) [4]	745.3	-21.5	15.6	-2.8	38.6	35.4	57.3	17.1	na
					(In per cent of GDP)				
Broad money (M2, end-year)	13.1	11.4	9.9	9.0	6.9	10.2	9.1	8.2	na
Interest and exchange rates					*(In per cent per annum, end-year)*				
Refinancing rate	230.0	52.5	35.0	18.5	25.0	18.0	14.0	9.0	8.0
Treasury bill rate (3-month maturity) [5]	456.4	58.7	32.2	16.0	25.8	14.3	7.9	5.8	na
Deposit rate [6]	na	44.4	29.3	12.0	14.5	13.5	15.6	11.0	na
Lending rate [6]	na	58.3	53.6	22.8	18.4	21.3	19.9	15.4	na
					(Tenges per US dollar)				
Exchange rate (end-year)	54.3	64.0	73.8	75.9	84.0	138.3	145.4	150.9	na
Exchange rate (annual average)	36.4	61.1	67.8	75.6	78.6	120.1	142.3	147.1	153.6
External sector					*(In millions of US dollars)*				
Current account	-904	-213	-750	-799	-1,225	-169	411	-1,748	-1,350
Trade balance [7]	-929	114	-335	-276	-801	344	2,440	896	1,000
Merchandise exports	3,285	5,440	6,292	6,899	5,871	5,989	9,288	9,120	9,400
Merchandise imports	4,214	5,326	6,627	7,176	6,672	5,645	6,848	8,224	8,400
Foreign direct investment, net	635	964	1,137	1,320	1,143	1,584	1,245	2,760	2,500
Gross reserves (end-year), excluding gold	838	1,136	1,295	1,697	1,461	1,479	1,594	1,997	2,547
External debt stock [8]	4,474	4,765	7,096	9,027	9,845	12,034	12,570	14,100	14,400
					(In months of imports of goods and services)				
Gross reserves (end-year), excluding gold [9]	2.1	2.2	2.1	2.5	2.2	2.6	2.1	2.2	2.7
					(In per cent of exports of goods and services)				
Debt service	4.2	7.9	15.9	24.5	22.4	27.3	16.9	11.9	12.2
Memorandum items					*(Denominations as indicated)*				
Population (end-year, millions)	16.2	16.0	15.7	15.5	15.2	14.9	14.8	14.8	14.4
GDP (in millions of tenges)	423,469	1,014,190	1,415,750	1,672,142	1,733,264	2,016,456	2,599,902	3,285,383	3,748,611
GDP per capita (in US dollars)	721	1,040	1,333	1,429	1,452	1,127	1,231	1,505	1,698
Share of industry in GDP (in per cent)	23.6	23.5	23.5	24.0	23.9	23.6	na	na	na
Share of agriculture in GDP (in per cent)	15.0	12.3	11.7	11.4	9.4	11.0	9.7	na	na
Current account/GDP (in per cent)	-7.8	-1.3	-3.6	-3.6	-5.6	-1.0	2.2	-7.8	-5.5
External debt - reserves, in US$ millions	3,637	3,630	5,801	7,330	8,384	10,555	10,976	12,103	11,853
External debt/GDP (in per cent)	38.4	28.7	34.0	40.8	44.6	71.7	68.8	63.1	59.0
External debt/exports of goods and services (in per cent)	120.2	79.8	101.9	116.6	145.3	173.9	120.6	135.7	134.0

[1] General government includes the state, municipalities and extra-budgetary funds.

[2] Government balance includes quasi-fiscal operations (zero after 1995). Balance excludes privatisation revenues and transfers to the National Fund. In 2001, the two items amounted to 0.9 per cent and 5.5 per cent of GDP respectively.

[3] Expenditures include extra-budgetary funds after 1998, leading to a break in the series. Following the old series, expenditures increased by only 1.4 per cent of GDP in 1998.

[4] Domestic credit from International Financial Statistics. Break in series in 1996-97.

[5] Three-month T-bill rate until December 1998, 60-40 day NBK note yield thereafter.

[6] Deposit rate for time deposits of individuals. Lending rate for short-term credits. Following a change in definition, data for 1997 are not comparable to previous years.

[7] Exports are at declared customs prices and are not corrected for under-invoicing of oil and gas exports, estimated at some US$ 200 million for 2001 by the IMF.

[8] Includes inter-company debt by branches of non-resident foreign enterprises. Public debt was around US$ 3.9 billion in 2000.

[9] Excluding National Fund.

Kyrgyz Republic

Key reform challenges

- Further efforts to foster integration with neighbouring countries are needed, both in terms of trade and regional FDI, to stimulate the private sector, which has suffered from lack of regional market access.

- While immediate debt servicing difficulties have been eased by a Paris Club agreement, implementation of the debt management strategy agreed with the IMF is key to achieving a more sustainable debt burden over the medium term.

- Progress must be made on the long-delayed restructuring and privatisation of the utilities in order to raise the level of FDI and attract funds for maintenance of the infrastructure.

Liberalisation, stabilisation, privatisation

1991
Aug   Independence from Soviet Union declared
Dec   Small-scale privatisation begins

1992
Jan   Most prices liberalised

1993
Apr   Free trade agreement with Russia signed
May   Exchange rate unified
May   New currency (som) introduced
May   Treasury bills market initiated

1994
Apr   Interest rates liberalised
May   Most export taxes eliminated
Jul   First IMF ESAF programme introduced

1995
Mar   Full current account convertibility introduced

1996
Jan   VAT introduced
Jul   New tax code introduced

1997
Jul   Customs union with Russia, Kazakhstan and Belarus established

1998
Jan   New Central Bank law adopted
Jul   All remaining foreign exchange controls abolished
Oct   Private land ownership passed in referendum
Dec   WTO membership granted

1999
Jul   Comprehensive Development Framework initiative launched

2001
Jun   Interim poverty reduction strategy adopted

2002
Feb   New privatisation law approved by parliament
Mar   Paris Club debt rescheduled

Liberalisation

Trade barriers threaten to strain relations with regional neighbours.

The Kyrgyz Republic has not yet reaped the full benefits from its liberal trade regime and WTO membership. Exports to Kazakhstan have fallen by more than 50 per cent in dollar terms since 1998, even though Kazakhstan has grown strongly during this period and terms of trade have not substantially changed. The trend suggests that there are growing trade restrictions, a suspicion that is corroborated by anecdotal evidence of corruption in customs services. Trade with Uzbekistan is complicated by the lack of convertibility of the Uzbek som. Much of the trade consists of complex gas-for-electricity barter transactions. Frequent disputes and supply disruptions have caused the Kyrgyz government to launch a programme for the replacement of imported gas by hydro electricity. The goal is to reach energy self-sufficiency by 2005. If fully implemented, the plan would require the Kyrgyz Republic to use its hydro-power in winter. This would affect summer irrigation in Uzbekistan and may potentially have destabilising regional consequences.

Stabilisation

Paris Club agreement grants some relief to bring public finances in order.

The Paris Club agreed in March 2002 to a non-concessional flow rescheduling of the Kyrgyz debt. Debt service due to bilateral creditors for 2001–04 will be reduced to US$ 5 million from the original US$ 130 million. Although no principal was written off, the agreement includes a goodwill clause for a stock rescheduling upon the successful completion of the current poverty reduction and growth facility (PRGF) in 2004. At the core of the PRGF is a fiscal adjustment that should reduce the general government deficit to 3.1 per cent of GDP in 2004 from 6.3 per cent of GDP in 2001. The programme is so far on track, but further revenue improvements are needed. In an attempt to raise tax collection, the authorities have decided to merge the state customs committee, the tax inspectorate, the financial police and the collection branch of the social fund into a single entity under the Ministry of Finance. The broadening of the tax base by extending VAT to all agricultural products is also under consideration.

External deficit narrowed, as inflation falls.

Average inflation fell to 3.4 per cent in June 2002. Taking seasonal effects into account, current levels of inflation imply deflation for the summer months. There has also been a marked narrowing in the external balance, in spite of weak export performance. The current account deficit fell from 7.5 per cent of GDP in 2000 to 3.3 per cent in 2001 and is expected to shrink further this year. The main reasons are lower imports mostly related to a reduction in public investments, a higher service balance due to the Western military base and lower interest payments due to the Paris Club debt restructuring. As a result, reserves rose by US$ 20 million in 2001 supporting a 5 per cent strengthening of the currency against the US dollar between January 2001 and July 2002. Renewed confidence in the currency has also allowed interest rates to fall to 6 per cent in July 2002.

Privatisation

Privatisation of strategic enterprises slowly moving forward.

At the end of December 2001, the government issued a new privatisation programme for 2002–03. In February 2002, the parliament passed a law on the privatisation of state property that takes precedence over earlier legislation that had prohibited the sale of certain enterprises classified as strategic. The authorities plan to sell 400 companies, including Kyrgyztelekom, Kyrgyzgas, the national airline and the four energy distribution companies. The government values its remaining stakes in these companies at KGS 8.7 billion (US$ 200 million). This year the government plans to sell a 51 per cent stake in national telecommunications operator Kyrgyztelekom. After a failed attempt in 1999, a new international tender for Kyrgyztelekom will be called in November 2002. Besides planned privatisations of utility companies, the government is concentrating on the divestiture of its tourism assets, which are mostly located at Lake Issykul.

Enterprises, infrastructure, finance and social reforms

1991
Jun — Banking laws adopted

1992
Dec — Comprehensive Central Bank law adopted

1994
Jan — Kyrgyz State Energy Holding Company established
Feb — Telecommunications company corporatised
Apr — Competition law introduced
May — Enterprise restructuring agency established

1995
May — Stock exchange begins trading
Jun — BIS capital adequacy enacted
Oct — First enterprises liquidated

1996
Sep — Securities and Exchange Commission established

1997
Jan — Electricity law adopted
May — Utilities privatisation suspended
Jun — State energy company restructured
Jul — IAS introduced
Oct — New bankruptcy law adopted
Oct — National Agency for Communication established

1998
Jun — Pension law amended significantly
Oct — New telecommunications law adopted
Dec — Foreign investor advisory council established

1999
Feb — Largest bank placed under conservatorship

Enterprise reform

International assistance is focused on improvements in governance ...

Corruption and weak governance at both the corporate and state levels have been singled out as the most important internal impediment to growth. The PRGF has a strong focus on transparency and accountability of public finances, while the Asian Development Bank's (ADB) corporate governance and enterprise reform programme focuses on creditor's rights, judicial reform and the legal, accounting and auditing frameworks. The ADB's customs modernisation project addresses inefficiencies and governance problems in the customs administration.

... while the government has initiated restructuring of some industrial assets.

The state remains the majority owner in several medium-sized industrial companies. These include enterprises in the textile and light industries, an auto repair workshop, a producer of antibiotics and a cable plant. Most of the companies are not financially viable in their current form and have substantial debts to the state and other creditors such as utilities. The companies are supposed to draw up debt rescheduling plans, separate viable from non-viable parts and spin off under-utilised assets. The initiative is being monitored by a government working group that has the authority to issue recommendations to the companies involved. Non-compliance with these recommendations is expected to result in the automatic opening of bankruptcy proceedings.

Infrastructure

Restructuring of air transportation to be followed by partial privatisation.

The air transport industry has been restructured into a national air carrier Kyrgyzstan Aba Zholdoru, the air navigation company Kyrgyzaeronavigatsia, and the international airport Manas. Joint ventures with private investors have been formed to supply fuel and lubricants (Aalam Service) and handle cargo and in-flight services (Manas Management). The state will keep a controlling stake in the airport, but intends to sell a majority stake in the airline. However, after being separated from the profit-making airport and air traffic control operations, the airline is currently not profitable.

Electricity prices adjusted.

Recent increases in electricity tariffs have reduced the quasi-fiscal deficit in the sector from 6.1 per cent of GDP in 2000 to 4.1 per cent of GDP in 2001. The deficit in domestic operations has so far been financed through cross subsidies from electricity exports to Uzbekistan and credits by multilateral and bilateral donors. However, both of these sources of finance are declining. Electricity exports to Uzbekistan reportedly fell between 5 and 10 per cent in 2001 and cuts in the public investment programme reduced the availability of loans to the electricity sector. Later this year the government intends to sell the electricity distributor Sever-elektro, which serves Bishkek and the Chui Valley. The privatisation of the distribution sector should help to raise collection rates and, together with recent tariff adjustments, improve the finances of the electricity sector as a whole.

Financial institutions

Banking sector reforms advanced.

Assets held in the banking sector have started to grow again, although from a very low base (less than 7 per cent of GDP). For the first time since 1998 the sector made profits in 2001. Several measures have been taken to strengthen creditor rights and the supervisory powers of the National Bank of Kyrgyzstan (NBKR). Inconsistencies between the law on pledges and the civil code, relating to bank lending, have been resolved. Legislative amendments are to be presented to parliament giving the NBKR the authority to judge a bank's financial position in liquidation cases. In the past, enforcement actions could be dismissed by the courts based on the judge's own assessment of a bank's finances. In April 2002, the NBKR revoked the licences of two problem banks – Kramds and Issyk-Kul.

Social reform

Social expenditures set to increase.

The Kyrgyz Republic is the second-poorest country of the CIS, both in terms of per capita income and poverty incidence. According to the World Bank, 18 per cent of the population lived in extreme poverty in 2000 (food only poverty line), while 84 per cent were below the more general poverty line (absolute poverty rate). GDP growth in recent years has failed to significantly lift average consumption levels. Incomes in rural areas, where poverty is concentrated, have been falling, while growth has been driven by gold exports with limited trickle-down effects. In April 2002, the authorities adopted a set of measures to increase the lowest government salaries and compensate vulnerable population groups for a 42 per cent increase in household electricity tariffs. Wages for social workers were increased by 15 per cent, social benefits by about 20 per cent and pensions by about 8 per cent on average. Social spending in 2002 is expected to grow by 5 per cent.

Liberalisation

Current account convertibility – **full**

Interest rate liberalisation – **full**

Wage regulation – **no**

Stabilisation

Share of general government tax revenue in GDP – **21.8 per cent**

Exchange rate regime – **managed float**

Privatisation

Primary privatisation method – **vouchers**

Secondary privatisation method – **MEBOs**

Tradability of land – **limited de facto**

Enterprises and markets

Competition Office – **no**

Infrastructure

Independent telecoms regulator – **yes**

Separation of railway accounts – **no**

Independent electricity regulator – **yes**

Financial sector

Capital adequacy ratio – **12 per cent**

Deposit insurance system – **no**

Secured transactions law – **yes**

Securities commission – **yes**

Social reform

Share of the population in poverty – **84.1 per cent**

Private pension funds – **yes**

	1993	1994	1995	1996	1997	1998	1999	2000	2001
Liberalisation									
Share of administered prices in CPI (in per cent)	na	na	na	na	na	na	na	na	na
Number of goods with administered prices in EBRD-15 basket	4.0	1.0	1.0	1.0	1.0	1.0	1.0	1.0	na
Share of trade with non-transition countries (in per cent)	na	40.2	17.6	19.4	33.5	57.7	55.7	56.9	45.4
Share of trade in GDP (in per cent)	na	62.5	55.6	66.1	71.5	77.4	79.4	74.0	62.7
Tariff revenues (in per cent of imports)	na	1.0	2.3	2.0	2.2	2.4	1.4	na	na
EBRD index of price liberalisation	3.0	3.0	3.0	3.0	3.0	3.0	3.0	3.0	3.0
EBRD index of forex and trade liberalisation	2.0	3.0	4.0	4.0	4.0	4.0	4.0	4.0	4.0
Privatisation									
Privatisation revenues (cumulative, in per cent of GDP)	0.2	0.6	0.9	1.2	1.3	1.5	1.7	2.3	na
Private sector share in GDP (in per cent)	25.0	30.0	40.0	50.0	60.0	60.0	60.0	60.0	60.0
Private sector share in employment (in per cent)	52.4	41.7	68.5	72.5	74.2	76.3	77.3	na	na
EBRD index of small-scale privatisation	3.0	4.0	4.0	4.0	4.0	4.0	4.0	4.0	4.0
EBRD index of large-scale privatisation	2.0	3.0	3.0	3.0	3.0	3.0	3.0	3.0	3.0
Enterprises									
Budgetary subsidies and current transfers (in per cent of GDP)	na	1.9	2.0	1.7	2.2	2.4	2.2	na	na
Effective statutory social security tax (in per cent)	na	53.0	67.5	60.5	67.7	66.5	60.3	na	na
Share of industry in total employment (in per cent)	16.0	14.7	12.5	11.1	10.2	8.9	9.2	na	na
Change in labour productivity in industry (in per cent) [1]	-17.0	-14.5	-11.4	16.5	48.8	18.8	-7.9	na	na
Investment rate/GDP (in per cent)	13.4	5.6	20.7	22.6	12.6	12.2	18.0	16.0	na
EBRD index of enterprise reform	1.0	2.0	2.0	2.0	2.0	2.0	2.0	2.0	2.0
EBRD index of competition policy	1.0	2.0	2.0	2.0	2.0	2.0	2.0	2.0	2.0
Infrastructure									
Main telephone lines per 100 inhabitants	8.0	7.3	7.6	7.5	7.6	7.8	7.6	7.7	7.7
Railway labour productivity (1990=100)	41.8	26.4	16.9	18.8	18.4	17.4	15.4	15.3	15.0
Electricity tariffs, USc kWh (collection rate in per cent)	na	0.74 (na)	1.00 (na)	2.25 (na)	2.00 (na)	0.48 (na)	0.37 (na)	0.40 (45)	0.59 (na)
GDP per unit of energy use (PPP in US dollars per kgoe)	3.0	3.4	3.8	3.6	4.3	4.1	5.0	na	na
EBRD index of infrastructure reform	1.0	1.3	1.3	1.3	1.3	1.3	1.3	1.3	1.3
Financial institutions									
Number of banks (foreign owned)	20 (1)	18 (3)	18 (3)	18 (3)	20 (3)	23 (6)	23 (5)	22 (6)	20 (5)
Asset share of state-owned banks (in per cent)	na	77.3	69.7	5.0	9.3	8.1	24.9	15.1	16.0
Non-performing loans (in per cent of total loans) [2]	na	92.2	72.0	26.1	7.6	0.2	6.4	16.4	13.8
Domestic credit to private sector (in per cent of GDP)	na	na	11.1	7.9	3.4	5.3	5.0	na	2.1
Stock market capitalisation (in per cent of GDP) [3]	na	na	na	3.0	0.5	0.8	0.4	0.3	0.3
EBRD index of banking sector reform	1.0	2.0	2.0	2.0	2.7	2.7	2.3	2.3	2.3
EBRD index of reform of non-banking financial institutions	1.0	1.0	1.7	2.0	2.0	2.0	2.0	2.0	2.0
Legal environment									
EBRD rating of legal extensiveness (company law)	na	na	na	na	3.0	3.0	3.3	3.3	na
EBRD rating of legal effectiveness (company law)	na	na	na	na	2.0	2.0	3.0	3.0	na
Social sector									
Expenditures on health and education (in per cent of GDP)	6.8	8.7	9.3	7.7	8.0	7.6	6.3	5.8	na
Life expectancy at birth, total (years)	67.2	66.0	65.8	66.5	66.9	67.1	67.0	67.3	na
Basic school enrolment ratio (in per cent)	85.3	86.3	87.7	89.2	89.6	90.0	89.5	95.9	na
Earnings inequality (GINI-coefficient)	44.5	44.3	39.5	42.8	43.1	42.9	46.6	47.0	na

[1] The increase in industrial labour productivity in 1997 was primarily due to the rise in production at the Kumtor gold mine.

[2] In 1998, all bad loans in the banking system were transferred to a special bank managed by NBKR. The data reported by the Central Bank are likely to exclude these bad loans.

[3] The listing of the state energy company, Kyrgyzenergo, accounts for the large increase in capitalisation in 1998.

	1994	1995	1996	1997	1998	1999	2000	2001 Estimate	2002 Projection
Output and expenditure					*(Percentage change in real terms)*				
GDP	-20.1	-5.4	7.1	9.9	2.1	3.7	5.1	5.3	2.0
Private consumption	-20.9	-17.8	6.0	-8.9	na	na	na	na	na
Public consumption	-14.4	-8.7	7.3	-4.5	na	na	na	na	na
Gross fixed investment	-30.2	55.4	-13.0	-29.2	na	na	na	na	na
Exports of goods and services	-19.0	-17.4	6.7	21.1	na	na	na	na	na
Imports of goods and services	-22.2	-18.4	6.9	-20.2	na	na	na	na	na
Industrial gross output	-23.5	-24.7	3.9	39.6	5.3	-4.3	6.0	5.4	na
Agricultural gross output	-15.0	-2.0	15.2	12.3	2.9	8.2	2.7	6.8	na
Employment					*(Percentage change)*				
Labour force (end-year)	0.2	1.4	2.6	1.9	4.1	1.9	1.7	na	na
Employment (end-year) [1]	-2.1	-0.2	0.6	2.3	0.9	0.8	2.9	na	na
					(In per cent of labour force)				
Unemployment (end-year) [2]	3.1	4.4	6.0	4.3	4.3	5.4	5.6	na	na
Prices and wages					*(Percentage change)*				
Consumer prices (annual average)	228.7	40.7	31.3	25.5	12.0	35.8	18.7	7.0	2.5
Consumer prices (end-year)	95.7	32.3	34.9	14.7	18.4	39.9	9.5	3.8	3.4
Producer prices (annual average)	196.7	37.6	26.1	29.0	4.8	14.9	na	na	na
Producer prices (end-year)	96.7	17.0	23.0	26.0	8.0	53.0	31.5	11.2	na
Gross average monthly earnings in economy (annual average)	178.5	57.8	33.3	38.6	16.0	34.0	14.4	24.5	na
Government sector [3]					*(In per cent of GDP)*				
General government balance [3]	-8.6	-17.3	-9.5	-9.1	-9.4	-11.8	-9.6	-6.0	-4.9
General government expenditure [3]	29.4	42.1	33.4	33.0	33.8	35.8	29.9	28.0	na
General government debt	37.0	40.0	44.2	54.0	76.3	98.7	119.0	113.0	na
Monetary sector					*(Percentage change)*				
Broad money (M3, end-year)	na	80.1	21.3	25.4	17.2	33.9	10.2	3.0	na
Domestic credit (end-year)	na	71.0	20.9	4.1	32.2	7.2	-4.6	-18.6	na
					(In per cent of GDP)				
Broad money (M3, end-year)	11.5	15.1	13.1	13.5	14.2	13.3	11.1	10.5	na
Interest and exchange rates					*(In per cent per annum, end-year)*				
Refinancing rate [4]	89.5	45.8	45.9	23.5	32.9	55.1	38.3	na	na
Treasury bill rate (3-month maturity)	73.0	44.0	52.3	23.5	32.9	65.5	32.0	14.0	na
Deposit rate [5]	na	na	24.8	32.0	29.5	na	na	na	na
Lending rate [5]	na	na	58.3	50.1	42.5	na	na	na	na
					(Soms per US dollar)				
Exchange rate (end-year)	10.7	11.2	16.7	17.4	29.4	45.5	48.4	47.7	na
Exchange rate (annual average)	10.8	10.8	12.8	17.4	20.8	39.0	47.8	48.3	na
External sector					*(In millions of US dollars)*				
Current account	-84.3	-234.8	-424.8	-139.2	-416.5	-247.4	-158.4	-50.5	-45.4
Trade balance	-86.1	-122.0	-251.7	-16.0	-220.0	-84.0	8.8	40.0	-10.0
Merchandise exports	340.0	408.9	531.2	630.0	535.0	462.0	510.9	480.0	460.0
Merchandise imports	426.1	530.9	782.9	646.0	755.0	546.0	502.1	440.0	470.0
Foreign direct investment, net	38.2	96.1	47.2	83.2	86.4	38.3	-6.0	22.0	25.0
Gross reserves (end-year), including gold	67.3	114.5	110.4	141.8	123.1	184.3	205.5	221.7	na
External debt stock	413.8	763.9	1,151.2	1,356.1	1,472.6	1,682.2	1,738.5	1,875.5	na
					(In months of imports of goods and services)				
Gross reserves (end-year), excluding gold	1.6	1.8	1.2	1.9	1.4	2.8	3.3	4.7	na
					(In per cent of exports of goods and services)				
Debt service	4.8	22.3	15.5	12.1	21.8	24.8	20.5	24.4	na
Memorandum items					*(Denominations as indicated)*				
Population (end-year, millions)	4.5	4.5	4.6	4.6	4.7	4.7	4.7	4.8	na
GDP (in millions of soms)	13,281	18,279	25,546	30,993	34,606	49,504	65,358	70,900	74,136
GDP per capita (in US dollars)	275.3	374.4	435.0	386.0	354.6	270.3	289.2	307.9	na
Share of industry in GDP (in per cent)	18.7	10.8	10.1	16.4	16.1	21.4	23.3	25.7	na
Share of agriculture in GDP (in per cent)	35.0	36.6	42.4	40.8	35.6	34.3	34.2	42.5	na
Current account/GDP (in per cent)	-6.9	-13.9	-21.4	-7.8	-25.0	-19.5	-11.6	-3.4	-2.9
External debt - reserves, in US$ millions	347	649	1,041	1,214	1,350	1,498	1,533	1,654	na
External debt/GDP (in per cent)	33.8	45.2	57.9	76.0	88.4	132.5	127.0	127.7	na
External debt/exports of goods and services (in per cent)	111.0	170.5	204.6	200.9	246.3	319.2	303.6	335.6	na

[1] An industrial sector enterprise survey conducted by the ILO in 1995 found that employment fell by about one-third between 1991 and 1994.

[2] Registered unemployed. The true rate of unemployment is unofficially estimated to be around 20 per cent.

[3] General government includes the state, municipalities and extra-budgetary funds. It also includes expenditure under the foreign financed Public Investment Programme. General government expenditure includes net lending.

[4] Simple average of National Bank's credit auction rates. Credit auctions were discontinued at the end of January 1997 and the three-month Treasury bill rate has become the official reference rate.

[5] Weighted average over all maturities.

Latvia

Key reform challenges

- Improvements in medium-term planning and the control of local government finances will be key to containing vulnerabilities associated with large current account deficits and to achieving a balanced budget over the medium term.

- Important progress has been made in improving the investment climate, but continued efforts are needed in implementing the new commercial code, improving transparency and corporate governance and fighting corruption.

- Further restructuring of infrastructure enterprises, particularly those in the energy sector, is needed to foster competition and attract private investment on a sustainable basis.

Stabilisation

Budget planning and controls have improved.

Over the medium term the authorities are committed to moving towards a balanced budget by improving medium-term planning, imposing tighter controls on local government and moving cautiously in reducing the tax burden. There has been some progress under the public administration reform strategy, following the approval in December 2001 of a detailed action plan and the law on framework of public administration in June 2002. In addition, there have been moves to tighten the control and monitoring of local governments after the spending overrun by the City of Riga in 2001. In June 2002, parliament approved amendments to the law on local government budgets, which clarify that local government borrowing requires the approval of the Ministry of Finance and is subject to the overall local government limit under the annual budget law. However, the President of Latvia used her power to send the law back to parliament for revisions. In addition, other enhancements to medium-term budget planning and the adoption of regulations to implement the new civil service pay scale are advancing more slowly.

Privatisation

Privatisation of the Latvian Shipping Company completed.

Following several failed privatisation attempts, the public offering for 32 per cent of shares against privatisation vouchers in the Latvian Shipping Company (LASCO) was held in April 2002. A cash auction of 51 per cent of shares in LASCO was also held on the Riga Stock Exchange in June 2002. The cash sale yielded LVL 35 million (around €63 million) in privatisation receipts. Full privatisation of the company will be completed when current and retired employees subscribe for the remaining 6 per cent in the company, with a deadline of mid-November 2002. However, the privatisation has proved controversial. The Latvian oil conglomerate Ventspils Nafta (itself 43.6 per cent state-owned) ended up owning almost 50 per cent of the shares while Fernandero Ltd., a Cypriot shipping company, claimed that it was unfairly excluded from the sale and started legal action. The Latvian Privatisation Agency (LPA) as seller and the Riga Stock Exchange as organiser contested this allegation, arguing that Fernandero did not comply with the auction deadline. Eventually, the claim was revoked and the auction results remain as approved.

Enterprise reform

Further efforts made to improve the business environment.

After some delay, a new commercial code came into effect in January 2002, which streamlines administrative procedures, enhances minority shareholder rights and further protects creditor interests. Although these simplifications may remove some of the shortcomings with regard to inconsistent interpretation of commercial laws, efforts will also be needed to strengthen the ability of the courts to implement the new legislation. In addition, the government has implemented 68 of the 77 suggested measures in its 1999 action plan to improve the business environment. The Cabinet of Ministers is currently considering the adoption of a new action plan. Following further high-level corruption cases over the past year, the government has also stepped up its efforts to fight corruption. These efforts have included the adoption of key legislation, such as a law on the prevention of conflict of interest and the establishment of the Office for the Prevention of and Fight against Corruption (OPFC) in May 2002.

Infrastructure

Further stake in the gas utility sold.

The government's last remaining 3 per cent stake in Latvijas Gaze was sold in February 2002 at auction against privatisation vouchers. Currently, the German companies Ruhrgas and E.ON Energie hold 29 per cent and 18 per cent respectively, while Russia's gas company Gazprom and Itera Latvia hold 25 per cent each. Ruhrgas has announced its intention to increase its stake. Gas tariff increases to cost recovery levels are still proving controversial. A court ruling in June 2002 rejected a claim made by Latvijas Gaze against the public services regulator committee for refusing a requested increase in tariffs. The rulings are being contested by the company.

Restructuring of Latvenergo progressing.

The government is implementing a restructuring programme, due to be completed by December 2002, for the energy monopoly

Enterprises, infrastructure, finance and social reforms

1991
Dec   Competition law adopted

1992
May   Two-tier banking system established
May   Banking law adopted
Oct   IAS accounting introduced

1993
May   Company law adopted
Dec   Stock exchange established

1994
Jan   BIS capital adequacy requirement introduced

1995
May   Banking crisis ensues
Jul   Stock exchange begins trading
Oct   New banking law adopted
Oct   IAS accounting for banks introduced
Oct   First state-owned bank privatised

1996
Jun   Energy Regulation Council established
Sep   Bankruptcy law adopted

1997
Jun   New competition law adopted
Aug   First corporate Eurobond issued
Nov   Electricity tariffs adjusted significantly
Dec   First corporate GDR issue undertaken

1998
Jan   Anti-monopoly office established
Jul   Private pension law adopted
Sep   New energy law adopted
Sep   New insurance law adopted
Nov   Railway law adopted

1999
Aug   PAYG pension system reformed

2000
Feb   Law on second pension pillar passed
May   Law on unified financial sector supervision adopted

2001
Jul   Financial and Capital Markets Commission commences operations
Jul   First contributions to second pillar of pensions scheme made
Jul   European Social Charter adopted
Sep   Single regulatory agency for public utilities created

2002
Jan   New commercial code enacted
Apr   New law on credit institutions adopted
Jun   Riga Stock Exchange acquired by Helsinki Exchange

Latvenergo. Steps have been taken to establish separate units and accounting systems for distribution, transmission and power generation. Furthermore, the government has adopted an EU directive on common rules for the internal market and other measures to further liberalise the sector. The government has increased the scope for bilateral trade among large customers and plans to further open the market next year, thereby significantly increasing the number of customers that can directly contract for electricity with independent generation companies. Work should continue to establish policy and regulatory clarity for the method of third-party access to the energy transmission and distribution grids and to establish separate prices for transmission and distribution services. In addition, the recently adopted principles for tariff setting should be implemented to increase tariffs further towards full cost-recovery levels, with the next tariff increase of around 10 per cent likely in 2004.

New regulatory agency for public utilities set up.
In September 2001, the single regulatory agency with responsibility for public utilities, including telecommunications, postal services, railway transportation and the energy sector (except district heating) was created. The law for this agency foresees that the regulator will act independently from any government institution, that any of its decisions can be revoked only by a court and that it is financed by an automatic state duty for public service regulation imposed on the public service providers.

Financial institutions

Further regulatory improvements have been made in the financial sector.
The unified Financial and Capital Markets Commission (FCMC), which started operations in July 2001, has continued to make progress in implementing the recommendations of the joint World Bank/IMF Financial Sector Assessment Programme of 2001. The adoption of amendments to the law on credit institutions in April 2002 should bring Latvia into full compliance with the Basel Core Principles. The FCMC intends to harmonise all sector-specific legislation, regulations and supervisory methods across sectors by end-December 2002 in order to reap the full benefits of unified supervision. Further improvements have also been made in enhancing the anti-money laundering framework, with the adoption in June 2002 of amendments to the law on the prevention of laundering of proceeds from criminal activity, which is in full compliance with the OECD Financial Action Task Force, UN and EU requirements. Potential cases of money laundering are identified by the Office for the Prevention of Laundering of Proceeds of Criminal Activity, based in the Chief Prosecutor's Office.

Helsinki Stock Exchange has acquired the Riga Stock Exchange.
Following its take-over of the Tallinn Stock Exchange last year, the Helsinki Stock Exchange further consolidated its holdings in the Baltics by buying a 93 per cent stake in the Riga Stock Exchange (RSE) in June 2002. The deal is conditional on RSE buying out all other existing shareholders in the Latvian Central Depository (LCD). Five shareholders of the Riga bourse who are also shareholders of the LCD have signed the share purchase agreement to sell their LCD shares to the RSE, giving it 81 per cent of LCD shares. The remaining 19 per cent are held by the LPA, which approved the sale of its shares in July 2002. The RSE has received the required regulatory approval from the FCMC. Once the deal is completed, HEX Group will become the majority owner of the RSE Group, consisting of the stock exchange and the depository. Of the 63 listed companies on the Riga Exchange, the most actively traded are the oil shipping concern Ventspils Nafta, the monopoly natural gas utility Latvijas Gaze and the Latvian Shipping Company.

Social reform

Pension reform has advanced with the introduction of a mandatory funded pillar.
In July 2001, a compulsory funded pension scheme ("second pillar") was introduced. Contributions to the second pillar are planned to rise gradually from 2 per cent of income to 10 per cent by 2010, with the first pillar being reduced accordingly. Participation in the scheme is mandatory for those who are subject to state pension insurance and under the age of 30, but optional for those aged between 30 and 49 years. For the first 18 months the State Treasury is managing the accumulated capital, but from 2003 the management will be entrusted to private investment companies. In the first year of the scheme, contributions reached LVL 7.3 million (around €13 million) and have accrued interest through investments in Treasury bills and term deposits at an average annual rate of 4.9 per cent.

Liberalisation
Current account convertibility – **full**
Interest rate liberalisation – **full**
Wage regulation – **no**

Stabilisation
Share of general government tax revenue
  in GDP – **30.4 per cent**
Exchange rate regime – **fixed**

Privatisation
Primary privatisation method – **direct sales**
Secondary privatisation method – **vouchers**
Tradability of land – **full except foreigners**

Enterprises and markets
Competition Office – **yes**

Infrastructure
Independent telecoms regulator – **yes**
Separation of railway accounts – **yes**
Independent electricity regulator – **no**

Financial sector
Capital adequacy ratio – **10 per cent**
Deposit insurance system – **yes**
Secured transactions law – **restricted**
Securities commission – **yes**

Social reform
Share of the population in poverty –
  34.8 per cent
Private pension funds – **yes**

	1993	1994	1995	1996	1997	1998	1999	2000	2001
Liberalisation									
Share of administered prices in CPI (in per cent)	6.1	16.6	16.6	17.8	19.6	20.4	22.0	22.3	22.0
Number of goods with administered prices in EBRD-15 basket	2.0	2.0	2.0	2.0	2.0	2.0	2.0	2.0	2.0
Share of trade with non-transition countries (in per cent)	43.6	46.4	49.5	50.0	56.7	66.4	72.9	79.8	68.6
Share of trade in GDP (in per cent)	96.7	64.3	75.1	74.1	80.4	84.6	72.3	72.2	76.2
Tariff revenues (in per cent of imports)	2.9	3.2	1.8	1.5	1.4	1.1	0.9	0.8	0.7
EBRD index of price liberalisation	3.0	3.0	3.0	3.0	3.0	3.0	3.0	3.0	3.0
EBRD index of forex and trade liberalisation	3.0	4.0	4.0	4.0	4.0	4.0	4.3	4.3	4.3
Privatisation									
Privatisation revenues (cumulative, in per cent of GDP)	na	0.3	0.7	0.8	2.2	3.3	3.5	4.1	4.5
Private sector share in GDP (in per cent)	30.0	40.0	55.0	60.0	60.0	65.0	65.0	65.0	65.0
Private sector share in employment (in per cent)	na	58.0	60.0	63.0	66.0	68.0	70.0	na	na
EBRD index of small-scale privatisation	3.0	4.0	4.0	4.0	4.0	4.0	4.0	4.3	4.3
EBRD index of large-scale privatisation	2.0	2.0	2.0	3.0	3.0	3.0	3.0	3.0	3.0
Enterprises									
Budgetary subsidies and current transfers (in per cent of GDP)	na	0.2	0.4	0.8	5.2	4.7	5.2	6.4	5.2
Effective statutory social security tax (in per cent)	na	70.0	73.9	68.3	76.4	79.0	81.7	na	na
Share of industry in total employment (in per cent)	23.1	21.0	20.4	19.8	20.2	18.4	17.8	18.1	na
Change in labour productivity in industry (in per cent)	-9.2	13.7	8.1	8.4	8.6	12.5	-1.7	2.6	na
Investment rate/GDP (in per cent) [1]	9.2	19.1	17.6	18.8	22.8	27.6	26.3	26.7	29.0
EBRD index of enterprise reform	2.0	2.0	2.0	3.0	2.7	2.7	2.7	2.7	2.7
EBRD index of competition policy	2.0	2.0	2.0	2.0	2.3	2.3	2.3	2.3	2.3
Infrastructure									
Main telephone lines per 100 inhabitants	26.6	25.8	28.0	29.8	29.8	30.2	30.0	30.3	30.8
Railway labour productivity (1989=100)	54.0	48.8	50.2	65.6	75.4	72.0	73.6	84.5	90.5
Electricity tariffs, USc kWh (collection rate in per cent)	na	2.7 (85)	4.7 (85)	5.6 (94)	6.4 (98)	6.6 (99)	6.7 (na)	6.4 (na)	6.5 (99)
GDP per unit of energy use (PPP in US dollars per kgoe)	2.5	2.7	3.2	3.2	3.3	3.5	4.1	na	na
EBRD index of infrastructure reform	1.0	2.0	2.0	2.3	2.3	2.7	2.7	2.7	2.7
Financial institutions									
Number of banks (foreign owned)	62 (na)	56 (na)	42 (11)	35 (14)	32 (15)	27 (15)	23 (12)	21 (12)	23 (10)
Asset share of state-owned banks (in per cent)	na	7.2	9.9	6.9	6.8	8.5	2.6	2.9	3.2
Non-performing loans (in per cent of total loans)	na	11.0	19.0	20.0	10.0	6.8	6.8	5.0	3.1
Domestic credit to private sector (in per cent of GDP)	na	15.9	7.5	6.9	10.6	15.1	16.0	19.5	31.8
Stock market capitalisation (in per cent of GDP)	na	na	0.2	3.0	6.1	6.1	5.9	8.0	9.2
EBRD index of banking sector reform	2.0	3.0	3.0	3.0	3.0	2.7	3.0	3.0	3.3
EBRD index of reform of non-banking financial institutions	1.0	2.0	2.0	2.0	2.3	2.3	2.3	2.3	2.3
Legal environment									
EBRD rating of legal extensiveness (company law)	na	na	na	na	3.3	3.3	3.7	4.0	3.7
EBRD rating of legal effectiveness (company law)	na	na	na	na	3.0	2.0	3.0	3.7	4.0
Social sector									
Expenditures on health and education (in per cent of GDP)	10.1	10.0	10.9	9.7	9.5	11.0	12.4	11.6	na
Life expectancy at birth, total (years)	67.6	66.7	66.8	69.3	69.9	69.7	70.4	70.4	na
Basic school enrolment ratio (in per cent)	88.7	88.2	88.6	90.6	91.4	91.5	93.9	96.3	na
Earnings inequality (GINI-coefficient)	28.3	32.5	34.6	34.9	33.6	33.2	33.3	33.7	na

[1] Source: World Bank Development Indicators. Gross capital formation.

	1994	1995	1996	1997	1998	1999	2000	2001	2002
								Estimate	*Projection*
Output and expenditure				*(Percentage change in real terms)*					
GDP	2.2	-0.9	3.7	8.4	4.8	2.8	6.8	7.7	4.0
Private consumption	3.2	0.6	9.9	4.9	1.1	3.7	7.4	7.1	na
Public consumption	-0.9	7.7	1.8	0.3	6.1	0.0	-1.9	-2.1	na
Gross fixed investment	0.8	8.7	22.3	20.7	44.0	-4.0	20.0	17.0	na
Exports of goods and services	-8.4	3.3	20.2	13.1	4.9	-6.4	12.0	6.9	na
Imports of goods and services	-0.7	1.3	28.5	6.8	19.0	-5.2	4.9	12.6	na
Industrial gross output	-7.1	1.6	2.5	12.5	3.5	-5.7	4.4	8.8	na
Agricultural gross output	-15.0	11.7	-7.0	6.4	-3.6	-3.7	11.3	5.0	na
Employment				*(Percentage change)*					
Labour force (end-year)	-1.5	-1.9	-1.0	-3.6	-0.4	-1.0	-0.4	-0.2	na
Employment (end-year)	-10.1	-3.5	-2.7	1.9	0.6	-0.5	0.0	-0.1	na
				(In per cent of labour force)					
Unemployment (end-year)	16.7	18.1	19.4	14.8	14.0	13.5	13.2	13.1	na
Prices and wages				*(Percentage change)*					
Consumer prices (annual average)	35.9	25.0	17.6	8.4	4.7	2.4	2.6	2.5	2.3
Consumer prices (end-year)	26.3	23.1	13.1	7.0	2.8	3.2	1.8	3.2	3.0
Producer prices (annual average)	16.9	11.9	13.7	4.1	1.9	-4.0	0.6	1.7	na
Producer prices (end-year)	10.7	15.9	7.7	3.6	-1.9	-1.1	1.0	1.8	na
Gross average monthly earnings in economy (annual average)	52.2	24.5	10.3	21.6	11.1	5.8	6.1	6.5	na
Government sector [1]				*(In per cent of GDP)*					
General government balance	-4.4	-4.0	-1.8	0.3	-0.8	-3.9	-3.3	-1.9	-2.5
General government expenditure	40.5	41.5	39.5	41.0	43.3	44.1	42.0	37.6	na
General government debt	14.1	16.3	14.5	12.0	10.5	13.0	13.1	15.0	na
Monetary sector				*(Percentage change)*					
Broad money (M2, end-year)	47.4	-23.1	19.9	38.7	5.9	8.0	27.9	29.0	na
Domestic credit (end-year)	72.3	-28.2	6.0	39.3	30.6	15.2	43.6	35.6	na
				(In per cent of GDP)					
Broad money (M2, end-year)	33.4	22.5	22.4	26.7	25.7	25.6	29.3	32.4	na
Interest and exchange rates				*(In per cent per annum, end-year)*					
Refinancing rate	25.0	24.0	9.5	4.0	4.0	4.0	3.5	3.5	na
Inter-bank market rate [2]	37.8	21.1	9.7	3.9	7.0	2.7	3.3	5.4	na
Deposit rate (short-term, under 1 year)	18.8	15.0	10.0	5.3	6.5	4.2	4.2	5.7	na
Lending rate (short-term, under 1 year)	36.7	31.1	20.3	12.1	16.4	12.5	11.8	9.9	na
				(Lats per US dollar)					
Exchange rate (end-year)	0.55	0.54	0.56	0.59	0.57	0.58	0.61	0.64	na
Exchange rate (annual average)	0.56	0.53	0.55	0.58	0.59	0.59	0.61	0.63	na
External sector				*(In millions of US dollars)*					
Current account	201	-16	-279	-345	-650	-654	-493	-735	-680
Trade balance	-301	-580	-798	-848	-1,130	-1,027	-1,058	-1,351	-1,450
Merchandise exports	1,022	1,368	1,488	1,838	2,011	1,889	2,058	2,216	2,437
Merchandise imports	1,322	1,947	2,286	2,686	3,141	2,916	3,116	3,566	3,887
Foreign direct investment, net	279	245	379	515	303	331	400	170	250
Gross reserves (end-year), excluding gold	545	506	622	704	728	840	851	1,149	na
External debt stock [3]	825	1,538	2,091	2,756	3,098	3,821	4,713	5,578	na
				(In months of imports of goods and services)					
Gross reserves (end-year), excluding gold	4.0	2.8	2.5	2.5	2.2	2.8	2.6	3.2	na
				(In per cent of exports of goods and services)					
Debt service	3.9	8.1	10.0	10.5	10.1	13.5	15.5	19.6	na
Memorandum items				*(Denominations as indicated)*					
Population (end-year, millions)	2.5	2.5	2.5	2.5	2.4	2.4	2.4	2.3	na
GDP (in millions of lats)	2,043	2,329	2,807	3,269	3,592	3,890	4,348	4,759	5,062
GDP per capita (in US dollars)	1,442	1,763	2,054	2,289	2,538	2,792	3,032	3,233	na
Share of industry in GDP (in per cent)	25.4	28.4	26.6	27.4	23.4	19.9	18.6	18.7	na
Share of agriculture in GDP (in per cent)	9.5	9.9	8.2	5.6	4.4	4.3	4.9	4.7	na
Current account/GDP (in per cent)	5.5	-0.4	-5.5	-6.1	-10.7	-9.8	-6.9	-9.7	-8.5
External debt - reserves, in US$ millions	280	1,032	1,469	2,052	2,370	2,981	3,862	4,429	na
External debt/GDP (in per cent)	22.6	34.9	41.1	49.0	50.9	57.5	65.7	73.5	na
External debt/exports of goods and services (in per cent)	49.1	73.7	80.0	96.0	99.3	131.1	144.1	161.6	na

[1] General government includes the state, municipalities and extra-budgetary funds. Privatisation revenues are not included in revenues. General government expenditure includes net lending.

[2] Weighted average interest rates in the inter-bank market.

[3] Includes non-resident currency and deposits, liabilities to affiliated enterprises and liabilities to direct investors.

Lithuania

Stabilisation

Litas re-pegged against the euro.
Lithuania's currency was successfully re-pegged from the US dollar to the euro in February 2002. Financial markets reacted positively to the move, with the spread of euro-denominated Lithuanian government Eurobonds narrowing against the benchmark German government bond. The Bank of Lithuania intends to maintain this currency board arrangement until the country accedes to the EU and joins the ERM II. The sustainability of the currency board hinges on the maintenance of sound fiscal policies (notwithstanding the additional fiscal burden associated with NATO and EU accessions) and further implementation of structural reforms to enhance external competitiveness. In recent years, the authorities have been successful in reducing the fiscal deficit, which dropped to 1.9 per cent in 2001 from 8.5 per cent of GDP in 1999.

Privatisation

Progress in the privatisation of large-scale enterprises.
At the end of 2001, the state property fund still managed 1,140 entities (including real estate assets). During the first half of 2002, LTL 242 million (€70 million) was raised from the sale of stakes in 469 companies and banks. The two largest deals were the partial sell-off of Lietuvos Dujos (Lithuanian Gas) and the privatisation of Agricultural Bank. In June 2002, the state's share in the Mazeikiu Nafta oil refinery was reduced further from 60 per cent to 40.7 per cent. Preparations for the privatisation of Lithuanian Gas (the second phase), Lithuanian Airlines, Lithuanian Energy, two shipping companies and four large state-owned alcohol producers are under way with a view to completing the sales by end-2003.

Enterprise reform

Participation of Yukos in Mazeikiu oil refinery may enhance performance.
The Mazeikiu Nafta oil refinery (MN), the largest enterprise in the country, recorded net losses of LTL 179 million (€52 million) and LTL 277 million (€80 million) in 2000 and 2001 respectively. The US company William International (WI) had management control and a 33 per cent stake during this period, but ownership and control are about to be transferred to Russian oil company Yukos. The agreement with Yukos on its equity participation and a long-term supply agreement was finalised in June 2002 when the company gained a 27 per cent stake in MN in return for a US$ 75 million cash injection. The government's stake has been reduced from 59 per cent to 41 per cent. Yukos also has provided a US$ 75 million loan for the modernisation of the refinery. In September, WI sold its entire stake and the operational control rights to Yukos.

Investment climate improves.
Between 1993 and 2001, Lithuania's cumulative foreign direct investment (FDI) net inflows per capita were one of the lowest among the ten EU accession countries of the region. In order to attract more FDI, the government is taking steps to improve the investment climate. A new civil code, effective from July 2001, has simplified the rules for the registration of legal entities. In January 2002, the parliament adopted the national anti-corruption programme, in order to make the fight against corruption more coordinated and effective. Since administrative corruption is the main area of concern, implementation is likely to concentrate on fighting corruption in the fields of public procurement and customs. In order to simplify the tax regime and lower the tax burden on businesses, as of 1 January 2002 the corporate profit tax rate has been lowered from 24 per cent to 15 per cent and exemptions on reinvested earnings have been eliminated. Since the new laws on bankruptcy and enterprise restructuring became effective in July 2001, the effectiveness of the bankruptcy procedures has improved. The number of bankruptcy cases filed at courts increased from 291 to 533 and the number of completed cases rose from 48 to 234 in 2000 and 2001 respectively.

Liberalisation, stabilisation, privatisation

1990
Feb	Central Bank established
Mar	Independence from Soviet Union declared
May	Personal income tax introduced

1991
Feb	Privatisation law adopted
Feb	Voucher privatisation begins
Jul	Restitution law adopted

1992
Apr	Export surrender requirement abolished
Oct	Most prices liberalised

1993
Jul	Litas becomes sole legal tender
Jul	Trade regime liberalised
Nov	Free trade agreement with Russia signed

1994
Apr	Currency board introduced
May	VAT introduced
May	Full current account convertibility introduced
Jul	Treasury bills market initiated
Jul	Land law adopted
Oct	Export duties abolished
Dec	Law on Central Bank adopted

1995
Jan	EFTA membership granted
Jun	First phase of privatisation completed
Jul	Cash privatisation begins
Dec	First sovereign Eurobond issued

1997
Nov	Privatisation law amended

1998
Oct	Tariffs increased on imports from CIS countries

1999
Jan	Capital gains tax introduced

2000
Mar	IMF Stand-By Arrangement reached
Dec	WTO membership granted

2002
Feb	Currency repegged from US dollar to euro
Jun	Mazeikiu oil refinery privatised

Enterprises, infrastructure, finance and social reforms

1992
Sep	Two-tier banking system re-established
Sep	Bankruptcy law adopted
Sep	Stock exchange established
Nov	Electricity prices readjusted significantly
Nov	Competition law adopted
Nov	Competition Office established

1993
Sep	Stock exchange begins trading

1994
Jul	Company law adopted

1995
Jan	New law on commercial banks adopted
Mar	Energy law adopted
Dec	Banking crisis ensues
Dec	Energy utilities and railways corporatised

1996
Jan	IAS accounting for banks introduced
Feb	Independent securities regulator established
Mar	BIS capital adequacy requirement introduced
Jul	First GDR issue undertaken
Aug	First major bank becomes majority foreign-owned

1997
Feb	Independent energy regulator established
Feb	First corporate Eurobond issued
Jul	Lithuanian Telecom corporatised
Oct	New bankruptcy law adopted

1998
Apr	Company law amended
Apr	Pledge law enacted
Apr	Mortgage registry established
Jun	Lithuanian Telecom privatised
Jun	IAS accounting for listed companies introduced
Aug	New telecommunications law adopted

1999
Apr	New competition law adopted
Jun	Private pension funds law adopted

2000
Oct	New gas law adopted
Dec	New electricity law adopted

2001
May	Independent telecommunications regulator established
Jul	Bankruptcy and restructuring laws strengthened
Dec	Lithuanian Energy Company unbundled

2002
Jan	Anti-corruption programme adopted
Mar	Banking sector privatisation completed
Jun	New labour code adopted

Infrastructure

Lithuanian Gas partially privatised.

In May 2002, the government sold a 34 per cent stake in the gas transmission and distribution monopoly, Lithuanian Gas, to a consortium of Germany's Ruhrgas and E.ON Energie for LTL 152 million (€44 million). According to the privatisation agreement, the consortium will subscribe to another LTL 70 million (€20 million) capital increase upon the sale of a further 34 per cent stake to a gas supplier. In August 2002, the government accepted that Gazprom of Russia qualified as a bidder in the second phase of privatisation and their preliminary offer was submitted in mid-September 2002. The privatisation of the company will enhance competition, but the regulatory authorities still have to ensure third-party access to transmission and distribution networks.

Lithuanian Energy Company unbundled.

In December 2001, the Lithuanian Energy Company (LE) was unbundled into two regional distribution companies, two generation companies and a transmission company. The government is clarifying the financial liabilities, assets and investment plans of the separated entities, with the goal of starting the privatisation of distribution companies in 2003. Under the plan, the new transmission company (LE in its new form) will remain under state ownership. It will undertake dispatching responsibilities and also act as the market operator and a licensed exporter of electricity until the market is fully liberalised. At the municipal level, the privatisation of district heating companies is also moving forward. In July 2002, a consortium of two German strategic investors and a local gas supplier participated in the capital increase of Klaipeda Energy, thereby diluting the shareholding of the municipality from 94 per cent to 76 per cent. In August 2002, a consortium led by Gazprom was awarded a leading bid for the acquisition of the combined heat and power plant of Kaunas Energy.

Steps taken to improve municipal finances.

In October 2001, the parliament adopted the amended law on municipal budget revenues determination methodology. The new law clarifies the amount of revenues from personal income tax that each municipality is able to retain. It also defines the methodologies for establishing the costs of service provision mandated by the state, such as education (for which the central government will provide about 45 per cent through transfers). These measures enhance the scope for the municipalities to undertake and finance investments. However, in spite of these improvements, municipalities are still likely to suffer from inadequate financing.

Financial institutions

Banking sector fully privatised …

In March 2002, the authorities sold their 76 per cent stake in Agricultural Bank, the third-largest bank in Lithuania in terms of assets, for LTL 71 million (€20 million) to NordLB of Germany. The sale completes the privatisation of the banking system and is expected to enhance competition in the sector. An IMF report issued in February 2002 found that bank supervision was adequate and that banks were adopting a conservative approach to lending and risk management. Nevertheless, in response to further recommendations provided by the IMF and an EU Progress Report, the authorities introduced in July 2002 a prudential limit on bank lending to connected parties. Plans have also been made to enhance anti-money laundering measures. These measures are particularly important as domestic credit is increasing strongly albeit from a low base.

… but the non-bank sector lacks depth.

The capital market in Lithuania is relatively undeveloped, reflecting in part a weak institutional investor base. Stock market capitalisation at the end of 2001 was only 10 per cent of GDP, lower than in most of the other advanced transition countries. At the same time, there were nine life insurance companies and 26 non-life insurance companies, but the total insurance premiums underwritten in 2001 were less than 1 per cent of GDP. No private pension funds have yet been established, although legislation on private voluntary pension funds became effective at the beginning of January 2000. The government is considering further reform of the pension system and the introduction of a privately managed voluntary pillar that will be matched by supplementary government contributions and tax incentives. On regulatory issues, the IMF expressed concerns about the quality of insurance sector regulation and supervision and recommended that financial sector supervision should be unified in the long term.

Social reform

New labour code adopted.

In June 2002, parliament adopted a new labour code in line with the EU *acquis,* which will become effective at the beginning of 2003. The new code regulates the contractual relationship between employers and employees and outlines the enforcement mechanism of labour legislation, implementation of labour rights, social partnership, collective contracts and dispute settlements. The new regulation on dismissals is expected to increase the flexibility of the labour market while sufficiently protecting the rights of employees.

Liberalisation
Current account convertibility – **full**
Interest rate liberalisation – **full**
Wage regulation – **no**

Stabilisation
Share of general government tax revenue
  in GDP – **27.4 per cent**
Exchange rate regime – **currency
  board (euro)**

Privatisation
Primary privatisation method – **vouchers**
Secondary privatisation method –
  direct sales
Tradability of land – **full** [1]

Enterprises and markets
Competition Office – **yes**

Infrastructure
Independent telecoms regulator – **yes**
Separation of railway accounts – **yes**
Independent electricity regulator – **yes**

Financial sector
Capital adequacy ratio – **10 per cent**
Deposit insurance system – **yes**
Secured transactions law – **yes**
Securities commission – **yes**

Social reform
Share of the population in poverty –
  22.5 per cent
Private pension funds – **no**

	1993	1994	1995	1996	1997	1998	1999	2000	2001
Liberalisation									
Share of administered prices in CPI (in per cent)	na	na	na	na	na	na	na	na	na
Number of goods with administered prices in EBRD-15 basket	6.0	6.0	2.0	2.0	2.0	2.0	2.0	2.0	2.0
Share of trade with non-transition countries (in per cent)	75.0	35.0	43.0	38.8	54.6	46.6	50.9	65.9	59.9
Share of trade in GDP (in per cent)	157.7	100.3	101.4	97.8	99.4	87.8	72.2	81.6	90.8
Tariff revenues (in per cent of imports) [2]	1.1	3.2	1.4	1.2	1.3	1.1	1.1	0.7	na
EBRD index of price liberalisation	3.0	3.0	3.0	3.0	3.0	3.0	3.0	3.0	3.0
EBRD index of forex and trade liberalisation	3.0	4.0	4.0	4.0	4.0	4.0	4.0	4.0	4.3
Privatisation									
Privatisation revenues (cumulative, in per cent of GDP)	0.9	1.3	1.4	1.4	1.6	6.9	8.0	9.8	10.8
Private sector share in GDP (in per cent)	35.0	60.0	65.0	70.0	70.0	70.0	70.0	70.0	70.0
Private sector share in employment (in per cent)	na	na	na	na	na	na	na	na	na
EBRD index of small-scale privatisation	3.3	4.0	4.0	4.0	4.0	4.0	4.3	4.3	4.3
EBRD index of large-scale privatisation	3.0	3.0	3.0	3.0	3.0	3.0	3.0	3.0	3.3
Enterprises									
Budgetary subsidies and current transfers (in per cent of GDP)	1.4	1.7	1.1	1.3	0.9	0.5	0.4	0.2	0.2
Effective statutory social security tax (in per cent)	65.8	81.5	70.3	73.0	70.8	78.8	78.3	na	na
Share of industry in total employment (in per cent)	25.7	22.5	20.9	20.7	21.6	21.2	20.7	20.5	21.2
Change in labour productivity in industry (in per cent)	-23.1	-11.1	14.1	6.5	2.4	8.0	-8.8	11.7	17.7
Investment rate/GDP (in per cent)	23.1	23.1	23.0	23.0	24.4	24.4	22.7	20.6	na
EBRD index of enterprise reform	2.0	2.0	2.0	3.0	2.7	2.7	2.7	2.7	2.7
EBRD index of competition policy	2.0	2.0	2.0	2.0	2.3	2.3	2.3	2.7	3.0
Infrastructure									
Main telephone lines per 100 inhabitants	23.1	24.1	25.4	26.8	28.3	30.1	31.2	32.1	31.3
Railway labour productivity (1989=100)	50.7	35.4	32.3	35.9	38.2	36.3	34.9	41.3	39.1
Electricity tariffs, USc kWh (collection rate in per cent)	na	na	5.0 (85)	5.0 (85)	5.5 (85)	5.5 (90)	5.5 (90)	6.1 (na)	6.3 (91)
GDP per unit of energy use (PPP in US dollars per kgoe)	2.4	2.6	2.5	2.5	2.8	2.8	3.1	na	na
EBRD index of infrastructure reform	1.0	1.0	1.7	1.7	2.0	2.3	2.3	2.7	2.7
Financial institutions									
Number of banks (foreign owned)	26 (0)	22 (0)	15 (0)	12 (3)	12 (4)	12 (5)	13 (4)	13 (6)	14 (4)
Asset share of state-owned banks (in per cent)	53.6	48.0	61.8	54.0	48.8	44.4	41.9	38.9	12.2
Non-performing loans (in per cent of total loans)	na	27.0	17.3	32.2	28.3	12.5	11.9	10.8	7.4
Domestic credit to private sector (in per cent of GDP)	13.8	17.6	12.6	9.4	9.3	9.6	11.1	10.1	11.5
Stock market capitalisation (in per cent of GDP)	na	1.0	2.6	11.4	17.8	10.0	10.7	14.0	10.0
EBRD index of banking sector reform	2.0	2.0	3.0	3.0	3.0	3.0	3.0	3.0	3.0
EBRD index of reform of non-banking financial institutions	1.7	2.0	2.0	2.0	2.3	2.3	2.7	3.0	3.0
Legal environment									
EBRD rating of legal extensiveness (company law)	na	na	na	na	4.0	4.0	4.0	4.0	3.7
EBRD rating of legal effectiveness (company law)	na	na	na	na	3.0	3.0	3.0	3.3	3.7
Social sector									
Expenditures on health and education (in per cent of GDP)	7.8	9.3	9.3	8.8	9.7	11.2	11.1	10.4	na
Life expectancy at birth, total (years)	69.0	68.7	69.3	70.4	71.2	71.6	72.1	72.6	na
Basic school enrolment ratio (in per cent)	91.1	91.4	92.7	93.0	94.9	95.9	95.5	97.6	na
Earnings inequality (GINI-coefficient)	na	39.0	37.4	35.0	34.5	35.7	36.8	na	na

[1] Full for non-agricultural land but ownership of agricultural land is constitutionally prohibited
   for foreigners and partially restricted for Lithuanian legal persons.

[2] Refers to all taxes on foreign trade.

	1994	1995	1996	1997	1998	1999	2000	2001 Estimate	2002 Projection
Output and expenditure					*(Percentage change in real terms)*				
GDP	-9.8	3.3	4.7	7.3	5.1	-3.9	3.8	5.9	5.2
Private consumption	na	na	na	9.2	4.0	2.1	4.6	3.0	na
Public consumption	na	na	na	1.5	22.9	-17.5	-0.8	0.4	na
Gross fixed investment	na	na	na	22.0	9.9	-6.3	-3.9	10.6	na
Exports of goods and services	na	na	na	18.7	0.7	-16.1	12.9	20.8	na
Imports of goods and services	na	na	na	25.0	6.9	-13.1	4.5	17.7	na
Industrial gross output	-26.5	5.3	5.0	3.3	8.2	-11.2	5.3	16.9	na
Agricultural gross output	-20.0	11.0	12.6	8.6	-5.2	-14.5	5.4	-8.5	na
Employment [1]					*(Percentage change)*				
Labour force (end-year)	-6.4	0.7	-2.1	-5.7	0.8	1.0	-3.7	-1.9	na
Employment (end-year)	-5.8	-1.9	-0.7	-3.1	1.7	0.1	-5.0	-3.8	na
					(In per cent of labour force)				
Unemployment (end-year)	3.8	17.5	16.4	14.1	13.3	14.1	15.4	17.0	na
Prices and wages					*(Percentage change)*				
Consumer prices (annual average)	72.1	39.6	24.6	8.9	5.1	0.8	1.0	1.3	0.9
Consumer prices (end-year)	45.0	35.7	13.1	8.4	2.4	0.3	1.4	2.0	0.4
Producer prices (annual average) [2]	44.8	28.3	16.5	6.0	-3.9	3.0	18.0	1.3	na
Producer prices (end-year) [2]	33.8	20.3	12.3	0.9	-8.3	23.3	2.6	-4.5	na
Gross average monthly earnings in economy (annual average)	95.9	47.8	28.5	25.9	19.5	6.2	-1.7	2.1	na
Government sector [3]					*(In per cent of GDP)*				
General government balance	-4.8	-4.5	-4.5	-1.8	-5.9	-8.5	-2.8	-1.9	-1.4
General government expenditure	37.4	36.8	34.2	33.7	38.1	40.2	33.2	31.4	na
General government debt	na	na	na	na	22.8	29.0	28.9	29.2	na
Monetary sector					*(Percentage change)*				
Broad money (M2, end-year)	63.0	28.9	-3.5	34.1	14.5	7.7	16.5	21.4	na
Domestic credit (end-year)	na	na	1.8	37.6	16.8	24.5	1.7	13.7	na
					(In per cent of GDP)				
Broad money (M2, end-year)	25.8	23.3	17.2	19.0	19.4	21.0	23.2	26.5	na
Interest and exchange rates					*(In per cent per annum, end-year)*				
Inter-bank interest rate	na	na	na	na	na	7.7	10.4	5.5	na
Treasury bill rate (3-month maturity)	22.4	10.7	7.6	5.8	6.1	4.6	4.7	3.0	na
Deposit rate [4]	7.6	7.4	4.3	1.9	2.4	1.6	1.0	0.7	na
Lending rate [5]	29.8	23.9	16.0	11.9	12.6	13.0	11.0	8.1	na
					(Litai per US dollar)				
Exchange rate (end-year)	4.0	4.0	4.0	4.0	4.0	4.0	4.0	4.0	na
Exchange rate (annual average)	4.0	4.0	4.0	4.0	4.0	4.0	4.0	4.0	na
External sector					*(In millions of US dollars)*				
Current account	-94	-614	-723	-981	-1,298	-1,194	-675	-574	-800
Trade balance	-205	-698	-896	-1,147	-1,518	-1,405	-1,104	-1,108	-1,240
Merchandise exports	2,029	2,706	3,413	4,192	3,962	3,147	4,050	4,889	5,207
Merchandise imports	2,234	3,404	4,309	5,340	5,480	4,551	5,154	5,997	6,447
Foreign direct investment, net [6]	31	72	152	328	921	478	375	439	395
Gross reserves (end-year), excluding gold	525	757	772	1,010	1,409	1,195	1,312	1,618	na
External debt stock [7]	529	1,374	2,401	3,299	3,795	4,540	4,884	5,262	na
					(In months of imports of goods and services)				
Gross reserves (end-year), excluding gold	2.4	2.3	1.9	1.9	2.7	2.7	2.7	2.9	na
					(In per cent of current account revenues, excluding transfers)				
Debt service	2.3	3.7	6.9	10.5	17.8	19.4	20.1	27.3	na
Memorandum items					*(Denominations as indicated)*				
Population (end-year, millions)	3.6	3.6	3.6	3.6	3.5	3.5	3.5	3.5	na
GDP (in millions of litai)	16,904	24,103	31,569	38,340	42,990	42,655	45,148	47,968	50,930
GDP per capita (in US dollars)	1,166	1,667	2,200	2,691	3,039	3,036	3,237	3,450	na
Share of industry in GDP (in per cent)	25.5	23.9	23.7	22.5	21.1	20.4	23.3	25.6	na
Share of agriculture in GDP (in per cent)	10.1	10.7	11.2	10.5	9.1	7.5	7.0	6.3	na
Current account/GDP (in per cent)	-2.2	-10.2	-9.2	-10.2	-12.1	-11.2	-6.0	-4.8	-5.8
External debt - reserves, in US$ millions	4	617	1,628	2,289	2,386	3,345	3,573	3,644	na
External debt/GDP (in per cent)	12.4	22.8	30.4	34.4	35.3	42.6	43.3	43.9	na
External debt/exports of goods and services (in per cent)	22.5	43.1	57.0	63.2	74.8	107.1	95.6	87.0	na

[1]   Based on the labour force survey data.
[2]   Producer prices excluding electricity, gas and water until 1995; total industry from 1996.
[3]   Cash basis. General government sector includes the state, municipalities and extra-budgetary funds. General government expenditure includes net lending.
[4]   Average interest rate on demand deposits in litai.

[5]   Average interest rate on loans in litai.
[6]   Covers only investment in equity capital for 1994; equity capital and reinvested earnings for 1995 onwards.
[7]   Includes non-resident currency and deposits and loans to foreign subsidiaries.

Moldova

Key reform challenges

- Resumption of official lending has eased external financing constraints, but successful implementation of key structural reforms is vital to achieve sustainable growth.

- For the effective implementation of recently approved reforms, administrative capacity has to be strengthened and state interference in the operation of privatised enterprises reduced.

- The independence of the newly created regulatory agencies for energy and telecommunications needs to be strengthened to sustain reform progress in these key sectors.

Liberalisation

Implementation of pre-shipment inspections under scrutiny.

The implementation of pre-shipment inspections (PSI), which were initially introduced as a requirement of an IMF agreed programme, has been the subject of intense debate by government officials and businesses. To assess the growing concerns, specialists from the Department of Commercial Relations have been nominated to act as the liaison between business representatives and SGS, the private foreign company implementing PSI. These specialists will be responsible for monitoring the activity of SGS and identifying any related business complaints. At the end of September 2002, the constitutional court declared the introduction of PSI by government decree unconstitutional. According to the ruling, PSI should be based on a special law adopted by parliament.

Stabilisation

Access to official funding resumed ...

The IMF resumed loan disbursements under the poverty reduction and growth facility (PRGF) in July 2002. The IMF commended the prudent fiscal and monetary policies that had been applied over the past year and the adoption of several laws intended to strengthen the institutional infrastructure, including the civil code. The resumption of the PRGF enabled the World Bank to disburse funds from the third Structural Adjustment Credit (SAC III), which assists the government in consolidating economic stabilisation, bolstering foreign reserves and servicing external debt. In June 2002, the World Bank also approved a rural investment and services project, which seeks to promote rural entrepreneurship, agricultural production and economic diversification in rural areas.

... but the country still faces serious external debt problems.

The need to repay about US$ 35 million out of a US$ 75 million Eurobond is the main reason for the sharp rise in scheduled external debt repayments in 2002, which amount to over 60 per cent of central government revenues. However, the government was unable to meet these obligations and was forced to reschedule its debt with private and official creditors. Following the restructuring of the Eurobond in August 2002, a positive outcome of negotiations with bilateral and unilateral creditors and the Paris Club is now necessary to ease the debt burden further and to create a basis for debt sustainability over the medium term.

Privatisation

Implementation of the privatisation programme moving slowly.

The 2002 privatisation programme includes more than 500 companies. They are to be privatised either through sales via the stock exchange (if the state holds up to 30 per cent of the share capital) or through international tenders (if the state has a majority ownership). The privatisation revenues raised in the first half of 2002 are about US$ 4 million, less than half the targeted amount. However, substantial privatisations in the wineries, electricity and telecommunications sectors have yet to be launched.

Enterprise reform

The implementation of new laws faces major challenges ...

The absence of a proper registrar for the registration of pledges and of specialised bankruptcy courts and judges is holding back the effective implementation of the newly adopted pledge and bankruptcy laws. For instance insufficient training on the newly required on-line registration procedures, which became effective in July 2002 after a nine-month transition period, has caused major disruptions in the pledge registration process.

... and Moldovan enterprises still face a very difficult business environment.

A World Bank report on the cost of doing business in Moldova, which was presented to representatives of government, business and non-governmental organisations in July 2002, concluded that Moldovan enterprises face more expensive registration and licensing procedures than businesses in neighbouring countries such as Georgia, Ukraine and Belarus. Moldovan enterprises are also subject to excessive state regulation,

Liberalisation, stabilisation, privatisation

1991
Aug	Independence from Soviet Union declared

1992
Jan	Most prices liberalised
Jan	State trading monopoly abolished
Jun	New tax system introduced
Sep	Exchange rate unified

1993
Mar	Cash privatisation begins
Mar	Privatisation with patrimonial bonds begins
Apr	Most quantity controls on exports removed
Nov	New currency (leu) introduced

1995
Jan	VAT introduced
Mar	Treasury bills market initiated
Jun	Full current account convertibility introduced

1996
Jan	New Central Bank law adopted

1997
Jun	First sovereign Eurobond issued
Jul	New VAT law enacted
Jul	New land law adopted
Sep	New privatisation law adopted

1998
Feb	National land cadastre introduced
Jun	Open market operations begin
Aug	Most tax and duty exemptions removed
Dec	VAT and income taxes amended

1999
Apr	All remaining trade restrictions removed
Nov	EFF programme suspended by IMF

2000
Jul	Parliamentary republic introduced
Dec	PRGF programme agreed with IMF

2001
May	PRGF programme suspended by IMF
Jun	WTO membership granted

2002
Jul	PRGF programme resumed by IMF
Aug	Eurobond restructured

especially in the form of frequent state inspections. On average, there are 16 inspections a year, which together can last for up to three months. The report found that the number of inspections

Enterprises, infrastructure, finance and social reforms

1991
Jun   Two-tier banking system established

1992
Feb   Competition law adopted

1994
Jul   Securities and Exchange Commission established

1995
Jun   Stock exchange established
Jun   Trade in listed shares begins
Jun   Enterprise restructuring agency established

1996
Jan   New financial institutions law adopted

1997
Aug   Independent energy regulator established

1998
Jan   IAS introduced
Oct   Restrictions on bank accounts abolished
Dec   Law on energy sector privatisation adopted
Dec   Pension reform launched

1999
May   Moldovgaz privatised

2000
Jan   Minimum bank capital requirements raised
Feb   Electricity distribution companies privatised
Jun   Regulation on bank mergers approved
Aug   Independent telecommunications regulator established

2001
Nov   Bankruptcy and pledge law amended

increases sharply with the size of the company and the size of the private ownership stake.

Infrastructure

New electricity tariffs raise concerns ...
A Western strategic investor, which owns three power distribution companies, has expressed concern about the new power tariff approved by the national energy regulator ANRE, announced in August 2002. According to the company, the new tariff is substantially lower than previously agreed in June 2002 and violates their privatisation contract, since

it was not calculated according to the agreed methodology. The company maintains that the delay in introducing new tariffs (originally due in April 2002) has implied substantial costs. Independently, ANRE has reduced tariffs for the two electricity distribution companies that remain in state hands.

... and the privatisation of two electricity distribution companies has been delayed.
In May 2002, the parliament amended the terms of the privatisation of the two remaining state-owned energy distribution companies. In an attempt to attract further interest, the parliament increased the stake to be privatised to 75 per cent plus one share and allowed companies other than international energy corporations to participate in the offer. A new financial adviser for the privatisation was appointed in August 2002 and the sale of the two utilities is expected by the end of 2002. If the offer fails to result in a sale, direct negotiations with interested parties will be started.

Competition in the telecommunications sector remains restricted ...
Progress towards greater liberalisation of the telecommunications sector depends on the enforcement of interconnection agreements and the funding of universal service obligations. While the government has committed to liberalise the sector by 2004, a temporary ban on the provision of internet telephony by all telecom providers (except Moldtelecom) is still in place and is holding back competition in this market segment. The national telecom regulator ANRTI is acting, in a temporary capacity and until the new economy-wide competition policy body is set up, as the competition authority in the telecommunications sector. It is currently developing the definition of dominant position and abuse of dominant position.

... but the tender for the privatisation of Moldtelecom has been launched.
The tender for the privatisation of the fixed-line monopoly Moldtelecom was announced in June 2002. The tender is open to local and foreign telecommunications operators with a minimum of 1 million subscribers, an annual turnover of more than US$ 150 million and assets exceeding US$ 300 million. However, only one bidder, a Russian company, has pre-qualified and negotiations with the company are still under way. According to the terms of the privatisation, the winner of the tender will acquire 51 per cent of the shares and management control.

Financial institutions

Bank restructuring proceeding.
Following the increase in minimum capital requirements (which vary according to licence type), the banking sector is undergoing a process of consolidation and restructuring. According to the National Bank of Moldova, 19 finance institutions currently have licences to provide bank services. The assets of the banking system increased by more than 20 per cent in the first half of 2002 and the amount of overdue credits was reduced by almost 7 per cent. In July 2002, the National Bank revoked the licence of BTR-Moldova, a Romanian-Turkish joint venture, for failing to comply with regulatory requirements and initiated bankruptcy proceedings against it.

Social reform

Salaries and pension increases put pressure on the budget.
In July, the parliament amended the 2002 budget to allow further government spending. The main new expenditure item was an extra US$ 12 million for salaries in the social sector, partly offset by a US$ 3.3 million reduction in spending on servicing public debt, capital investments, credits to farms, subsidies for viticulture and the tobacco fund. In May 2002, pensions were increased by 20 per cent after an unused surplus from last year was carried forward. Under existing legislation, these funds cannot be used for any purpose other than pensions and pension rises. However, an improvement in tax collection will be needed to support the higher projected level of expenditures.

New measures to fight poverty devised.
In July 2002, the government approved a bill on social support in coordination with the World Bank and the EU. The bill defines the low-income population categories entitled to receive social benefits and is expected to form the basis for a broader social security system. According to a World Bank study, 87 per cent of the population have disposable incomes of less than the monthly subsistence minimum (the lei equivalent of US$ 35). Poverty rates have risen since the 1998 crisis and about 20 per cent of the population are considered "newly" poor, that is, they have fallen into poverty between 1999 and 2001.

Liberalisation

Current account convertibility – **full**

Interest rate liberalisation – **full**

Wage regulation – **yes**

Stabilisation

Share of general government tax revenue in GDP – **19.7 per cent**

Exchange rate regime – **independently floating**

Privatisation

Primary privatisation method – **vouchers**

Secondary privatisation method – **direct sales**

Tradability of land – **full**

Enterprises and markets

Competition Office – **no**

Infrastructure

Independent telecoms regulator – **yes**

Separation of railway accounts – **no**

Independent electricity regulator – **yes**

Financial sector

Capital adequacy ratio – **12 per cent**

Deposit insurance system – **no**

Secured transactions law – **restricted**

Securities commission – **yes**

Social reform

Share of the population in poverty – **84.6 per cent**

Private pension funds – **no**

	1993	1994	1995	1996	1997	1998	1999	2000	2001
Liberalisation									
Share of administered prices in CPI (in per cent)	na	na	na	na	na	na	na	na	na
Number of goods with administered prices in EBRD-15 basket	11.0	11.0	11.0	11.0	11.0	10.0	10.0	10.0	8.0
Share of trade with non-transition countries (in per cent)	na	8.9	16.5	15.4	19.4	29.2	40.3	44.0	42.9
Share of trade in GDP (in per cent)	88.7	110.6	91.2	98.9	97.1	86.8	91.0	88.0	91.3
Tariff revenues (in per cent of imports) [1]	2.1	1.1	1.4	1.9	2.2	2.0	3.4	na	na
EBRD index of price liberalisation	3.0	3.0	3.0	3.0	3.0	3.0	3.0	3.3	3.3
EBRD index of forex and trade liberalisation	2.0	2.0	4.0	4.0	4.0	4.0	4.0	4.0	4.3
Privatisation									
Privatisation revenues (cumulative, in per cent of GDP)	0.0	0.5	0.8	1.3	3.6	4.4	5.5	11.3	11.3
Private sector share in GDP (in per cent)	15.0	20.0	30.0	40.0	45.0	50.0	45.0	50.0	50.0
Private sector share in employment (in per cent)	na	na	na	na	na	na	na	na	na
EBRD index of small-scale privatisation	1.0	2.0	3.0	3.0	3.0	3.3	3.3	3.3	3.3
EBRD index of large-scale privatisation	2.0	2.0	3.0	3.0	3.0	3.0	3.0	3.0	3.0
Enterprises									
Budgetary subsidies and current transfers (in per cent of GDP)	na	na	na	na	na	na	na	na	na
Effective statutory social security tax (in per cent)	47.1	73.9	77.0	78.2	68.4	71.0	70.5	na	na
Share of industry in total employment (in per cent)	14.5	13.8	16.0	14.7	14.3	14.3	na	na	na
Change in labour productivity in industry (in per cent)	7.3	-23.6	12.0	8.6	10.5	-7.5	na	na	na
Investment rate/GDP (in per cent)	15.5	19.3	16.0	19.4	19.9	21.9	na	na	na
EBRD index of enterprise reform	1.0	2.0	2.0	2.0	2.0	2.0	2.0	2.0	2.0
EBRD index of competition policy	1.7	1.7	2.0	2.0	2.0	2.0	2.0	2.0	2.0
Infrastructure									
Main telephone lines per 100 inhabitants	12.0	12.6	13.1	14.0	14.4	15.0	12.7	13.3	15.4
Railway labour productivity (1989=100)	43.0	32.2	28.3	26.5	27.6	25.2	15.6	18.7	23.2
Electricity tariffs, USc kWh (collection rate in per cent)	na	4.3 (na)	3.2 (na)	3.1 (na)	4.7 (na)	5.2 (na)	4.4 (na)	4.0 (55)	5.2 (na)
GDP per unit of energy use (PPP in US dollars per kgoe)	2.5	2.1	2.4	2.1	2.1	2.2	3.2	na	na
EBRD index of infrastructure reform	1.0	1.0	1.0	1.3	2.0	2.0	2.0	2.0	2.0
Financial institutions									
Number of banks (foreign owned)	16 (na)	21 (na)	25 (na)	22 (na)	22 (na)	23 (7)	20 (10)	20 (11)	19 (10)
Asset share of state-owned banks (in per cent)	na	na	na	na	na	0.3	7.9	9.8	10.2
Non-performing loans (in per cent of total loans) [2]	na	31.0	36.0	45.5	26.0	32.0	29.3	20.6	9.9
Domestic credit to private sector (in per cent of GDP) [3]	5.0	3.7	5.8	6.8	14.8	15.8	12.4	12.6	14.8
Stock market capitalisation (in per cent of GDP) [4]	na	na	na	2.3	3.4	4.0	3.6	na	2.4
EBRD index of banking sector reform	2.0	2.0	2.0	2.0	2.0	2.3	2.3	2.3	2.3
EBRD index of reform of non-banking financial institutions	1.0	2.0	2.0	2.0	2.0	2.0	2.0	2.0	2.0
Legal environment									
EBRD rating of legal extensiveness (company law)	na	na	na	na	3.0	4.0	3.7	3.0	3.3
EBRD rating of legal effectiveness (company law)	na	na	na	na	2.0	3.0	3.0	2.0	3.7
Social sector									
Expenditures on health and education (in per cent of GDP)	11.0	14.9	12.6	14.9	14.1	9.9	7.4	6.5	7.1
Life expectancy at birth, total (years)	67.4	66.0	65.7	66.6	66.5	66.5	67.8	67.8	na
Basic school enrolment ratio (in per cent)	78.3	78.3	79.0	79.2	92.5	92.5	94.1	93.5	na
Earnings inequality (GINI-coefficient)	43.7	37.9	39.0	41.4	na	42.6	44.1	39.2	na

[1] Refers to all taxes on foreign trade.

[2] Changes in non-performing loans data compared with previous *Transition Reports* are due to the change of loan categories included in non-performing loans (see definitions).

[3] Credits to individuals and enterprises excluding banks and government.

[4] Data from survey to Moldovan Stock Exchange, including government securities. Data from IFC give a figure of 4.56 per cent of GDP for listed companies in 1997.

	1994	1995	1996	1997	1998	1999	2000	2001 Estimate	2002 Projection
Output and expenditure				*(Percentage change in real terms)*					
GDP	-31.2	-1.4	-5.9	1.6	-6.5	-3.4	2.1	6.1	3.5
Private consumption	na	na	na	na	na	na	na	na	na
Public consumption	na	na	na	na	na	na	na	na	na
Gross fixed investment	na	na	na	na	na	na	na	na	na
Exports of goods and services	na	na	na	na	na	na	na	na	na
Imports of goods and services	na	na	na	na	na	na	na	na	na
Industrial gross output	-27.7	-3.9	-6.5	0.0	-15.0	-11.6	7.7	14.2	na
Agricultural gross output	-24.6	1.9	-11.6	11.4	-11.0	-8.0	-3.3	4.0	na
Employment				*(Percentage change)*					
Labour force (end-year)	0.0	-0.2	-0.8	-0.6	0.0	-10.8	-9.4	na	na
Employment (end-year)	-0.4	-0.5	-0.8	-0.8	-0.2	-11.2	-9.3	na	na
				(In per cent of labour force)					
Unemployment (end-year) [1]	1.1	1.4	1.8	1.5	1.9	2.3	2.1	na	na
Prices and wages				*(Percentage change)*					
Consumer prices (annual average)	329.7	30.2	23.5	11.8	7.7	39.0	31.3	9.8	9.0
Consumer prices (end-year)	116.1	23.8	15.1	11.1	18.2	43.8	18.5	6.4	12.0
Producer prices (annual average)	205.1	52.9	31.2	14.9	9.7	44.0	28.5	5.7	na
Producer prices (end-year)	214.5	46.6	20.4	13.6	13.6	58.6	24.2	na	na
Gross average monthly earnings in economy (annual average)	247.4	32.1	31.2	16.3	14.6	21.6	33.9	27.3	na
Government sector [2]				*(In per cent of GDP)*					
General government balance	-19.2	-13.1	-15.2	-14.1	-5.7	-6.1	-2.6	-0.5	-2.7
General government expenditure	49.5	39.6	38.7	43.2	38.7	36.4	30.2	27.4	na
General government debt	58.8	46.0	50.8	70.7	91.1	121.2	119.4	103.3	na
Monetary sector				*(Percentage change)*					
Broad money (M2, end-year)	94.1	63.8	16.7	34.6	-22.0	33.3	39.0	37.8	na
Domestic credit (end-year)	101.5	64.7	17.4	27.8	43.0	3.6	18.3	na	na
				(In per cent of GDP)					
Broad money (M2, end-year)	14.3	14.7	14.6	17.2	13.1	14.7	14.1	16.8	na
Interest and exchange rates				*(In per cent per annum, end-year)*					
Refinancing rate	na	21.0	19.5	16.0	28.4	na	31.0	na	na
Inter-bank interest rate (up to 30 days maturity)	na	na	31.2	24.5	30.9	na	32.6	na	na
Deposit rate (1 year)	na	32.5	25.4	23.5	21.7	na	27.5	na	na
Lending rate (1 year)	na	41.9	36.7	33.3	30.8	na	35.5	na	na
				(Lei per US dollar)					
Exchange rate (end-year)	4.3	4.5	4.7	4.7	8.3	11.6	12.4	13.1	na
Exchange rate (annual average)	4.1	4.5	4.6	4.6	5.4	10.5	na	12.9	na
External sector				*(In millions of US dollars)*					
Current account	-82	-115	-188	-275	-322	-34	-121	-145	-170
Trade balance	-53	-55	-252	-347	-388	-128	-307	-318	-350
Merchandise exports	619	739	823	890	644	469	477	571	650
Merchandise imports	672	794	1,075	1,237	1,032	597	783	889	1,000
Foreign direct investment, net	18	73	23	71	88	34	128	60	100
Gross reserves (end-year), excluding gold	179	257	315	366	140	181	206	227	na
External debt stock	620	668	815	1,335	1,466	1,457	1,547	1,464	na
				(In months of imports of goods and services)					
Gross reserves (end-year), excluding gold	2.9	3.0	3.0	3.1	1.4	2.9	2.5	2.5	na
				(In per cent of exports of goods and services)					
Debt service	2.3	8.2	5.7	13.8	27.9	37.4	24.7	30.4	na
Memorandum items				*(Denominations as indicated)*					
Population (end-year, millions)	4.4	4.3	4.3	4.3	4.3	4.3	3.6	3.6	na
GDP (in millions of lei)	4,737	7,550	8,830	10,120	10,370	12,322	17,815	20,572	24,060
GDP per capita (in US dollars)	268	387	443	507	449	274	398	444	na
Share of industry in GDP (in per cent)	31.4	25.0	23.1	20.2	16.7	16.2	na	na	na
Share of agriculture in GDP (in per cent)	27.3	29.3	27.5	26.0	25.8	22.3	na	na	na
Current account/GDP (in per cent)	-7.0	-6.8	-9.8	-12.6	-16.7	-2.9	-8.4	-9.1	-9.2
External debt - reserves, in US$ millions	441	412	500	969	1,326	855	1,341	1,237	na
External debt/GDP (in per cent)	53.1	39.7	42.5	60.9	75.9	105.7	108.0	91.6	na
External debt/exports of goods and services (in per cent)	95.1	77.2	87.0	130.4	192.1	240.8	241.6	200.8	na

[1] Figures refer to registered unemployed.

[2] General government includes the state, municipalities and extra-budgetary funds.

Poland

Stabilisation

Fiscal policy remains expansionary while monetary policy has eased.

The Monetary Policy Council has cut interest rates repeatedly during 2001 and 2002, from the recent peak of 19 per cent in February 2001 to 8 per cent in August 2002, as annual inflation declined from 6.6 per cent to 1.2 per cent over the same period. Parliament discussed in the first half of 2002 the appropriateness of monetary policy and the possible need for legislative changes, including reducing the independence of the Central Bank. At the same time, fiscal deficits remained large, due in part to recent low growth rates, further increasing the tensions between the Central Bank and the government. New measures announced by the government in August 2002, including tax and social contribution arrears forgiveness, state credit and tax deferral for small enterprises, and an increase in state guarantees for enterprise debt, are likely to further increase fiscal deficits. These deficits are financed primarily by debt issuance and the stock of public debt now stands at over 45 per cent of GDP. At a debt ratio of 50 per cent of GDP, there are legal triggers for restrictions on fiscal policy, including limits on central and local budget deficits.

Privatisation

The state continues to have a large impact on the enterprise sector.

Privatisation has advanced in recent years, but the state has retained a controlling stake in over 2,000 companies, including three banks, a dominant insurance company, all major steel companies, the copper and silver mining company KGHM, and several other large enterprises, most of them unrestructured and in financial difficulties. Since the new government assumed power in September 2001, the privatisation process has stalled. Privatisation revenues in the first eight months of 2002 reached only about PLZ 0.8 billion (US$ 0.3 billion), equivalent to 12 per cent of the 2002 target.

Enterprise reform

Improvements to the business environment proposed.

The business environment for foreign investors remains difficult compared with other central European transition countries. Corruption remains a significant and widespread problem and public procurement continues to lack transparency and accountability. In its February 2002 economic programme, the government proposed a series of measures to reduce administrative barriers and to increase income limits for lump-sum taxpayers and extend them to additional businesses. In mid-2002, the government also approved measures to streamline the bankruptcy process and to provide additional funds and guarantees to ailing enterprises willing to enter state supported restructuring programmes and to small, newly established firms.

The rural economy continues to lag behind.

Limited restructuring has been achieved in the agricultural sector and there is no consensus on reforms in the rural economy. Farms continue to benefit from significant state subsidies, including pension contributions for farmers at 10 per cent of the level for regular pension system contributors and subsidised loans. There are still about 2 million small, mostly non-viable farms, with an average size of 8 hectares. As a result, the agricultural sector is inefficient, employing about 19 per cent of the labour force and producing 3.7 per cent of GDP, resulting in labour productivity in agriculture at 13 per cent of the EU average.

Infrastructure

Public spending on infrastructure expected to increase.

The government proposed in its February 2002 economic programme to increase substantially infrastructure investment over the next four years, including PLZ 36 billion (US$ 12 billion) on road construction. A new National Road Authority is to be established, financed by a universal fee for the use of express and national roads.

Liberalisation, stabilisation, privatisation

1990
Jan	Most prices liberalised
Jan	Most foreign trade controls removed
Jan	Small-scale privatisation begins
Jan	Fixed exchange rate introduced
Apr	Privatisation law adopted

1991
May	Treasury bills market initiated
May	Crawling peg exchange rate regime introduced

1992
Jan	Corporate and personal income taxes reformed
Mar	EU Association Agreement signed
Mar	CEFTA membership granted

1993
Apr	Mass privatisation programme begins
Jul	VAT introduced
Nov	EFTA agreement signed

1994
Oct	Major external debt restructuring
Dec	National investment funds (NIFs) established

1995
Jan	Wage restrictions redefined
May	Agricultural import restrictions changed
May	Managed float with fluctuation band introduced
Jun	First sovereign Eurobond issued
Jun	Full current account convertibility introduced
Jul	WTO membership granted
Jul	State enterprises allocated to NIFs

1996
Aug	New privatisation law adopted
Nov	OECD membership granted

1997
Jun	NIF shares listed on WSE

1998
Feb	Independent Monetary Policy Council established
Mar	EU accession negotiations commence

1999
Jan	New foreign exchange law enacted
Dec	Import tariffs on agricultural products increased

2000
Jan	Corporate tax reform implemented
Apr	Exchange rate floated

2002
Jan	Capital gains tax introduced

Enterprises, infrastructure, finance and social reforms

1990
Jan   Competition law adopted
Jan   Competition agency established
Dec   Insurance law adopted

1991
Jan   Telecommunications law adopted
Mar   Securities law adopted
Apr   Stock exchange begins trading
Sep   Banking law adopted

1992
Dec   Banking law amended

1993
Feb   Financial restructuring law adopted
Apr   First bank privatised
May   BIS capital adequacy adopted

1994
Sep   IAS introduced

1995
May   Telecommunications law amended
Jul   Railway law adopted
Oct   Insurance law amended

1996
Apr   First corporate Eurobond issued
Aug   Gdansk Shipyard declared bankrupt

1997
Mar   First toll motorway concession awarded
May   Energy law adopted
Jun   Securities law amended
Dec   Electricity law adopted

1998
Jan   Banking act amended
Jan   Independent banking regulator established
Jan   Bankruptcy law amended
Feb   Investment funds law adopted
Nov   Telecommunications privatisation begins
Nov   Mine restructuring law adopted

1999
Jan   Pension reforms implemented
Jan   Health care system reformed
Jan   Insurance law amended

2000
May   New telecommunications law adopted
Jul   Stake in TPSA acquired by strategic investor
Jul   Railway reform plan approved

2001
Jan   New commercial legislation adopted

2002
Apr   New power sector strategy approved

New power sector strategy approved.
In April 2002, the government approved a new strategy for the power sector. Mergers between three major power plants, a large lignite-fuelled power plant with the mine supplying fuel, and several regional distributors are envisaged. In addition, the privatisation timetable for the power industry has been altered, with a completion date in 2004 instead of 2002 as previously planned. The government also plans to retain a blocking minority stake of 25 per cent plus one share in each power distribution company. So far, only four power plants and one distribution company have been privatised.

Financial institutions

Privatisation in the financial sector has stalled recently.
The share of state-owned banks measured by total assets has declined to about 25 per cent, but the state still owns the largest savings bank PKO BP, the rural economy bank BGZ and the development bank BGK. The government is currently considering the sale of minority stakes in BGZ and PKO BP over the medium term, but the two banks are expected to remain majority owned by the state. BGZ is the main, and in many places the only, bank providing credit to agricultural and rural enterprises, as well as to small municipalities. Its restructuring and eventual privatisation are key to support rural development and restructuring of the agricultural sector. In addition, the present government cancelled the sale of further state shares in PZU to a minority strategic investor led by Eureko, to maintain the state control of this dominant insurance provider and reverse the decision of the previous government.

Bad loans increased during the economic slowdown.
The share of non-performing loans increased to 20.1 per cent of total loans at the end of 2001 from 16.8 per cent at the end of 2000, as a result of economic slowdown and deterioration of financial performance of enterprises. The vulnerability of the banking sector may increase further as a result of the government's intention to use state-owned banks to finance its economic programme, particularly to support ailing enterprises in the steel, chemical and shipbuilding industries. A 20 per cent capital gains tax, introduced in January 2002, is generating lower revenues than expected.

Social reform

Labour market reform increasingly urgent.
The unemployment rate increased to over 18 per cent in the first half of 2002 due in part to the recent slowdown in economic growth. Other contributing factors were the downsizing of privatised companies after employment guarantee contracts expired, the increase in the working age population and the limited flexibility of the labour market, including a relatively high minimum wage, high payroll taxes (which included social taxes) and restrictions on temporary work contracts. In February 2002, the government proposed a number of measures, which were later approved by parliament, to address labour market deficiencies, focusing on support for first-time job seekers. The government is also changing the labour code to allow lower overtime pay and permission for employers to suspend some labour code regulations when threatened by bankruptcy. However, the strength of trade unions has led to company-level rigidities which hinder labour restructuring, particularly in state-owned companies, and these will be difficult to resolve.

Health care reform proposed.
The government intends to replace the existing health funds with one centralised fund, featuring regional branches and a streamlined hospital network. The existing funds were introduced in 1999 to collect health insurance premiums and to pay for health care services through contracts with hospitals and other providers. The proposed health care reforms also include further rationalisation measures, including a greater role for family doctors, clearer specialist consultation procedures and increased monitoring of health care providers.

Public expenditures on social welfare remain high and inefficient.
The share of public expenditure on education, health, housing, social protection and welfare is, at approximately 70 per cent of the total, one of the highest among the OECD countries. Spending on early retirement, disability and sickness benefits and subsidies for farmer pensions are untargeted, inefficient and in need of reform. The farmer pension fund, KRUS, was not included in the 1999 pension reform and remains a pay-as-you-go system, including a subsidy covering 95 per cent of KRUS pension obligations and equivalent to 8.7 per cent of total public expenditure or 2.1 per cent of GDP in 2001. Although 3.2 per cent of GDP was spent on disability benefits, only two-thirds of recipients perceive themselves as disabled, according to a recent World Bank report.

Liberalisation	Privatisation	Infrastructure	Social reform
Current account convertibility – **full**	Primary privatisation method – **direct sales**	Independent telecoms regulator – **yes**	Share of the population in poverty –
Interest rate liberalisation – **full**	Secondary privatisation method – **MEBOs**	Separation of railway accounts – **yes**	**18.4 per cent**
Wage regulation – **no**	Tradability of land – **full except foreigners**	Independent electricity regulator – **yes**	Private pension funds – **yes**

Stabilisation	Enterprises and markets	Financial sector	
Share of general government tax revenue in GDP – **33.1 per cent**	Competition Office – **yes**	Capital adequacy ratio – **8 per cent**	
Exchange rate regime – **floating**		Deposit insurance system – **yes**	
		Secured transactions law – **yes**	
		Securities commission – **yes**	

	1993	1994	1995	1996	1997	1998	1999	2000	2001
Liberalisation									
Share of administered prices in CPI (in per cent)	10.6	12.0	12.0	11.6	10.6	10.6	9.0	2.6	1.2
Number of goods with administered prices in EBRD-15 basket	3.0	3.0	2.0	2.0	2.0	1.0	0.0	0.0	0.0
Share of trade with non-transition countries (in per cent)	87.7	86.3	82.3	79.3	75.5	77.4	79.3	81.1	80.9
Share of trade in GDP (in per cent)	34.5	37.7	40.0	42.4	48.5	47.0	43.5	43.9	40.2
Tariff revenues (in per cent of imports)	15.0	12.0	9.6	7.4	5.6	4.0	3.4	2.8	2.4
EBRD index of price liberalisation	3.0	3.0	3.0	3.0	3.0	3.3	3.3	3.3	3.3
EBRD index of forex and trade liberalisation	4.0	4.0	4.0	4.3	4.3	4.3	4.3	4.3	4.3
Privatisation									
Privatisation revenues (cumulative, in per cent of GDP)	0.9	1.7	2.6	3.6	5.1	6.4	7.7	11.6	12.4
Private sector share in GDP (in per cent)	50.0	55.0	60.0	60.0	65.0	65.0	65.0	70.0	75.0
Private sector share in employment (in per cent)	57.0	59.0	61.4	63.0	66.7	69.2	70.9	72.0	72.0
EBRD index of small-scale privatisation	4.0	4.0	4.0	4.3	4.3	4.3	4.3	4.3	4.3
EBRD index of large-scale privatisation	2.0	3.0	3.0	3.0	3.3	3.3	3.3	3.3	3.3
Enterprises									
Budgetary subsidies and current transfers (in per cent of GDP)	1.4	1.2	1.1	0.8	3.3	2.9	2.7	2.3	2.4
Effective statutory social security tax (in per cent)	na	71.7	76.1	77.7	76.4	72.7	78.8	na	na
Share of industry in total employment (in per cent)	24.6	22.5	23.1	22.2	21.9	21.7	21.1	21.1	21.0
Change in labour productivity in industry (in per cent)	13.8	13.0	6.5	9.1	11.6	4.3	9.1	10.4	4.4
Investment rate/GDP (in per cent)	14.9	18.0	18.7	20.9	23.6	25.3	26.4	26.3	26.0
EBRD index of enterprise reform	3.0	3.0	3.0	3.0	3.0	3.0	3.0	3.0	3.3
EBRD index of competition policy	3.0	3.0	3.0	3.0	3.0	3.0	3.0	3.0	3.0
Infrastructure									
Main telephone lines per 100 inhabitants	11.5	13.0	14.8	16.9	19.4	22.8	26.0	28.2	29.5
Railway labour productivity (1989=100)	70.4	72.6	77.4	78.2	80.8	78.2	78.4	84.3	86.7
Electricity tariffs, USc kWh (collection rate in per cent)	na	4.94 (90)	6.19 (95)	6.53 (97)	6.24 (97)	6.68 (na)	6.42 (na)	8.4 (na)	7.8 (na)
GDP per unit of energy use (PPP in US dollars per kgoe)	2.2	2.5	2.6	2.6	2.9	3.2	3.5	na	na
EBRD index of infrastructure reform	2.0	2.0	2.7	2.7	3.0	3.0	3.0	3.3	3.3
Financial institutions									
Number of banks (foreign owned) [1]	87 (10)	82 (11)	81 (18)	81 (25)	83 (29)	83 (31)	77 (39)	74 (47)	64 (46)
Asset share of state-owned banks (in per cent)	86.2	80.4	71.7	69.8	51.6	48.0	24.9	23.9	24.4
Non-performing loans (in per cent of total loans)	36.4	34.0	23.9	14.7	11.5	11.8	14.5	16.8	20.1
Domestic credit to private sector (in per cent of GDP)	12.2	12.0	12.7	15.9	17.1	17.6	18.8	18.7	18.4
Stock market capitalisation (in per cent of GDP)	3.7	3.5	3.9	6.6	9.6	13.1	20.0	18.7	14.0
EBRD index of banking sector reform	3.0	3.0	3.0	3.0	3.0	3.3	3.3	3.3	3.3
EBRD index of reform of non-banking financial institutions	2.0	2.0	3.0	3.0	3.3	3.3	3.3	3.7	3.7
Legal environment									
EBRD rating of legal extensiveness (company law)	na	na	na	na	4.0	4.0	4.0	3.7	3.7
EBRD rating of legal effectiveness (company law)	na	na	na	na	4.3	4.0	3.0	4.0	3.0
Social sector									
Expenditures on health and education (in per cent of GDP)	10.4	10.7	9.7	10.8	11.2	9.9	na	na	na
Life expectancy at birth, total (years)	71.6	71.7	71.9	72.2	72.6	73.0	73.0	73.3	na
Basic school enrolment ratio (in per cent)	97.2	97.1	97.2	97.4	98.0	98.1	98.3	98.6	na
Earnings inequality (GINI-coefficient)	25.6	28.1	29.0	30.2	30.0	29.4	30.5	na	na

[1] Data for 2000 include Slaski Bank Hipoteczny SA, a banking organisation that previously did not file reports on ownership.

	1994	1995	1996	1997	1998	1999	2000	2001	2002
								Estimate	Projection
Output and expenditure					*(Percentage change in real terms)*				
GDP [1]	3.9	7.1	3.9	-6.1	-5.4	-3.2	1.8	5.3	3.5
Private consumption	2.6	13.1	8.0	-3.1	-4.6	-4.9	-1.2	6.4	na
Public consumption	11.0	1.0	1.5	-11.6	14.1	-2.5	4.2	-1.9	na
Gross fixed investment	20.7	6.9	5.7	-3.0	-18.1	-5.1	5.5	6.6	na
Exports of goods and services	19.0	17.0	2.0	11.4	na	9.7	23.9	10.6	na
Imports of goods and services	2.8	16.3	8.7	7.5	na	-5.1	29.1	17.5	na
Industrial gross output, unadjusted series	3.3	9.5	9.8	-5.6	-17.3	-8.8	8.2	na	na
Agricultural gross output	0.2	4.5	1.3	3.4	-7.6	5.5	-14.1	na	na
Employment					*(Percentage change)*				
Labour force (end-year)	0.1	-6.6	-4.3	-1.3	-0.7	-2.9	0.9	-1.1	na
Employment (end year)	-0.5	-5.2	-1.2	-3.8	-2.3	-4.5	2.5	0.8	na
					(In per cent of labour force)				
Unemployment (end-year) [2]	10.9	9.5	6.6	8.9	10.3	11.8	10.5	8.6	na
Prices and wages					*(Percentage change)*				
Consumer prices (annual average)	136.7	32.3	38.8	154.8	59.1	45.8	45.7	34.5	22.7
Consumer prices (end-year)	61.7	27.8	56.9	151.4	40.6	54.8	40.7	30.2	17.6
Producer prices (annual average)	140.5	35.1	49.9	156.6	33.2	42.2	51.5	40.9	na
Producer prices (end-year)	73.4	32.0	60.4	154.3	19.8	62.9	48.6	29.9	na
Gross average monthly earnings in economy (annual average)	135.6	50.5	54.2	98.2	60.3	44.3	46.9	48.9	na
Government sector					*(In per cent of GDP)*				
General government balance	-2.2	-2.5	-3.9	-4.6	-5.0	-3.5	-3.7	-3.5	-3.0
General government expenditure	33.9	34.7	33.8	34.0	34.9	35.6	35.1	34.6	na
General government debt	na	17.6	28.1	27.7	27.8	33.6	31.6	29.8	na
Monetary sector					*(Percentage change)*				
Broad money (M2, end-year)	138.1	71.6	66.0	104.9	48.9	45.0	38.0	46.2	na
Domestic credit (end-year)	109.2	123.6	82.1	82.1	95.2	26.8	7.5	31.5	na
					(In per cent of GDP)				
Broad money (M2, end-year)	21.4	25.3	27.9	24.6	24.9	24.9	23.2	24.0	na
Interest and exchange rates					*(In per cent per annum, end-year)*				
Discount rate	58.0	35.0	35.0	40.0	35.0	35.0	35.0	35.0	na
1-week BUBOR	na	na	51.7	102.4	159.0	68.9	47.3	39.3	na
Deposit rate (average)	49.5	36.5	38.1	51.6	38.3	45.4	32.7	23.4	na
Lending rate (average)	61.8	48.6	55.8	63.7	56.9	65.9	53.5	40.6	na
					(Lei per US dollar)				
Exchange rate (end-year)	1,767	2,578	4,035	8,023	10,951	18,255	25,926	31,597	na
Exchange rate (annual average)	1,655	2,033	3,083	7,168	8,875	15,333	21,693	29,061	na
External sector					*(In millions of US dollars)*				
Current account	-428	-1,774	-2,584	-2,137	-2,917	-1,296	-1,347	-2,349	-2,065
Trade balance	-411	-1,577	-2,494	-1,980	-2,625	-1,092	-1,684	-2,969	-2,573
Merchandise exports	6,151	7,910	8,061	8,431	8,302	8,503	10,366	11,385	12,068
Merchandise imports	6,562	9,487	10,555	10,411	10,927	9,595	12,050	14,354	14,641
Foreign direct investment, net	341	417	415	1,267	2,079	1,025	1,051	1,154	1,200
Gross reserves (end-year), excluding gold	536	278	547	2,194	1,375	1,526	2,497	3,960	na
External debt stock	5,509	6,484	8,345	9,502	9,902	9,091	10,602	11,822	na
					(In months of imports of goods and services)				
Gross reserves (end-year), excluding gold	0.8	0.3	0.5	2.1	1.3	1.6	2.1	2.9	na
					(In per cent of exports of goods and services)				
Debt service [3]	na	10.5	13.5	20.4	23.3	28.5	25.3	20.5	na
Memorandum items					*(Denominations as indicated)*				
Population (mid-year, millions)	22.7	22.7	22.6	22.6	22.5	22.5	22.4	22.3	na
GDP (in billions of lei)	49,773	72,136	108,920	252,926	371,194	539,357	796,534	1,127,729	1,431,974
GDP per capita (in US dollars)	1,323	1,564	1,563	1,565	1,859	1,566	1,636	1,743	na
Share of industry in GDP (in per cent)	36.2	32.9	34.2	35.6	27.5	27.8	27.6	na	na
Share of agriculture in GDP (in per cent)	19.9	19.8	19.1	18.8	14.5	13.9	11.4	na	na
Current account/GDP (in per cent)	-1.4	-5.0	-7.3	-6.1	-7.0	-3.7	-3.7	-6.1	-5.0
External debt - reserves, in US$ millions	4,973	6,206	7,798	7,308	8,527	7,564	8,105	7,862	na
External debt/GDP (in per cent)	18.3	18.3	23.6	26.9	23.7	25.8	28.9	30.5	na
External debt/exports of goods and services (in per cent)	76.6	68.9	86.7	95.4	104.0	92.1	87.5	88.7	na

[1] From 2001, growth rates are calculated by the National Statistical Institute using a new methodology in compliance with European standards of national accounting. As a result, the official growth figure for 2000 was revised upwards to 1.8 per cent from 1.6 per cent.

[2] Registered unemployed. Based on ILO methodology, unemployment was lower (8.0, 6.7, 6.0, 6.3 and 6.8 per cent for 1995, 1996, 1997, 1998 and 1999 respectively).

[3] Debt service payments on private and public external debt.

Russia

Key reform challenges

- While reform plans have been adopted in several areas, their smooth and timely implementation is key to unlock productivity gains and ensure long-term growth. Restraining the political influence of the large and growing business conglomerates will be necessary to ensure the effective implementation of reforms.

- Deeper integration with the world economy would accelerate restructuring, promote investment and build a constituency for reform. Early accession to the WTO at fair terms will be central to this process.

- Expanding the provision of finance to the real economy requires an accelerated pace of banking reform, including better capitalisation, stronger regulation and the creation of a level playing field through the introduction of comprehensive deposit insurance.

Liberalisation

The timing of WTO accession remains uncertain.

The process of aligning the legislative framework with WTO rules is gathering momentum. Over 20 bills are to be submitted to the Duma over the next year. Important draft laws, including the customs code, an amended law on the liberalisation of currency controls, and new legislation on technical regulation, certification and standardisation will be discussed during the autumn parliamentary session. Negotiations on a range of sensitive issues such as financial services, agriculture, energy subsidies and the protection of intellectual property rights continue. However, while the government is committed to an early entry, there is growing opposition from protected industries.

Breakthrough on land reform.

Following the introduction in early 2002 of a new land code on industrial and residential land, a new law on the sale of agricultural land has been adopted in July 2002. The law covers the ownership, use and management of farm land and is expected to lead to the creation of a market for agricultural mortgages. Foreigners are only permitted to lease agricultural land for up to 49 years. Regional and local authorities have preferential rights in buying farm land, unless the plot is auctioned.

Privatisation

Privatisation set to accelerate.

The planned sale of the government's remaining 5.9 per cent stake in Lukoil was called off in August 2002 due to poor market conditions. The privatisation of oil company Slavneft, scheduled for later this year, has been tainted by a recent management scandal. However, the privatisation programme for 2003, recently approved by the government, should reinvigorate the privatisation process. It envisages the partial or full privatisation of over 1,000 companies, including Slavneft, the telecommunications company Svyazinvest and the metal producer MMK. The government still fully owns 9,500 enterprises and

holds stakes worth an estimated US$ 60 billion in another 3,500 companies. The privatisation revenue target for next year is RUR 51 billion (US$ 1.6 billion), similar to the original target of RUR 65 billion (US$ 2.1 billion) for this year. However, given that key privatisations, including the sale of Lukoil, have been postponed, this year's actual privatisation revenues will most likely only amount to half the original target.

Enterprise reform

Laws on shareholder protection and corporate governance improved ...

Amendments to the law on joint-stock companies have reduced the risk of shareholder abuse. Minority shareholders were granted pre-emptive rights against the dilution of their shareholding. They also enjoy stronger protection in the case of spin-offs and split-ups and in transactions with related parties. A new corporate governance code entered into force in April. The regulations governing the disclosure of information have been tightened in the context of recent amendments to the criminal code. A revised bankruptcy law is at an advanced stage of approval and promises better protection for shareholders and creditors by ending the use of the bankruptcy mechanism as a channel for hostile take-overs.

... but their implementation remains problematic.

Despite a better formal legal basis, there remain a number of factors that make improvements in corporate governance standards difficult to achieve in practice. The still unsettled ownership and control positions in many companies, the continuing property distribution process, the large number of loss-making companies and the inter-relationship between politics and business continue to create significant obstacles to transparent and efficient corporate governance. The spread and strengthening of vertically integrated business conglomerates may constitute a barrier to enterprise reform. These institutions, created partly because of the lack of trust among independent businesses, serve to concentrate economic and political power.

Liberalisation, stabilisation, privatisation

1990
Jun	Sovereignty proclaimed

1991
Oct	Reform programme introduced
Dec	Soviet Union dissolved

1992
Jan	VAT introduced
Jan	Most prices liberalised
Jan	State trading monopoly abolished
Jun	Mass privatisation programme adopted
Jul	Exchange rate unified
Oct	Voucher privatisation begins

1993
May	Treasury bills market initiated
Jul	New currency (rouble) introduced
Nov	Rouble zone collapsed

1994
Jul	Cash-based privatisation begins
Oct	Currency crisis ensues

1995
Jun	First shares-for-loans auctions conducted
Nov	Currency corridor introduced

1996
Mar	IMF three-year programme agreed
Apr	Foreign trade liberalisation completed
Jun	Full current account convertibility introduced
Nov	First sovereign Eurobond issued

1997
May	First regional Eurobond issued
Sep	Admission to Paris Club granted

1998
Jun	Western financing package provided
Aug	Financial crisis ensues

1999
Jan	New tax code (Part I) enacted
Jan	Dual exchange rate regime introduced
Jun	Exchange rate re-unified
Aug	New IMF programme approved
Dec	Parliamentary election held

2000
Feb	Agreement with London Club on long-term debt restructuring reached
May	New government appointed
Jul	Government reform programme adopted

2001
Jan	Income and social tax regime reformed
Jun	Large-scale privatisation resumed

2002
Jan	Land code enacted
Jul	Law on farmland sale adopted

Enterprises, infrastructure, finance and social reforms

1992
Jan	Federal Energy Commission established
Feb	Law on subsoil resources adopted
Nov	Bankruptcy law adopted
Nov	RAO UES and Gazprom transformed into joint-stock companies

1994
Jan	60 per cent of Gazprom shares sold to the public
Oct	New civil code adopted
Nov	Federal Securities Commission established

1995
Aug	Inter-bank market crisis ensues
Aug	Law on natural monopolies adopted
Dec	Law on joint-stock companies adopted
Dec	Securities law adopted

1996
Jan	Federal telecommunications regulator established
Feb	Federal transport regulator established

1997
Jul	First corporate Eurobond issued

1998
Mar	New bankruptcy law adopted
Aug	Banking crisis ensues, following GKO default
Oct	Agency for bank restructuring established

1999
Feb	Law on insolvency of financial institutions adopted
Feb	Law on protection of securities market investors adopted
Jul	Law on restructuring of credit organisations adopted
Jul	Law on foreign investment adopted
Jul	Mortgage law introduced

2000
Jun	Anti-oligarch campaign commences
Jul	Law on reforming the federal power structure adopted

2001
May	Banking laws amended
Jun	Judiciary reform initiated
Jul	Deregulation package adopted
Jul	Law on profit tax adopted
Sep	Agency for regulating natural monopoly tariffs established

2002
Jan	Amendments to JSC law enacted
Jan	Pension reform begins
Feb	New labour code adopted
Apr	Corporate governance code endorsed

They tend to lack organisational and financial transparency and have an in-built preference for intra-holding resource allocation instead of seeking potentially more profitable opportunities in the economy.

Market power of large companies hampering entry.
Distorted competition caused by various forms of state-intervention remains a key weakness in the business environment. Large enterprises typically enjoy privileged regulatory treatment by the regional and local authorities and the degree of monopolisation remains large. According to a recent World Bank study the top four firms in regional markets typically account for more than 95 per cent of sales. In such an environment entry by new firms, especially small and medium-sized businesses, is extremely difficult and the inflow of FDI remains limited.

More attention placed on SME development.
Growth in Russia still comes primarily from large companies. However, the government is stepping up efforts to promote SMEs and has made small business development a policy and reform priority. New laws on licensing, registration and state inspections have entered into force, although according to initial indications they have not yet greatly impacted upon these areas. Significant improvements are also expected from the introduction of new taxation and accounting procedures for SMEs in early 2003.

Infrastructure

Power sector reform delayed.
There was significant progress on power sector reform over the past year, but some of the momentum was lost this summer. The process of merging the 72 power plants owned by UES into ten power generating companies is under way. The formation of the market operator, the grid company and the system operator – all separate entities – is also going ahead and the debate about the restructuring of the distribution companies (energos) is at an advanced stage. However, the parliamentary discussion of new electricity legislation has been postponed to the Duma's autumn session.

Railway reforms progress.
Several pieces of legislation that form the basis for the three-stage railway sector restructuring have been adopted in the first reading during the spring session of the Duma. According to the reform plan, the railway ministry will be split into two separate entities responsible for regulation and operation respectively. By 2005, the operating entity, Russian Railroads, is to be further divided into financially independent subsidiaries responsible for cargo, passenger trains, repairs, social institutions and the track infrastructure. A competitive market is to be established by 2010.

Financial institutions

New, reform-minded management takes charge at the Central Bank.
The change at the helm of the Central Bank of Russia (CBR) in April 2002 has paved the way for the acceleration of banking reform. The CBR wants to use the application process for a deposit insurance system, to be introduced in 2004, as a device that will ultimately lead to the consolidation of the sector. The transformation of pocket banks into independent financial organisations and the development of regional banks have become priorities. The transition to IAS accounts in both the enterprise and banking sector is also planned for 2004. The transfer of ownership of Vneshtorgbank from the CBR to the government is expected to take place before the end of the year. No decision has, however, been taken on the future role of Sberbank in the banking system.

Pension reform boosts capital market development.
Over the past year, the legislative basis for the new pension system has been put in place. In the beginning of 2002, workers were allocated individual pension accounts for their social security contributions. During the summer, the Duma adopted the regulation governing the investment of accumulated pension funds. While the private sector will only be allowed to participate in the management of pension funds in 2004, this prospect is already having a positive impact on the industry. Interest from foreign fund managers and insurance companies to enter the market has significantly increased.

Social reform

New labour code replaces Soviet era rules.
A new labour code, which came into force in February 2002, alters significantly the regulation of employment relations in Russia. Under the new rules, employers are liable to pay compensation if wages are not paid on time. The code provides a legal framework consistent with a market economy for employment decisions, rules on collective bargaining and more demanding health and safety regulations. It is applicable for all employees up to the level of CEO. At the same time the code expanded employers' rights to lay off workers in case of misconduct or a change in market conditions. The code will have major implications on other social legislation and changes to over 30 related laws are under preparation.

Liberalisation
Current account convertibility – **full**
Interest rate liberalisation – **full**
Wage regulation – **no**

Stabilisation
Share of general government tax revenue
in GDP – **38 per cent**
Exchange rate regime – **managed float**

Privatisation
Primary privatisation method – **vouchers**
Secondary privatisation method –
  direct sales
Tradability of land – **limited de facto**

Enterprises and markets
Competition Office – **yes**

Infrastructure
Independent telecoms regulator – **no**
Separation of railway accounts – **no**
Independent electricity regulator – **yes**

Financial sector
Capital adequacy ratio – **8 per cent**
Deposit insurance system – **no**[1]
Secured transactions law – **yes**
Securities commission – **yes**

Social reform
Share of the population in poverty –
  29 per cent
Private pension funds – **yes**

	1993	1994	1995	1996	1997	1998	1999	2000	2001
Liberalisation									
Share of administered prices in CPI (in per cent)	na	na	na	na	na	na	na	na	na
Number of goods with administered prices in EBRD-15 basket	7.0	6.0	5.0	5.0	5.0	2.0	2.0	2.0	2.0
Share of trade with non-transition countries (in per cent)	na	66.6	68.2	67.0	65.4	66.9	70.5	68.5	71.4
Share of trade in GDP (in per cent)	64.7	42.7	43.1	37.9	37.6	49.1	59.5	58.0	50.7
Tariff revenues (in per cent of imports)[2]	10.8	15.0	10.7	7.9	7.2	7.1	8.9	18.5	na
EBRD index of price liberalisation	3.0	3.0	3.0	3.0	3.0	2.7	2.7	3.0	3.0
EBRD index of forex and trade liberalisation	3.0	3.0	3.0	4.0	4.0	2.3	2.3	2.3	2.7
Privatisation									
Privatisation revenues (cumulative, in per cent of GDP)	1.1	1.3	1.5	1.7	2.7	3.4	3.5	3.8	na
Private sector share in GDP (in per cent)	40.0	50.0	55.0	60.0	70.0	70.0	70.0	70.0	70.0
Private sector share in employment (in per cent)	na	na	na	na	na	na	na	na	na
EBRD index of small-scale privatisation	3.0	3.0	4.0	4.0	4.0	4.0	4.0	4.0	4.0
EBRD index of large-scale privatisation	3.0	3.0	3.0	3.0	3.3	3.3	3.3	3.3	3.3
Enterprises									
Budgetary subsidies and current transfers (in per cent of GDP)[3]	na	na	na	na	na	na	5.3	na	na
Effective statutory social security tax (in per cent)	67.9	64.3	62.2	57.8	71.3	62.4	59.3	na	na
Share of industry in total employment (in per cent)	29.3	27.1	26.8	26.4	24.8	20.3	22.4	22.7	na
Change in labour productivity in industry (in per cent)	-11.9	-11.4	4.5	0.8	12.0	19.1	7.3	6.0	na
Investment rate/GDP (in per cent)	20.4	21.8	20.9	21.0	19.1	17.5	16.1	17.8	19.6
EBRD index of enterprise reform	1.0	1.7	2.0	2.0	2.0	2.0	1.7	2.0	2.3
EBRD index of competition policy	2.0	2.0	2.0	2.0	2.3	2.3	2.3	2.3	2.3
Infrastructure									
Main telephone lines per 100 inhabitants	15.8	16.2	17.0	17.5	19.2	19.9	21.0	21.8	24.3
Railway labour productivity (1989=100)	75.4	57.7	56.8	54.6	58.6	60.9	72.1	78.8	85.0
Electricity tariffs, USc kWh (collection rate in per cent)[4]	na	2.20 (50)	2.33 (50)	3.00 (50)	3.20 (50)	2.7 (87)	1.1 (na)	0.9 (85)	na
GDP per unit of energy use (PPP in US dollars per kgoe)	1.6	1.7	1.7	1.7	1.8	1.8	1.9	na	na
EBRD index of infrastructure reform	1.3	1.7	1.7	2.0	2.0	2.0	2.0	2.0	2.0
Financial institutions									
Number of banks (foreign owned)	na	na	2,297 (21)	2,029 (22)	1,697 (26)	1,476 (30)	1,349 (32)	1,311 (33)	1,319 (35)
Asset share of state-owned banks (in per cent)	na	na	na	na	37.0	41.9	na	na	na
Bad loans (in per cent of total loans)	na	na	12.3	13.4	12.1	30.9	25.8	15.3	12.1
Domestic credit to enterprises (in per cent of GDP)	11.8	12.1	8.7	7.4	9.1	12.1	10.1	11.2	14.6
Stock market capitalisation (in per cent of GDP)[5]	0.0	0.1	4.8	9.7	31.0	16.5	41.7	15.3	25.7
EBRD index of banking sector reform	1.0	2.0	2.0	2.0	2.3	2.0	1.7	1.7	1.7
EBRD index of reform of non-banking financial institutions	1.7	1.7	2.0	3.0	3.0	1.7	1.7	1.7	1.7
Legal environment									
EBRD rating of legal extensiveness (company law)	na	na	na	na	3.3	3.7	3.7	3.7	3.0
EBRD rating of legal effectiveness (company law)	na	na	na	na	3.0	2.0	2.3	3.0	3.7
Social sector									
Expenditures on health and education (in per cent of GDP)	7.2	7.7	6.3	7.4	8.7	7.4	6.6	5.9	na
Life expectancy at birth, total (years)	65.2	64.0	64.8	66.0	66.7	67.0	66.0	65.3	na
Basic school enrolment ratio (in per cent)	87.5	87.8	88.4	88.7	88.7	88.5	88.8	89.4	na
Earnings inequality (GINI-coefficient)	46.1	44.6	47.1	48.3	na	na	na	na	na

[1] Although there is no general deposit insurance, deposits in Sberbank are covered by a formal deposit insurance scheme.
[2] Refers to all taxes on international trade.
[3] Expenditures on national economy of the consolidated budget (including industry, agriculture, the energy sector and housing subsidies of regional budgets).

[4] Figures are averages of the Siberian, Northern, Southern, Volga, Far East and Ural regions and the Federation; collection ratios are estimated.
[5] Includes listings on the Moscow Interbank Currency Exchange, Moscow Stock Exchange and RTS Stock Exchange.

	1994	1995	1996	1997	1998	1999	2000	2001 Estimate	2002 Projection
Output and expenditure					*(Percentage change in real terms)*				
GDP	-13.5	-4.1	-3.4	0.9	-4.9	5.4	8.3	4.9	4.1
Private consumption	1.2	-2.8	-4.5	5.1	-2.4	-4.2	8.5	8.4	na
Public consumption	-2.9	1.1	0.8	-2.4	0.6	3.0	1.6	-1.1	na
Gross fixed investment	-26.0	-7.5	-19.3	-5.7	-9.8	4.7	15.5	11.5	na
Exports of goods and services	na	7.3	-2.0	4.2	2.7	-4.5	6.0	na	na
Imports of goods and services	na	16.6	6.9	10.6	-14.1	-21.7	16.0	na	na
Industrial gross output	-20.9	-3.3	-4.0	1.9	-5.2	8.1	9.0	4.9	na
Agricultural gross output	-12.0	-7.6	-5.1	0.1	-12.3	2.4	4.0	6.8	na
Employment					*(Percentage change)*				
Labour force (end-year)	-1.4	-5.3	-2.3	-1.8	-1.5	8.9	-1.0	-0.2	na
Employment (end-year)	-3.4	-6.4	-3.4	-3.1	-2.7	8.0	1.4	1.3	na
					(In per cent of labour force)				
Unemployment (end-year)	7.8	8.5	9.6	10.8	11.9	12.6	10.5	9.0	na
Prices and wages					*(Percentage change)*				
Consumer prices (annual average)	311.4	197.7	47.8	14.7	27.6	86.1	20.8	21.6	16.3
Consumer prices (end-year)	204.4	128.6	21.8	10.9	84.5	36.8	20.1	18.8	15.3
Producer prices (annual average)	337.4	236.5	50.8	19.7	21.5	56.3	18.4	22.7	na
Producer prices (end-year)	233.0	175.0	25.6	7.4	21.5	56.3	33.0	14.8	na
Gross average monthly earnings in economy (annual average)	277.3	119.5	48.4	20.2	15.2	44.4	40.6	47.6	na
Government sector [1]					*(In per cent of GDP)*				
General government balance	-10.4	-6.1	-8.9	-8.0	-8.0	-3.3	3.0	2.9	1.5
General government expenditure	45.1	40.2	42.4	45.1	41.4	38.4	35.8	35.8	na
General government debt (domestic)	68.5	58.9	60.6	58.6	88.0	108.1	74.7	61.4	na
Monetary sector					*(Percentage change)*				
Broad money (M2, end-year)	200.0	125.8	30.6	29.8	19.8	57.2	62.4	40.1	na
Domestic credit (end-year)	335.6	87.8	48.3	22.2	68.2	34.1	13.8	26.5	na
					(In per cent of GDP)				
Broad money (M2, end-year)	16.0	14.3	13.4	15.1	16.6	14.8	15.7	17.7	na
Interest and exchange rates					*(In per cent per annum, end-year)*				
Central Bank refinance rate (uncompounded)	180.0	160.0	48.0	28.0	60.0	55.0	25.0	25.0	na
Treasury bill rate (all maturities) [2]	263.0	104.1	33.6	36.6	48.1	na	na	na	na
Lending rate	na	320.0	146.8	32.0	41.7	38.3	18.0	16.5	na
Deposit rate	na	102.0	55.1	16.8	17.1	9.4	5.0	5.2	na
					(Roubles per US dollar)				
Exchange rate (end-year) [3]	3.6	4.6	5.6	6.0	20.7	26.8	28.2	30.2	na
Exchange rate (annual average) [3]	2.2	4.6	5.1	5.8	10.0	24.6	28.2	29.2	na
External sector					*(In millions of US dollars)*				
Current account [4]	8,431	7,487	11,753	2,060	680	24,641	46,337	35,092	27,100
Trade balance [4]	17,374	20,310	22,471	17,025	16,868	36,129	60,703	49,430	42,000
Merchandise exports [4]	67,826	82,913	90,563	89,008	74,883	75,666	105,565	103,194	100,000
Merchandise imports [4]	50,452	62,603	68,092	71,983	58,015	39,537	44,862	53,764	58,000
Foreign direct investment, net	na	1,460	1,657	1,679	1,496	1,103	-496	-137	1,000
International reserves (end-year), excluding gold	5,300	15,700	12,900	14,800	7,800	9,500	25,000	34,500	na
External debt stock [5]	127,500	128,000	136,100	134,600	158,200	154,600	140,700	134,000	na
					(In months of imports of goods and services)				
International reserves (end-year), excluding gold	1.0	2.3	1.8	1.9	1.3	2.2	4.8	5.5	na
					(In per cent of current account revenues, excluding transfers)				
Public debt service due [6]	23.5	19.6	16.6	10.9	14.2	20.2	12.1	12.0	na
Public debt service paid [6]	4.6	6.5	6.4	5.5	8.5	10.9	9.8	14.1	na
Memorandum items					*(Denominations as indicated)*				
Population (end-year, millions) [7]	148.4	148.3	148.0	147.5	146.4	145.7	145.4	144.8	na
GDP (in millions of roubles)	610,700	1,540,000	2,146,000	2,479,000	2,696,000	4,767,000	7,302,000	9,041,000	10,620,103
GDP per capita (in US dollars)	1,867	2,276	2,829	2,903	1,848	1,330	1,784	2,137	na
Share of industry in GDP (in per cent)	32.8	29.5	28.2	26.8	26.7	27.6	28.2	25.6	na
Share of agriculture in GDP (in per cent)	6.5	7.4	7.0	7.0	5.1	7.0	6.4	7.1	na
Current account/GDP (in per cent)	3.0	2.2	2.8	0.5	0.3	12.7	17.9	11.3	8.0
External debt - reserves, in US$ millions	132,200	132,300	153,200	149,800	182,100	176,200	146,800	131,500	na
External debt/GDP (in per cent)	49.6	43.8	39.7	38.4	70.2	95.8	66.2	53.6	na
External debt/exports of goods and services (in per cent)	180.3	158.3	160.0	159.7	217.6	219.2	149.1	145.5	na

[1] General consolidated government includes the federal, regional and local budgets and extra-budgetary funds and excludes transfers.

[2] The 1998 figure is the yield on obligations of the Central Bank of Russia.

[3] Data in new (denominated) roubles per US dollar. From 1 January 1998, one new rouble = 1,000 old roubles.

[4] Data from the consolidated balance of payments, which covers transactions with both CIS and non-CIS countries.

[5] Data include public debt only. Debt to former COMECON countries is included.

[6] Difference between due and paid arises from accumulation of arrears on debt servicing.

[7] Data as of 1 January of the following year.

Slovak Republic

Stabilisation

Fiscal policy remains expansionary and has led to monetary tightening.

The government had agreed with the IMF, under the Staff Monitored Programme adopted in June 2001, on a 2002 target for the general government deficit of 3.5 per cent of GDP. However, the deficit is likely to increase to about 4.5 per cent as a result of higher spending on social welfare and lower non-tax revenues. The government also continues to use state guarantees, the stock of which currently stands at 15 per cent of GDP, to cover the operating losses of certain public enterprises. The combination of expansionary fiscal policy and a large trade deficit has led the Central Bank to increase its headline interest rate to 8.25 per cent in April 2002, despite the current low level of inflation. For 2002, high privatisation revenues, mostly from the gas and power sectors, are likely to more than cover the fiscal deficit, but most state assets eligible for privatisation, except for the dominant power generating company, have already been sold off.

Enterprise reform

Enterprise regulation remains complex and non-transparent.

Transparency and integrity issues remain major problems. Corruption appears to be widespread in the areas related to regulation, licensing, registration and certification of various business permits. A recent World Bank survey of entrepreneurs and civil servants concluded that state subsidies are often granted on the basis of bribes, political influence and political contacts. To combat this, the authorities adopted a national anti-corruption plan in September 2001, but this needs to be implemented effectively at all levels of the government and in the judiciary to be successful. Corporate governance standards also remain poor, resulting from the non-transparent manner of privatisation in the past, weak enforcement of shareholder rights, connected lending practices before the state-owned banks were privatised and the persistence of old management structures. Amendments to the commercial code that were enacted in January 2002 will lead to an alignment with all the EU directives related to company legislation by 2003.

New labour code adopted.

New labour market legislation came into force in April 2002, bringing the Slovak Republic closer to compliance with the *acquis communautaire*. However, further changes in labour market policies are necessary to increase flexibility in the labour market and lower the persistently high level of unemployment. The unemployment rate has been close to 20 per cent of the labour force since 1999 as a result of enterprise restructuring, inflexible labour markets including inefficient housing and transport sectors, and an extensive social safety net. Average unemployment benefits last up to nine months and are equivalent to 40 per cent of the average net wage, while social benefits for the long-term unemployed in 2000 were on average equal to 33 per cent of the average net wage. The Slovak Republic is also characterised by large regional disparities in unemployment. Some regions report unemployment close to a third of the labour force while the capital, Bratislava, had an unemployment rate of 5.8 per cent at the end of 2001.

Infrastructure

Privatisation in the energy sector has progressed ...

In March 2002, the government sold a 49 per cent ownership stake and management control in the gas monopoly company SPP to a consortium of Gaz de France, Ruhrgas and Gazprom for SKK 130 billion (€3 billion), about 12 per cent of GDP. SPP combines the transit of approximately 80 per cent of Russian gas exports to western Europe with local gas distribution. The government also sold in April 2002 a 49 per cent ownership stake, again with management control, in its three regional power distribution companies. The western distributor, ZSE, was sold to E.ON of Germany; the central distributor, SSE, was sold to Electricite de France; and the smaller eastern distributor, VSE, was sold to RWE of Germany. The three sales generated a total of about €600 million for the government. The privatisation of Slovenske Elektrarne, the dominant producer of electric energy and operator of the national power grid, which is scheduled for late 2002 or 2003,

will complete both the privatisation in the energy sector and the privatisation of large Slovak enterprises. The water companies are currently being corporatised and the shares given to the municipalities, which have the option to either privatise partially or invite private operators.

Enterprises, infrastructure, finance and social reforms

1991
Aug   Bankruptcy law adopted

1992
Jan   Commercial code adopted
Feb   Banking law adopted

1993
Apr   Stock exchange begins trading
Jun   New bankruptcy law adopted

1994
Jan   First corporate Eurobond issued
Feb   New banking law adopted
Aug   New competition law enacted

1995
Dec   First municipal Eurobond issued

1996
Dec   BIS capital adequacy requirements
       adopted

1997
Aug   Enterprise revitalisation law enacted
Dec   IRB (third-largest bank) collapses

1998
Feb   Bankruptcy law amended
Nov   Enterprise revitalisation law cancelled
Nov   Steel producer VSZ defaults

1999
Aug   Restructuring programme approved
Sep   Privatisation law amended

2000
Jan   New investment law adopted
Feb   Utility prices increased significantly
May   New telecommunications law adopted
Jul   Slovak Telecom acquired by strategic
       investor
Aug   New bankruptcy law adopted
Sep   Major steel company sold to strategic
       investor
Nov   Independent financial markets regulator
       established
Dec   Largest bank sold to strategic investor

2001
Jul   New banking law adopted
Dec   Dominant insurance company privatised

2002
Jan   Commercial code amendments enacted
Jan   Independent network industries regulator
       established
Jan   Electricity market partially opened
Jan   New investment funds law adopted
Mar   Gas monopoly privatised
Apr   Power distribution companies privatised
Apr   New financial market regulation enacted
Apr   New labour market legislation adopted

... and liberalisation in the energy sector has started.

A new regulation on network industries law was enacted in January 2002 and an independent regulator was established. The country's largest electricity users, purchasing more than 100 GWh of electricity per year, are now free to choose their power suppliers. This move liberalises about 30 per cent of the market. The 15 companies included in the arrangement are large industrial enterprises such as the Slovalco smelter, US Steel Kosice, the oil refiner Slovnaft, the gas-company SPP and Slovak Railways. Market liberalisation will proceed with free choice of power suppliers for companies consuming more than 40 GWh starting on 1 January 2003.

Financial institutions

Banking and insurance sector privatisation mostly completed.

The former third-largest bank, IRB, which went into forced administration in December 1997, was sold to the Hungarian OTP Bank for €16 million in early December 2001. The government is also selling its stakes in two small banks, Postova Banka and Banka Slovakia. As a result of these and previous banking sector privatisations, over 90 per cent of banking sector assets will be controlled by foreign strategic investors. At the end of December 2001, the government also approved the privatisation of Slovenska Poistovna, the dominant insurance company, to German company Allianz, for approximately €200 million. The parliament also approved an amendment to the bank deposit guarantee scheme in November 2001, making it compatible with EU legislation, and in August 2002, the parliament approved new legislation on secured transactions. This will allow banks to take security over moveable assets and should lead to increased lending, especially to SMEs.

A number of unregulated investment companies collapsed.

Consumer confidence in the financial sector was damaged in the first quarter of 2002 when six unregulated investment companies, which had together attracted approximately SKK 20 billion (close to €500 million) from over 250,000 small retail investors, collapsed. However, the clients of the failed investment companies were not eligible for the deposit insurance scheme that covers ordinary bank depositors and, therefore, there was no risk to the stability of the financial system. Up until January 2002, the collapsed companies were not legally required to disclose client numbers, how much they had collected in deposits or what they were doing with the deposits. However, with the enactment of the new law on securities and investment services on 1 January 2002, the government has tried to tighten the relevant supervision requirements.

Social reform

Increasing poverty becomes a pressing problem.

The poverty rate, defined as the percentage of population living on less than US$ 4.30 a day, has increased from 1 per cent in the early stages of transition to over 8 per cent in recent years. There are large regional disparities in the level of development as well as poverty, partly due to concentration of economic activity and foreign direct investment in and around the capital. While the Bratislava region has a GDP per capita, in Purchasing Power Parity terms, level with the EU average, some rural areas in the eastern part of the country are characterised by high unemployment and have GDP at about a third of the capital. The high levels of rural poverty are closely linked to unemployment rates and lack of investments outside the capital, partly the result of insufficient infrastructure and an inadequate skill base in some regions.

Progress in health care reform mixed.

The government intends to reform the provision of health care in two phases under the plan announced in April 2002. In the first phase, control of hospitals and clinics without debts is to be transferred to municipalities and this process is now under way. In the second phase, the indebted providers of health care will receive debt relief. However, additional measures are needed to lower healthcare costs, particularly those related to pharmaceutical expenditures. The government has approved the transfer of SKK 3.7 billion (€80 million) to alleviate the indebtedness in the health sector, but it is estimated that the debt of the health insurance companies to pharmacies alone has already reached SKK 6 billion (€130 million). An important reason behind the financial difficulties of the health care system is the large arrears in health care insurance premiums.

Liberalisation

Current account convertibility – **full**

Interest rate liberalisation – **full**

Wage regulation – **no**

Stabilisation

Share of general government tax revenue
in GDP – **34.2 per cent**

Exchange rate regime – **floating**

Privatisation

Primary privatisation method – **direct sales**

Secondary privatisation method – **vouchers**

Tradability of land – **full except foreigners**

Enterprises and markets

Competition Office – **yes**

Infrastructure

Independent telecoms regulator – **yes**

Separation of railway accounts – **yes**

Independent electricity regulator – **yes**

Financial sector

Capital adequacy ratio – **8 per cent**

Deposit insurance system – **yes**

Secured transactions law – **yes**

Securities commission – **yes**

Social reform

Share of the population in poverty –
8.6 per cent

Private pension funds – **yes**

	1993	1994	1995	1996	1997	1998	1999	2000	2001
Liberalisation									
Share of administered prices in CPI (in per cent)	21.8	21.8	21.8	21.8	20.8	17.8	17.8	17.8	17.8
Number of goods with administered prices in EBRD-15 basket	5.0	5.0	5.0	5.0	5.0	4.0	4.0	3.0	3.0
Share of trade with non-transition countries (in per cent)	39.5	44.9	45.6	49.4	54.2	62.0	62.0	64.0	62.0
Share of trade in GDP (in per cent)	93.2	91.6	94.7	100.9	104.6	110.9	109.1	128.4	137.3
Tariff revenues (in per cent of imports) [1]	2.3	3.4	3.3	2.9	3.3	2.6	2.7	2.2	0.5
EBRD index of price liberalisation	3.0	3.0	3.0	3.0	3.0	3.0	3.0	3.0	3.0
EBRD index of forex and trade liberalisation	4.0	4.0	4.0	4.3	4.0	4.3	4.3	4.3	4.3
Privatisation									
Privatisation revenues (cumulative, in per cent of GDP)	4.7	6.7	8.4	9.7	10.2	10.8	11.0	14.7	18.2
Private sector share in GDP (in per cent)	45.0	55.0	60.0	70.0	75.0	75.0	75.0	80.0	80.0
Private sector share in employment (in per cent)	40.8	52.8	59.6	63.1	64.6	68.9	70.0	75.0	75.0
EBRD index of small-scale privatisation	4.0	4.0	4.0	4.3	4.3	4.3	4.3	4.3	4.3
EBRD index of large-scale privatisation	3.0	3.0	3.0	3.0	4.0	4.0	4.0	4.0	4.0
Enterprises									
Budgetary subsidies and current transfers (in per cent of GDP)	3.7	3.0	2.6	2.3	2.4	2.0	1.9	4.0	2.7
Effective statutory social security tax (in per cent)	73.9	75.0	89.7	94.1	93.3	86.9	80.7	na	na
Share of industry in total employment (in per cent)	27.8	27.5	28.1	27.7	25.0	26.6	24.4	23.0	25.1
Change in labour productivity in industry (in per cent)	-1.1	9.0	4.0	2.5	3.8	7.8	2.6	7.2	3.6
Investment rate/GDP (in per cent)	32.7	29.4	27.4	36.9	38.6	40.8	33.8	30.1	32.5
EBRD index of enterprise reform	3.0	3.0	3.0	3.0	2.7	2.7	3.0	3.0	3.0
EBRD index of competition policy	2.0	3.0	3.0	3.0	3.0	3.0	3.0	3.0	3.0
Infrastructure									
Main telephone lines per 100 inhabitants	16.7	18.7	20.8	23.2	25.8	28.5	30.7	31.4	28.8
Railway labour productivity (1989=100)	65.4	60.7	68.7	60.8	63.1	60.8	53.0	61.0	62.4
Electricity tariffs, USc kWh (collection rate in per cent)	na	2.9 (95)	3.1 (95)	3.2 (95)	2.9 (95)	2.8 (na)	3.5 (na)	5.9 (na)	5.0 (102)
GDP per unit of energy use (PPP in US dollars per kgoe)	2.3	2.5	2.7	2.8	3.1	3.2	3.2	na	na
EBRD index of infrastructure reform	1.0	1.0	1.7	1.7	1.7	1.7	2.0	2.0	2.3
Financial institutions									
Number of banks (foreign owned)	28 (13)	29 (14)	33 (18)	29 (14)	29 (13)	27 (11)	25 (10)	23 (13)	19 (12)
Asset share of state-owned banks (in per cent)	70.7	66.9	61.2	54.2	48.7	50.0	50.7	49.1	4.9
Non-performing loans (in per cent of total loans)	12.2	30.3	41.3	31.8	33.4	44.3	32.9	26.2	24.3
Domestic credit to private sector (in per cent of GDP)	30.4	23.0	26.3	30.4	42.1	43.9	40.5	37.6	27.6
Stock market capitalisation (in per cent of GDP) [2]	na	7.3	6.7	11.5	9.3	4.7	3.8	3.9	3.3
EBRD index of banking sector reform	2.7	2.7	2.7	2.7	2.7	2.7	2.7	3.0	3.3
EBRD index of reform of non-banking financial institutions	2.0	2.7	2.7	2.7	2.3	2.3	2.3	2.3	2.3
Legal environment									
EBRD rating of legal extensiveness (company law)	na	na	na	na	3.0	3.0	4.0	3.0	3.3
EBRD rating of legal effectiveness (company law)	na	na	na	na	3.0	2.0	3.3	3.0	3.3
Social sector									
Expenditures on health and education (in per cent of GDP)	9.1	8.5	8.9	11.1	10.7	10.2	9.9	9.6	9.5
Life expectancy at birth, total (years)	72.4	72.3	72.3	72.7	72.7	72.6	72.9	73.1	na
Basic school enrolment ratio (in per cent)	98.5	97.9	97.5	96.8	98.7	101.3	107.5	107.4	na
Earnings inequality (GINI-coefficient)	na	na	na	na	na	na	na	na	na

[1] Refers to import tariffs, customs duties and import surcharge.

[2] Data from Bratislava Stock Exchange.

	1994	1995	1996	1997	1998	1999	2000	2001	2002
								Estimate	Projection
Output and expenditure					*(Percentage change in real terms)*				
GDP	5.3	4.1	3.5	4.6	3.8	5.2	4.6	3.0	2.7
Private consumption	4.0	9.1	2.0	2.8	3.3	6.0	0.8	1.7	na
Public consumption	2.1	2.5	3.4	4.3	5.8	4.6	3.1	3.2	na
Gross fixed investment	14.1	16.8	8.9	11.6	11.3	19.1	0.2	-1.9	na
Exports of goods and services	9.4	1.1	3.6	11.6	6.7	1.7	12.7	6.2	na
Imports of goods and services	6.0	11.3	2.1	11.9	10.4	8.2	6.1	2.1	na
Industrial gross output	6.4	2.0	1.0	1.0	3.7	-0.5	6.2	2.9	na
Agricultural gross output [1]	4.2	1.6	1.0	-3.0	3.2	-2.1	-1.0	-2.1	na
Employment [2]					*(Percentage change)*				
Labour force (mid-year)	0.5	1.7	-0.6	2.1	1.8	-2.0	0.0	0.9	na
Employment (mid-year)	0.7	3.6	-0.5	2.3	1.0	-1.7	0.2	2.2	na
					(In per cent of labour force)				
Unemployment (mid-year)	9.1	7.4	7.3	7.1	7.6	7.4	7.2	5.9	na
Prices and wages					*(Percentage change)*				
Consumer prices (annual average)	21.0	13.5	9.9	8.4	7.9	6.1	8.9	8.4	7.4
Consumer prices (end-year)	19.5	9.0	9.0	8.8	6.5	8.0	8.9	7.0	7.4
Producer prices (annual average)	17.7	12.8	6.8	6.1	6.0	2.1	7.6	9.0	na
Producer prices (end-year)	18.2	7.9	5.8	6.8	3.6	3.5	9.2	7.5	na
Gross average monthly earnings in economy (annual average) [3]	25.4	18.4	15.3	11.7	9.6	9.6	10.6	11.9	na
Government sector [4]					*(In per cent of GDP)*				
General government balance	-0.2	-0.3	-0.2	-1.7	-1.4	-0.9	-1.3	-1.2	-2.9
General government expenditure	43.6	43.4	42.9	43.8	44.4	44.5	44.1	44.3	na
General government debt	18.5	18.8	22.7	23.2	23.7	24.5	25.1	26.9	na
Monetary sector					*(Percentage change)*				
Broad money (M2, end-year)	43.3	28.1	20.5	24.3	19.8	13.2	15.3	30.4	na
Domestic credit (end-year)	27.2	35.1	13.2	14.2	22.4	19.3	16.7	16.9	na
					(In per cent of GDP)				
Broad money (M2, end-year)	39.7	42.4	44.4	48.5	51.9	52.4	54.7	63.0	na
Interest and exchange rates					*(In per cent per annum, end-year)*				
Discount rate	16.0	10.0	10.0	10.0	10.0	8.0	10.0	11.0	na
Inter-bank market rate (average)	24.7	15.9	10.2	9.8	5.6	6.9	7.2	4.7	na
Deposit rate (31-90 days)	27.9	20.8	11.2	13.9	7.0	9.6	10.9	8.5	na
Lending rate (short-term working capital)	38.5	28.0	18.3	20.3	12.3	15.2	16.3	13.7	na
					(Tolars per US dollar)				
Exchange rate (end-year)	126.5	126.0	141.5	169.2	161.2	196.8	227.4	250.9	na
Exchange rate (annual average)	128.8	118.5	135.4	159.7	166.1	181.8	222.7	242.7	na
External sector					*(In millions of US dollars)*				
Current account	574	-100	31	12	-147	-783	-612	-67	251
Trade balance	-336	-953	-825	-776	-789	-1,245	-1,139	-622	-335
Merchandise exports	6,832	8,350	8,353	8,408	9,091	8,623	8,808	9,342	9,529
Merchandise imports	7,168	9,303	9,178	9,184	9,880	9,868	9,947	9,964	9,864
Foreign direct investment, net	131	183	188	340	250	144	110	338	553
Gross reserves (end-year), excluding gold [5]	1,499	1,821	2,297	3,315	3,639	3,168	3,196	4,330	na
External debt stock	2,258	2,970	3,981	4,123	4,915	5,400	6,217	6,717	na
					(In months of imports of goods and services)				
Gross reserves (end-year), excluding gold [5]	2.2	2.0	2.6	3.8	3.8	3.3	3.4	4.6	na
					(In per cent of current account revenues, excluding transfers)				
Debt service [6]	4.7	6.5	8.5	8.4	13.0	7.7	9.1	14.0	na
Memorandum items					*(Denominations as indicated)*				
Population (end-year, millions)	1.9	2.0	2.0	2.0	2.0	2.0	2.0	2.0	na
GDP (in millions of tolars)	1,852,997	2,221,459	2,555,369	2,907,277	3,253,751	3,648,401	4,035,518	4,566,191	5,037,921
GDP per capita (in US dollars)	7,592	9,418	9,501	9,172	9,900	10,098	9,106	9,509	na
Share of industry in GDP (in per cent)	30.3	28.3	27.9	28.0	28.1	27.3	27.7	27.4	na
Share of agriculture in GDP (in per cent)	4.0	3.9	3.9	3.7	3.6	3.2	2.9	2.7	na
Current account/GDP (in per cent)	4.0	-0.5	0.2	0.1	-0.8	-3.9	-3.4	-0.4	1.2
External debt - reserves, in US$ millions	759	1,149	1,684	808	1,277	2,232	3,021	2,387	na
External debt/GDP (in per cent)	15.7	15.8	21.1	22.6	25.1	26.9	34.3	35.7	na
External debt/exports of goods and services (in per cent)	26.1	28.6	38.0	39.4	44.2	51.3	58.1	59.5	na

[1] Agricultural value added.

[2] Based on labour force survey data. These figures have been consistently lower than those calculated as officially registered unemployed.

[3] Data for all enterprises employing three or more persons.

[4] General government includes the state, municipalities and extra-budgetary funds. Privatisation revenues from state and socially owned enterprises are placed below the line. Balances from 1999 are based upon the new budget classifications.

[5] Total reserves excluding gold of the Bank of Slovenia.

[6] Long-term debt only.

Tajikistan

Key reform challenges

- **Investment opportunities remain constrained by obstacles to trade, which will require concerted regional efforts and continued domestic market liberalisation to be overcome.**

- **Improvements in tax collection and some debt reduction efforts have reduced immediate fiscal pressures, but prudent fiscal management must continue to create room for priority public investments.**

- **Implementing the government's poverty reduction strategy will require strengthening of governance and administrative capacity.**

Liberalisation

Despite further liberalisation, trade remains hampered by non-tariff barriers and regional tensions.

Import tariffs were unified at 5 per cent in May 2002 and the sales tax on cotton and aluminium was reduced from 15 per cent to 10 per cent in January 2002. However, private importers and exporters continue to face non-tariff barriers, such as import/export licences, visa requirements, double taxation and corruption in the customs service. Due to security concerns, Kazakhstan temporarily blocked railway transit from Tajikistan to Russia via its territory, while Uzbekistan maintains restrictions on road and railway traffic and has mined border areas used by shuttle traders. Because of these obstacles, trade turnover fell 12 per cent in 2001. Various regional organisations, including the Shanghai Co-operation Organisation and the Eurasian Economic Community, are engaged in promoting regional economic cooperation, but to little effect so far. Having gained observer status in the WTO in May 2001, Tajikistan is presently working on its trade memorandum, the document explaining its trade policies and institutions to WTO members.

Stabilisation

While public finances have improved, significant vulnerabilities remain.

Debt reduction and rescheduling negotiations with Uzbekistan, Kazakhstan and Russia have reduced the debt stock by around US$ 200 million to US$ 1 billion (100 per cent of GDP). At the same time, tax collection has improved. The Ministry of National Incomes and Duties was established in early 2002 to further progress fiscal management and enable the public investment spending foreseen under the government's poverty reduction strategy. However, macroeconomic stability remains at risk from external financing shortfalls, with Tajikistan vulnerable to price fluctuations in its major commodities, aluminium and cotton, and entirely dependent on official financial assistance. Tajikistan recently completed an IMF Staff Monitored Programme and a resumption of financing could be possible in late 2002, should it make sufficient progress on structural reforms.

Privatisation

Progress in privatisation uneven.

Privatisation slowed down in the second half of 2001 as the government focused on political stability and anti-terrorism activities. However, it regained some momentum in 2002 in a bid to meet targets agreed with the World Bank. A total of 216 companies (86 of which are medium and large-scale) were privatised during the first half of 2002, mostly in the construction, transportation, industrial and trade sectors. However, only two large enterprises were sold during this period: a sewing factory for US$ 0.5 million and a construction company for US$ 0.4 million. Around half of all medium and large-scale enterprises remain state-owned. A new privatisation strategy for the next two years was approved in July 2002, which contains commercialisation and privatisation plans for most medium and large-scale enterprises, including some strategic companies. In June 2002, the government signed an action plan with the World Bank, under which it commits itself to prepare a tender for a management contract or strategic stake in TADAZ, an aluminium smelter and by far the largest company in the country.

Enterprise reform

Productivity increasing in several sectors ...

Production in both agriculture and industry increased significantly in 2001, by 11 per cent and 15 per cent growth respectively, while employment fell. The cotton sector is one example of the positive impact of structural reforms on productivity. Following continued progress in land reform, raw cotton yields increased from 1.3 tonnes per hectare in 1999 to 1.4 tonnes in 2000 and 1.8 tonnes in 2001. Similarly, after the privatisation of the cotton ginneries, the share of cotton fibre extracted from raw cotton increased from 30 per cent in 2000 to 32 per cent in 2001. Aluminium production, which rose from 160,000 tonnes in 1997 to 300,000 tonnes in 2000, increased further to 324,000 tonnes in 2001. Following the end of the civil war, TADAZ has benefited from improved access to raw material and working capital financing under an exclusive supply and off-take agreement with Ansol, a foreign trading company.

Liberalisation, stabilisation, privatisation

1991
Oct — Small-scale privatisation begins
Dec — Central Bank law adopted

1992
Jan — Most prices liberalised
Jan — VAT introduced
Jul — Civil war declared

1993
Jan — Price liberalisation partially reversed
Dec — Wage indexation introduced

1994
Sep — Interim cease-fire arranged

1995
May — New currency (Tajik rouble) introduced
May — Exchange rate unified
May — State trading monopoly abolished
Jun — Most consumer prices liberalised
Aug — Licences for agricultural trade eliminated
Dec — Interest rates fully liberalised

1996
Feb — Export surrender requirement abolished
Mar — Price controls on grain and bread lifted
May — Large-scale privatisation programme launched
May — IMF programme adopted
Dec — Land privatisation started

1997
May — Privatisation law revised
Jun — Peace agreement concluded
Sep — Treasury system reformed

1998
Apr — Customs union membership granted
Jul — Free tradability of land rights granted
Nov — Regular credit auctions introduced

1999
Jan — New tax code adopted
Jun — State cotton trading company liquidated

2000
Jul — Official exchange rate unified with curb market rate
Aug — Privatisation of cotton ginneries completed
Oct — New currency (somoni) introduced
Dec — New treasury system set up

2001
May — WTO observer status granted

2002
May — Import tariff rates unified
Jul — New privatisation strategy approved

Enterprises, infrastructure, finance and social reforms

1991
Feb   Banking legislation adopted
Dec   Joint-stock companies law adopted

1992
Mar   Bankruptcy law adopted

1993
Dec   Competition law adopted

1994
Jun   Law on mortgages adopted

1995
Aug   Banking regulations adopted

1996
Jul   Electricity tariffs reduced below average cost

1998
Apr   Banking regulations amended
May   New banking law adopted

1999
Apr   Major bank liquidated
Jul   Financial audit of state banks completed
Sep   Road link to China completed
Oct   Decree prohibiting National Bank from direct lending issued

2000
Jan   Prudential regulations on banks tightened
Feb   Directed credits by NBT renewed
Oct   Energy and transport sector restructured
Oct   Anti-monopoly agency established

2001
Mar   Public audit office established

2002
Apr   New telecommunications law adopted
May   Poverty reduction strategy paper adopted

... but foreign investment remains limited.
Apart from capital repatriation by Tajiks living abroad, foreign direct investment is minimal, with per capita FDI flows of just US$ 1 in 2001. Foreign investors continue to have concerns over a weak legal environment, poor governance, widespread corruption and high security risks in the country. Administrative capacity to implement new legislation is poor and the authorities have sometimes lacked focus on the key economic reform priorities. More recently, foreign investors have complained about delays in procuring inputs and accessing export markets, which are the result of transit and trade restrictions by regional neighbours.

Infrastructure

Tajik Rail facing financial difficulties ...
Traffic volumes within and through Tajikistan have decreased dramatically in the past decade. Freight traffic fell from 10.7 billion tonne-kilometres in 1990 to 1.3 billion tonne-kilometres in 2000. Passenger traffic also decreased from 842 million passenger-kilometres to 83 million passenger-kilometres during the same period. Cash collection for railway services has been weak and government agencies have accumulated significant payment arrears. Moreover, the government has used Tajik Rail as a vehicle for servicing debts to Uzbekistan by offering transit services, for which Tajik Rail has not been sufficiently compensated. As a result, there has been virtually no investment in rolling stock, tracks and locomotives in recent years. However, this has now changed. In 2002, a new head was appointed to Tajik Rail and a restructuring plan developed. A special commission was set up in May 2002 to control the sale of train tickets and the Prime Minister has ordered government institutions to clear arrears to the railway.

... while reform of telecommunications has made some progress.
A new telecommunications law was passed by parliament in April 2002. A regulatory agency has been created, initially within the Ministry of Communications, but with the intention of making it independent by 2004. Tariff reform has also begun, with monthly subscription, local call and related charges increasing by 174 per cent in June 2002. A formula for automatic adjustments of tariffs has been agreed by the Ministry of Communications and the Anti-monopoly Committee, which will reflect the financing costs for new investments undertaken by the incumbent operator, Tajiktelecom. Tajiktelecom has also made strenuous efforts to increase its revenue collections, which reached 88 per cent of total billings in the first half of 2002. However, collections from state entities are much lower and substantial payment arrears remain from previous years, affecting the financial health of the company. Privatisation is regarded as premature in the present environment, as a tender would be unlikely to attract competent private bidders.

Financial institutions

Confidence in local banks increasing, but bank restructuring has slowed.
Banking sector reforms over the past few years have resulted in consolidation of the commercial banking sector. The number of commercial banks decreased to 14 in January 2002 from 24 in 1994. The rise in deposits by 84 per cent in 2001 testifies to the gradual increase in confidence in the sector. However, the effectiveness of the regulatory framework remains uncertain, as the National Bank of Tajikistan (NBT) has been reluctant to close non-viable financial institutions. For example, the NBT postponed the deadline for adherence to the US$ 2.5 million minimum capital requirement by one year to the end of 2003. At present, half of the commercial banks fall below this requirement and there are concerns over related party lending and the protection of minority shareholders. Also, several banks are still to provide the required independent audits of their accounts.

Social reform

Poverty reduction strategy paper approved.
Tajikistan remains one of the poorest countries in the region. The average monthly salary was 25 somoni (US$ 10.40) in 2001. The monthly pension allowance was 6.01 somoni (US$ 2.50) and there are significant payment arrears. To increase real incomes and living standards and to target better government assistance to the poor, the government approved a poverty reduction strategy paper (PRSP) in July 2002. This strategy forms the basis for future official donor assistance and outlines key policy priorities over the medium term. Particular emphasis is placed on improving the rural economy and the agriculture sector on which the majority of poor people depend. Ultimately, however, effective poverty reduction will require sustained growth and new employment opportunities in the private sector, which remains small outside the rural economy.

Liberalisation

Current account convertibility – **full**
Interest rate liberalisation – **full**
Wage regulation – **yes**

Stabilisation

Share of general government tax revenue
 in GDP – **14.1 per cent**
Exchange rate regime – **managed floating**

Privatisation

Primary privatisation method – **direct sales**
Secondary privatisation method – **MEBOs**
Tradability of land – **limited de facto**

Enterprises and markets

Competition Office – **yes**

Infrastructure

Independent telecoms regulator –
 yes, limited
Separation of railway accounts – **no**
Independent electricity regulator – **no**

Financial sector

Capital adequacy ratio – **12 per cent**
Deposit insurance system – **no**
Secured transactions law – **yes**
Securities commission – **yes**

Social reform

Share of the population in poverty –
 95.8 per cent
Private pension funds – **no**

	1993	1994	1995	1996	1997	1998	1999	2000	2001
Liberalisation									
Share of administered prices in CPI (in per cent)	na	na	na	na	na	na	na	na	na
Number of goods with administered prices in EBRD-15 basket	2.0	2.0	1.0	1.0	1.0	1.0	1.0	na	na
Share of trade with non-transition countries (in per cent)	na	75.6	58.9	52.7	44.7	47.9	36.2	33.4	29.9
Share of trade in GDP (in per cent)	157.7	135.9	260.5	147.8	138.5	99.4	125.1	163.7	135.9
Tariff revenues (in per cent of imports)	0.9	4.0	1.2	0.6	2.6	6.2	2.1	1.8	2.8
EBRD index of price liberalisation	1.7	1.7	2.7	3.0	3.0	3.0	3.0	3.0	3.0
EBRD index of forex and trade liberalisation	1.0	1.0	2.0	2.0	2.0	2.7	2.7	3.3	3.3
Privatisation									
Privatisation revenues (cumulative, in per cent of GDP)	0.9	1.1	1.4	1.6	2.1	2.7	4.0	5.0	5.3
Private sector share in GDP (in per cent)	10.0	15.0	25.0	30.0	30.0	30.0	40.0	40.0	45.0
Private sector share in employment (in per cent)	na	na	53.0	55.0	58.0	57.0	63.0	58.0	60.0
EBRD index of small-scale privatisation	2.0	2.0	2.0	2.0	2.3	3.0	3.0	3.3	3.7
EBRD index of large-scale privatisation	1.0	1.0	2.0	2.0	2.0	2.0	2.3	2.3	2.3
Enterprises									
Budgetary subsidies and current transfers (in per cent of GDP) [1]	8.0	10.9	6.9	0.7	1.1	0.6	0.8	0.7	0.5
Effective statutory social security tax (in per cent)	69.8	109.9	17.8	22.1	47.7	33.8	na	na	na
Share of industry in total employment (in per cent)	11.5	11.1	9.9	10.5	9.2	8.2	7.7	6.9	7.4
Change in labour productivity in industry (in per cent)	8.2	-22.5	-3.2	-23.1	8.0	19.8	16.8	21.2	5.7
Investment rate/GDP (in per cent)	23.1	22.3	14.7	na	na	na	na	na	na
EBRD index of enterprise reform	1.0	1.0	1.0	1.0	1.0	1.7	1.7	1.7	1.7
EBRD index of competition policy	2.0	2.0	2.0	2.0	2.0	2.0	2.0	2.0	1.7
Infrastructure									
Main telephone lines per 100 inhabitants	4.6	4.5	4.5	4.2	3.8	3.7	3.5	3.6	3.6
Railway labour productivity (1994=100)	na	100.0	121.7	87.3	70.8	75.5	62.9	62.9	57.2
Electricity tariffs, USc kWh (collection rate in per cent)	na	na	na	na	na	na	na	na	0.2 (na)
GDP per unit of energy use (PPP in US dollars per kgoe)	1.4	2.2	2.1	1.6	1.8	1.8	1.9	na	na
EBRD index of infrastructure reform	1.0	1.0	1.0	1.0	1.0	1.0	1.0	1.0	1.0
Financial institutions									
Number of banks (foreign owned)	15 (na)	17 (na)	18 (na)	23 (na)	28 (5)	20 (5)	20 (3)	17 (4)	17 (3)
Asset share of state-owned banks (in per cent)	na	na	na	5.3	30.3	29.2	6.9	6.8	4.8
Non-performing loans (in per cent of total loans)	na	na	na	2.9	3.0	3.2	15.8	10.8	12.5
Domestic credit to private sector (in per cent of GDP)	na	na	na	4.0	4.8	7.7	10.0	11.3	13.6
Stock market capitalisation (in per cent of GDP)	na	na	na	na	na	na	na	na	na
EBRD index of banking sector reform	1.0	1.0	1.0	1.0	1.0	1.0	1.0	1.0	1.0
EBRD index of reform of non-banking financial institutions	1.0	1.0	1.0	1.0	1.0	1.0	1.0	1.0	1.0
Legal environment									
EBRD rating of legal extensiveness (company law)	na	na	na	na	na	2.0	na	2.0	2.0
EBRD rating of legal effectiveness (company law)	na	na	na	na	na	3.0	na	1.7	2.0
Social sector									
Expenditures on health and education (in per cent of GDP)	8.5	12.8	3.9	3.5	3.4	3.3	3.1	3.2	3.3
Life expectancy at birth, total (years)	66.8	66.0	68.3	68.4	68.4	na	na	68.8	na
Basic school enrolment ratio (in per cent)	85.5	86.4	87.0	85.9	85.8	89.7	89.1	88.4	na
Earnings inequality (GINI-coefficient)	na	na	na	na	na	35.0	na	na	na

[1] Data from IMF. Excludes special cotton financing from the National Bank of Tajikistan.

	1994	1995	1996	1997	1998	1999	2000	2001 Estimate	2002 Projection
Output and expenditure					*(Percentage change in real terms)*				
GDP	-18.9	-12.5	-4.4	1.7	5.3	3.7	8.3	10.3	7.0
Private consumption	na	na	na	na	na	na	na	na	na
Public consumption	na	na	na	na	na	na	na	na	na
Gross fixed investment	na	na	na	na	na	na	na	na	na
Exports of goods and services	na	na	na	na	na	na	na	na	na
Imports of goods and services	na	na	na	na	na	na	na	na	na
Industrial gross output	-25.4	-13.6	-24.0	-2.1	8.1	5.0	10.3	14.4	na
Agricultural gross output	-6.5	-25.9	2.0	3.6	6.3	3.8	12.4	11.0	na
Employment					*(Percentage change)*				
Labour force (end-year)	0.5	0.2	-6.0	3.5	0.8	-3.5	0.2	1.0	na
Employment (end-year)	-0.1	0.5	-6.6	3.4	0.3	-3.3	0.5	1.4	na
					(In per cent of labour force)				
Unemployment (end-year) [1]	1.7	2.0	2.6	2.8	3.2	3.0	2.7	2.4	na
Prices and wages					*(Percentage change)*				
Consumer prices (annual average)	350.0	609.0	418.0	88.0	43.2	27.6	32.9	38.6	12.8
Consumer prices (end-year)	1.1	2,133.3	40.5	163.6	2.7	30.1	60.8	12.5	13.7
Producer prices (annual average)	327.8	1,080.0	449.0	95.7	27.8	41.2	43.5	28.7	na
Producer prices (end-year)	301.9	628.3	77.7	121.7	5.9	64.0	33.9	9.4	na
Gross average monthly earnings in economy (annual average)	116.1	164.2	219.6	68.3	84.8	26.6	37.7	23.7	na
Government sector [2]					*(In per cent of GDP)*				
General government balance	-4.6	-3.3	-5.8	-3.3	-3.8	-3.1	-0.6	-0.1	-1.0
General government expenditure	52.2	20.8	19.0	17.0	15.8	16.6	15.2	16.3	na
General government debt	na	na	na	na	na	na	na	na	na
Monetary sector					*(Percentage change)*				
Broad money (M2, end-year) [3]	159.4	-19.4	93.2	110.7	53.9	19.7	55.2	54.6	na
Domestic credit (end-year)	na	na	94.0	201.8	363.6	-5.3	32.7	66.1	na
					(In per cent of GDP)				
Broad money (M2, end-year) [3]	81.7	20.5	8.3	8.6	8.1	7.4	8.6	9.5	na
Interest and exchange rates					*(In per cent per annum, end-year)*				
Monetary policy rate	na	152.5	72.0	81.0	36.4	20.1	20.6	20.0	na
Deposit rate (up to 3 months) [4]	30.0	100.0	109.0	89.0	15.7	11.4	21.8	31.1	na
Lending rate (up to 3 months) [4]	30.0	500.0	122.0	74.0	49.7	23.2	15.6	20.4	na
					(Tajik somoni per US dollar)				
Exchange rate (end-year) [5]	0.036	0.294	0.328	0.748	0.977	1.436	2.200	2.536	na
Exchange rate (annual average) [5]	0.022	0.104	0.293	0.564	0.777	1.238	1.823	2.395	na
External sector					*(In millions of US dollars)*				
Current account	-163	-99	-75	-61	-120	-36	-63	-72	-44
Trade balance	-127	-59	-16	-60	-139	-27	-46	-121	-89
Merchandise exports	559	779	770	746	586	666	788	652	739
Merchandise imports	686	838	786	806	725	693	834	773	828
Foreign direct investment, net	12	10	18	18	25	21	24	9	20
Gross reserves (end-year), excluding gold	1	4	14	30	65	58	87	96	na
External debt stock	760	869	948	1,108	1,213	1,230	1,231	1,023	na
				(In months of imports of goods and services, excluding alumina and electricity)					
Gross reserves (end-year), excluding gold	0.0	0.1	0.3	0.6	1.5	1.7	2.1	1.9	na
				(In per cent of exports of goods and services, excluding alumina and electricity)					
Debt service	12.1	36.1	34.1	15.1	15.7	11.9	13.8	19.2	na
Memorandum items					*(Denominations as indicated)*				
Population (end-year, millions)	5.8	5.9	5.9	6.0	6.1	6.1	6.2	6.9	na
GDP (in millions of somoni)	20.2	64.8	308.5	632.0	1,025.2	1,345.0	1,806.8	2,512.1	2,950.0
GDP per capita (in US dollars)	159.1	105.9	177.0	186.6	216.3	177.4	159.8	164.5	na
Share of industry in GDP (in per cent) [6]	22.0	34.0	25.7	19.7	18.1	19.1	20.4	18.7	na
Share of agriculture in GDP (in per cent) [6]	19.1	36.2	36.0	27.1	19.8	16.8	17.4	22.1	na
Current account/GDP (in per cent)	-17.8	-16.0	-7.1	-5.4	-9.1	-3.4	-6.4	-6.9	-4.1
External debt - reserves, in US$ millions	759.0	865.0	934.0	1,078.0	1,147.7	1,171.9	1,143.8	927.7	na
External debt/GDP (in per cent)	83.0	140.0	90.0	98.9	91.9	113.2	124.2	97.6	na
External debt/exports of goods and services (in per cent) [7]	193.3	217.2	169.1	218.3	290.2	303.7	297.3	320.8	na

[1] Officially registered unemployed. The World Bank estimates the true unemployment rate in 1998 at about 30 per cent of the labour force.

[2] Excludes transfers from the state budget to the Pension Fund and Employment Funds.

[3] Series before 1998 is for broad money only, subsequently includes foreign currency deposits.

[4] Interest rates were set by the parliament until June 1995. Thereafter, rates refer to one- to three-month maturity.

[5] Both Russian roubles (until 1994) and Tajik roubles (until October 2000) are converted to Tajik somoni.

[6] Figures are based on current prices. Variations in the shares thus reflect changes in relative prices.

[7] Export of goods and services excluding alumina and electricity.

Turkmenistan

Key reform challenges

- The dual exchange rate, which remains the largest single price distortion in the economy and a major obstacle to private investment, must be unified.

- Comprehensive price liberalisation is fundamental to providing appropriate price signals and, therefore, more effective use of the country's natural resource wealth.

- Against the background of rapid population growth, private sector job creation needs to be accelerated through the reduction of business obstacles and a restarting of the privatisation process.

Liberalisation

State control over prices and resources remains pervasive.

Access to foreign exchange and provision of large subsidies to domestic consumers for water, gas, electricity, fuel and other public services remain under government control. Together the implicit fiscal transfers embodied in price and exchange rate distortions may account for around 30 to 40 per cent of GDP (20 to 25 per cent for the energy sector and 10 to 15 per cent in agriculture). This is in addition to the 25 per cent of GDP raised in official taxation and the 7 to 10 per cent of GDP in taxes on the gas sector that are transferred to the Foreign Exchange Reserve Fund (FERF). These figures highlight the degree of state control over resource allocation. The large distortions have encouraged smuggling of fuel, wheat and cotton, in particular across the border to Iran and Uzbekistan, forcing the government to re-introduce restrictions on individual travel to these countries. The prevalence of output targets is another manifestation of the prevailing central planning mode in the country.

Stabilisation

Despite rising gas exports, the underlying fiscal position appears vulnerable.

Rising gas exports boosted public sector revenues in 2001. The FERF currently receives half of all cash payments for gas exports, amounting to some US$ 400 million in 2001 alone. While official data on foreign debt and reserves held by the FERF point to a substantial improvement in the net foreign asset position of the country, this is inconsistent with balance of payments data showing a US$ 620 million net increase in short-term obligations. Large foreign borrowing and a significant expansion of directed credits to agriculture in mid-2001 suggest a continuously weak underlying fiscal position. This gives rise to concern, as recent high growth rates may not be sustainable in the face of constraints on further gas export expansion.

Privatisation

Privatisation stalled and no longer on the policy agenda.

No enterprise sales have taken place since the responsibility for privatisation moved back to the Ministry of Economy and Finance in 2001. All strategic assets remain state-owned and the government tends to hold at least a 50 per cent stake in all new commercial investments. According to official figures, private sector employment reached 63 per cent of the total in 2001. However, this figure includes estimates for people employed in their own household and rural Dayhan farms (25 per cent of total employment), where commercial autonomy is limited. Their land rights are not tradable and they are typically reliant on the state for all inputs and are subject to strict output quotas. Outside agriculture, the private sector role in the economy is very limited.

Enterprise reform

Foreign investment increasing ...

According to official numbers, FDI reached US$ 170 million in 2001, up 30 per cent on 2000. Hydro-carbon investments made under the five Production Sharing Agreements (PSAs) with Dragon Oil, Burren Energy, Exxon Mobil, Petronas and Mitro International accounted for the bulk of the inflow. However, Exxon Mobil left the country in early 2002, citing disappointing drilling results and a rationalisation of its Caspian exposure. Another company, Wintershall, was in negotiations over an offshore PSA, but has failed to make progress because of territorial disagreements between Turkmenistan and Azerbaijan over the respective exploration block. Foreign involvement has given a boost to the textiles industry, which grew by 27 per cent in 2001. However, given the substantial exchange rate distortions, which reduce the effective cost paid for imported capital equipment to a fraction of its true value, the real value added of this new domestic industry is in doubt.

Liberalisation, stabilisation, privatisation

1991
Oct	Independence from Soviet Union declared

1993
Oct	Gas exports to Europe interrupted
Oct	VAT introduced
Nov	New currency (manat) introduced
Nov	Foreign exchange law adopted

1994
May	Small-scale privatisation begins
Aug	State trading monopoly reinforced
Sep	National privatisation programme adopted

1995
Jan	State treasury system introduced
Jul	Flat rate income tax introduced

1996
Jan	Exchange rate unified legally
Jan	Most prices liberalised
May	Barter trade in cotton, oil and wool banned
Aug	First Treasury bill issued
Dec	Land reform decreed

1997
Mar	Gas deliveries halted to non-paying CIS customers
Apr	Large-scale privatisation law adopted

1998
Apr	Exchange rate unified
Sep	Large forex premium on parallel market re-emerges

1999
Jan	Gas exports to Ukraine resumed
Apr	Gas exports to Ukraine interrupted
Dec	Gas export agreement with Gazprom concluded
Dec	Niyazov made President for life
Dec	Soviet-style ten-year plan adopted
Dec	Public sector wages doubled

2000
Nov	Gas exports to Ukraine resumed

... while domestic businesses go into hiding.

Faced with numerous administrative barriers and constant government interference, 8,000 companies de-registered in 2001, around a third of the total. More may be inactive or operating in the informal sector, although given tight policing, the scope for tax evasion may be more limited than elsewhere in the region.

Enterprises, infrastructure, finance and social reforms

1992
Jun   Bankruptcy law adopted

1993
Oct   Company legislation enacted
Nov   Two-tier banking system established

1995
Dec   Inter-bank market established

1996
Apr   BIS capital adequacy enacted

1997
Mar   Hydrocarbon resources law adopted
Dec   Gas pipeline to Iran opened

1998
Dec   Directed credits officially abolished
Dec   Merger of private and state bank decreed by government
Dec   New civil code adopted

1999
Mar   Gas sale agreement signed with Turkey
Jul   Construction agreement for Trans-Caspian gas pipeline signed
Dec   President Bank created

2000
Jun   Trans-Caspian pipeline consortium (PSG) presence reduced
Jun   Directed credits renewed
Jun   Citizens banned from holding foreign bank accounts
Dec   Private licences for Internet services revoked

2002
May   Trans-Afghan pipeline plans revived

Public officials face a crackdown on corruption.

A nationwide crackdown on corruption has revealed numerous cases of misuse of office. Significant parallel incomes have been made in the public sector through over-invoicing or the diversion of goods from state channels to private traders. The Turkmen Council of Elders, the supreme legislative body in the country, is to consider proposals for new selection criteria for public officials, including "integrity checks" on officials and their relatives. However, corruption charges are routinely used to dislodge political opponents and subsequent wide-scale amnesties for all low-profile cases are the norm.

Infrastructure

Trans-Afghan pipeline plans revived ...

Turkmenistan's gas export prospects received a potential boost when the replacement of the Taliban regime in Afghanistan rekindled interest in a gas pipeline from Eastern Turkmenistan via Afghanistan to Pakistan and possibly onwards to India. The Asian Development Bank (ADB) has agreed to finance a feasibility study and serve as a strategic partner for the 1,500 kilometre pipeline, estimated to cost around US$ 2 billion and have a capacity of 30 billion cubic metres per annum. The study, which will also include an assessment of a parallel oil pipeline, is due in May 2003. However, political risks remain high and some observers have suggested that only the extension to India would make the project commercially interesting. If it goes ahead, the project would significantly boost Turkmenistan's gas exports, currently limited by Ukraine's ability to pay for, and Gazprom's willingness to transport, Turkmen gas.

... while Turkmenistan remains cool to a Eurasian gas "OPEC".

Turkmenistan has been reluctant so far to join a Russian-sponsored gas alliance, reflecting concerns over access to Russian transport routes and potentially growing competition from Uzbekistan and Kazakhstan, through which Turkmenistan's gas exports must transit. Russia has recently raised transit tariffs for exporters by 25 per cent to USc 0.98 for 1,000 cubic metres and 100 kilometres. This has affected the competitiveness of Turkmen gas in other CIS countries and raises doubts over the commercial future of Itera, the Russian gas company, which is Turkmenistan's main partner in shipping gas abroad. Uzbekistan recently also threatened to limit Turkmenistan's access to the Central Asian gas pipeline, which carries gas shipments to the Russian and Ukrainian markets.

Construction of the Turkmen "lake" pressing ahead.

The planned construction of a new lake in the middle of the Karakum desert is perhaps the most conspicuous of Turkmenistan's state-led infrastructure investments. According to official reports, TMM 42 billion (US$ 80 million at the official exchange rate) has been invested in the project so far in 2002. The lake is due to take in the first flow of drainage water collected in feeder canals by 2004, with an annual inflow target of 10 cubic kilometres. This compares with the water quota of 22 cubic kilometres allocated to Turkmenistan under the water sharing agreements for the Amur Darya. Given the enormous inefficiencies and maintenance problems in the existing irrigation infrastructure, there are doubts over

the project's economic rationale. There are also concerns that inflow targets might be met by increasing Turkmenistan's off-take from the Amur Darya rather than collecting drainage water. Other priority projects in the state-led investment drive are a 650 kilometre highway and railway connection linking Dashoguz in the north to Ashgabat, and several new power plants geared in part for future increased power exports.

Financial institutions

Easing of convertibility restrictions may unblock the EBRD credit line.

Together with some limited bilateral support, the funds extended under the EBRD's SME credit line are virtually the only source of long-term funding for domestic private sector investment. Restricted access to foreign exchange to pay back loans extended under the programme led to its disruption in August 2000. Since early 2002, convertibility restrictions have eased somewhat, raising the possibility of renewed lending later in the year. The vast majority (95 per cent) of bank credits go to state-owned enterprises, with rates often controlled by the government. Most banks are reported to make larger profits through fees charged for foreign exchange operations than from lending operations.

Social reform

Military conscription expanded to absorb the unemployed.

Given Turkmenistan's rapidly growing population, it is becoming increasingly difficult for the 140,000 annual school leavers to find a job. The government's education policy focuses on "training on the job" schemes, rather than enhanced higher education facilities, particularly through the military. Military conscription is planned to include work placements in public services such as train conductors, construction, or even training in technical skills such as electrical engineering. An advantage for the government is that soldiers are paid only minimum salaries and are effectively still supported by their families.

Liberalisation
Current account convertibility – **limited**
Interest rate liberalisation – **limited de jure**
Wage regulation – **yes**

Stabilisation
Share of general government tax revenue
in GDP – **25.2 per cent**
Exchange rate regime – **fixed**

Privatisation
Primary privatisation method – **MEBOs**
Secondary privatisation method –
  direct sales
Tradability of land – **limited de jure**

Enterprises and markets
Competition Office – **no**

Infrastructure
Independent telecoms regulator – **no**
Separation of railway accounts – **no**
Independent electricity regulator – **no**

Financial sector
Capital adequacy ratio – **10 per cent**[1]
Deposit insurance system – **no**
Secured transactions law – **restricted**
Securities commission – **no**

Social reform
Share of the population in poverty –
  34.4 per cent[2]
Private pension funds – **no**

	1993	1994	1995	1996	1997	1998	1999	2000	2001
Liberalisation									
Share of administered prices in CPI (in per cent)	18.8	18.8	18.8	18.8	16.7	6.3	6.4	na	na
Number of goods with administered prices in EBRD-15 basket	6.0	5.0	5.0	5.0	5.0	4.0	4.0	na	na
Share of trade with non-transition countries (in per cent)	na	23.3	31.8	32.4	38.8	72.6	61.0	47.1	42.0
Share of trade in GDP (in per cent)	78.1	184.9	137.2	140.9	72.7	68.1	107.7	162.2	159.7
Tariff revenues (in per cent of imports)[3]	na	na	0.3	0.3	0.4	0.3	0.5	na	na
EBRD index of price liberalisation	1.0	1.7	2.0	2.0	2.0	2.0	2.0	2.0	2.0
EBRD index of forex and trade liberalisation	1.0	1.0	1.0	1.0	1.0	1.0	1.0	1.0	1.0
Privatisation									
Privatisation revenues (cumulative, in per cent of GDP)	na	0.1	0.2	0.2	0.2	0.2	0.3	0.6	0.6
Private sector share in GDP (in per cent)	10.0	15.0	15.0	20.0	25.0	25.0	25.0	25.0	25.0
Private sector share in employment (in per cent)	na	na	na	na	na	na	na	na	na
EBRD index of small-scale privatisation	1.0	1.0	1.7	1.7	2.0	2.0	2.0	2.0	2.0
EBRD index of large-scale privatisation	1.0	1.0	1.0	1.0	2.0	1.7	1.7	1.7	1.0
Enterprises									
Budgetary subsidies and current transfers (in per cent of GDP)	na	1.6	1.7	0.8	0.6	1.6	na	na	na
Effective statutory social security tax (in per cent)	na	na	na	na	na	na	na	na	na
Share of industry in total employment (in per cent)	10.4	10.0	10.1	10.3	11.2	12.5	12.6	na	na
Change in labour productivity in industry (in per cent)	-5.9	-25.9	14.0	25.9	-39.5	11.4	11.0	33.0	na
Investment rate/GDP (in per cent)	na	na	na	na	na	na	na	na	na
EBRD index of enterprise reform	1.0	1.0	1.0	1.0	1.7	1.7	1.7	1.0	1.0
EBRD index of competition policy	1.0	1.0	1.0	1.0	1.0	1.0	1.0	1.0	1.0
Infrastructure									
Main telephone lines per 100 inhabitants	6.8	7.6	7.1	7.4	8.0	8.2	8.2	8.2	8.0
Railway labour productivity (1991=100)	60.4	41.2	34.0	28.7	27.9	27.8	26.9	27.8	24.7
Electricity tariffs, USc kWh (collection rate in per cent)[4]	na	na	na	na	na	0.8 (na)	0.5 (na)	0.5 (30)	0.5 (na)
GDP per unit of energy use (PPP in US dollars per kgoe)	1.8	1.2	1.1	1.2	1.1	1.2	1.2	na	na
EBRD index of infrastructure reform	1.0	1.0	1.0	1.0	1.0	1.0	1.0	1.0	1.0
Financial institutions									
Number of banks (foreign owned)[5]	na	na	67 (3)	68 (4)	67 (4)	13 (4)	13 (4)	13 (4)	13 (4)
Asset share of state-owned banks (in per cent)	na	na	26.1	64.1	68.3	77.8	96.6	97.1	96.5
Non-performing loans (in per cent of total loans)	na	na	11.2	11.4	13.9	2.2	0.5	0.6	0.3
Domestic credit to private sector (in per cent of GDP)[6]	na	na	na	5.7	7.8	9.5	na	2.0	1.9
Stock market capitalisation (in per cent of GDP)	na	na	na	na	na	na	na	na	na
EBRD index of banking sector reform	1.0	1.0	1.0	1.0	1.0	1.0	1.0	1.0	1.0
EBRD index of reform of non-banking financial institutions	1.0	1.0	1.0	1.0	1.0	1.0	1.0	1.0	1.0
Legal environment									
EBRD rating of legal extensiveness (company law)	na	na	na	na	na	na	na	na	2.0
EBRD rating of legal effectiveness (company law)	na	na	na	na	na	na	na	na	3.0
Social sector									
Expenditures on health and education (in per cent of GDP)	6.3	5.3	5.1	4.4	8.0	9.8	7.1	10.8	na
Life expectancy at birth, total (years)	na	na	65.7	na	65.7	na	na	66.3	na
Basic school enrolment ratio (in per cent)	81.8	80.8	81.5	81.0	80.6	79.9	78.9	na	na
Earnings inequality (GINI-coefficient)	na	na	na	na	24.9	20.9	26.5	na	na

[1] Calculated with a risk weight of zero for all loans to state-owned enterprises which are
    thus assumed to be implicitly guaranteed by the state.
[2] 1998 estimate.
[3] Refers to differential excise taxes on imports; Turkmenistan does not levy import tariffs.
[4] Households are entitled to free electricity allowance of 35 kWh per family member per month;
    excess usage is charged at just under 1 US cent per kWh (at the official exchange rate).

[5] The number of banks until 1997 includes all branches of Agricultural Bank.
    In 1998, these were unified into one Agricultural Bank.
[6] Manat credit to state-owned and private firms.

	1994	1995	1996	1997	1998	1999	2000	2001 Estimate	2002 Projection
Output and expenditure					*(Percentage change in real terms)*				
GDP	-17.3	-7.2	-6.7	-11.3	5.0	16.0	17.6	12.0	13.5
Private consumption	na	na	na	na	na	na	na	na	na
Public consumption	na	na	na	na	na	na	na	na	na
Gross fixed investment	na	na	na	na	na	na	na	na	na
Exports of goods and services	na	na	na	na	na	na	na	na	na
Imports of goods and services	na	na	na	na	na	na	na	na	na
Industrial gross output	-27.9	21.4	30.7	-33.0	25.8	13.0	29.0	11.0	na
Agricultural gross output	-17.6	4.5	-45.2	123.7	8.7	35.0	17.0	15.0	na
Employment					*(Percentage change)*				
Labour force (end-year)	2.5	9.2	-0.1	0.2	5.5	-1.6	3.1	5.0	na
Employment (end-year)	1.4	5.0	1.8	2.0	1.3	0.7	na	na	na
					(In per cent of labour force)				
Unemployment[1]	na	na	na	na	na	na	na	na	na
Prices and wages					*(Percentage change)*				
Consumer prices (annual average)	1,748.0	1,005.3	992.4	83.7	16.8	24.2	8.3	11.6	9.6
Consumer prices (end-year)	1,327.9	1,261.5	445.8	21.5	19.8	21.2	7.4	11.7	9.5
Producer prices (annual average)	na	na	na	na	na	na	na	na	na
Producer prices (end-year)	na	1,293.0	na	na	10.3	na	na	na	na
Gross average monthly earnings in economy (annual average)	587.7	639.8	757.1	220.0	46.3	21.9	60.3	35.0	na
Government sector[2]					*(In per cent of GDP)*				
General government balance	-2.3	-2.6	0.3	0.0	-2.6	0.0	0.4	0.8	-2.0
General government expenditure	19.2	23.1	16.3	25.3	24.6	19.4	25.3	24.4	na
General government debt	na	na	na	na	na	na	na	na	na
Monetary sector					*(Percentage change)*				
Broad money (M3, end-year)	983.9	448.0	411.7	81.2	83.2	22.6	81.9	17.5	na
Domestic credit (end-year)	915.0	402.8	1,389.3	88.4	77.8	24.6	24.4	15.0	na
					(In per cent of GDP)				
Broad money (M3, end-year)	25.6	18.8	8.1	10.2	14.9	12.7	20.3	18.1	na
Interest and exchange rates					*(In per cent per annum, end-year)*				
Refinance rate	50.0	15.0	105.0	35.0	30.0	27.0	20.0	12.0	na
Inter-bank market rate	na	55.0	121.4	45.2	30.0	27.0	15.0	7.7	na
Deposit rate (1 year)[3]	206.0	80.0	130.0	41.1	24.2	27.1	na	na	na
Lending rate (1 year)[3]	300.0	70.0	200.0	52.6	58.6	41.8	11.3	na	na
					(Manats per US dollar)				
Exchange rate (end-year)[4]	75	2,442	5,126	5,222	8,148	8,200	9,790	10,060	na
Exchange rate (annual average)[4]	42	240	3,546	4,627	5,500	8,524	9,013	10,158	na
External sector					*(In millions of US dollars)*				
Current account	84	24	2	-608	-952	-583	386	-74	30
Trade balance	485	441	304	-259	-539	-210	644	325	450
Merchandise exports	2,176	2,084	1,692	743	597	1,162	2,383	2,526	2,800
Merchandise imports	1,691	1,644	1,388	1,003	1,136	1,372	1,739	2,201	2,350
Foreign direct investment, net	103	233	108	108	62	125	126	133	150
Gross reserves (end-year), excluding gold[5]	927	1,165	1,172	1,285	1,379	1,555	1,808	2,055	na
External debt stock	418	550	668	1,356	1,749	2,047	2,230	2,400	na
					(In months of imports of goods and services)				
Gross reserves (end-year), excluding gold[5]	4.5	5.8	7.0	9.2	9.0	9.1	9.3	8.8	na
					(In per cent of exports of goods and services)				
Debt service	1.7	11.7	13.6	28.1	41.0	38.6	18.7	30.9	na
Memorandum items					*(Denominations as indicated)*				
Population (end-year, millions)	4.0	4.6	4.7	4.9	5.0	5.2	5.4	5.6	na
GDP (in millions of manats)	87,200	652,000	7,751,700	11,108,800	13,995,000	20,056,000	22,900,000	30,062,905	39,276,260
GDP per capita (in US dollars)	517.0	591.9	464.1	495.1	509.9	452.5	473.3	524.8	na
Share of industry in GDP (in per cent)	38.1	52.8	54.4	32.9	27.6	32.0	38.0	37.0	na
Share of agriculture in GDP (in per cent)	32.7	16.2	12.6	20.2	25.2	27.0	26.0	23.0	na
Current account/GDP (in per cent)	4.0	0.9	0.1	-25.3	-37.4	-24.8	15.2	-2.5	0.8
External debt - reserves, in US$ millions	-509.0	-615.0	-504.0	70.5	370.0	492.0	422.0	345.0	na
External debt/GDP (in per cent)	20.0	20.2	30.6	56.5	68.7	87.0	87.8	81.1	na
External debt/exports of goods and services (in per cent)	16.9	22.9	33.5	133.5	209.9	150.3	84.2	86.4	na

Note: Data dissemination by Turkmen authorities has become increasingly restrictive. Recent data are, therefore, subject to considerable uncertainty. Data for 2002 are EBRD estimates.

[1] Every Turkmen citizen is guaranteed employment. Therefore, official unemployment does not exist. According to a household survey, unemployment was 19 per cent in 1998.

[2] Significant off-budget expenditures occur through extra-budgetary funds and directed lending. The overall public sector borrowing requirement has been estimated at 8 per cent of GDP in 2001.

[3] Deposit and lending rates are quoted for legal entities at joint-stock banks. For 1996-99, data are average for loans and deposits of three to six months' maturity. Lending and deposit rates for 1993-96 are the highest of the total range. All interest rates are annual uncompounded.

[4] Turkmenistan operates a dual exchange rate system. The series refers to a weighted average between the official exchange rate and the commercial rate, given as the buying rate offered at commercial banks until September 1998 and the black market rate thereafter. Weights are variable depending on the relative size of official and shuttle trade.

[5] Foreign exchange reserves of the Central Bank plus the foreign exchange reserve fund.

Ukraine

Liberalisation

Progress on accession to the WTO remains slow.

In February 2002, a presidential decree outlining the measures required to accelerate Ukraine's accession into the WTO was announced and in July the President passed a revised version of the customs code, further extending the powers of the Customs Service. The law, to take effect at the beginning of 2003, will enable the Service to check the business activities of enterprises engaged in international trade. However, the process of harmonising national laws and regulations with WTO requirements remains incomplete. The government also needs to complete negotiations on the bilateral protocols relating to market access and to resolve the dispute over intellectual property rights of US producers of media products. Although the Rada approved a law to combat media piracy in January (which took effect in May), the US trade representative claimed the law was inadequate and imposed trade sanctions on some Ukraine exports to the United States.

Stabilisation

New tax code yet to be approved.

A new tax code failed to pass its third reading in December 2001 because, in part, of concerns that the proposed lower tax rates under the "small tax code" could result in an initial fall in total revenues. The government concluded that while lower rates would improve incentives, the tax base had to be broadened, including fewer tax exemptions. A further concern has been the growth in tax arrears to almost UAH 10 billion (US$ 1.8 billion) by mid 2002 after the tax amnesty of 2001. In recent months, the Rada has reviewed government proposals to amend specific tax legislation, including the laws relating to both VAT and corporate tax.

Privatisation

Large-scale privatisations delayed.

In 2001, the State Property Fund (SPF) sold stakes in 1,658 entities, mainly at auctions. Almost half of these were small-scale privatisations, while just 86 were large-scale privatisations. As a result, the proceeds amounted to only UAH 2.2 billion (US$ 410 million), less than 40 per cent of the original target. At the beginning of 2002, the government announced its intention to continue with the large-scale privatisation programme and raise UAH 5.8 billion (US$ 1.1 billion) for the budget. Originally, the intention was to sell the remaining power distribution companies, Ukrtelecom and stakes in a number of strategic industrial companies. However, delays to the privatisation of the utilities led the SPF in July to revise its estimate for privatisation receipts to just UAH 1 billion (US$ 190 million) with greater emphasis on selling the stakes in the industrial enterprises. Small-scale privatisation has continued with over 64,000 such enterprises privatised by the first quarter of 2002.

New land code confirms the principle of private land ownership.

The new land code, which took effect at the beginning of 2002, allows for the sale of agricultural land from 2005. The lag was introduced to give the authorities time to develop the necessary procedures and institutions to enable a land market to function. These include establishing a land registry, approving procedures for assessing land use and commencing land valuations. One of the main benefits of the new land code will be to allow the use of land as collateral, thereby attracting additional finance to this sector. By July, 42 per cent of land owners had completed the formal registration of ownership of their plots. Although foreigners may not own agricultural land, they can own industrial land on which their enterprises are located.

Enterprise reform

Approval of the civil and commercial codes delayed.

Progress with legislation to improve the business environment has been mixed. The President did not approve either the civil or commercial codes that the Rada had passed towards the end of 2001, even though the former had provided a more market-oriented legal framework for the operations of both private and state-owned enterprises.

Liberalisation, stabilisation, privatisation

1994
Oct	Most prices liberalised
Oct	Most export quotas and licences abolished
Oct	Exchange rate unified
Nov	Voucher privatisation begins

1995
Jan	New corporate profits tax introduced
Mar	Treasury bills market initiated
Dec	Indicative export prices removed

1996
Jan	Licensing requirement for grain exports abolished
Sep	New currency (hryvnia) introduced

1997
Apr	Full current account convertibility introduced
Jun	Export surrender requirement revoked
Jul	New corporate tax rate introduced
Oct	VAT rate changed

1998
Mar	Limits on auto imports imposed
Sep	Foreign exchange restrictions re-introduced
Sep	Currency band widened
Sep	Domestic debt rescheduling starts
Dec	Agricultural sector given VAT exemption

1999
Feb	Currency band widened further
Mar	Inter-bank currency market liberalised
Jun	New Central Bank law approved
Dec	Presidential decree on reform of agricultural collectives issued

2000
Feb	Introduction of floating exchange rate regime confirmed
Mar	Commercial debt rescheduling agreement signed

2001
Jan	National programme for SME support initiated
Jan	VAT exemption for agricultural products extended
Feb	Law on settlement of tax liabilities signed
Jul	External debt restructuring agreement signed
Jul	Budget code enacted

2002
Feb	Amended law on competition policy enacted
Jul	Revised customs code signed by President

Enterprises, infrastructure, finance and social reforms

1992
Feb	Competition agency established
May	Bankruptcy law adopted
Jun	Stock exchange begins trading

1995
Jun	Securities and Exchange Commission established

1996
Mar	Grado Bank placed under forced administration

1997
Mar	Land code amended
Aug	First sovereign Eurobond issued

1998
Jan	IAS introduced for commercial banks
May	Limits on foreign ownership of banks lifted

1999
Apr	Utility tariffs increased
Jul	Law on concessions adopted
Aug	Presidential decree on privatisation of electric power utilities issued
Oct	Law on production sharing agreement adopted

2000
Jan	New bankruptcy law adopted
Feb	Law providing tax breaks to joint ventures repealed
Jun	Law on payments reform in the electricity sector adopted
Jul	Law on telecommunications privatisation enacted
Jul	Presidential decree on development of the banking sector issued
Oct	Rights of minority shareholders improved, following adoption of Securities Commission regulation
Dec	Law on banks and banking approved by Rada
Dec	Chernobyl nuclear plant closed

2001
Apr	Majority stakes in six power utilities sold to strategic investors
Apr	Law on mutual investment institutions adopted
Jul	Licence of Bank Ukraina withdrawn
Jul	Presidential decree on measures to improve investment climate issued
Sep	Law on individual deposit insurance adopted
Dec	Poverty alleviation strategy approved

2002
Jan	Land code adopted

Monetisation in the economy increased.
Cash collections have continued to improve in the energy sector. In the gas sector, the majority of collections were in cash in 2001. The share of barter in industrial sales has continued to fall, amounting to 8 per cent by the end of 2001, compared with 33 per cent two years earlier. At the same time, the amount of overdue enterprise receivables has fallen as a share of GDP. More monetisation should contribute to greater efficiency in the conduct of economic transactions.

Government promotes small businesses.
In September 2001, the government announced a programme to develop small businesses, including UAH 49 million (US$ 9 million) to support micro businesses and a network of regional funds to finance business development, especially in the coal mining areas. The small business sector has continued to develop, assisted by a unified tax scheme. In July, the President requested the government prepare legislation to further reduce the burden of regulation and taxation on the sector. According to official data, there are some 220,000 such companies (excluding those owned by natural persons) accounting for 5.2 per cent of total output and 9.3 per cent of employment.

Infrastructure

Privatisation of Ukrtelecom requires progress with regulation.
Following the completion of sales of preferred stock in the telecommunications utility to employees, the government agreed that a further 42.9 per cent share could be sold to a consortium of strategic and financial investors. The government listed the criteria for strategic investors and, at the end of July, also introduced some tariff revisions. In August, however, partly because of the difficult market conditions in the sector, the SPF confirmed that the privatisation would be postponed until next year. Progress now depends on approving legislation to establish a suitable regulatory framework and on completing a comprehensive audit of the utility.

Government meets its obligations to strategic investors in the power sector ...
Electricity tariffs for industrial consumers were raised by at least 8 per cent at the end of 2001, thereby meeting one of the commitments to investors who participated in the first round of privatisations in April 2001. However, tariffs for residential consumers were not changed and substantial cross-subsidisation of residential consumers by industrial users persists. In July, however, the National Electricity Regulation Commission proposed that tariffs for residential users should be raised from 2003. Cash collections in the Energomarket have continued to improve, increasing to an average of 76 per cent by the end of June this year, compared with 66 per cent for 2001 as a whole.

... but the next stage of privatisation has been delayed.
Towards the end of 2001, the government decided to proceed with the sale of controlling stakes (to strategic investors) in nine of the 12 regional power distribution companies that remain under state ownership. In July, the government confirmed the tender terms for the sale. However, most of the companies have substantial debts and in August the SPF confirmed that the sales would be delayed until the debt problems have been resolved. The government also plans to sell 25 per cent stakes, on the stock exchange, of five of the first seven power companies that were privatised to domestic financial investors in 1998.

Financial institutions

Banking regulation strengthened, but further consolidation is required.
There were some positive regulatory developments during 2001, including a strengthening of the supervisory powers of the National Bank of Ukraine (NBU). From October 2001, the deposit insurance scheme was extended to banks other than the Savings Bank and, from this year, the amount covered was increased to UAH 1,200 (US$ 225). By August, 149 banks had joined the Individual Deposit Guarantee Fund. In 2001, there was further rapid growth in credit to the private sector (an increase of over 40 per cent). However, inadequate collateral limited the access some borrowers had to these loans. As a result, the sector's capital base remains small. In May, there were still 154 licensed banks (excluding those undergoing liquidation) with the seven largest banks (including the two state-owned banks) accounting for almost half the assets. More bank mergers are likely as all banks must comply with the current capital requirements (between €1-5 million depending on the type of bank) by January 2003.

Social reform

Alleviating poverty a main objective.
About 27 per cent of the population remain below the national poverty line, according to official data. Progress has been made in lowering the outstanding stock of wage arrears, which fell from UAH 4.5 billion (US$ 840 million) in April 2001 to UAH 2.5 billion (US$ 470 million) in August 2002. The government has also developed proposals to reform funding of the social sector, which are to be implemented by 2006. These include improving the targeting of social benefits, which currently cover over 40 per cent of the population. Draft laws on pension reform passed their first reading last year.

Liberalisation

Current account convertibility – **full**

Interest rate liberalisation – **full**

Wage regulation – **no**

Stabilisation

Share of general government tax revenue in GDP – **27.1 per cent (excluding pension fund)**

Exchange rate regime – **managed float**

Privatisation

Primary privatisation method – **vouchers**

Secondary privatisation method – **MEBOs**

Tradability of land – **limited de facto**

Enterprises and markets

Competition Office – **yes**

Infrastructure

Independent telecoms regulator – **no**

Separation of railway accounts – **no**

Independent electricity regulator – **yes**

Financial sector

Capital adequacy ratio – **8 per cent**

Deposit insurance system – **yes**

Secured transactions law – **yes**

Securities commission – **yes**

Social reform

Share of the population in poverty – **27.2 per cent**[1]

Private pension funds – **yes**[2]

	1993	1994	1995	1996	1997	1998	1999	2000	2001
Liberalisation									
Share of administered prices in CPI (in per cent)	na	na	na	na	na	na	na	na	na
Number of goods with administered prices in EBRD-15 basket	11.0	6.0	2.0	2.0	2.0	2.0	na	na	na
Share of trade with non-transition countries (in per cent)	na	38.7	40.3	45.5	57.1	53.6	57.4	52.0	49.6
Share of trade in GDP (in per cent)	85.1	82.8	84.1	79.4	69.9	71.7	80.4	98.1	90.4
Tariff revenues (in per cent of imports)[3]	1.2	1.1	1.7	1.2	1.9	2.4	2.3	na	na
EBRD index of price liberalisation	1.0	2.0	3.0	3.0	3.0	3.0	3.0	3.0	3.0
EBRD index of forex and trade liberalisation	1.0	1.0	3.0	3.0	3.0	2.7	3.0	3.0	3.0
Privatisation									
Privatisation revenues (cumulative, in per cent of GDP)	1.3	1.3	1.4	1.7	1.8	2.3	2.9	4.3	5.5
Private sector share in GDP (in per cent)	15.0	40.0	45.0	50.0	55.0	55.0	55.0	60.0	60.0
Private sector share in employment (in per cent)	na	na	na	na	na	na	na	na	na
EBRD index of small-scale privatisation	2.0	2.0	2.0	3.0	3.3	3.3	3.3	3.3	3.3
EBRD index of large-scale privatisation	1.0	1.0	2.0	2.0	2.3	2.3	2.3	2.7	3.0
Enterprises									
Budgetary subsidies and current transfers (in per cent of GDP)[4]	na	13.3	5.8	6.5	5.0	na	na	na	na
Effective statutory social security tax (in per cent)	81.2	88.5	79.4	78.7	79.9	76.7	80.2	na	na
Share of industry in total employment (in per cent)	29.3	28.2	26.2	25.6	24.6	21.2	19.9	19.3	na
Change in labour productivity in industry (in per cent)	-3.0	-20.3	-4.5	2.5	7.3	2.1	13.7	19.2	na
Investment rate/GDP (in per cent)	24.3	25.5	23.3	20.7	19.8	19.3	na	na	na
EBRD index of enterprise reform	1.0	1.0	2.0	2.0	2.0	2.0	2.0	2.0	2.0
EBRD index of competition policy	2.0	2.0	2.0	2.0	2.3	2.3	2.3	2.3	2.3
Infrastructure									
Main telephone lines per 100 inhabitants	15.2	15.7	16.1	18.1	18.5	19.1	19.9	20.7	21.2
Railway labour productivity (1989=100)	53.3	46.9	46.1	40.7	42.4	42.2	41.7	44.9	46.5
Electricity tariffs, USc kWh (collection rate in per cent)	na	na (60)	na (65)	2.46 (70)	3.13 (80)	2.89 (79)	2.25 (84)	2.0 (na)	2.21 (78)
GDP per unit of energy use (PPP in US dollars per kgoe)	1.4	1.3	1.2	1.1	1.2	1.2	1.2	na	na
EBRD index of infrastructure reform	1.0	1.0	1.0	1.0	1.3	1.3	1.3	2.0	2.0
Financial institutions									
Number of banks (foreign owned)	211 (na)	228 (1)	230 (1)	229 (6)	227 (12)	175 (12)	161 (15)	154 (14)	152 (16)
Asset share of state-owned banks (in per cent)	na	na	na	na	13.5	13.7	12.5	11.9	11.8
Non-performing loans (in per cent of total loans)[5]	na	na	na	na	na	34.6	34.2	32.5	na
Domestic credit to private sector (in per cent of GDP)	1.4	4.6	1.5	1.4	2.5	7.8	8.6	9.9	12.0
Stock market capitalisation (in per cent of GDP)[6]	na	na	na	na	7.4	1.9	4.5	6.0	3.6
EBRD index of banking sector reform	1.0	1.0	2.0	2.0	2.0	2.0	2.0	2.0	2.0
EBRD index of reform of non-banking financial institutions	1.7	1.7	2.0	2.0	2.0	2.0	2.0	2.0	2.0
Legal environment									
EBRD rating of legal extensiveness (company law)	na	na	na	na	2.0	2.0	2.0	3.3	3.3
EBRD rating of legal effectiveness (company law)	na	na	na	na	2.0	2.0	2.0	2.0	3.0
Social sector									
Expenditures on health and education (in per cent of GDP)	8.5	10.1	10.0	8.7	9.5	7.9	6.6	7.1	na
Life expectancy at birth, total (years)	67.9	67.9	67.1	67.3	67.3	68.2	68.2	68.3	na
Basic school enrolment ratio (in per cent)	91.0	90.7	90.9	90.8	90.2	89.0	na	na	na
Earnings inequality (GINI-coefficient)	36.4	na	na	41.3	40.6	39.1	42.7	46.2	na

[1] Based on an international poverty line. The poverty rate based on the national poverty line is 26.7 per cent.

[2] Private pension funds are unregulated.

[3] Refers to taxes on international trade and transactions.

[4] Refers to consumer and producer subsidies.

[5] Changes in non-performing loans data compared with previous *Transition Reports* are due to the change of loan categories included in non-performing loans (see definitions).

[6] Data from Stock Market Survey.

	1994	1995	1996	1997	1998	1999	2000	2001	2002
								Estimate	Projection
Output and expenditure					*(Percentage change in real terms)*				
GDP	-22.9	-12.2	-10.0	-3.0	-1.9	-0.2	5.9	9.1	4.5
Private consumption	na	5.1	-9.5	-1.6	1.3	-2.2	2.3	8.9	na
Public consumption	na	-0.3	-5.4	-2.3	-3.5	-7.9	1.0	9.0	na
Total investment	na	-11.3	-25.7	2.1	2.6	0.1	12.4	8.3	na
Exports of goods and services	na	-16.9	16.9	-5.4	1.2	-2.2	21.5	2.9	na
Imports of goods and services	na	20.0	15.8	-4.6	2.0	-16.7	23.8	2.2	na
Industrial gross output	-27.3	-12.0	-5.1	-1.8	-1.0	4.3	12.5	14.2	na
Agricultural gross output	-16.5	-3.6	-9.5	-1.9	-9.8	-5.7	7.6	10.2	na
Employment					*(Percentage change)*				
Labour force (end-year)	0.1	2.4	-0.7	-0.5	0.4	0.3	0.1	-0.7	na
Employment (end-year)	-3.8	3.0	-2.1	-2.7	-1.1	-2.4	-2.5	-0.9	na
					(In per cent of labour force)				
Unemployment (end-year)	0.3	0.3	1.3	2.3	3.7	4.3	4.2	3.7	na
Prices and wages					*(Percentage change)*				
Consumer prices (annual average)	891.0	377.0	80.0	15.9	10.5	22.7	28.2	12.0	1.6
Consumer prices (end-year)	401.0	181.7	39.7	10.1	20.0	19.2	25.8	6.1	3.0
Producer prices (annual average)	1,144.0	488.0	52.0	7.7	13.2	32.0	20.9	8.9	na
Producer prices (end-year)	774.0	172.0	17.3	5.0	35.4	15.7	20.8	0.9	na
Gross average monthly earnings in economy (annual average)	786.1	483.9	71.4	13.3	7.2	6.3	29.2	35.2	na
Government sector [1]					*(In per cent of GDP)*				
General government balance	-8.7	-6.1	-3.2	-5.4	-2.8	-2.4	-1.3	-1.6	-1.8
General government expenditure	50.6	37.8	39.9	44.2	38.7	36.1	36.4	36.6	na
General government debt	na	26.7	22.7	26.6	45.7	55.3	45.6	38.5	na
Monetary sector					*(Percentage change)*				
Broad money (M2, end-year)	567.0	113.0	36.6	33.9	25.3	40.4	45.4	42.0	na
Domestic credit (end-year)	539.9	191.2	42.3	32.5	47.1	38.0	23.5	18.9	na
					(In per cent of GDP)				
Broad money (M2, end-year)	26.8	12.6	11.5	13.4	15.3	16.9	18.5	21.9	na
Interest and exchange rates					*(In per cent per annum, end-year)*				
Refinancing rate	252.0	110.0	40.0	35.0	60.0	45.0	27.0	12.5	na
Treasury bill rate (3-month maturity) [2]	na	164.0	51.0	22.1	40.0	45.0	18.0	17.1	na
Deposit rate [3]	209.0	70.0	34.0	18.0	22.0	21.0	14.0	10.8	na
Lending rate [3]	250.0	123.0	80.0	49.0	55.0	55.0	42.0	29.6	na
					(Hryvnas per US dollar)				
Exchange rate (end-year) [4]	1.04	1.79	1.89	1.90	3.43	5.22	5.44	5.29	na
Exchange rate (annual average) [4]	0.33	1.47	1.83	1.86	2.45	4.13	5.44	5.37	na
External sector					*(In millions of US dollars)*				
Current account	-1,163	-1,152	-1,185	-1,335	-1,296	834	1,481	1,402	1,600
Trade balance	-2,575	-2,702	-4,296	-4,205	-2,584	-482	779	198	100
Merchandise exports	13,894	14,244	15,547	15,418	13,699	12,463	15,722	17,091	17,800
Merchandise imports	16,469	16,946	19,843	19,623	16,283	12,945	14,943	16,893	17,700
Foreign direct investment, net	151	257	516	581	747	489	594	769	750
Gross reserves (end-year), excluding gold	651	1,051	1,960	2,341	761	1,046	1,353	2,956	na
External debt stock	5,164	8,025	9,003	10,017	12,364	13,549	11,821	11,831	na
					(In months of imports of goods and services)				
Gross reserves (end-year), excluding gold	0.4	0.7	1.1	1.3	0.5	0.8	0.9	1.7	na
					(In per cent of exports of goods and services)				
Debt service	11.2	8.0	6.6	7.5	11.2	16.6	10.0	8.1	na
Memorandum items					*(Denominations as indicated)*				
Population (end-year, millions)	51.7	51.5	51.3	50.9	50.5	50.1	49.3	49.0	na
GDP (in millions of hryvnas)	12,038	54,516	81,519	93,365	102,593	130,442	170,070	201,927	214,390
GDP per capita (in US dollars)	456	720	869	985	828	631	634	767	na
Share of industry in GDP (in per cent)	30.0	34.4	na	34.3	35.4	38.4	38.5	38.2	na
Share of agriculture in GDP (in per cent)	16.0	14.5	12.2	14.4	14.2	12.8	12.5	12.5	na
Current account/GDP (in per cent)	-4.9	-3.1	-2.7	-2.7	-3.1	2.6	4.7	3.7	4.0
External debt - reserves, in US$ millions	4,513	6,974	7,043	7,676	11,603	12,503	10,468	8,875	na
External debt/GDP (in per cent)	21.9	21.6	20.2	20.0	29.6	42.9	37.8	31.5	na
External debt/exports of goods and services (in per cent)	31.0	47.0	44.2	49.2	70.2	83.0	60.6	56.1	na

[1] General government includes the state, municipalities and, from 1994, extra-budgetary funds.
Data are on a cash basis until 1995, and on an accrual basis thereafter.
[2] Treasury bills were introduced in March 1995.

[3] Weighted average over all maturities.
[4] The hryvna replaced the karbovanets in September 1996, but the rates prior to 1996 are shown in hryvna for convenience.

Uzbekistan

Key reform challenges

- **The full liberalisation of the foreign exchange market remains the key policy challenge to kick-starting structural reforms, attracting more private investment and creating sustainable growth.**

- **Currency convertibility will need to be supported by tight budget management and significant reductions in quasi-fiscal deficits, as well as accelerated privatisation and agricultural reforms to spur productivity improvements.**

- **The banking system must be restructured to deal with the overhang of state-directed credits, increase the demand for domestic currency and encourage domestic saving.**

Liberalisation

Some progress towards foreign exchange convertibility, but more remains to be done.

Since January this year, the authorities have been working with the IMF under a Staff Monitored Programme (SMP). While the Uzbek authorities have observed the monetary and fiscal targets set in the programme, the IMF was less satisfied with progress on structural reforms relating to cotton procurement, the abolition of cash withdrawal limits in the banking sector and the foreign trade regime. Following the completion of the SMP in August, the IMF sent a mission to Uzbekistan in September. Upon the mission's conclusion, the IMF announced that it would not begin discussing a stand-by facility with the country until the currency market had been fully liberalised.

Concerns remain over the sustainability of present policies.

The recent reduction in the wedge between the official and black market exchange rates has been achieved, to a large extent, through lower cash emissions and tighter monetary policy rather than liberalising the foreign exchange market. Uzbekistan maintains tight controls on cash withdrawals from banks by companies. This has allowed the authorities to liberalise the cash market while keeping a separate exchange rate for non-cash transactions. The "cash" rate stood at around UZS 1,060/US$ at the end of September 2002, close to the black market rate of UZS 1,110/US$. The "non-cash" rate was around UZS 800/US$.

Trade restrictions move away from rationing to tariffs.

The list of consumer good imports for which no foreign currency is available through official channels was abolished in June 2002 and the number of goods that cannot be exported was reduced. The system of import registration has also been changed, reducing direct state control. However, a flat 30 per cent ad valorem tariff was introduced in July for imports by legal entities of non-food consumer goods and barter payment was disallowed. The authorities have also imposed a punitive tax on individual "shuttle" trade

transactions of up to 70 per cent. The state procurement of cotton and grain has been changed to 50 per cent of the actual harvest, rather than 50 per cent of the (usually over-optimistic) output target and the prices paid by the state are now linked to world market prices. However, the extent to which these changes have been implemented for the 2002 harvest remains unclear.

Stabilisation

Budget transfers cushion the impact of devaluation ...

The depreciation of the official exchange rates throughout the year has increased debt servicing costs both for the budget and for companies with foreign debt. To date, government assistance to these companies in 2002 has run up to UZS 22.5 billion (US$ 24 million) or about 1 per cent of GDP. The authorities have committed themselves to limit transfers to UZS 40.5 billion (US$ 43 million) for the year and phase them out over time. Public sector wages, pensions and social assistance were increased by 15 per cent in April and by another 15 per cent in August. These payments are expected to push up the budget deficit to a projected 3.0 per cent of GDP. Given the slow progress of negotiations with the IMF, it is not clear how the deficit will be financed without recourse to monetary financing.

... but highlight the need for fundamental budgetary reforms.

Public finances continue to be characterised by significant quasi-fiscal operations and the direct control of enterprise cash flows. The abolition of implicit subsidies through trade and exchange rate liberalisation and the planned reforms in the agricultural and banking sectors will necessitate thorough budgetary reform to maintain fiscal balance. As an initial reform step, a budget system law has been passed and there are plans to create a Treasury to improve public cash management. Starting in 2002, profit and personal income taxes were lowered, agricultural taxes were unified into a single land tax and private pre-shipment customs inspections were established. Major outstanding challenges include the clarification of fiscal

relations with the regions, the shift from direct to indirect taxes and the improved collection of income tax.

Privatisation

Privatisation plans dependent on foreign exchange convertibility.

Faced with difficulties in repatriating profits, long delays in obtaining vital inputs and a generally difficult investment climate, many foreign investors have left Uzbekistan over the last few years. Investor interest would

Liberalisation, stabilisation, privatisation

1991
Sep	Independence from Soviet Union declared

1994
Jan	New currency (som) introduced
May	Foreign investment law adopted

1995
May	Foreign investment law amended
Oct	IMF programme adopted

1996
Jun	Privatisation programme adopted
Oct	IMF programme suspended

1997
Nov	Custom duties and export licensing abolished; tariffs increased
Dec	Customs code enacted

1998
Jan	Tax code enacted
Feb	Import tariffs further increased
Dec	Tender for six large enterprises announced

1999
Jan	Export surrender increased to 50 per cent
Feb	Trade barriers against Kazakh and Kyrgyz imports introduced
Jun	Tender for large copper plant cancelled
Jul	EU partnership and cooperation agreement adopted
Dec	New privatisation programme for 27 large enterprises initiated

2000
May	Two administrative exchange rates unified
Jun	Access to subsidised hard currency restricted

2002
Apr	Cash currency market partially liberalised

Enterprises, infrastructure, finance and social reforms

1990
Jun   Decree on joint-stock companies adopted

1991
Feb   Company law adopted

1992
Jul   Competition law adopted
Dec   Pledge law adopted

1993
Sep   Securities law adopted

1994
Apr   Stock exchange established
May   Bankruptcy law adopted
Jul   Decree on securities market issued

1995
Aug   Telecommunications law adopted

1996
Mar   First Treasury bills issued
Apr   Banking law adopted
Apr   Land law amended
Aug   Bankruptcy law amended

1997
Mar   Bank accounting standards adopted

1998
Aug   Law on depositories enacted
Oct   Presidential decree to reform commercial banks issued

1999
Apr   Largest commercial bank partially privatised

2000
Jul   National and international telecommunications companies merged

2001
Mar   State railway company restructured

recover, however, if convertibility were achieved, allowing the privatisation programme to accelerate. A new privatisation plan for the sale of 38 large companies was adopted in March 2001. So far, majority stakes in two of the listed companies, Andizhankabel and AO Foton, have been sold to Russian investors. Privatisation advisers have been hired for another nine companies, including Commerzbank for the privatisation of Uztelekom, BNP Paribas for the gas company Uzbekneftegaz, Raiffeisen for Uzbekkabel and Maxwell Stamp for the chemical company Uzkhimprom.

Enterprise reform

State procurement of cotton and grain to move closer to market principles.
The changes in state procurement policies, if fully implemented and combined with convertibility, should improve terms of trade for cotton and grain farmers in 2003. However, for the reforms to really take effect, the dominance of state-owned farms will need to be reduced. The government has reorganised the former sovkhozes and kolkhozes into new forms of collective farms (shirkats), whose subdivisions are farmed by extended families. The former household plots of farm labourers have been turned into peasant farms (dekhan), which have become the main source of dynamism in the agricultural sector. In 2000, the government exempted the export of fruits and vegetables from foreign exchange surrender requirements and this has markedly boosted export earnings.

Improvements in the business climate spur SME growth.
Although small and medium-sized enterprise (SME) development has for several years been a policy priority, the number of SMEs fell during 1997–99, due to the weak investment climate. Factors contributing to this fall included limited access to foreign exchange, discretionary government intervention and large market distortions. Since 2000, reporting requirements have been reduced, as have the number of regulatory authorities and inspections. Taxes have been simplified and foreign exchange surrender requirements eliminated for SME exports. In addition, a large increase in subsidised credit has been directed towards SMEs and, in June 2002, some restrictions on cash withdrawals from bank accounts were lifted for microenterprises. These measures have resulted in a large increase in the number of registered SMEs, although consolidation is likely once convertibility is introduced.

Infrastructure

Water sector reforms spearhead commercialisation in public utilities ...
In the water supply and waste-water sector, progress has been made on decentralisation and private sector participation. The metering of water consumption has been introduced. The government has decentralised the management of urban water utilities to the municipalities and has outlined new principles for tariff setting. Some municipalities have started implementing these measures by completing corporate development plans and introducing new tariff policies. This has resulted in sharp hikes in residential tariffs (four- to five-fold since early 1999), reduced cross-subsidies and improved collection rates. However, the agriculture irrigation sector, the dominant water consumer, remains unreformed.

... while the transport sector also sees improvements.
The regulatory and operational responsibilities for urban transport services have been separated and competition has been introduced through a programme of bus route franchising. Restructuring of the railway Uztemiryollari (UTY) has continued with the spin off of non-core businesses, labour retrenchment and the rationalisation of tariffs. The corporatisation of UTY and its subsidiaries has also begun. In road and air transport, the focus has been on the modernisation of air traffic control, airline equipment and airport facilities, the rehabilitation of several trunk roads and the construction of a key road link to the Fergana valley. However, apart from urban transport, the transport sector is still dominated by state-owned enterprises and there is no appropriate financial, regulatory or institutional framework for the competitive provision of transport services.

Financial institutions

Steps taken to strengthen banking regulation and to reduce directed credits.
Restrictions to limit legal entities to just one bank account have been lifted, a computerised inter-bank payments system has been introduced, international accounting standards have been adopted and an increasing number of banks have undergone independent audits. The government has set a timetable to phase out bank cross-shareholdings, reduce limits on bank ownership by enterprises and increase minimum capital requirements. The sale of significant state shares in the two largest banks, National Bank of Uzbekistan and Asaka Bank, is also being prepared but privatisation will be difficult until the currency and credit markets are further liberalised. Directed credits through the state banks have in principle been phased out under the SMP. However, restrictions on cash withdrawals from enterprise bank accounts severely constrain financial intermediation, encourage informal transactions outside the banking system and impose high monitoring costs.

Social reform

Poverty remains concentrated in rural areas.
Around 31 per cent of the population are estimated to live in poverty. The incidence of poverty is highest in rural areas, where two-thirds of poor households are located, and in western regions such as Karakalpakstan and Khorezm. A group that is relatively well protected is pensioners, who receive substantial transfers. However, the cost of this safety net is high. Pension spending is around 7 per cent of GDP and payroll taxes to finance pensions represent almost 40 per cent of salaries. Compliance rates are correspondingly low, placing an even higher burden on those who do contribute.

Liberalisation
Current account convertibility – **limited**
Interest rate liberalisation –
 limited de facto
Wage regulation – **yes**

Stabilisation
Share of general government tax revenue
 in GDP – **32 per cent**
Exchange rate regime – **multiple
 exchange rates**

Privatisation
Primary privatisation method – **MEBOs**
Secondary privatisation method –
 direct sales
Tradability of land – **limited de jure**

Enterprises and markets
Competition Office – **yes**

Infrastructure
Independent telecoms regulator – **no**
Separation of railway accounts – **yes**
Independent electricity regulator – **no**

Financial sector
Capital adequacy ratio – **8 per cent**
Deposit insurance system – **no**
Secured transactions law – **yes**
Securities commission – **yes**

Social reform
Share of the population in poverty –
 31 per cent [1]
Private pension funds – **no**

	1993	1994	1995	1996	1997	1998	1999	2000	2001
Liberalisation									
Share of administered prices in CPI (in per cent)	na	na	na	na	na	na	na	na	na
Number of goods with administered prices in EBRD-15 basket	5.0	5.0	1.0	1.0	1.0	na	na	na	na
Share of trade with non-transition countries (in per cent)	na	45.6	34.9	47.3	38.2	47.4	53.5	37.8	46.8
Share of trade in GDP (in per cent)	120.4	99.6	73.2	62.1	69.3	52.2	65.0	81.4	86.8
Tariff revenues (in per cent of imports) [2]	2.4	2.5	2.6	1.6	1.6	1.9	0.7	na	na
EBRD index of price liberalisation	2.0	3.0	3.0	3.0	2.7	2.0	2.0	2.0	2.0
EBRD index of forex and trade liberalisation	1.0	2.0	2.0	2.0	1.7	1.7	1.0	1.0	1.7
Privatisation									
Privatisation revenues (cumulative, in per cent of GDP)	0.2	0.7	1.6	2.4	2.5	2.6	2.7	2.7	na
Private sector share in GDP (in per cent)	15.0	20.0	30.0	40.0	45.0	45.0	45.0	45.0	45.0
Private sector share in employment (in per cent)	na	na	na	na	na	na	na	na	na
EBRD index of small-scale privatisation	2.0	3.0	3.0	3.0	3.0	3.0	3.0	3.0	3.0
EBRD index of large-scale privatisation	1.0	2.0	2.7	2.7	2.7	2.7	2.7	2.7	2.7
Enterprises									
Budgetary subsidies and current transfers (in per cent of GDP)	7.6	2.7	3.4	4.0	3.2	na	na	na	na
Effective statutory social security tax (in per cent)	5.4	na	33.5	35.9	na	na	na	na	na
Share of industry in total employment (in per cent)	14.1	13.1	12.9	12.9	12.8	12.7	12.8	12.6	na
Change in labour productivity in industry (in per cent)	2.3	10.5	-1.6	4.4	6.3	5.3	5.0	2.9	na
Investment rate/GDP (in per cent)	14.6	18.3	27.3	29.3	21.7	19.2	na	25.0	na
EBRD index of enterprise reform	1.0	1.0	2.0	2.0	2.0	2.0	2.0	1.7	1.7
EBRD index of competition policy	2.0	2.0	2.0	2.0	2.0	2.0	2.0	2.0	2.0
Infrastructure									
Main telephone lines per 100 inhabitants	7.1	7.0	6.7	6.7	6.5	6.4	6.6	6.7	6.6
Railway labour productivity (1989=100)	52.3	33.1	28.1	27.3	26.9	27.1	26.6	34.2	35.5
Electricity tariffs, USc kWh (collection rate in per cent)	na	na	na	na	1.7 (na)	1.9 (80)	1.2 (90)	0.7 (na)	na
GDP per unit of energy use (PPP in US dollars per kgoe)	1.0	1.0	1.2	1.1	1.2	1.0	1.1	na	na
EBRD index of infrastructure reform	1.0	1.0	1.0	1.0	1.0	1.3	1.3	1.3	1.7
Financial institutions									
Number of banks (foreign owned)	21 (1)	29 (1)	31 (1)	29 (2)	30 (4)	33 (4)	35 (5)	34 (6)	na
Asset share of state-owned banks (in per cent)	15.9	46.7	38.4	75.5	70.6	67.3	65.8	77.5	na
Non-performing loans (in per cent of total loans)	0.0	0.0	0.0	0.0	0.4	0.1	0.1	0.0	na
Domestic credit to private sector (in per cent of GDP)	na	na	na	na	na	na	na	na	na
Stock market capitalisation (in per cent of GDP)	na	na	na	0.4	0.5	2.1	4.3	0.6	0.6
EBRD index of banking sector reform	1.0	1.0	1.7	1.7	1.7	1.7	1.7	1.7	1.7
EBRD index of reform of non-banking financial institutions	1.0	2.0	2.0	2.0	2.0	2.0	2.0	2.0	2.0
Legal environment									
EBRD rating of legal extensiveness (company law)	na	na	na	na	2.3	2.3	2.7	3.0	3.0
EBRD rating of legal effectiveness (company law)	na	na	na	na	2.0	2.0	2.3	2.3	3.0
Social sector									
Expenditures on health and education (in per cent of GDP)	13.4	11.8	11.0	11.1	10.4	10.7	10.4	na	na
Life expectancy at birth, total (years)	na	na	69.2	na	69.2	na	na	69.7	na
Basic school enrolment ratio (in per cent)	87.3	87.5	88.0	88.4	88.9	89.2	88.9	97.0	na
Earnings inequality (GINI-coefficient)	na	na	na	na	na	na	na	na	na

[1] Refers to national poverty line. Internationally comparable data not available.

[2] Refers to custom duties and export taxes.

	1994	1995	1996	1997	1998	1999	2000	2001	2002
								Estimate	Projection
Output and expenditure					*(Percentage change in real terms)*				
GDP	-4.2	-0.9	1.6	2.5	4.4	4.1	4.0	4.5	2.5
Private consumption	na	-30.2	22.8	15.9	8.3	na	na	na	na
Public consumption	na	6.7	-2.2	-17.2	16.0	na	na	na	na
Gross fixed investment	na	na	na	17.0	20.0	na	na	na	na
Exports of goods and services	na	na	na	na	na	na	na	na	na
Imports of goods and services	na	na	na	na	na	na	na	na	na
Industrial gross output	1.0	0.2	6.3	6.5	5.8	6.1	3.5	8.1	na
Agricultural gross output	2.2	2.3	-6.5	5.8	4.0	5.9	3.2	4.5	na
Employment					*(Percentage change)*				
Labour force (end-year)	-1.3	3.7	1.4	1.4	1.4	0.4	1.7	na	na
Employment (end-year)	-1.3	3.7	1.3	1.4	1.4	0.4	1.6	na	na
					(In per cent of labour force)				
Unemployment (end-year) [1]	0.4	0.4	0.4	0.4	0.5	0.5	0.6	na	na
Prices and wages					*(Percentage change)*				
Consumer prices (annual average)	1,568.0	304.6	54.0	58.9	17.8	29.1	24.2	26.2	22.8
Consumer prices (end-year)	1,281.4	116.9	64.3	27.6	26.1	25.2	28.0	24.2	20.3
Producer prices (annual average)	1,428.0	499.0	107.0	52.0	48.4	35.5	40.0	na	na
Producer prices (end-year)	1,425.0	217.4	75.4	40.3	48.4	34.5	36.0	na	na
Gross average monthly earnings in economy (annual average)	1,314.6	276.6	99.7	75.2	57.5	60.2	24.2	26.2	na
Government sector [2]					*(In per cent of GDP)*				
General government balance	-6.1	-4.1	-7.3	-2.4	-3.0	-2.7	-1.2	-0.5	-2.5
General government expenditure	35.3	38.7	41.6	32.5	33.1	32.0	30.4	32.5	na
General government debt	na	na	23.9	28.3	34.3	49.7	64.6	71.1	na
Monetary sector					*(Percentage change)*				
Broad money (M3, end-year)	725.9	144.3	113.3	45.6	28.1	32.1	37.1	50.0	na
Domestic credit (end-year)	525.3	80.0	188.8	51.4	74.7	35.0	13.8	na	na
					(In per cent of GDP)				
Broad money (M3, end-year)	34.7	18.2	21.0	17.5	15.4	13.6	12.4	12.7	na
Interest and exchange rates					*(In per cent per annum, end-year)*				
Refinancing rate	na	84.0	60.0	48.0	48.0	36.0	24.0	34.5	na
Treasury bill rate (3-month maturity)	na	na	36.0	26.0	17.6	16.0	na	na	na
Deposit rate (1 year)	60.0	90.0	28.0	15.0	12.0	12.0	na	na	na
Lending rate (1 year)	100.0	105.0	50.0	28.0	33.0	30.0	na	na	na
					(Soms per US dollar)				
Exchange rate (end-year) [3]	28.0	39.3	65.7	108.5	178.7	348.4	631.3	937.6	na
Exchange rate (annual average) [3]	11.4	33.0	44.7	90.7	131.8	257.2	483.5	774.8	na
External sector					*(In millions of US dollars)*				
Current account	119	-21	-979	-583	-38	-163	185	-30	35
Trade balance	213	237	-706	-72	171	203	494	276	350
Merchandise exports	2,940	3,475	3,534	3,695	2,888	2,790	2,935	2,755	2,850
Merchandise imports	2,727	3,238	4,240	3,767	2,717	2,587	2,441	2,479	2,500
Foreign direct investment, net	73	-24	90	167	140	121	73	71	75
Gross reserves (end-year), excluding gold	676	815	772	374	533	783	810	800	na
External debt stock	1,107	1,771	2,381	2,594	3,484	4,310	4,363	4,533	na
					(In months of imports of goods and services)				
Gross reserves (end-year), excluding gold	3.0	2.9	2.2	1.1	2.2	3.3	3.5	3.5	na
					(In per cent of export of goods and services)				
Debt service	10.5	17.0	9.0	9.0	13.0	17.8	28.3	30.4	na
Memorandum items					*(Denominations as indicated)*				
Population (annual average, millions)	22.3	22.7	23.1	23.6	24.0	24.5	25.0	25.4	na
GDP (in millions of soms)	64,878	302,787	559,071	976,830	1,416,157	2,128,659	3,194,504	4,671,800	5,879,732
GDP per capita (in US dollars)	255.4	404.4	541.0	457.1	447.7	338.2	264.3	237.4	na
Share of industry in GDP (in per cent)	19.8	20.0	20.0	19.0	21.0	20.8	21.0	na	na
Share of agriculture in GDP (in per cent)	38.0	32.0	26.0	29.0	26.0	28.0	27.0	na	na
Current account/GDP (in per cent)	2.1	-0.2	-7.8	-5.4	-0.4	-2.0	2.8	-0.5	0.6
External debt - reserves, in US$ millions	431	956	1,609	2,220	2,951	3,527	3,553	3,733	na
External debt/GDP (in per cent)	19.5	19.3	19.0	24.1	32.4	52.1	66.0	75.2	na
External debt/exports of goods and services (in per cent)	35.9	47.1	60.8	64.0	108.9	154.5	148.7	164.5	na

[1] Officially registered unemployed. No labour force survey based estimates available.

[2] Includes extra-budgetary funds but excludes local government.

[3] Since 1996, dual exchange rates have been in operation. Data show the weighted average of the official exchange rate (40 per cent), the bank rate (30 per cent) and the parallel market rate (30 per cent). Starting from 2001, the weights have changed to official rate (20 per cent), the so called "over the counter" (OTC) rate (50 per cent) and black market rate (30 per cent).

Methodological notes

Definitions and data sources for macroeconomic indicators

Liberalisation

Current account convertibility
Options: full (full compliance with Article VIII of IMF Agreement), limited (restrictions on payments or transfers for current account transactions).

Source: International Monetary Fund, International Financial Statistics.

Interest rate liberalisation
Options: full (banks are free to set deposit and lending rates), limited de facto (no legal restrictions on banks to set deposit and lending rates, but limitations arise from substantial market distortions, such as directed credits or poorly functioning or high illiquid money or credit markets), limited de jure (restrictions on the setting of interest rates by banks through law, decree or central bank regulation).

Source: EBRD staff assessments.

Wage regulation
Restrictions or substantial taxes on the ability of some enterprises to adjust the average wage or wage bill upward; options: yes, no.

Source: EBRD staff assessments.

Stabilisation

Share of general government tax revenue in GDP
General government includes central government, extra-budgetary funds and local government.

Source: See the Macroeconomic Indicators tables.

Exchange rate regime
Options: currency board, fixed, fixed with band, crawling peg, crawling peg with band, managed float, floating.

Source: International Monetary Fund, International Financial Statistics.

Privatisation

Primary privatisation method since the start of transition
Options: vouchers (distribution of investment coupons at a symbolic price), direct sales (sales to outsiders), MEBOs (management /employee buy-outs), liquidations.

Source: EBRD staff assessments.

Secondary privatisation method since the start of transition
Options and definitions as above.

Source: EBRD staff assessments.

Tradability of land
Options: full (no substantial restrictions on the tradability of land rights beyond administrative requirements; no discrimination between domestic and foreign subjects), full except foreigners (as "full", but with some differential treatment of foreigners), limited de facto (substantial de facto limitations on the tradability of land, for example due to the lack of enforceability of land rights, a non-existent land market, or significant obstruction by government officials), limited de jure (legal restrictions on the tradability of land rights), no (land trade prohibited).

Source: EBRD staff assessments.

Enterprises and markets

Competition Office
Competition or anti-monopoly office exists separately from any ministry, though it may not be fully independent; options: yes, no.

Source: EBRD staff assessments.

Infrastructure

Independent telecommunications regulator
Independent body, but the scope of power may differ across countries; options: yes, no.

Source: EBRD staff assessments.

Separation of railway accounts
Accounts for freight and passenger operations are separated; options: yes, no.

Source: EBRD staff assessments.

Independent electricity regulator
Independent body, but the scope of power may differ across countries; options: yes, no.

Source: EBRD staff assessments.

Financial sector

Capital adequacy ratio
Ratio of bank regulatory capital to risk-weighted assets; regulatory capital includes paid-in capital, retentions and some forms of subordinated debt.

Source: EBRD staff assessments.

Deposit insurance system
Deposits in all banks are covered by a formal deposit insurance scheme; options: yes, no.

Source: EBRD staff assessments.

Secured transactions law
Non-possessory security over movable assets permitted; options: yes, restricted, no.

Source: EBRD regional survey of secured transactions laws.

Securities commission
Securities and exchange commission exists separately from any ministry, although it may not be fully independent; options: yes, no.

Source: EBRD staff assessments.

Social reform

Share of the population in poverty
Percentage of population living on less than US$ 4.3 (in 1995 US$ at PPP) a day per person. Selected years 1995–99.

Source: Household survey data compiled by the World Bank.

Private pension funds
Options: yes, no.

Source: EBRD staff assessments.

Liberalisation

Share of administered prices in CPI (in per cent)
Administered prices are defined as those prices subject to regulation by the state.

Sources: EBRD survey of national authorities and IMF country reports.

Number of goods with administered prices in EBRD-15 basket
The EBRD-15 basket consists of flour/bread, meat, milk, gasoline/petrol, cotton textiles, shoes, paper, cars, television sets, cement, steel, coal, wood, rents, inter-city bus service.

Source: EBRD survey of national authorities.

Share of trade with non-transition economies (in per cent)
Ratio of merchandise exports and imports with non-transition economies to total trade (exports plus imports).

Source: IMF, Directions of Trade Statistics. Data for CIS countries suffer from under-reporting of intra-CIS trade for the early 1990s and are reported for 1994 onwards only.

Share of trade in GDP (in per cent)
Ratio of exports plus imports to GDP.

Source: See the Macroeconomic Indicators tables.

Tariff revenues (in per cent of imports)
Tariff revenues include all revenues from international trade. Imports are those of merchandise goods.

Sources: EBRD surveys of national authorities and IMF country reports.

Privatisation

Privatisation revenues (cumulative, in per cent of GDP)
Government revenues from cash sales of enterprises, not including investment commitments.

Sources: EBRD survey of national authorities and IMF country reports.

Definitions and data sources for structural and institutional indicators

Private sector share in GDP (in per cent)
The "private sector shares" of GDP represent rough EBRD estimates, based on available statistics from both official (government) sources and unofficial sources. The underlying concept of private sector value added includes income generated by the activity of private registered companies, as well as by private entities engaged in informal activity in those cases where reliable information on informal activity is available.

Sources: EBRD staff estimates, 1994-2000, and IMF staff estimates, 1989-93.

Private sector share in employment (in per cent)
The "private sector shares" of employment represent rough EBRD estimates, based on available statistics from both official (government) sources and unofficial sources. The underlying concept of private sector employment includes employment in private registered companies, as well as in private entities engaged in informal activity in those cases where reliable information on informal activity is available.

Sources: EBRD staff estimates, 1994-2000, and IMF staff estimates, 1989-93.

Enterprises

Budgetary subsidies (in per cent of GDP)
Budgetary transfers to enterprises and households, excluding social transfers.

Sources: EBRD surveys of national authorities and IMF country reports.

Effective statutory social security tax (in per cent)
Ratio of effective collection of social security taxes over total labour income in the economy, divided by the statutory social security tax rate. A collection of 6 per cent of total payroll for a statutory rate of 10 per cent would give an efficiency of tax collection of 0.6. The EU average is 0.65.

Sources: IMF, Government Finance Statistics, OECD, Revenue Statistics, UN, National Account Statistics, World Bank, World Bank Atlas, World Bank, CIS Statistical Yearbook, national statistical publications and IMF country reports.

Share of industry in total employment (in per cent)
Industry includes electricity, water, power, mining and manufacturing.

Sources: ILO, Labour Statistics Yearbook, UN, National Account Statistics, national statistical publications and IMF country reports.

Change in labour productivity in industry (in per cent)
Labour productivity is calculated as the ratio of industrial production to industrial employment and the changes in productivity are calculated on the basis of annual averages.

Sources: National statistical publications and IMF country reports.

Infrastructure

Main telephone lines per 100 inhabitants
Fixed lines only, excluding mobile telephones.

Sources: International Telecommunications Union, World Telecommunications Development Report.

Railway labour productivity (1989=100)
Productivity measured as the ratio of the number of traffic units (passenger-kilometres plus freight tonne-kilometres) and the total number of railway employees.

Sources: National authorities and World Bank.

Electricity tariff, US cents per kilowatt-hour (collection rate in per cent)
The average retail tariff; the collection rate is defined as the ratio of total electricity payments received in cash and total electricity charges.

Sources: Financial Times, Power in Eastern Europe, national authorities and World Bank.

GDP per unit of energy use
The ratio of GDP in Purchasing Power Parity terms and total energy consumption.

Source: World Development Indicators.

Financial institutions

Number of banks (foreign-owned)
Number of commercial and savings banks, excluding cooperative banks. Foreign-owned banks are defined as those with foreign ownership exceeding a 50 per cent share, end-of-year.

Source: EBRD survey of central banks.

Asset share of state-owned banks (in per cent)
Share of total bank assets of majority state-owned banks in total bank sector assets. The state is defined to include the federal, regional and municipal levels, as well as the state property fund and the state pension fund. State-owned banks are defined as banks with state ownership exceeding 50 per cent, end-of-year.

Source: EBRD survey of central banks.

Non-performing loans (in per cent of total loans)
Ratio of non-performing loans to total loans. Non-performing loans include substandard, doubtful and loss classification categories for loans, but excludes loans transferred to a state rehabilitation agency or consolidation bank, end-of-year.

Source: EBRD survey of central banks.

Domestic credit to private sector (in per cent of GDP)
Ratio of total outstanding bank credit to the private sector at end-of-year, including households and enterprises, to GDP.

Sources: IMF, International Financial Statistics and IMF country reports.

Stock market capitalisation (in per cent of GDP)
Market value of all shares listed on the stock market as a percentage of GDP, end-of-year.

Source: EBRD survey of national stock markets. In some cases, the data differ notably from capitalisation as reported by the Standard & Poor's/IFC Handbook of Emerging Markets. The difference in most cases is due to the exclusion in the Standard & Poor's/IFC data of companies listed on the third tier.

Social sector

Expenditures on health and education (in per cent of GDP)
Expenditures of general government, excluding those by state-owned enterprises.

Sources: EBRD survey to ministries of finance, IMF country reports, World Bank, World Development Indicators.

Life expectancy at birth, total (years)
Life expectancy is defined as the average age reached by an individual after the first day of life, excluding deaths at birth.

Source: World Bank, World Development Indicators.

Basic school enrolment ratio (in per cent)
Gross rates of school enrolment in per cent of the relevant population between 7 and 15 years old. Basic school includes 8 years of schooling from the age of 7/8 to 14/15.

Sources: UNICEF, International Child Development Centre, TransMONEE Database.

Earnings inequality (GINI coefficient)
The GINI coefficient measures the distribution of employees' earnings. A higher coefficient implies a higher degree of earnings inequality. The GINI coefficient is derived from the cumulative distribution of earnings across the workforce ranked in order of ascendance. It is defined as one half of the mean difference between any two observations in the earnings distribution divided by average earnings. Its possible values range between 0 and 1. The GINI coefficients presented in the table are calculated using monthly earnings data as reported by employers. Small employers are often excluded, and some data refer to the public sector only.

Sources: UNICEF, International Child Development Centre, TransMONEE Database.

EBRD transition indicators

The transition indicator scores from 1 to 4 with a 0.3 decimal points added or subtracted for + and – ratings that were first introduced in 1997 and retroactively added to years 1989-96 in the *Transition Report* 2000. For definitions of the rating scores, see Tables 2.1 and 2.2 and Annex 2.2 (for legal transition indicators). The infrastructure rating is an unweighted average of four sector-specific reform ratings (power, roads,

Methodological notes

Definitions and data sources for country snapshot variables

telecommunications and water) for the period 1993-97 and five sector-specific reform ratings (power, railways, roads, telecommunications and water) from 1998 onward.

Source: EBRD staff assessments.

Data for 1993-2000 represent official estimates of out-turns as reflected in publications from the national authorities, the International Monetary Fund, the World Bank, the OECD, the Institute of International Finance and Tacis Economic Trends. Data for 2001 reflect EBRD staff assessments, based in part on information from these sources. Because of frequent revisions to official data sources, there may be changes to all series published in the *Transition Report* and *Transition Report Update* from year to year.

Country-specific notes can be found under each country table.

Output and expenditure

Official estimates of GDP, industrial and agricultural production. Growth rates can lack precision in the context of transition due to large shifts in relative prices, the failure to account for quality improvements and the substantial size and change in the informal sector. In some countries, national authorities have started to incorporate the informal sector into their estimates of GDP.

Employment

For most countries, data reflect official employment records from the labour registries. In many countries, small enterprises are not recorded by official data. A number of countries have moved towards ILO-consistent labour force surveys in recording changes in labour force, employment and unemployment. Where available these data are presented.

Prices and wages

Data from the statistical offices or IMF. In some countries, notably Belarus, Turkmenistan and Uzbekistan, official CPI data may underestimate underlying inflation because of price controls and inadequate measurement of price increases in informal markets. Wage data are from national authorities and often exclude small enterprises as well as the informal sector.

Government sector

Data for the general government, including local government and extra-budgetary funds, where available. Data for most countries are from IMF country reports. Budget balance data can differ from official estimates due to different budgetary accounting, in particular with respect to privatisation revenues and foreign lending.

Monetary sector

Broad money is the sum of money in circulation outside banks and demand deposits other than those of the central government. It also includes quasi-money time, savings and foreign currency deposits of the resident sectors other than the central government. Data from IMF, International Financial Statistics, IMF country reports and monetary authorities.

Interest and exchange rates

Deposit and lending rates from most countries are weighted averages across maturities. For some countries, weighted averages are not available and rates are quoted for the most frequently used instruments. Turkmenistan and Uzbekistan operate dual exchange rate systems or have substantial parallel markets with significant premiums on the official exchange rate. Please refer to the table footnotes for details on the reported exchange rates. Data from the IMF, International Financial Statistics, IMF country reports and monetary authorities.

External sector

Trade data in many countries can differ between balance of payments and customs statistics, because of differences in recording and of informal border trade, which is typically not recorded by customs statistics. Country notes provide further details. Trade data are on a balance of payments basis as published by the monetary authorities and IMF country reports. External debt are EBRD staff estimates based on IMF country reports and national authorities.